T0155879

Lecture Notes in Computer Science 13619

Founding Editors

Gerhard Goos
Juris Hartmanis

Editorial Board Members

Elisa Bertino, *Purdue University, West Lafayette, IN, USA*
Wen Gao, *Peking University, Beijing, China*
Bernhard Steffen⑩, *TU Dortmund University, Dortmund, Germany*
Moti Yung⑩, *Columbia University, New York, NY, USA*

The series Lecture Notes in Computer Science (LNCS), including its subseries Lecture Notes in Artificial Intelligence (LNAI) and Lecture Notes in Bioinformatics (LNBI), has established itself as a medium for the publication of new developments in computer science and information technology research, teaching, and education.

LNCS enjoys close cooperation with the computer science R & D community, the series counts many renowned academics among its volume editors and paper authors, and collaborates with prestigious societies. Its mission is to serve this international community by providing an invaluable service, mainly focused on the publication of conference and workshop proceedings and postproceedings. LNCS commenced publication in 1973.

Joaquin Garcia-Alfaro ·
Guillermo Navarro-Arribas · Nicola Dragoni
Editors

Data Privacy Management, Cryptocurrencies and Blockchain Technology

ESORICS 2022 International Workshops, DPM 2022 and CBT 2022
Copenhagen, Denmark, September 26–30, 2022
Revised Selected Papers

 Springer

Editors
Joaquin Garcia-Alfaro 🆔
Samovar, Télécom SudParis
Institut Polytechnique de Paris
Palaiseau, France

Guillermo Navarro-Arribas 🆔
Universitat Autonoma de Barcelona
Bellaterra, Spain

Nicola Dragoni 🆔
Technical University of Denmark
Lyngby, Denmark

ISSN 0302-9743 ISSN 1611-3349 (electronic)
Lecture Notes in Computer Science
ISBN 978-3-031-25733-9 ISBN 978-3-031-25734-6 (eBook)
https://doi.org/10.1007/978-3-031-25734-6

© The Editor(s) (if applicable) and The Author(s), under exclusive license
to Springer Nature Switzerland AG 2023
This work is subject to copyright. All rights are reserved by the Publisher, whether the whole or part of
the material is concerned, specifically the rights of translation, reprinting, reuse of illustrations, recitation,
broadcasting, reproduction on microfilms or in any other physical way, and transmission or information
storage and retrieval, electronic adaptation, computer software, or by similar or dissimilar methodology now
known or hereafter developed.
The use of general descriptive names, registered names, trademarks, service marks, etc. in this publication
does not imply, even in the absence of a specific statement, that such names are exempt from the relevant
protective laws and regulations and therefore free for general use.
The publisher, the authors, and the editors are safe to assume that the advice and information in this book
are believed to be true and accurate at the date of publication. Neither the publisher nor the authors or the
editors give a warranty, expressed or implied, with respect to the material contained herein or for any errors
or omissions that may have been made. The publisher remains neutral with regard to jurisdictional claims in
published maps and institutional affiliations.

This Springer imprint is published by the registered company Springer Nature Switzerland AG
The registered company address is: Gewerbestrasse 11, 6330 Cham, Switzerland

Foreword from the DPM 2022 Program Chairs

This volume contains the post-proceedings of the 17th Data Privacy Management International Workshop (DPM 2022), which was organized within the 27th European Symposium on Research in Computer Security (ESORICS 2022). The DPM series started in 2005 when the first workshop took place in Tokyo (Japan). Since then, the event has been held in different venues: Atlanta, USA (2006); Istanbul, Turkey (2007); Saint Malo, France (2009); Athens, Greece (2010); Leuven, Belgium (2011); Pisa, Italy (2012); Egham, UK (2013); Wroclaw, Poland (2014); Vienna, Austria (2015); Crete, Greece (2016); Oslo, Norway (2017); Barcelona, Spain (2018); Luxembourg (2019); and held virtually in Guildford, UK (2020) and Darmstadt, Germany (2021).

This 2022 edition was held in Copenhagen, Germany. The workshop was back to an in-person format, with the exception of three presentations that where held online due, mostly, to restrictions for authors from the COVID-19 pandemic.

In response to the call for papers, we received 21 submissions. Each submission was evaluated on the basis of significance, novelty, and technical quality. The program committee performed a thorough review process and selected ten full papers. The result was a technical program covering a wide area of data privacy, from federated learning and differential privacy to blockchain, genetic scores, or Internet exams.

We would like to thank everyone who helped organize the event, including all the members of the organizing committee of both ESORICS and DPM 2022. Our gratitude goes to Christian D. Jensen and Weizhi Meng, General Chairs of ESORICS 2022, Mauro Conti and Jianying Zhou, Workshop Chairs of ESORICS 2022, and all the people in the ESORICS 2022 organization. Very special thanks go as well to all the DPM 2022 Program Committee members, additional reviewers, all the authors who submitted papers, and to all the workshop attendees.

Finally, we want to acknowledge the support received from sponsoring by the following institutions: Institut Mines-Telecom and Institut Polytechnique de Paris (Télécom SudParis and SAMOVAR), Universitat Autònoma de Barcelona, and Cybercat. We acknowledge support as well from the Spanish Government project SECURING/NET PID2021-125962OB-C33.

November 2022

Guillermo Navarro-Arribas
Joaquin Garcia-Alfaro

Organization

17th International Workshop on Data Privacy Management – DPM 2022

Program Committee Chairs

Joaquin Garcia-Alfaro | Intitut Polytechnique de Paris, France
Guillermo Navarro-Arribas | Universitat Autònoma de Barcelona, Spain

Program Committee

Esma Aïmeur	University of Montreal, Canada
Ken Barker	University of Calgary, Canada
Elisa Bertino	Purdue University, USA
Jordi Casas-Roma	Universitat Oberta de Catalunya, Spain
Jordi Castellá-Roca	Universitat Rovira i Virgili, Spain
Mauro Conti	University of Padua, Italy
Mathieu Cunche	University of Lyon, France
Frédéric Cuppens	Polytechnique de Montréal, Canada
Sabrina De Capitani di Vimercati	Università degli Studi di Milano, Italy
Josep Domingo-Ferrer	Universitat Rovira i Virgili, Spain
Nicolas E. Diaz Ferreyra	Hamburg University of Technology, Germany
Jose M. De Fuentes	Universidad Carlos III de Madrid, Spain
Sebastien Gambs	Université du Québec à Montréal, Canada
Guy-Vincent Jourdan	University of Ottawa, Canada
Marc Juarez	University of Edinburgh, UK
Nesrine Kaaniche	Intitut Polytechnique de Paris, France
Christos Kalloniatis	University of the Aegean, Greece
Florian Kammueller	Middlesex University London and TU Berlin, Germany
Bruce Kapron	University of Victoria, Canada
Sokratis Katsikas	Norwegian University of Science and Technology, Norway
Muhammad Imran Khan	Insight Centre for Data Analytics, Ireland
Christophe Kiennert	Intitut Polytechnique de Paris, France
Hiroaki Kikuchi	Meiji University, Japan

Marc-Olivier Killijian	Université du Québec à Montréal, Canada
Evangelos Kranakis	Carleton University, Canada
Alptekin Küpçü	Koç University, Turkey
Romain Laborde	University Paul Sabatier Toulouse III, France
Patrick Lacharme	École nationale supérieure d'ingénieurs de Caen, France
Costas Lambrinoudakis	University of Piraeus, Greece
Maryline Laurent	Intitut Polytechnique de Paris, France
Giovanni Livraga	University of Milan, Italy
Brad Malin	Vanderbilt University, USA
Lukas Malina	Brno University of Technology, Czech Republic
David Megias	Universitat Oberta de Catalunya, Spain
Benjamin Nguyen	National Institute and School of Applied Sciences of the Centre Loire Valley, France
Gerardo Pelosi	Politecnico di Milano, Italy
Isabel Praça	GECAD / ISEP, Portugal
Silvio Ranise	Universy of Trento and Fundazione Bruno Kessler, Italy
Kai Rannenberg	Goethe University Frankfurt, Germany
Ruben Rios	Universidad de Malaga, Spain
Pierangela Samarati	Università degli Studi di Milano, Italy
Natalia Stakhanova	University of Saskatchewan, Canada
Nadia Tawbi	Laval University, Canada
Vicenç Torra	Umeå University, Sweden
Alexandre Viejo	Universitat Rovira i Virgili, Spain
Isabel Wagner	University of Basel, Switzerland
Jens Weber	University of Victoria, Canada
Lena Wiese	Goethe-Universität Frankfurt, Germany
Nicola Zannone	Eindhoven University of Technology, The Netherlands

Steering Committee

Josep Domingo-Ferrer	Universitat Rovira i Virgili, Spain
Joaquin Garcia-Alfaro	Intitut Polytechnique de Paris, France
Guillermo Navarro-Arribas	Universitat Autònoma de Barcelona, Spain
Vicenç Torra	Umeå University, Sweden

Additional Reviewers

Zongxiong Chen
Amrita Ghosal
Youcef Korichi

Foreword from the CBT 2022 Program Chairs

This volume contains the proceedings of the 6th International Workshop on Cryptocurrencies and Blockchain Technology (CBT 2022), held in Copenhagen, Denmark, the 29th of September of 2022, in conjunction with the 27th European Symposium on Research in Computer Security (ESORICS 2022) and the 17th International Workshop on Data Privacy Management (DPM 2022).

The CBT workshop started in 2017, with the aim of providing a forum for researchers with a specific focus on the use of cryptocurrencies and blockchain technologies, in areas such as identification and tracking of distributed autonomous organizations. Papers published in previous venues carefully analyzed current issues in such domains, and proposed scientific updates for the consolidation of security and privacy in the blockchain research area.

In response to the call for papers, CBT 2022 received 18 submissions that were carefully reviewed by the members of the program committee and the help of additional reviewers. Each submission was evaluated on the basis of its significance, novelty, and technical quality. Based on the reviews and the discussion, seven papers were accepted for presentation at the workshop as regular papers, complemented by three short papers.

The organization was made possible through the support received from the Institut Polytechnique de Paris (Telecom SudParis and SAMOVAR), the Technical University of Denmark, and the BART initiative (supported by Inria, IRT SystemX and Institut Mines-Télécom). We would like to thank all people involved in CBT 2022. We are grateful to the Program Committee members and the external reviewers for their help in providing detailed and timely reviews of the submissions. We also thank all the members of the ESORICS 2022 local organization team for all their help and support. Thanks go as well to Springer for their support throughout the entire process. Last but by no means least, we thank all the authors who submitted papers and all the workshop attendees.

November 2022

Nicola Dragoni
Joaquin Garcia-Alfaro

Foreword from the ISBE 2022 Program Chair

Organization

6th International Workshop on Cryptocurrencies and Blockchain Technology – CBT 2022

Program Committee Chairs

Nicola Dragoni	Technical University of Denmark, Denmark
Joaquin Garcia-Alfaro	Intitut Polytechnique de Paris, France

Program Committee

Lennart Ante	Blockchain Research Lab, Germany
Daniel Augot	Inria Saclay, France
Artem Barger	IBM Research, Israel
Alex Biryukov	University of Luxembourg, Luxembourg
Rainer Böhme	Universität Innsbruck, Austria
Karima Boudaoud	University of Nice, France
Jéferson Campos-Nobre	Federal University of Rio Grande do Sul, Brazil
Alexandre Chepurnoy	IOHK Research, Russia
Richard Chbeir	Université de Pau et des Pays de l'Adour, France
James Chiang	Technical University of Denmark, Denmark
Jeremy Clark	Concordia University, Canada
Mauro Conti	University of Padua, Italy
Vanesa Daza	Universitat Pompeu Fabra, Spain
Matteo Dell'Amico	EURECOM, France
Sven Dietrich	City University of New York, USA
Jeremie Decouchant	Delft University of Technology, The Netherlands
Kaoutar Elkhiyaoui	EURECOM, France
Joshua Ellul	University of Malta, Malta
Nour El-Madhoun	EPITA Engineering School, France
Antonio Faonio	EURECOM, France
Paula Fraga	University of A Coruna, Spain
Victor Garcia	Universitat Oberta de Catalunya, Spain
Hannes Hartenstein	Karlsruhe Institute of Technology, Germany
Ryan Henry	University of Calgary, Canada
Jordi Herrera-Joancomarti	Universitat Autonoma de Barcelona, Spain

Sandra Johnson	ConsenSys, Australia
Ghassan Karame	Ruhr-Universität Bochum, Germany
Jiasun Li	George Mason University, USA
Daniel-Xiapu Luo	Hong Kong Polytechnic University, Hong Kong, China
Darya Melnyk	Aalto University, Finland
Shin'ichiro Matsuo	Georgetown University, USA
Jose Luis Muñoz-Tapia	Universitat Politecnica de Catalunya, Spain
Guillermo Navarro-Arribas	Universitat Autonoma de Barcelona, Spain
Aafaf Ouaddah	Institut National des Postes et Telecommunications, Morocco
Dongming Peng	University of Nebraska-Lincoln, USA
Cristina Pérez-Solà	Universitat Oberta de Catalunya, Spain
Alfredo Rial	University of Luxembourg, Luxembourg
Motoyoshi Sekiya	Fujitsu Limited, USA
Matteo Signorini	Nokia Bell Labs, France
Weidong Shi	University of Houston, USA
Hitesh Tewari	Trinity College Dublin, Ireland
Eirini Tsiropoulou	University of New Mexico, USA
Dimitrios Vasilopoulos	IMDEA Software Institute, Spain
Edgar Weippl	SBA Research, Austria

Steering Committee

Rainer Böhme	Universität Innsbruck, Austria
Joaquin Garcia-Alfaro	Intitut Polytechnique de Paris, France
Hannes Hartenstein	Karlsruher Institut für Technologie, Germany
Jordi Herrera-Joancomartí	Universitat Autònoma de Barcelona, Spain

Additional Reviewers

Ankit Gangwal
Marc Leinweber
Peter Robinson
Oliver Stengele

Contents

DPM Workshop: Differential Privacy and Data Analysis

Enhancing Privacy in Federated Learning with Local Differential Privacy for Email Classification

Sascha Löbner$^{(\boxtimes)}$ [ID], Boris Gogov [ID], and Welderufael B. Tesfay [ID]

Chair of Mobile Business and Multilateral Security, Goethe University,
60323 Frankfurt am Main, Germany
{sascha.loebner,welderufael.tesfay}@m-chair.de, bgogo@protonmail.com

Abstract. With federated learning, information among different clients can be accessed to train a central model that aims for an optimal use of data while keeping the clients' data local and private. But since its emergence in 2017, several threats such as gradient attacks or model poisoning attacks against federated learning have been identified. Therefore, federated learning cannot be considered as stand alone privacy preserving machine learning technique. Thus, we analyse how and where local differential privacy can compensate for the drawbacks of federated learning while keeping its advantage of combining data from different sources. In this work, we analyse the different communication channels and entities in the federated learning architecture that may be attacked or try to reveal data from other entities. Thereby, we evaluate where local differential privacy is helpful. Finally, for our spam and ham email classification model with local differential privacy, we find that setting a local threshold of F1-Score on the clients' level can reduce the consumption of privacy budget over several rounds, and decrease the training time. Moreover, we find that for the central model a significantly higher F1-Score than those set on the local level for the clients can be achieved.

Keywords: Federated learning · Differential privacy · Phishing and spam prevention

1 Introduction

To achieve a good model performance of machine learning (ML) applications, large and up to date datasets are required. Especially for time critical applications, such as spam filters or intrusion detection, up to date ML models are crucial. In these fields, a co-evolutional problem exists so that ML is used in an arms race between attackers and defenders [5]. This is where the adaptability of Federated Learning (FL) [12,27] is a key feature to improve existing spam and

This work was supported by the European Union's Horizon 2020 Research and Innovation Program through the Project CyberSec4Europe under Agreement 830929.

© The Author(s), under exclusive license to Springer Nature Switzerland AG 2023
J. Garcia-Alfaro et al. (Eds.): DPM 2022/CBT 2022, LNCS 13619, pp. 3–18, 2023.
https://doi.org/10.1007/978-3-031-25734-6_1

ham classification approaches that are based on spam mail detection. While in the past, data among clients was often treated as separated islands or required significant effort for anonymisation, FL aims to build a joint, and up to date central model, while simultaneously keeping the data of each client private. Thereby, clients train their models locally and share only the models' gradients with a central server that calculates a central model that is re-distributes to the clients [27]. The result is an up to date spam and ham classification model that can take the data of many separated databases into account, without sending the data to a central location [21]. Thus, the core of FL for spam and ham classification is the gradient update that is used to keep local data private. But recent research has shown that it is possible to elicit training data and labels from the models gradients [29]. Thus, FL as a stand alone technique is not sufficiently privacy preserving in general [9]. Therefore, an additional layer of privacy is required when aiming to make use of the benefits of FL as a privacy preserving machine learning (PPML) technique.

Especially for content based spam filters that utilise ML to classify emails in spam or ham, performance, communication overhead, and required computational power are the key feature. When clients' data is used to update a model, it is important that the data is kept private. A common techniques for PPML is Differential Privacy (DP) [10,14]. Although some research that combines FL and DP has been carried out [23], to the best of our knowledge no model that enriches FL with local DP (LDP) for private email classification exists.

With the insights generated by this work we contribute to overcome the privacy shortcomings in FL by extending the architecture with LDP. This is relevant because with FL spam mail detection can become more up to date while the privacy risk for each client is reduced at the same time. We use qualitative evaluation criteria to identify, against which threads and entities LDP can help to overcome the weaknesses of plain FL. Thus, we identify where additional steps are necessary to build a privacy preserving spam mail detection model. Moreover, we aim to provide an idea of how a FL and LDP model can be set up for spam and ham email classification and how the parameters interact with each other. Finally, we propose a local F1-Score threshold for the clients model to make FL in combination with DP even more efficient. Our contribution is as follows:

R1 Improved Privacy: **With requirement 1, we aim to identify which privacy weaknesses of FL can be overcome with the addition of LDP for application of spam and ham classification.** For the application of spam and ham detection we have evaluated privacy of client, privacy of the model and privacy of results (for details see Sect. 4.1). We find an increase of privacy especially for global privacy when clients can trust the central server. Within local privacy where data is required to be kept private against all other parties, we find a need of improvement in the privacy of model and privacy of results.

R2 Efficiency: **With requirement 2, we aim to identify how the combination of LDP and FL can become more efficient what is important for an implementation in practice.** For the application of spam and ham classification we introduce a local F1-Score threshold of 0.85 on the clients' models to overcome the negative impact of LDP on the computation time and effort. We find that this approach still achieves an F1-Score of 0.94 for a noise multiplier of 0.99 and an ϵ value of 23 after 20 federated rounds for 10 clients, while simultaneously increasing performance and efficiency compared to a noise multiplier of 0.7.

2 Attacks Against Federated Learning

In this section we will have a closer look at attacks that are designed specifically against FL. In general, the attacks can be separated into those that aim to reveal user data and those that aim to manipulate the model's predictions.

Gradient Attacks: Wei et al. [26] assert that the sharing of gradients in a FL model can be a privacy risk because of gradient leakage attacks that aim to reveal a worker's training data. If the central server is honest, an adversary could still be able to intercept parameter updates before they reach the central server. Also, an adversary might be able to access locally saved data about the model, e.g. stored gradients, on a compromised worker without seeing the training data. They test the mitigation strategies of gradient perturbation by adding noise and the gradient squeezing with controlled local training iterations. They find that both methods disturb the quality of their privacy leakage attack against the workers. Geiping et al. [9] show for trained deep networks that it is possible to reconstruct high-resolution images from the gradients of models that were trained with deep learning. Moreover, it is possible to completely reconstruct the input to any connected layer of the neuronal network, using gradient inversion attacks. Zhu et al. [29] show how to obtain training data and respective labels after a view rounds of iterations with a deep gradient attack. They obtain images pixel wise and sentences token wise matching texts from the gradients. With LDP for image data, they find that a defensive level of noise has a significant impact on accuracy.

Data Poisoning Attacks: Tolpegin et al. [22] show that data poisoning attacks can significantly reduce the accuracy metrics, e.g. accuracy and recall, of a federated classification model even with only a small number of malicious workers. In such an attack, malicious workers poison the central model by sending gradients trained on mislabeled data. Awan et al. [3] further differentiate between an untargeted attack that aims to reduce the overall testing accuracy of the FL model and targeted attacks that aim to cause misclassification in a certain class. Possible countermeasures proposed are reputation based learning [3] or the identification of malicious participants utilising e.g., loss or error functions [22] or gradient outlier detection [26]. Moreover, Dong et al. [7] propose a solution to overcome the trust problem in byzantine attacks with a dishonest majority.

3 Related Literature

In this section, we present literature related to phishing and spam detection with FL. We also consider alternative machine learning approaches for spam detection as well as other FL models that combine DP with FL.

We identify a view studies that already implement phishing detection with FL. Makkar et al. [15] propose a model for internet attack utilising FL for image spam detection. Moreover, they see especially phishing email detection as a promising application for FL because FL can enhance privacy resulting in an increase of willingness of users to participate in data sharing and thus increase the model's accuracy. Thapa et al. [21] already implemented a FL based phishing mail detection model. Their contribution mainly focuses on different data distributions among clients, different numbers of clients, the scalability of the model and lastly the communication overhead. They find that an increased number of workers influences the convergence of the model's accuracy slightly negatively. Moreover, they point out that there exists a trade off between communication overhead and privacy. Furthermore, they assert that transfer learning can increase the convergence of the model's accuracy. The integration of other privacy preserving techniques such as Homomorphic Encryption (HE) or DP are identified as future work to further improve the model's privacy-protection.

Also other approaches for spam email detection with ML exist. Following the Text Retrieval Conference (TREC), spam can be defined as any indiscriminately sent, unsolicited email. The authors find that most of the techniques for email spam filtering are based on reputation, textual content or multimedia content, where ML belongs to the group of content based filters [5]. In their work, they identify Naive Bayes, Support Vector Machines and Decision Trees as technologies of choice. Also, Dada et al. [6] analyse different ML approaches and find that most state-of-the-art techniques for email spam filters cannot learn in real-time.

FL is combined with differential privacy also by other researchers. Geyer et al. [10] focus on the probability of attacks against a FL model performed by any entity participating in the FL architecture. They try to hide the contribution of the workers during the training by using DP on the local client data. In their results, they assert that LDP can reach high accuracy if the group of participating workers is high enough. Basu et al. [4] propose a contextualised transformer based text classification model based on FL, including DP utilising financial text data. They find that the performance increases with an increasing ϵ and decreasing noise. Wei et al. [25] also introduce a (ϵ, δ)-differential privacy based model that adds noise to the client's parameters. They calculate a convergence bound on the loss function of their FL model. First they find, that with increased privacy the accuracy is reduced, second that with the number of workers the convergence performance increases, and third that an optimal number of maximum aggregation times exists, with regard to convergence performance and level of protection.

To the best of our knowledge, no model exists that combines FL and DP for a spam and ham email classification problem.

4   Methodology

In this section, we will take a closer look at the requirements of this paper, which aims to contribute to the current state of research in spam and ham email classification. Furthermore, we present our metrics to evaluate our requirements.

4.1   Requirement Elicitation

R1: Improved Privacy: With this requirement, we aim to identify which privacy weaknesses of FL can be overcome with the addition of LDP. To fulfil R1 we have derived qualitative evaluation criteria that represent the different levels at which privacy can be leaked.

R2: Efficiency: A combination of LDP and FL is only useful in practice if it is efficient. We evaluate efficiency by comparing different quantitative evaluation parameters, e.g., run time, the evaluation metric F1-Score, or the achieved ϵ value. On the one hand, a high F1-Score is required for a reliable spam and ham classification, on the other hand, the clients' data needs to be kept private while at the same time the costs of communication and computation are kept low.

4.2   Evaluation Criteria

Qualitative Metrics of Privacy: To evaluate R1 we introduce a framework of qualitative privacy metrics that is provided in Fig. 1. In general, Tanuwidjaja et al. [20] differentiate between three different qualitative metrics of privacy in PPML from which we elicit the following three metrics for our approach:

First, we investigate the privacy of the clients who share their gradients with the central server and use the spam filter to keep their emails private. Neither central server nor other clients should be able to reveal data from any clients' email. If no entity can access the clients data, this is defined as local privacy. Local privacy is of great importance if the central server is malicious. Global privacy is the protection against third parties, except the central server [12].

Second, the privacy of the model relates to the model that is built by the central server. No party, including the central server, should know the logic of the model. Tanuwidjaja et al. [20], and Yang et al. [27] propose HE or Secure Multiparty Computation (SMPC) to overcome this thread. With regard to FL, we understand privacy of the model as the precise weights of a client's local model.

Third, the protection of the privacy of the results specifies that no entity should be able to know the classification results for a certain instance [20]. Again, on a local privacy level, this includes all entities participating in the architecture, such as central server, and clients as well as third parties from outside.

Quantitative Evaluation Metrics: As evaluation metric for our machine learning model, we have chosen the F1-Score that is defined as the harmonic mean of precision and recall and that prevents the model from hiding false positives or false negatives [19]. Especially false positives can cause much worse problems and costs in spam email detection [5]. To evaluate the achieved level of privacy we will use the ϵ value as it is derived by the opacus implementation [28]. Moreover, we take also training time and number of required federated rounds into account.

5   Approach

In this section, we describe the data set, local data preparation and our model.

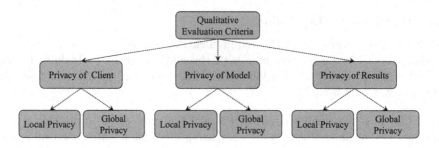

Fig. 1. Qualitative evaluation criteria, elicited from [12,20,27].

Data and Computation: For our model, we have use the improved Enron dataset 2020 as provided by the Natural Language Processing Group of Athens University of Economics[1]. Their version already contains spam and ham labeled data, with 33,722 messages out of which 17,171 are labeled as spam (50.9%) and 16,545 messages are labeled as ham (49,1%). The ham messages in the Enron dataset are benchmarked to protect the original messages and their content. From a statistical point of view, benchmarked messages are in their sequence of tokens very close to the original ones [17]. Our model runs on a CPU: Intel 8700K (6 cores), RAM: 32 GB, and GPU: nVidia 1080Ti (11 GB VRAM, CUDA 11.2).

FL and LDP Architecture: In Fig. 2, we provide the architecture of our privacy preserving spam mail detection demonstrator including the FL architecture and the local DP update process. For the spam and ham email classification problem, our architecture follows the horizontal FL structure [27].

Before starting Algorithm 1, data is collected on the local devices. In our demonstrator, we simulate the devices with different independent clients on one server. Therefore, we do not take data exchange problems caused by different devices or applications into account. We assume that the user who is using an email service has labelled the spam email by putting them into the spam folder. The emails in the spam folder we define as spam. All other emails are treated as ham. Thus, we work with already labelled datasets, the labelling of data does not take place but is provided for a better understanding of our process. McMahan et al. [16] have introduced a federated averaging algorithm that we used as a starting point for our model that we will describe in the following (see Algorithm 1):

First, the central server initialises the starting weights w_0 for the global model, the number of clients K to which the data will be distributed and the number of training rounds T after the algorithm stops (see line 2). In practice, the stopping criteria can be different, e.g. F1-Score, for testing we use T.

Second, for each training round t all clients $k \in K$ do in parallel the computation of the local model `client_update`(k, w_t) (see line 5). McMahan et al. [16] show an extension in the selection of k by using a random subset S_t of m clients. For testing purposes, we have not implemented this step in our model.

---

[1] http://nlp.cs.aueb.gr/software_and_datasets/Enron-Spam/index.html.

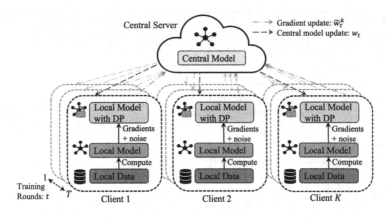

Fig. 2. Privacy preserving architecture, extending FL [27] with LDP.

Third, the function client_update$(k, w_t, \epsilon, \delta)$ takes the weight w from the current global model for each client k and the DP parameters ϵ and δ as input (see line 10). In general, ϵ can be interpreted as a parameter for privacy leakage we aim to keep as low as possible and δ as the probability of accidental privacy leakage. In our model, in parallel all clients perform the local Long Short-Term Memory (LSTM) model with the predefined local epochs E and the batch size B. $\eta \nabla l(w_t; b)$, thereby describing the optimisation function of the neuronal network. Later, we will extend the client date by adding a local threshold that stops the iteration over E if $F1-Score \geq threshold$ is satisfied. The F1-Score is calculated based on the local training data and the local model. The threshold is a tradeoff between privacy and achievable accuracy. Note that the accuracy in epoch i can be lower than the *threshold* but bigger in epoch $i + 1$.

Fourth, we use (δ, ϵ) DP to add noise to the gradients. With our approach, we follow the definition of Dwork et al. [8] for (δ, ϵ) privacy:

$$\forall x : \ \Pr[M(D) = x] \leq \exp(\epsilon) \cdot \ \Pr[M(D') = x] + \delta.$$

This statement implies that for assuming a dataset D' that differs in only 1 entry from dataset D, the probabilities of the x never differs more than $\exp(\epsilon)$ from each other. In our implementation, we use the Python library Opacus, an extension of Differential Privacy Stochastic Gradient Descent (DP-SGD) [1] that ensures that the condition given above is satisfied for every model update [28]. In general, in DP-SGD gradients are computed sample wise, their $l2$ norm is clipped and they are aggregated as batch gradients, adding Gaussian noise. While we have only indicated this procedure in line 15, more details can be found in [1,25].

Fifth, the central server uses the received gradients in round t from each client k and computes a central model using the weighted average as aggregation function (see line 6). The iteration over t continues until T is reached.

Data Pre-processing and Model Structure: In Fig. 3 we show the different steps of local pre-processing on each client. The example shows how a spam message is

Algorithm 1. $k \in \{1,2,...,K\} : K := \#$ clients; $B :=$ local minibatch size, $E :=$ # local epochs, $t \in \{1,2,...,T\} : T$ training rounds, and $\eta :=$ learning rate. [16]

```
1: central_server:
2: initialize w₀, K, T
3: for each round t = 1, 2, ... do
4:     for each client k ∈ K in parallel do
5:         w̃ᵏₜ₊₁ ← client_update(k, wₜ, ε, δ)
6:         wₜ₊₁ ← ∑ᴷₖ₌₁ (nₖ/n) w̃ᵏₜ₊₁
7: client_update(k, wₜ, ε, δ)
8: B ← (split Pₖ into batches of size B)
9: for each local epoch i form 1 to E do
10:    for batch b ∈ B do
11:        wᵏₜ₊₁ ← wₜ - η∇l(wₜ; b)
12:        w̃ᵏₜ₊₁ ← wᵏₜ₊₁ + noise
13: return w̃ᵏₜ₊₁ to server
```

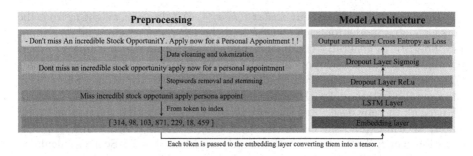

Fig. 3. Steps of pre-processing local data on each client.

altered during the pre-processing from data cleaning to indexing. After the pre-processing, the data is transferred to the embedding layer, where each word is mapped to its proper vector. We chose the LSTM architecture since it performs well on binary text classification [11], e.g., Amjad et al. [2] compared text classification methods with the result that LSTM slightly outperforms NB, MNN and CNN. Finally, we use dropout layers to prevent the model from overfitting. The model is implemented using PyTorch [18] and published via GitHub[2].

6   Results

In this section, we present the results of our model that combines LDP and FL for the application of privacy preserving spam and ham classification.

Figure 4a shows the test results of our model with regard to different levels of noise. The green line represents the values without any level of noise and is therefore without LDP. We will use this model as the base model. In Table 1

---

[2] https://github.com/supaboy1999/federated-spam-ham.

Table 1. Privacy budget (ϵ) and F1-Score of the central model after t rounds of federated training and with different levels of noise

Noise	Federated rounds								Time total
	5		10		20		40		
	ϵ	F1	ϵ	F1	ϵ	F1	ϵ	F1	
0	n/a	0.9843	n/a	0.9838	n/a	0.9837	n/a	0.9845	137 min
0.2	322	0.9344	580	0.9544	1201	0.9294	2185	0.955	148 min
0.7	24	0.8804	29	0.9044	44	0.9185	57	0.8853	152 min
0.99*	12	0.6763	17	0.9007	23	0.9438	34	0.9401	144 min

*Additional threshold at F1-Score of 0.85

we show the precise F1-Score scores after 5, 10, 20 and 40 rounds for the noise multiplier set to 0.2, 0.7 and 0.99. For the noise level of 0.99 we have implemented a local threshold of the F1-Score of 0.85 to increase the performance. More precisely, a client stops running a model locally if the local F1-Score of 0.85 is achieved. This is done to consume less privacy budget in each training round, to prevent overfitting, and to decrease the training time. In Table 1 also the noise level and respective ϵ value are shown as well. Where the noise multiplier is 0 and no DP is used, we have labeled the ϵ value as not applicable (n/a). A first result that can be noted is that for all test runs, the achieved F1-Score fluctuates within a certain range. With increasing amounts of noise added to the gradients the fluctuation increases as well. For the green line without any noise, the fluctuation is the lowest and in a range from 0.970 (10 rounds) to 0.986 (40 rounds). Up to 40 federated rounds, the F1-Score is increasing overall. The blue line shows a noise multiplier of 0.2. It can already be noticed that the blue line in Fig. 4a is much more fluctuating compared to the green line. The blue line is still converging fast and achieves a F1-Score of 0.955 after 40 rounds, 0.0295 lower than the green line. The orange line converges much later at federated round 5 and exhibits the worst F1-Score of 0.8853. More interestingly, the purple curve starts stronger fluctuation after round 32. Taking a closer look at Table 1 we can see that with more federated rounds, the ϵ increases significantly. This happens because with every additional federated round, more data is leaked. Therefore, it is of interest to have a limited number of training rounds to reduce data leakage.

While we can only observe a trend in Fig. 4a, the phenomenon becomes clearer when increasing the level of noise (see Fig. 4b). With an increasing noise multiplier, the model converges later and the F1-Score decreases. While at round 11 the noise multiplier of 1, 1.5 and 2.0 seem to converge equally, after 15 rounds, a significant loss in the accuracy metric of F1-Score can be noticed. At this stage, the model shows an F1-Score of 0.982 for the noise multiplier 0, an F1-Score of 0.94 for 1.0, an F1-Score of 0.92 for 1.5, and an F1-Score of 0.909 for 2.0. After 20 rounds the F1-Score of the black line, with a noise multiplier of 2.0 has significantly dropped. While there is a trend toward higher fluctuation and a slight decrease in performance, the blue line with a noise multiplier of 1.0 and the red line with a noise multiplier of 1.5 still provide good results.

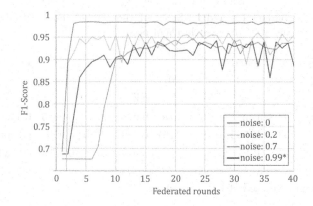

(a) Levels of noise: (0, 0.2, 0.7, 0.99*).

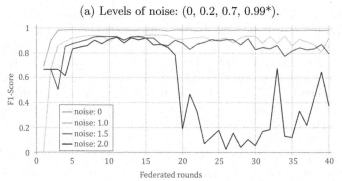

(b) Levels of noise: (0, 1.0, 1.5, 2.0).

Fig. 4. FL with LDP, 10 clients, showing F1-Score of central model after t rounds. (Color figure online)

In Fig. 5, we investigate the effect of varying numbers of clients. In the experiment, we always distributed the testing set with 33,716 among all clients. Thus, we had 6148 instances per client for the 5 clients test and 3072 instances for the 10 clients test. We can see that the F1-Scores for both tests stabilise after 11 federated rounds and start to drop after 30 rounds. Therefore, the most privacy preserving number of federated rounds in both cases lies between 11 and 20 federated rounds. In Table 2, it can be observed that the F1-Score of the central model is highest after 20 rounds. Taking a closer look at the ϵ values, epsilon is constantly increasing but until 40 rounds it is significantly lower than without the local F1-Score threshold. Comparing the ϵ values of 5 and 10 clients, the noise for 5 clients where the data sets are bigger is much lower. Therefore, in a real world implementation, it is important to set a limit of instances per client in each federated round, to not consume unnecessary privacy budget.

In Fig. 6 we show the local epochs and the F1-Score of two randomly selected clients that have participated in the same training as shown in Fig. 5. In addition,

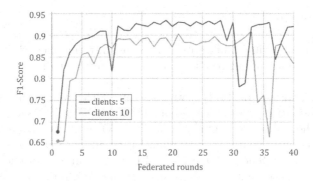

Fig. 5. FL combined with LDP and different number of clients (5, 10), local F1-Score threshold 0.8, F1-Score of the central model after t rounds.

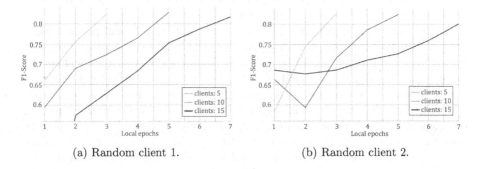

(a) Random client 1.   (b) Random client 2.

Fig. 6. Local F1-Score after t fed. rounds, showing the epochs of 2 random clients.

Table 2. Privacy budget (ϵ) and F1-Score of the central model after t rounds of FL, noise level 0.99, local F1-Score threshold of 0.8 and clients $k = 5$; $k = 10$.

Federated rounds	5		10		20		40	
Clients	Noise	ϵ	F1	ϵ	F1	ϵ	F1	ϵ	F1
5	0.99*	5.746	0.856	7.778	0.870	10.58	0.920	11.89	0.920
10	0.99*	7.367	0.891	10.12	0.817	12.95	0.873	25.71	0.8343

*Additional threshold at F1-Score of 0.80

we also provide the result for 15 clients in Fig. 6 where each client had 2048 instances for training. While the local model with 5 clients reaches the F1-Score threshold of 0.8 very fast, 10 and 15 clients take much more epochs. This implies that with more data, e.g. 6000 instances, the model is more efficient. It can also be observed that the accuracy is slightly above the threshold of 0.8. We have chosen 0.8 because we see this value as the best compromise between privacy and security. This happens because in our current implementation, the training stops if the F1-Score is equal or above the threshold in a certain epoch.

7   Discussion

In this section, we will evaluate our model against the elicited requirements, point out the impact of our results and illustrate future work.

R1 Improved Privacy: In Table 3, we show at which level, with regard to the qualitative evaluation criteria derived in Sect. 4.2, LDP can help in our approach to decrease the risk of revealing private data. Overall, we see an increase in privacy protection in comparison to plain FL by adding LDP to the FL model on the clients' level. The architecture of FL with in allows all clients' data to be kept local but does not protect against attacks. With our approach of using LDP on the gradients of the local model in combination with setting a threshold to the local F1-Score clients' private data is more likely to be protected. This is also reflected by the ϵ values presented in Table 2. Therefore, we see local privacy and global privacy enhanced for the clients' data.

Privacy of client we see improved for both, global and local privacy. Since the global model is trained on the gradients of the clients, the protection with regard to global privacy should be at a minimum as good as for the local clients. With global privacy, the probability that a certain client is attacked by another clients is reduced, due to the larger group and weighted central model gradients.

Privacy of model is in brackets for local privacy because the local privacy enhances if the ϵ is kept on a low level. But it has to be ensured that the central server cannot learn from the gradient updates over several federated rounds. Scenarios might exist, where the highest F1-Score possible, has to be achieved, thus, a lower ϵ is chosen. Therefore, we indicate this risk with brackets. For global privacy, we do not see this issue and have indicated an increase in privacy.

Privacy of results ensures that the classification result into spam or ham for a certain instance in the data is not revealed to any other party [20]. We evaluate the privacy of results equally to the privacy of model because again, over several federated rounds, the risk exists that the central server learns about the model. Learning about a certain client's model is much easier from for the central server compared to clients because clients are not obfuscated in the crowd. Therefore, we put the local privacy in brackets and evaluate global privacy as achieved.

To further increase the privacy of the central model against attacks from third parties, the implementation of DP on the gradients of the central model becomes important. This would also further lower the risk of an attack performed by another client because of the additional DP layer. Although, no global DP is implemented in our model, LDP already reduces the risk of gradient leakage.

With regard to gradient attacks, LDP is likely to protect the clients' data. Especially with introducing a local threshold, the noise level can be increased while ϵ is kept low over several rounds. Additional steps, e.g., obfuscating the clients' data in a bigger crowd to complicate the linkage of several training rounds of a certain client can help to protect their data. Also, HE and SMPC are suitable to extend our model, to solve the problem of dishonest central servers [27].

With regard to data poisoning attacks, LDP does not help because it does only protect the clients' privacy. Countermeasures [22], might be less effective

Table 3. Evaluation of qualitative privacy metrics. In global privacy, clients trust the central server while local privacy aims to keep data private against all parties.

Privacy	Privacy of client	Privacy of model	Privacy of results
Global Privacy	✓	✓	✓
Local Privacy	✓	(✓)	(✓)

because label flipping is less likely to be detected. Therefore, further mitigation strategies, e.g., gradient outlier detection [26], are required.

R2 Efficiency: The decrease of model performance caused by noise was already foreseen as also noted in other studies (see [4]). More interesting is that the model with LDP converges later, which has a negative impact on computation time and effort. But with regard to a spam filter the usability on different types of devices is essential. Especially mobile devices, e.g., smartphones and laptops, exhibit a limited battery charge and the computational power might also be required for more urgent or important tasks. Therefore, an increase of federated rounds has a negative impact on the implementation for such devices. Especially as users may not evaluate privacy as a key feature they tend to use a lower privacy level [13].

To keep the computational power required for training low, we propose to introduce a local threshold for the F1-Score as an additional step, so that the local training stops when the defined F1-Score (e.g. 0.8) is reached. We have shown in our results (see Table 2) that even with a low threshold for the F1-Score of 0.8, combining several local gradients will result in a high F1-Score for the central model. A small drawback of this method is that more federated training rounds are required until the model converges, which increases the communication overhead a little. Moreover, the local threshold might be exceeded in the epoch, when the preset F1-Score is reached. To overcome this issue and to guarantee the preset threshold the model that was trained 1 epoch earlier could be used instead. Besides these drawbacks, we provide a solution for FL spam email detection that achieves a high accuracy by using simultaneously a high noise level with an acceptable ϵ value. Especially for local devices, this can become a problem since the computation might take too much power and makes the device unusable.

Impact: For companies the ability to set different levels of privacy is of special interest, especially if certain departments require stricter privacy settings than others. E.g., a customer service does not want to be too restrictive to reduce false positives so that customers messages do not get lost. On the other hand, banks want to be more restrictive, as they are often attacked and need a higher security level, while false positives are more accepted in view of the risks. While internal privacy in a company is important, the sharing of gradients among companies is also of interest. As we have shown, even if gradients of a simplified model are shared, the combined model can exceed the accuracy of the participating companies. In a real world implementation, all entities e.g. private users, companies and governmental institutions could share their data to build the most up to date spam filter possible. By implementing our proposed approach, we foresee a positive impact on data protection rights and the sovereignty of clients. Also other domains e.g., spoofing detection can gain useful insights from our approach.

Limitations: Since the email text data the model is built on is exclusively in English, characteristics from other languages are not considered. This can lead to structural bias in the model and cause misclassifications. Also, the model cannot deal with data poisoning attacks, thus, additional mitigation steps to mitigate are necessary for a real world implementation. Moreover, the model was built in a stable testing environment. Real world devices and larger amounts of data can bring their own difficulties that should be considered in future implementations.

Future Work: In the future, we plan to test the qualitative evaluation metrics by realising the attacks against our prototype to have a more reliable evaluation based on a theoretical approach. This can also help to better understand the optimal ϵ value that should be achieved for each worker. So far, we preset the local F1-Score threshold for each client equally. As a next step, we plan to investigate how the model reacts to different local accuracy thresholds which enables us to increase the number of participants and to address the individual privacy needs of each client. Along with this approach we are interested to test for natural persons as users of the spam and ham classification, how the combination of other PPML techniques meets their personal preferences by comparing user acceptance criteria and PPML characteristics. Besides the F1-Score we also plan to introduce precision as threshold metric. Again, even with a very low threshold, the central model can still a high accuracy. Another extension, is the implementation of poisoning detection and identification of local model bias [24].

8   Conclusion

In this work, we identify the benefits and drawbacks from combining FL and LDP for clients' gradients in a spam and ham email classification model. This is highly relevant for future implementations because spam detection relies on up to date models that can be adapted quickly. FL is very strong in learning rare events and distributing them quickly among all clients. Nonetheless, it is vulnerable against gradient attacks from inside and outside the network. With our work, we show that local DP helps to minimise the clients' privacy risk, while F1-Score and performance are kept on a considerably high level. But besides this, additional countermeasures are required to increase also the protection level of the global model against malicious clients. Regarding the performance and a loss of accuracy, a major drawback of DP, we show that a local threshold can help to compensate these issues. We find that setting a local threshold for the F1-Score on the clients' level can reduce the consumption of privacy budget, reduces both:

the training time, and overfitting of the model. We find that DP, along with FL has a high potential to create strong, up to date spam filters among different entities. The next steps are to investigate different privacy thresholds among the clients, and to test the resilience against attacks of our model.

References

1. Abadi, M., et al.: Deep learning with differential privacy. In: Proceedings of the 2016 ACM SIGSAC Conference on Computer and Communications Security, pp. 308–318 (2016)
2. Amjad, M., Voronkov, I., Saenko, A., Gelbukh, A.: Comparison of text classification methods using deep learning neural networks. In: Proceedings of the 20th International Conference on Computational Linguistics and Intelligent Text Processing (CICLing) (2019)
3. Awan, S., Luo, B., Li, F.: CONTRA: defending against poisoning attacks in federated learning. In: Bertino, E., Shulman, H., Waidner, M. (eds.) ESORICS 2021. LNCS, vol. 12972, pp. 455–475. Springer, Cham (2021). https://doi.org/10.1007/978-3-030-88418-5_22
4. Basu, P., Roy, T.S., Naidu, R., Muftuoglu, Z.: Privacy enabled financial text classification using differential privacy and federated learning. arXiv preprint arXiv:2110.01643 (2021)
5. Bhowmick, A., Hazarika, S.M.: E-mail spam filtering: a review of techniques and trends. In: Kalam, A., Das, S., Sharma, K. (eds.) Advances in Electronics, Communication and Computing. LNEE, vol. 443, pp. 583–590. Springer, Singapore (2018). https://doi.org/10.1007/978-981-10-4765-7_61
6. Dada, E.G., Bassi, J.S., Chiroma, H., Adetunmbi, A.O., Ajibuwa, O.E., et al.: Machine learning for email spam filtering: review, approaches and open research problems. Heliyon 5(6), e01802 (2019)
7. Dong, Y., Chen, X., Li, K., Wang, D., Zeng, S.: FLOD: oblivious defender for private Byzantine-robust federated learning with dishonest-majority. Cryptology ePrint Archive (2021)
8. Dwork, C., McSherry, F., Nissim, K., Smith, A.: Calibrating noise to sensitivity in private data analysis. In: Halevi, S., Rabin, T. (eds.) TCC 2006. LNCS, vol. 3876, pp. 265–284. Springer, Heidelberg (2006). https://doi.org/10.1007/11681878_14
9. Geiping, J., Bauermeister, H., Dröge, H., Moeller, M.: Inverting gradients-how easy is it to break privacy in federated learning? In: Advances in Neural Information Processing Systems, vol. 33, pp. 16937–16947 (2020)
10. Geyer, R.C., Klein, T., Nabi, M.: Differentially private federated learning: a client level perspective. arXiv preprint arXiv:1712.07557 (2017)
11. Jain, G., Sharma, M., Agarwal, B.: Optimizing semantic LSTM for spam detection. Int. J. Inf. Technol. 11(2) (2019)
12. Li, T., Sahu, A.K., Talwalkar, A., Smith, V.: Federated learning: challenges, methods, and future directions. IEEE Signal Process. Mag. 37(3), 50–60 (2020)
13. Löbner, S., Tesfay, W.B., Nakamura, T., Pape, S.: Explainable machine learning for default privacy setting prediction. IEEE Access 9, 63700–63717 (2021)
14. Löbner, S., Tronnier, F., Pape, S., Rannenberg, K.: Comparison of de-identification techniques for privacy preserving data analysis in vehicular data sharing. In: Computer Science in Cars Symposium, pp. 1–11 (2021)

15. Makkar, A., Ghosh, U., Rawat, D.B., Abawajy, J.: FedLearnSP: preserving privacy and security using federated learning and edge computing. IEEE Consum. Electron. Mag. **11**, 21–27 (2021)

16. McMahan, B., Moore, E., Ramage, D., Hampson, S., Arcas, B.A.: Communication-efficient learning of deep networks from decentralized data. In: Artificial Intelligence and Statistics, pp. 1273–1282. PMLR (2017)

17. Metsis, V., Androutsopoulos, I., Paliouras, G.: Spam filtering with Naive Bayes-which Naive Bayes? In: CEAS, Mountain View, CA, vol. 17 (2006)

18. Paszke, A., et al.: PyTorch: an imperative style, high-performance deep learning library. In: Wallach, H., Larochelle, H., Beygelzimer, A., d'Alché-Buc, F., Fox, E., Garnett, R. (eds.) Advances in Neural Information Processing Systems, vol. 32, pp. 8024–8035. Curran Associates, Inc. (2019)

19. Powers, D.M.: Evaluation: from precision, recall and F-measure to ROC, informedness, markedness and correlation. preprint arXiv:2010.16061 (2020)

20. Tanuwidjaja, H.C., Choi, R., Baek, S., Kim, K.: Privacy-preserving deep learning on machine learning as a service-a comprehensive survey. IEEE Access **8**, 167425–167447 (2020)

21. Thapa, C., et al.: FedEmail: performance measurement of privacy-friendly phishing detection enabled by federated learning. arXiv - CS - Machine Learning (2020)

22. Tolpegin, V., Truex, S., Gursoy, M.E., Liu, L.: Data poisoning attacks against federated learning systems. In: Chen, L., Li, N., Liang, K., Schneider, S. (eds.) ESORICS 2020. LNCS, vol. 12308, pp. 480–501. Springer, Cham (2020). https://doi.org/10.1007/978-3-030-58951-6_24

23. Triastcyn, A., Faltings, B.: Federated learning with Bayesian differential privacy. In: 2019 IEEE International Conference on Big Data (Big Data), pp. 2587–2596. IEEE (2019)

24. Tronnier, F., Pape, S., Löbner, S., Rannenberg, K.: A discussion on ethical cybersecurity issues in digital service chains. In: Kołodziej, J., Repetto, M., Duzha, A. (eds.) Cybersecurity of Digital Service Chains. LNCS, vol. 13300, pp. 222–256. Springer, Cham (2022). https://doi.org/10.1007/978-3-031-04036-8_10

25. Wei, K., et al.: Federated learning with differential privacy: algorithms and performance analysis. IEEE Trans. Inf. Forensics Secur. **15**, 3454–3469 (2020)

26. Wei, W., et al.: A framework for evaluating client privacy leakages in federated learning. In: Chen, L., Li, N., Liang, K., Schneider, S. (eds.) ESORICS 2020. LNCS, vol. 12308, pp. 545–566. Springer, Cham (2020). https://doi.org/10.1007/978-3-030-58951-6_27

27. Yang, Q., Liu, Y., Chen, T., Tong, Y.: Federated machine learning: concept and applications. ACM Trans. Intell. Syst. Technol. (TIST) **10**(2), 1–19 (2019)

28. Yousefpour, A., et al.: Opacus: user-friendly differential privacy library in PyTorch. arXiv preprint arXiv:2109.12298 (2021)

29. Zhu, L., Liu, Z., Han, S.: Deep leakage from gradients. In: Advances in Neural Information Processing Systems, vol. 32 (2019)

Towards Measuring Fairness for Local Differential Privacy

Julián Salas[1(✉)], Vicenç Torra[2], and David Megías[1]

[1] Internet Interdisciplinary Institute (IN3), Universitat Oberta de Catalunya (UOC),
Barcelona, Spain
{jsalaspi,dmegias}@uoc.edu
[2] Department of Computing Science, Umeå Universitet, Umea, Sweden
vicenc.torra@umu.se

Abstract. Local differential privacy (LDP) approaches provide data subjects with the strong privacy guarantees of Differential Privacy under the scenario of untrusted data curators. They are used by companies (e.g., Google's RAPPOR) to collect potentially sensitive data from clients through randomized response. Randomized response was proposed as a method to allow respondents to surveys to answer questions about sensitive issues such as illegal behavior or private preferences. By randomizing their answers, the respondents are provided by plausible deniability, their answers about a sensitive issue may be "yes" either because it is true or by chance.

We study how randomized response mechanisms that provide LDP for a fixed ε, may provide different privacy guarantees to respondents depending on their sensitive attribute value, i.e., they have disparate impact regarding the privacy protection. We propose measures for fair privacy when applying LDP and show that the parameters on the randomized response matrix can be tuned to generate fairer-LDP mechanisms with the same global privacy guarantee ε. We show the effectiveness of our approach through an experimental evaluation in Machine Learning Classification tasks on three commonly used benchmark datasets: Adult Income, COMPAS and German Credit.

Keywords: Fair privacy · Local differential privacy · Randomized response · Algorithmic fairness

1 Introduction

Locally differentially private mechanisms obtained through randomized response are used to collect potentially sensitive data from clients by Google [10,12], Apple [1,23], and Microsoft [5]. Randomized response was proposed in [27] as a method to allow respondents to surveys to answer questions about sensitive issues such as illegal behavior or private preferences, while maintaining confidentiality. Still, it is possible to estimate the true proportion of affirmative and negative answers in the population, and also to collect and perform statistical and Machine Learning

© The Author(s), under exclusive license to Springer Nature Switzerland AG 2023
J. Garcia-Alfaro et al. (Eds.): DPM 2022/CBT 2022, LNCS 13619, pp. 19–34, 2023.
https://doi.org/10.1007/978-3-031-25734-6_2

(ML) models that relate public and private data from users. However, the privacy protection needed for an affirmative answer of a sensitive question may be higher than that of a negative answer.

In this paper, we study how randomized response mechanisms that provide ε-LDP, may offer different privacy guarantees to respondents depending on their sensitive attribute value. Therefore, we show that ε-LDP algorithms have a disparate treatment, regarding the privacy protection, to different groups of respondents. We measure such differences and show that the parameters on the randomized response matrix can be tuned to generate fairer-LDP mechanisms with the same global privacy guarantee ε.

We consider randomized response mechanisms with binary answers in statistical surveys. Binary answers are able to represent complex data through encodings, such as in RAPPOR algorithm [10], which first represents data encoded as a binary vector and then applies binary randomization to such data. We remark that when randomized response is applied by the data controller after collecting all the data it is called post-randomization (PRAM) and it is a well known method for statistical disclosure control.

We follow the agenda for equitable privacy towards answering the following two questions proposed by [9] to characterize the fairness of a particular privacy enhancement system (in this case LDP).

Q1: **Does the system provide comparable privacy protections to different groups of subjects?** This can be restated also as: Does the system protect all its users, or do some users obtain better protections than others? Do differences in protection capabilities result in members of protected classes being less protected than other subjects?

Q2: **Are privacy attacks more effective against members of protected classes?** This question puts the focus on attack capabilities instead of protection. In addition to considering the protections of a privacy-protection scheme, it is also relevant to examine the disparate effectiveness of privacy attacks.

The rest of the paper is organized as follows: Sect. 2 describes the required background information. Section 3 presents the concept of ε-tight that is used for the characterization of the pairs of values of the randomization probabilities p_{00} and p_{11} to provide ε-LDP. Section 4 provides definitions for fair-privacy and the theoretical analysis that will be used in the experiments in Sect. 5. Section 6 presents the related work and Sect. 7 summarizes the contributions.

2   Local Differential Privacy and Randomized Response

In this section, we provide the main definitions of local differential privacy and randomized response that are used through the following sections.

Definition 1 (Local differential privacy). *A randomized algorithm $\mathcal{A}$ satisfies (ε, δ)-local differential privacy if for all inputs i, j and all outputs $k \in Range(\mathcal{A})$:*

$$Pr[\mathcal{A}(i) = k] \leq e^{\varepsilon} Pr[\mathcal{A}(j) = k] + \delta \tag{1}$$

we say that $\mathcal{A}$ is locally (ε, δ)-differentially private or ε-locally differentially private (ε-LDP), when $\delta = 0$.

Any LPD algorithm obtained through randomized response is uniquely determined by its design matrix.

Definition 2 (Design matrix for randomized response). *The design matrix R for a binary randomized response mechanism is defined as follows:*

$$R = \begin{pmatrix} p_{00} & p_{01} \\ p_{10} & p_{11} \end{pmatrix}$$

where the entry $p_{jk} = Pr[X_i = k | x_i = j]$, and X_i is the random output for original random variable $x_i \in \{0, 1\}$.

Therefore, p_{00} denotes the probability that the randomized value is 0 and the original value is 0; p_{01} denotes the probability that the published value is 1 and the original value 0; and so on.

Remark 1. For the probability mass functions of each X_i to sum to 1, it is necessary that $p_{00} + p_{01} = 1$ and $p_{10} + p_{11} = 1$. The design matrix simplifies to:

$$P = \begin{pmatrix} p_{00} & 1 - p_{00} \\ 1 - p_{11} & p_{11} \end{pmatrix} \tag{2}$$

where $p_{00}, p_{11} \in [0, 1]$.

Definition 3 (Region of feasibility) [17]. *The set of pairs $(p_{00}, p_{11}) \in [0,1]^2$ for which the randomization mechanism P in (2) is ε-LDP is called the* region of feasibility $\mathcal{R}$. *It is defined by the following equations:*

$$\mathcal{R} = \begin{cases} p_{00} \leq e^{\varepsilon}(1 - p_{11}) \\ p_{11} \leq e^{\varepsilon}(1 - p_{00}) \\ 1 - p_{00} \leq e^{\varepsilon}(p_{11}) \\ 1 - p_{11} \leq e^{\varepsilon}(p_{00}) \end{cases} \tag{3}$$

We finish this section by presenting the optimal mechanisms (i.e., which minimize the estimation error) for ε and (ε, δ)-LDP.

Example 1 (Optimal mechanism) [25]. Let $p_{00} + p_{11} > 1$ and $\varepsilon > 0$. The ε-LDP randomized response mechanism which minimizes estimation error is given by the design matrix:

$$P_{rr} = \begin{pmatrix} \frac{e^{\varepsilon}}{e^{\varepsilon}+1} & \frac{1}{e^{\varepsilon}+1} \\ \frac{1}{e^{\varepsilon}+1} & \frac{e^{\varepsilon}}{e^{\varepsilon}+1} \end{pmatrix} \tag{4}$$

Example 2 (Optimal mechanism for (ε, δ)-LDP) [17]. The optimal Warner's randomized response mechanism (i.e., such that $p_{00} = p_{11}$) for (ε, δ)-LDP is given by the design matrix:

$$P_\delta = \begin{pmatrix} \frac{e^\varepsilon + \delta}{e^\varepsilon + 1} & \frac{1 - \delta}{e^\varepsilon + 1} \\ \frac{1 - \delta}{e^\varepsilon + 1} & \frac{e^\varepsilon + \delta}{e^\varepsilon + 1} \end{pmatrix} \tag{5}$$

3 ε-Tight Differentially Private Mechanisms

In this section, we generalize the boundary of the region of feasibility through the definition of ε-tight differentially private mechanisms. We show how to calculate the ε for which the randomization mechanisms are tight and we characterize all the possible values for which the randomized response mechanisms are ε-tight.

   We present an example in which the discretization of the Laplace mechanism yields ε'-tight mechanism with $\varepsilon' < \varepsilon$, which is smaller than the ε obtained by the composition theorem, that is, the discretization improves the privacy guarantees.

3.1   Characterization of ε-Tight Randomized Response Mechanisms

In [17], it is proved that optimal mechanisms are obtained when the parameters p_{00}, p_{11} belong to the boundary of the region of feasibility $\mathcal{R}$. We now generalize the concept of boundary, through the following definition.

Definition 4 (ε-Tight). *We say that a differentially private mechanism is ε-tight if it is ε-differentially private, but it is not ε'-differentially private for any $\varepsilon' < \varepsilon$.*

Proposition 1. *An ε-locally differentially private mechanism $\mathcal{A}$ is ε-tight if and only if for some output k, there are inputs i, j such that:*

$$Pr[\mathcal{A}(i) = k] = e^\varepsilon Pr[\mathcal{A}(j) = k] \tag{6}$$

Proof. We show the contrapositive. Assume that (6) is false. Since, $\mathcal{A}$ is ε-differentially private, then for all outputs k and all inputs i, j, the following equation holds:
$$Pr[\mathcal{A}(i) = k] < e^\varepsilon Pr[\mathcal{A}(j) = k]$$

   Therefore, let:

$$\varepsilon' = \ln(s), \text{ where } s = \max_{k,i,j} \left\{ \frac{Pr[\mathcal{A}(i) = k]}{Pr[\mathcal{A}(j) = k]} \right\}.$$

   Note that $e^\varepsilon > s$ and $e^{\varepsilon'} = s \geq \frac{Pr[\mathcal{A}(i)=k]}{Pr[\mathcal{A}(j)=k]}$ for all k, i, j. Hence, $\mathcal{A}$ is ε'-differentially private and $\varepsilon' < \varepsilon$. Thus, the mechanism $\mathcal{A}$ is not ε-tight. Finally, it is straightforward to verify that if (6) holds, $\mathcal{A}$ cannot be ε'-differentially private for any $\varepsilon' < \varepsilon$, finishing the proof.

From Proposition 1, we obtain as a Corollary a heuristic for calculating the value of ε for which a randomization mechanism is ε-tight.

Corollary 1 (How to calculate ε). *Let $\mathcal{A}$ be a randomization mechanism. Then $\mathcal{A}$ is ε-tight for:*

$$\varepsilon = \max_{k,i,j}\left\{\ln\left(\frac{Pr[\mathcal{A}(i) = k]}{Pr[\mathcal{A}(j) = k]}\right)\right\}, \tag{7}$$

where k is any output, and i, j any inputs of $\mathcal{A}$.

Example 3 (The optimal Warner's (ε, δ)-LDP mechanisms are also ε'-LDP). Applying Corollary 1 to P_δ in Example 2, it follows that:

$$\varepsilon' = \frac{e^\varepsilon + \delta}{1 - \delta}$$

Which is well defined for $\delta < 1$, therefore the optimal (ε, δ)-LDP Warner's mechanism from [17] is actually a pure ε'-LDP mechanism which is ε'-tight for $\varepsilon' = \frac{e^\varepsilon + \delta}{1 - \delta}$.

We obtain a complete characterization of the probabilities (p_{00}, p_{11}) for which the randomized response mechanisms are ε-tight in Theorem 1, see also Fig. 1. We use the following parametrization obtained from [17].

Lemma 1. *The line for which (p_{00}, p_{11}) is in the region of feasibility $\mathcal{R}$ and $p_{00} = e^\varepsilon(1 - p_{11})$ can be parametrized as:*

$$(p_{00}, p_{11}) \in \left(\frac{te^\varepsilon}{1 + e^\varepsilon}, 1 - \frac{t}{1 + e^\varepsilon}\right)_{0 < t \leq 1}$$

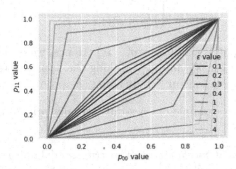

Fig. 1. Characterization of ε-tight randomized response mechanisms from Theorem 1. Note that for each ε there is a diamond-shaped set of values for pairs (p_{00}, p_{11}).

Theorem 1 (ε-tight characterization). *The pairs $(p_{00}(z), p_{11}(z))$ that define a randomization matrix $P(z)$ for which the randomized response mechanism, is ε-tight are of the form:*

$$(p_{00}(z), p_{11}(z)) = \begin{cases} (e^\varepsilon z, 1 - z); & or \\ (1 - z, e^\varepsilon z); & or \\ (1 - e^\varepsilon z, z); & or \\ (z, 1 - e^\varepsilon z) \end{cases} \Bigg\} \ for \ 0 < z \le \frac{1}{1 + e^\varepsilon} \qquad (8)$$

Proof. We separate the proof in two cases, when $p_{00} + p_{11} > 1$ and when $p_{00} + p_{11} < 1$. We do not show the case where $p_{00} + p_{11} = 1$ which is equivalent to $\varepsilon = 0$. In this case, all the rows in the matrix are the same, therefore the probability of returning either value (0 or 1) is independent of the input.

If $p_{00} + p_{11} > 1$, then $1 - p_{11} < p_{00}$, and assuming that the first inequality in (3) holds, then $1 - p_{11} < e^\varepsilon(p_{00})$. Similarly, $1 - p_{00} < e^\varepsilon(p_{11})$, hence (3) simplifies to:

$$\mathcal{R} = \begin{cases} p_{00} \le e^\varepsilon(1 - p_{11}) \\ p_{11} \le e^\varepsilon(1 - p_{00}) \end{cases}$$

From Proposition 1, either $p_{00} = e^\varepsilon(1 - p_{11})$ or $p_{11} = e^\varepsilon(1 - p_{00})$. If $p_{00} = e^\varepsilon(1 - p_{11})$, then from Lemma 1 and parametrizing the line with $z = \frac{t}{1+e^\varepsilon}$ we obtain that $(p_{00}(z), p_{11}(z)) = (e^\varepsilon z, 1 - z)$ for $0 < z \le \frac{1}{1+e^\varepsilon}$.

If $p_{11} = e^\varepsilon(1 - p_{00})$, by a similar argument, we obtain $(p_{00}(z), p_{11}(z)) = (1 - z, e^\varepsilon z)$ for $0 < z \le \frac{1}{1+e^\varepsilon}$.

In the case where $p_{00} + p_{11} < 1$, let $p'_{00} = 1 - p_{11}$ and $p'_{11} = 1 - p_{00}$ and replace them in (3). Then, it becomes:

$$\mathcal{R}' = \begin{cases} 1 - p'_{11} \le e^\varepsilon(p'_{00}) \\ 1 - p'_{00} \le e^\varepsilon(p'_{11}) \\ p'_{11} \le e^\varepsilon(1 - p'_{00}) \\ p'_{00} \le e^\varepsilon(1 - p'_{11}) \end{cases}$$

Also, since $p_{00} + p_{11} < 1$, then $p'_{00} + p'_{11} > 1$. Hence, we obtain the same set of equations as (3), but for p'_{00} and p'_{11}. Making the appropriate substitutions we obtain the last two equations in (8), finishing the proof.

We follow with an example of an ε-differentially private mechanism that is not ε-tight.

Example 4 (Not ε-tight mechanism). The truncated Laplace mechanism is an ε-differentially private mechanism that is not ε-tight. It is defined as follows in [26]:

$$y_i = \begin{cases} 0 \ if \ x_i + Lap(1/\varepsilon) < c \\ 1 \ if \ x_i + Lap(1/\varepsilon) \ge c \end{cases}$$

We consider the particular case when adding Laplace Noise and truncating at $c = 1/2$, hence it is ε-differentially private from the composition theorem [8] and is represented by the following randomization matrix:

$$P_{lm} = \begin{pmatrix} 1 - \frac{1}{2}e^{-\frac{\varepsilon}{2}} & \frac{1}{2}e^{-\frac{\varepsilon}{2}} \\ \frac{1}{2}e^{-\frac{\varepsilon}{2}} & 1 - \frac{1}{2}e^{-\frac{\varepsilon}{2}} \end{pmatrix} \tag{9}$$

We show that P_{lm} is not ε-tight for $c = 1/2$. In this case, $p_{00} = p_{11} = 1 - \frac{1}{2}e^{-\varepsilon/2}$. And considering Proposition 1, it is enough to show that the following inequality holds:

$$\frac{p_{00}}{1 - p_{00}} = \frac{p_{11}}{1 - p_{11}} = \frac{1 - \frac{1}{2}e^{-\varepsilon/2}}{\frac{1}{2}e^{-\varepsilon/2}} < e^{\varepsilon}$$

This is equivalent to:

$$2 < e^{\varepsilon/2} + \frac{1}{e^{\varepsilon/2}}$$

For $\varepsilon = 0$, we have $e^{\varepsilon/2} + \frac{1}{e^{\varepsilon/2}} = 2$ and since the derivative is positive for all ε, it is monotonically increasing, hence the inequality holds for all $\varepsilon > 0$ and the truncated Laplace mechanism is not ε-tight.

We finish this section with an example to show the relevance of considering the ε for which the mechanisms are ε-tight.

Example 5 (Comparison between Randomized Response and Laplace mechanism). Theorem 3 in [25] states that: Given ε, for the randomized response scheme based on P_{rr} and the Laplace mechanism based on P_{lm}, we have:

$$\text{ERROR}_{P_{rr}}(\hat{x}_i) \leq \text{ERROR}_{P_{lm}}(\hat{x}_i)$$

where, the error for the estimate $\hat{x}_i$ for x_i given the randomization mechanism A is defined as:

$$\text{ERROR}_A(\hat{x}_i) = \mathbb{E}[(\hat{x}_i - x_i)^2]$$

Based on this result, [25] concluded that the randomized response mechanism P_{rr} outperforms the Laplace noise mechanism P_{lm}. However, we have shown in Example 4 that the truncated Laplace mechanism P_{lm} is ε-LDP but is not ε-tight. This means that P_{lm} is actually ε'-LDP for some $\varepsilon' < \varepsilon$. Hence, the larger error of P_{lm} can be explained because the actual LDP guarantee ε' provided by P_{lm} is more strict than that of P_{rr} which is ε.

4 Fair Privacy Protection as Classification

In the previous section, we showed that for each ε there are several possible values for p_{00} and p_{11} for which the randomized response mechanisms are ε-differentially private. Hence, the global privacy guarantees provided for all users can be measured by ε in LDP, still different users may obtain different protection depending on their sensitive attribute values (as we show in Example 6). Therefore, in this section, we propose metrics for measuring fairness in LDP mechanisms, and provide a method to correct for disparate treatment.

Example 6 (Disparate privacy guarantees). The following design matrices P_1 and P_2 are (ε, δ)-private for all $\varepsilon \geq 0$ and $0 \leq \delta \leq 1$.

$$P_1 = \begin{pmatrix} \delta & 1 - \delta \\ 0 & 1 \end{pmatrix}$$

P_1 always returns the true value $X_i = 1$ for the users i with sensitive attribute $x_i = 1$, and randomizes $1 - \delta$ of the users with sensitive attribute $x_i = 0$. Hence, in this case an adversary observing the output $X_i = 0$ learns the true value of δ of the users with $x_i = 0$.

$$P_2 = \begin{pmatrix} 1 & 0 \\ 1 - \delta & \delta \end{pmatrix}$$

For P_2, similarly as in previous example, an adversary observing the output $X_i = 1$ learns the true value of δ of the users with $x_i = 1$.

In both cases the users are protected with (ε, δ)-LDP, for all $\varepsilon \geq 0$ and $0 \leq \delta \leq 1$. However, the users that have their sensitive attribute revealed when applying P_1 are the users with $x_i = 0$ while with P_2 are the users with $x_i = 1$.

4.1 Measuring Privacy Through Classification

While there are several definitions for algorithmic fairness [20], we only know of the following definition for fair privacy.

Definition 5 (Fair privacy protection) [9]. *A privacy system provides fair protection if the probability of failure and expected risk are statistically independent of the subject's membership in a protected class.*

The most similar fairness definition to this setting is equalized odds [16]. Following the literature of algorithmic fairness, we consider the case of advantaged and disadvantaged groups over a protected attribute (PA) variable (e.g., race or gender). Hence, a classifier $\hat{Y}$ satisfies *equalized odds* with respect to protected attribute PA and outcome Y, if $\hat{Y}$ and PA are independent conditional on Y.

However, in our case the PA is the sensitive attribute Y that the attacker intends to predict through the classifier $\hat{Y}$, that has been trained with the randomized protected attribute. Hence, providing fair protection means to have the same error rates for both predicted outcomes:

$$Pr(\hat{Y} = 1 \mid Y = 1) = Pr(\hat{Y} = 0 \mid Y = 0) \tag{10}$$

Since, this equality does not hold in general, we use further proxy measures for fair privacy to evaluate the randomization mechanisms. First, we formalize the attacker's model.

Definition 6 (Attacker's model). *We consider an attacker that has access to the randomization matrix P, to the collected randomized sensitive attributes X_i in Definition 2, and to other demographics that have been collected or linked to each user in a dataset.*

The attackers' aim is to predict the sensitive attribute of the user. Therefore, we consider that the attacker trains a classifier $\hat{Y}$ with the output of a randomized algorithm $\mathcal{A}$ to predict the sensitive attribute $Y = x_i$.

With this attacker's model, we consider the balanced error rate as a first measure for fair privacy, since it is an approach to having the same error rates for both predicted outcomes as in (10). Additionally, [13] showed that any decision exhibiting disparate impact can be converted into one where the protected attribute can be predicted with low balanced error rate.

Definition 7 (Balanced error rate). *The balanced error rate of a predictor is defined as the unweighted average class-conditioned error.*

$$\text{BER}(\hat{Y}) = \frac{FPR(\hat{Y}) + FNR(\hat{Y})}{2} = 1 - \frac{TPR(\hat{Y}) + TNR(\hat{Y})}{2}$$

Here, FPR denotes the false positive rate, FNR the false negative rate, TPR the true positive rate and TNR the true negative rate of the model.

The BER measures how accurate is the classifier for predicting true values and false values for a condition. Having a low BER is also a guarantee of having good utility. Additionally, when both prediction accuracies are balanced, we provide fair privacy as considered in Definition 5.

Besides this measure, we define the risk of disclosure as the attackers' confidence of inferring the sensitive attribute of a user, when observing the randomized sensitive attribute.

Definition 8 (Confidence of disclosure). *We define the* confidence of disclosure *as the probability that an attacker observing the randomized value $\hat{Y} = j$, correctly infers the sensitive attribute of the user $Y = j$. That is:*

$$\text{Confidence}(Y = j \mid \hat{Y} = j) = Pr[Y = j \mid \hat{Y} = j], \text{ for } j \in \{0,1\} \qquad (11)$$

Remark 2. Note that $Pr[Y = 1 \mid \hat{Y} = 1]$ and $Pr[Y = 0 \mid \hat{Y} = 0]$ are the Positive Predictive Value (PPV) and the Negative Predictive Value (NPV) of the attacker's classifier.

To provide similar privacy guarantees to the users, in terms of Definition 8, regardless of their group of responses (positive or negative), we should guarantee that the PPV and NPV are not very different. Hence, we propose the following measure of risk-disparity:

Definition 9 (Risk disparity). *We define the* risk-disparity (RD) *measure for a randomization mechanism $\mathcal{A}$, with respect to a classifier $\hat{Y}$ that has been trained with protected data obtained from the algorithm $\mathcal{A}$, as the difference of positive and negative predictive values of $\hat{Y}$:*

$$\text{RD}(\hat{Y}) = |PPV(\hat{Y}) - NPV(\hat{Y})|$$

4.2 Theoretical Bounds for Randomized Response

Before carrying out the experimental evaluation, we consider an attacker that uses only the randomized sensitive attributes X_i and the randomization matrix P in (2). Under these assumptions, we can obtain general theoretical results for all randomized response mechanisms regardless of the additional data.

In this case, the classifier is $\hat{Y} = X_i$, recall that x_i is the sensitive attribute, and we denote by n_j the number of users with $x_i = j$ and by N_j the number of users with $X_i = j$, for $j \in \{0, 1\}$.

Thus, we can estimate the expected values of the metrics in Sect. 4.1.

Proposition 2 (Expected values of the fair privacy metrics).

$$\mathrm{BER}(\hat{Y}) = 1 - \frac{p_{11} + p_{00}}{2}$$

$$\mathrm{RD}(\hat{Y}) = \left| \frac{p_{11} n_1}{p_{11} n_1 + (1 - p_{00}) n_0} - \frac{p_{00} n_0}{p_{00} n_0 + (1 - p_{11}) n_1} \right|$$

Proof. The proof for $\mathrm{BER}(\hat{Y})$ is straightforward from the calculation of $TPR(\hat{Y})$ and $TNR(\hat{Y})$. For calculating $\mathrm{RD}(\hat{Y})$, we consider the following equations obtained from the definition of the randomization matrix:

$$(1 - p_{00}) n_0 + p_{11} n_1 = N_1$$
$$p_{00} n_0 + (1 - p_{11}) n_1 = N_0$$

Then, $\mathrm{PPV}(\hat{Y}) = Pr[Y = 1 \mid \hat{Y} = 1] = \frac{p_{11} n_1}{N_1} = \frac{p_{11} n_1}{p_{11} n_1 + (1 - p_{00}) n_0}$. Similarly, $\mathrm{NPV}(\hat{Y}) = \frac{p_{00} n_0}{p_{00} n_0 + (1 - p_{11}) n_1}$.

From Proposition 2 and Theorem 1, we obtain the following:

Corollary 2. *For any ε-tight LDP algorithm $\mathcal{A}_z$ such that $p_{00} + p_{11} > 1$ and $p_{00} = e^{\varepsilon}(1 - p_{11})$, the expected value of the fair privacy measures as a function of $0 < z \leq \frac{1}{1+e^{\varepsilon}}$, can be calculated as follows:*

$$\mathrm{BER}(\mathcal{A}_z) = \frac{1}{2} + \frac{1 - e^{\varepsilon}}{2} z$$

$$\mathrm{RD}(\mathcal{A}_z) = \left| \frac{e^{\varepsilon} n_0}{e^{\varepsilon} n_0 + n_1} - \frac{n_1}{n_1 + (\frac{1 - e^{\varepsilon} z}{1 - z}) n_0} \right|$$

5 Experimental Evaluation

In this section, we carry out an experimental evaluation over three datasets commonly used as benchmarks in privacy and fairness literature: Adult Income (*Income*) [6], *COMPAS* [19] and German Credit (*Credit*) [6]. Each of them has different number of instances and features for training and is used for predicting a particular sensitive attribute, as reported in Table 1.

The experimental setting is defined as follows, for each dataset:

Table 1. Datasets used and sensitive attributes considered for the experiments.

Dataset	Sensitive attribute	Features	Instances
Income	Earns over $50k	12	48842
COMPAS	Recidivated	8	6907
Credit	Repaid loan	20	1000

1. Generate 30 random splits of the dataset in train (80%) and test (20%) of the instances.
2. Choose ε values. We chose four with high utility ($\varepsilon = 1, 2, 3, 4$) and four with high privacy ($\varepsilon = 0.1, 0.2, 0.3, 0.4$).
3. Apply the randomization matrix $P(z)$ from Theorem 1 to the sensitive attribute on the train set, for 10 equally spaced values of z given by (8) for each ε value.
4. Learn a classifier $\hat{Y}$ from the train set with randomized sensitive attributes, using the additional data features for training.
5. Predict the sensitive attribute on the test set, using the learnt classifier $\hat{Y}$.
6. Collect and average the metrics for all the experiments.
7. Additionally, we calculate the *theoretical bounds* for each of the three metrics using Corollary 2.

We consider only the case of $p_{00} + p_{11} > 1$, because it preserves better the utility, otherwise, the case $p_{00} + p_{11} < 1$ obtains poorer classifiers.

In all figures, the values of p_{00}, p_{11} and ε are related to each other. Having fixed two of these three parameters, defines the value of the third (e.g., the value of p_{00} and ε defines the value of p_{11}). They are related to each other through the equations in (8). Moreover, the possible values for p_{00} are limited by the ε (as in Fig. 1), and the range of possible values for p_{00} decreases with ε.

We tested three different classifiers $\hat{Y}$: Gaussian Naive Bayes (GNB) which was used in [4], Logistic Regression (LR), which was used in [13] and Random Forests (RF), since Decision Trees were used in [14], but Random Forests are more complex and better performing.

5.1 Empirical Results

In Fig. 2, we show the results on the balanced error rates (BER). The theoretical bound in Corollary 2 shows that BER can be minimized when the ε and p_{00} increase. This trend is followed by *COMPAS* and *Credit* but for *Income*, the minimal value of BER for $\varepsilon \geq 1$ is reached when p_{00} is close to its possible maximum but does not reaches it (e.g. for $\varepsilon = 4$ the best p_{00} is around 0.7). We remark that BER is related with the utility of the classifiers, and as the results show, the utility is better preserved (i.e., BER is smaller) when the added noise is smaller (i.e., for larger values of ε). We also note that the shapes of the functions (the concavity) are more similar depending on the dataset than on the classifier.

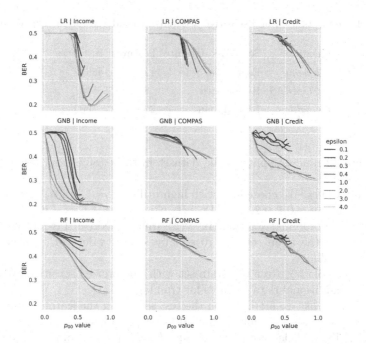

Fig. 2. Balanced error rates for all datasets and classifiers trained with the randomized sensitive attributes.

In Table 2 we present the best RD obtained when performing classification with LR and the corresponding BER values obtained by tuning the values of p_{00} for $\varepsilon = 0.1$ and 1. For $\varepsilon = 0.1$, we note that for *COMPAS* and *Income* the same value $p_{00} = p_{11} = 0.52$ obtains the best metrics for both BER and RD metrics, however the best BER for *Credit* is not reached when the RD is optimal. For $\varepsilon = 1$, we note that the best metrics for *COMPAS* are obtained for the same value $p_{00} = p_{11} = 0.73$. In this case, there is a compromise between BER and RD for both *Income* and *Credit*.

Table 2. Values of p_{00} and p_{11} to obtain the lowest risk disparity (RD) and their corresponding balanced error rates (BER), that provide $\varepsilon = 0.1$ and $\varepsilon = 1$, when using LR for classification (best scores in bold).

	$\varepsilon = 0.1$					$\varepsilon = 1$			
Dataset	p_{00}	p_{11}	BER	RD	Dataset	p_{00}	p_{11}	BER	RD
Income	0.52	0.52	**0.460**	**0.188**	*Income*	0.73	0.73	0.326	**0.149**
COMPAS	0.52	0.52	**0.417**	**0.072**	*COMPAS*	0.73	0.73	**0.338**	**0.007**
Credit	0.36	0.66	0.492	**0.334**	*Credit*	0.51	0.81	0.459	**0.146**

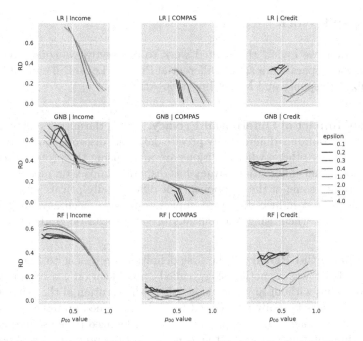

Fig. 3. Risk disparities on all datasets and classifiers trained with the randomized sensitive attributes.

In Fig. 3, we show the results on the risk disparities (RD). Which can be compared to the theoretical bounds calculated in Corollary 2, depicted in Fig. 4. The results for *Credit* are similar to the theoretical values, for all the three classifiers (LR, GNB and RF). The values of RD for *Income* obtained with RF are almost the same as the corresponding theoretical values on Fig. 4. Finally, when comparing Figs. 2 and 3, we observe that the dataset that has a larger range of BER for each ε (i.e., *Income*), is also the one with a larger range of RD.

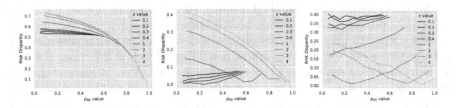

Fig. 4. Theoretical risk disparity measures obtained with the protected attribute on *Income, COMPAS* and *Credit* as a function of probability p_{00} and ε.

6 Related Work

In this section, we review the related work to our study, we considered works regarding the disparate impact of Differential Privacy, Local Differential Privacy, Randomized Response and Model Inversion Attacks.

Disparate Impact of Differential Privacy. In [21] the authors show that the noise added to obtain ε-differentially private data may disproportionately impact some groups over others, when decisions are made using the protected data. In [2] it is shown that differential privacy has disparate impact on model accuracy, and [24] studies some of the components of differentially private empirical risk minimization, that induce disparate impacts on model accuracy. In [28] show how to correct it when using differentially private stochastic gradient descent.

Local Differential Privacy. The first definition equivalent to LDP was proposed in [11], it was a methodology called "amplification", used for limiting privacy breaches without any knowledge of the distribution of the original data. However LDP was formally introduced by [18] and gained prominence since [7].

In [26], it was shown how to provide LDP randomized response mechanisms, while maximizing the accuracy of the estimation of the proportion π of people in the population possessing the sensitive attribute. More generally [17] obtain the randomized response mechanisms which minimize such estimation error, when providing (ε, δ)-differential privacy. Frequency estimation in LDP setting is also studied in [25], where the Optimized Local Hashing (OLH) protocol is introduced and it is shown to have much better accuracy than previous frequency estimation protocols satisfying LDP. Randomized response mechanisms for surveys and applied research were studied together with multivariate regression techniques in [3].

Model Inversion Attacks. To define an alternative measure of privacy that explains what it means for an ML model to breach privacy, we contemplated the works on model inversion [14,15] and membership inference attacks from [22] which consider that a privacy breach occurs if an adversary can use the model's output to infer the values of unintended (sensitive) attributes used as input to the model. Or, in other words, how ML models leak information about the individual data records on which they were trained. Also, [4] showed that an attacker may use data protected under differential privacy, to train an accurate classifier. The main difference with such work is that, in our setting, the attacker has access to the randomized train data and the model.

7 Conclusion

In this paper, we have proposed two metrics to analyze the fairness of binary randomized response algorithms that provide ε-local differential privacy. We have shown through such metrics, that the privacy protection guarantees of those algorithms may be different depending on the sensitive attribute of the individuals. We have obtained theoretical and empirical bounds on three different datasets, and analyzed an attackers' capabilities through classification in machine learning tasks. We have characterized all the values of the randomization matrix that provide ε-differential privacy, and shown that is possible to choose them in a way to correct the disparities of the privacy guarantees provided to different groups of individuals.

Acknowledgements. This research was partly supported by the by the Spanish Ministry of Science and Innovation under projects RTI2018-095094-B-C22 "CONSENT" and PID2021-125962OB-C31 "SECURING".

References

1. Apple Differential Privacy Team: Learning with privacy at scale (2017). https://machinelearning.apple.com/research/learning-with-privacy-at-scale
2. Bagdasaryan, E., Poursaeed, O., Shmatikov, V.: Differential privacy has disparate impact on model accuracy. In: Advances in Neural Information Processing Systems, vol. 32 (2019)
3. Blair, G., Imai, K., Zhou, Y.Y.: Design and analysis of the randomized response technique. J. Am. Stat. Assoc. **110**(511), 1304–1319 (2015)
4. Cormode, G.: Personal privacy vs population privacy: learning to attack anonymization. In: Proceedings of the 17th ACM SIGKDD International Conference on Knowledge Discovery and Data Mining, pp. 1253–1261 (2011)
5. Ding, B., Kulkarni, J., Yekhanin, S.: Collecting telemetry data privately. In: Advances in Neural Information Processing Systems, vol. 30 (2017)
6. Dua, D., Graff, C.: UCI machine learning repository (2017). http://archive.ics.uci.edu/ml
7. Duchi, J.C., Jordan, M.I., Wainwright, M.J.: Local privacy and statistical minimax rates. In: 2013 IEEE 54th Annual Symposium on Foundations of Computer Science, pp. 429–438. IEEE (2013)
8. Dwork, C., Roth, A.: The algorithmic foundations of differential privacy. Found. Trends Theor. Comput. Sci. **9**(3–4), 211–407 (2014)
9. Ekstrand, M.D., Joshaghani, R., Mehrpouyan, H.: Privacy for all: ensuring fair and equitable privacy protections. In: Proceedings of the 1st Conference on Fairness, Accountability and Transparency, pp. 35–47. PMLR (2018)
10. Erlingsson, U., Pihur, V., Korolova, A.: RAPPOR: randomized aggregatable privacy-preserving ordinal response. In: Proceedings of the 2014 ACM SIGSAC Conference on Computer and Communications Security, CCS 2014, pp. 1054–1067 (2014)
11. Evfimievski, A., Gehrke, J., Srikant, R.: Limiting privacy breaches in privacy preserving data mining. In: Proceedings of the Twenty-Second ACM SIGMOD-SIGACT-SIGART Symposium on Principles of Database Systems, PODS 2003, pp. 211–222 (2003)
12. Fanti, G., Pihur, V., Erlingsson, Ú.: Building a RAPPOR with the unknown: privacy-preserving learning of associations and data dictionaries. Proc. Priv. Enhancing Technol. **3**, 41–61 (2016)

13. Feldman, M., Friedler, S.A., Moeller, J., Scheidegger, C., Venkatasubramanian, S.: Certifying and removing disparate impact. In: Proceedings of the 21th ACM SIGKDD International Conference on Knowledge Discovery and Data Mining, KDD 2015, pp. 259–268 (2015)
14. Fredrikson, M., Jha, S., Ristenpart, T.: Model inversion attacks that exploit confidence information and basic countermeasures. In: Proceedings of the 22nd ACM SIGSAC Conference on Computer and Communications Security, pp. 1322–1333 (2015)
15. Fredrikson, M., Lantz, E., Jha, S., Lin, S., Page, D., Ristenpart, T.: Privacy in pharmacogenetics: an end-to-end case study of personalized warfarin dosing. In: 23rd USENIX Security Symposium (USENIX Security 2014), pp. 17–32 (2014)
16. Hardt, M., Price, E., Srebro, N.: Equality of opportunity in supervised learning. In: Advances in Neural Information Processing Systems, vol. 29 (2016)
17. Holohan, N., Leith, D.J., Mason, O.: Optimal differentially private mechanisms for randomised response. Trans. Info. For. Sec. **12**(11), 2726–2735 (2017)
18. Kasiviswanathan, S.P., Lee, H.K., Nissim, K., Raskhodnikova, S., Smith, A.: What can we learn privately? SIAM J. Comput. **40**(3), 793–826 (2011)
19. Larson, J., Mattu, S., Kirchner, L., Angwin, J.: How we analyzed the COMPAS recidivism algorithm. ProPublica **9** (2016)
20. Mitchell, S., Potash, E., Barocas, S., D'Amour, A., Lum, K.: Algorithmic fairness: choices, assumptions, and definitions. Ann. Rev. Stat. Appl. **8**, 141–163 (2021)
21. Pujol, D., McKenna, R., Kuppam, S., Hay, M., Machanavajjhala, A., Miklau, G.: Fair decision making using privacy-protected data. In: Proceedings of the 2020 Conference on Fairness, Accountability, and Transparency, pp. 189–199 (2020)
22. Shokri, R., Stronati, M., Song, C., Shmatikov, V.: Membership inference attacks against machine learning models. In: 2017 IEEE Symposium on Security and Privacy (SP), pp. 3–18. IEEE (2017)
23. Thakurta, A., et al.: Emoji frequency detection and deep link frequency. US Patent 9,705,908, 11 July 1988
24. Tran, C., Dinh, M., Fioretto, F.: Differentially private empirical risk minimization under the fairness lens. In: Advances in Neural Information Processing Systems, vol. 34 (2021)
25. Wang, T., Blocki, J., Li, N., Jha, S.: Locally differentially private protocols for frequency estimation. In: Proceedings of the 26th USENIX Conference on Security Symposium, SEC 2017, pp. 729–745. USENIX Association, USA (2017)
26. Wang, Y., Wu, X., Hu, D.: Using randomized response for differential privacy preserving data collection. In: EDBT/ICDT2016WS (2016)
27. Warner, S.L.: Randomized response: a survey technique for eliminating evasive answer bias. J. Am. Stat. Assoc. **60**(309), 63–69 (1965)
28. Xu, D., Du, W., Wu, X.: Removing disparate impact on model accuracy in differentially private stochastic gradient descent. In: Proceedings of the 27th ACM SIGKDD Conference on Knowledge Discovery & Data Mining, pp. 1924–1932 (2021)

Privacy-Preserving Link Prediction

Didem Demirag[1]([✉]), Mina Namazi[2], Erman Ayday[3], and Jeremy Clark[1]

[1] Concordia University, Montreal, QC, Canada
d_demira@encs.concordia.ca, j.clark@concordia.ca
[2] Open University of Catalonia, Barcelona, Spain
mnamaziesfanjani@uoc.edu
[3] Case Western Reserve University, Cleveland, OH, USA
exa208@case.edu

Abstract. Consider two data holders, ABC and XYZ, with graph data (*e.g.*, social networks, e-commerce, telecommunication, and bioinformatics). ABC can see that node A is linked to node B, and XYZ can see node B is linked to node C. Node B is the common neighbour of A and C but neither network can discover this fact on their own. In this paper, we provide a two party computation that ABC and XYZ can run to discover the common neighbours in the union of their graph data, however neither party has to reveal their plaintext graph to the other. Based on private set intersection, we implement our solution, provide measurements, and quantify partial leaks of privacy. We also propose a heavyweight solution that leaks zero information based on additively homomorphic encryption.

Keywords: Link prediction · Common neighbour · Privacy preserving graph mining · Private set intersection · Social network graphs

1 Introduction

Link prediction discovers important linkages between nodes in a graph. Based on the analysis of these linkages, it helps the data holder to forecast what future connections might emerge between the nodes, and to predict if there are missing links in the data. Some common applications include: (i) in social networks, to recommend links between users; (ii) in e-commerce or personalized advertisement, to recommend products to users; (iii) in telecommunication, to build optimal phone usage plans between the users; and (iv) in bioinformatics, to predict associations between diseases and attributes of patients or to discover associations between genes (or proteins) and different functions.

Link prediction is typically done on the local graph of a data holder or service provider. For instance, a social network, analyzing the common neighbours between its users decides whether to recommend links between the users. However, link prediction will be more accurate and correct by considering more information about the graph nodes. This can be achieved by merging two or

© The Author(s), under exclusive license to Springer Nature Switzerland AG 2023

J. Garcia-Alfaro et al. (Eds.): DPM 2022/CBT 2022, LNCS 13619, pp. 35–50, 2023.
https://doi.org/10.1007/978-3-031-25734-6_3

more graph databases that include similar information, leading to "distributed link prediction" between two or more graph databases. For instance, two social networks may utilize the connections in their combined graph to provide more accurate link prediction for their users. Furthermore, distributed link prediction will enable different uses of link prediction, such as building connections between users and products based on the tastes of other similar users (*e.g.,* friends of a user). Such an application may be possible between graph databases of a social network and an e-commerce service provider. In some cases, collaboration is mutually beneficial to both parties. In others, one party can pay the other party to participate—one party gets better data and the other gets to monetize its data.

Distributed link prediction, although is a promising approach for more accurate and richer link prediction applications, also results in privacy concerns since it implies combining two or more different graph databases. In this scenario, threats against privacy can be categorized into three groups [22]: identity disclosure, link disclosure, and attribute disclosure. All these threats should be considered in a distributed link prediction algorithm, since it involves privacy-sensitive databases from multiple parties.

One promising solution for this privacy concern is cryptography to achieve distributed link prediction in a privacy-preserving way. Thus, in this paper, our goal is to develop a cryptographic solution for privacy-preserving distributed link prediction between multiple graph databases. We propose a solution based on private set intersection (PSI) to tackle this problem by considering both the efficiency of the solution and its privacy.

Via evaluations, we show that this solution provides good efficiency. For example, it can run in under 1 s (ignoring communication latency) for graphs based on a Flickr dataset with 40K nodes.

The proposed protocol does not provide perfect privacy (it leaks some intermediary values) and so we quantify this leakage to better understand if it is consequential enough to move to a fully private solution (which we also sketch).

1.1   Use Cases

Privacy-preserving distributed link prediction can be utilized in different settings. Here, we explain some of the possible applications.

Social Networks. In this setting, there are two social networks, Graph 1 and Graph 2. Graph 1 aims to understand whether there will be a link formed between nodes x and y by also utilizing the similarity of x and y in Graph 2, as distributed link prediction provides better accuracy compared to performing this operation locally.

E-commerce. Another application can be between a social network and an e-commerce service. In the previous use case, the link between two users is the main concern of the protocol. Unlike the previous case, here the links between a user and products are determined at the end of the protocol. In the e-commerce graph, there are links between the users and the products that they have bought. The aim here is to provide better advertising to users. The network will recommend product n to the user x if this user's friends also purchased the same product. For this purpose, the e-commerce network has to know the friends of user x in the social network. Unlike the previous use case, here link prediction cannot be done locally on the e-commerce graph, as the knowledge of the social network's structure should be utilized in order to do the recommendation.

Telecommunication. In this use case, an advertising company wants to propagate an advertisement in the telecom network. If user x is a target for that advertisement, the company would like to know which nodes are likely to form links with user x, in order to decide which nodes it will send the advertisement. The aim is to maximize the number of nodes that learn about the advertisement. Another application involves a social network graph and a phone operator graph. The phone operator wants to find out friends of user x in the social network, so that it offers the special services (e.g., discounts) to the users that are similar to user x.

Bioinformatics. Here, the first graph consists of patients and diseases and the aim is to predict the link between the patient i and the disease j. In the second graph, there are similar patients to patient i. Using these similar patients, and their connection to disease j, the link between patient i and disease j can be inferred.

1.2   Related Work

There is a rich literature on link prediction algorithms (without consideration of privacy) in a variety of network structures: multiple partially aligned social networks [25]; coupled networks [11]; and heterogenous networks [21]. Other works consider node similarity when two nodes in the graph do not share common neighbours [17]; unbalanced, sparse data across multiple heterogeneous networks [10]; missing link prediction using local random walk [19]; and the intersection of link prediction and transfer learning [24].

Other research considers the use of cryptography for collaborating on graph-based data between two parties with privacy protections. However such works consider problems other than link prediction: merging and query performed on knowledge graphs owned by different parties [6]; whether one graph is a subgraph of the other graph [23]; single-source shortest distance and all-pairs shortest distance both in sparse and dense graphs [1]; all pairs shortest distance and single source shortest distance [4]; and transitive closure [14]; anonymous invitation-based system [2] and its extension to malicious adversarial model [3]. While it may be possible to transform some of these into finding common neighbours with a black-box approach, we provide a purpose-built protocol for common neighbour. Later in Sect. 2.3, we review potential cryptographic building blocks in the literature.

Table 1. Different similarity metrics in a graph.

Similarity metric	Definition
Common neighbours	$\|\Gamma(x) \cap \Gamma(y)\|$
Jaccard's coefficient	$\frac{\|\Gamma(x) \cap \Gamma(y)\|}{\|\Gamma(x) \cup \Gamma(y)\|}$
Adamic/Adar	$\sum_{z \in \|\Gamma(x) \cap \Gamma(y)\|} \frac{1}{log(\|\Gamma(z)\|)}$
$Katz_\beta$	$\sum_{l=1}^{\infty} \beta^l \cdot \|path_{x,y}^{\langle l \rangle}\|$
	where $path_{x,y}^{\langle l \rangle} := \{\text{paths of length exactly } l \text{ from } x \text{ to } y\}$
	weighted: $path_{x,y}^{\langle l \rangle} :=$ weight of the edge between x and y
	unweighted: $path_{x,y}^{\langle l \rangle} := 1$ iff x and y are 1-hop neighbours
	The weight is determined by the constant value β

2   Proposed Solution

2.1   Building Blocks from Data Mining

Link Prediction. Given a snapshot of a graph at time t, link prediction algorithms aim to accurately predict the edges that will be added to the graph during the interval from time t to a given future time t' [18].

Similarity Metrics. In Table 1, different metrics for calculating proximity are given. Common neighbours, Jaccard coefficient and Adamic-Adar index are regarded as the node-dependent indices and they only require the information about node degree and the nearest neighbourhood, whereas the Katz index is defined as path-dependent index that consider the global knowledge of the network topology [19]. While there are also other metrics that are used (some of which are shown in Table 1), we choose common neighbours, as it is one of the widely-used methods for link prediction.

Common Neighbours. Common neighbours is used to predict the existence of a link between two nodes based on the number of their common neighbours. If two nodes share common neighbours, it is more likely that they will be connected in the future. In a local graph, the result of the metric can directly be computed by determining the intersection of the neighbour sets of two nodes. Based on the cardinality of the set, the network decides whether to suggest a link between these two nodes. The cardinality is defined as

$$\text{common neighbours} = \|\Gamma(x) \cap \Gamma(y)\|,$$

where $\Gamma(x)$ and $\Gamma(y)$ are the set of neighbours of nodes x and y respectively.

Adapting Common Neighbours for Two Parties. For the use case in this paper, we look at the problem of computing common neighbours metric across two different graphs owned by different entities. For example, this could be two separate social networks, or a social network with an e-commerce network. Graph

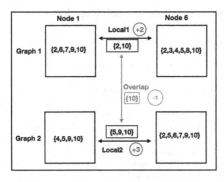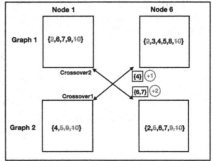

Fig. 1. An example computation between Graph 1 and Graph 2 to find the number of common neighbours of nodes 1 and 6 in their joint graph. Our contribution is to perform this computation in a privacy-preserving manner.

1 wants to perform link prediction between the nodes x and y by using the common neighbours information from Graph 2. CN denotes the total number of common neighbours that will be determined at the end of the protocol. We propose the following computation for two graphs, taking care to not double count any common neighbours:

$$CN = \text{local1} + \text{local2} + \text{crossover1} + \text{crossover2} - \text{overlap}$$

The variables are as follows:

- local1: number of common neighbours of node x and node y in Graph 1
- local2: number of common neighbours of node x and node y in Graph 2
- crossover1: number of common neighbours of node x from Graph 1 and node y from Graph 2
- crossover2: number of common neighbours of node y from Graph 1 and node x from Graph 2
- overlap: intersection of local1 and local2

Figure 1 illustrates an example of how CN is computed using the neighbours sets of both Graph 1 and Graph 2 (based on the graphs in Fig. 6). Graph 1 decides whether to suggest a link between nodes 1 and 6 based on this cardinality.

2.2 System Model

In our setting, there are two parties: Graph 1 and Graph 2, each having a graph structured network. Graph 1 wants to determine whether to suggest a link between the nodes x and y, not by only determining the common neighbours using its own graph, but also utilizing the graph structure of Graph 2. Graph 1 and Graph 2 compute common neighbours on their joint graphs without disclosing their respective graph structures. The result (number of common neighbours) is provided only to Graph 1, however the protocol can be run twice if

---

Table 2. PSI-based and Non-PSI based cryptographic building blocks

PSI based	PSI [9]	**Complexity:** Protocol complexity is linear in the sizes of the two sets. Both the client and the server performs exponentiations and modular multiplications. **Info leaked:** Intersection cardinality, no third party **Security setting:** semi-honest
	Delegated PSI [12]	**Complexity:** Computation and communication complexity of the protocol is linear in the size of the smaller set. For polynomial interpolation field operations are performed. Cloud server has to evaluate oblivious distributed key PRF instances, and unpack messages. The waiting time of packing messages by the backend server is the main computation cost **Info leaked:** Intersection cardinality, uses third party **Security setting:** semi-honest
	PSI with FHE [8]	**Complexity:** Communication overhead is logarithmic in the larger set size and linear in the smaller set size. While FHE is asymptotically efficient, it isn't in practice **Info leaked:** Input sizes and bit string length of the sets, no third party **Security setting:** Semi-honest
	PSI with OT [20]	**Complexity:** The circuit-based PSI protocol has linear communication complexity **Info leaked:** No info leaked as the result of a function on the intersection cardinality is the output, no third party **Security setting:** semi-honest
	Labeled PSI with FHE in malicious setting [7]	**Complexity:** Communication overhead is logarithmic in the larger set size and linear in the smaller set size. While FHE is asymptotically efficient, it isn't in practice **Info leaked:** No info is leaked, as the output is secret shared, no third party **Security setting:** Malicious
Non-PSI based	Privacy-preserving integer comparison [15] over each pair	**Complexity:** Privacy-preserving integer comparison protocol is run between every pair of nodes in the adjacency matrix created using the neighbour list from both graphs. The comparison protocol performs encryption, partial decryption, modular exponentiation, and multiplications **Info leaked:** No info is leaked, no third party **Security setting:** Malicious if ZKP added

Graph 2 also wants the result (otherwise, we assume Graph 1 is paying Graph 2 for this service). While creating our scheme, we make the following assumptions:

1. The identifiers in both graphs for the same nodes match. The graphs should prepare for the computation by sharing a schema and agreeing on unique identifiers (*e.g.,* an email address or phone number for human users).

2. Both graphs know the identity of the nodes for which the computation is being performed. In other words, edges involving these nodes are hidden, as well as all other edges and nodes.
3. If x and y are direct neighbours in Graph 1, Graph 1 has no need for the computation.
4. If x and y are direct neighbours in Graph 2, Graph 2 will halt before doing the computation and inform Graph 1. In this case, Graph 1 discovers a hidden link between x and y, which is stronger for prediction than the number of common neighbours.

Threat Model. The common public input to the computation will be the identifiers of two nodes known to Graph 1 and Graph 2. The private input of Graph 1 and Graph 2, respectively, is an assertion of their graph data. We assume Graph 1 and Graph 2 honestly input their correct data. This is a common assumption and resolving it involves having the data authenticated outside of the protocol, which is not a natural assumption for our use-cases. The second question is whether we can assume Graph 1 and Graph 2 follow the protocol correctly (semi-honest model) or exhibit arbitrary behaviour (malicious model). Given the strong assumption of data input, we find it natural to fit it to a semi-honest model of the protocol.

With these assumptions, we design the protocol so that Graph 2 learns nothing about Graph 1 other than the common input. On the other hand, Graph 1 learns the number of common neighbours on the joint set, which is the output of the multiparty computation (MPC). A fundamental limitation of MPC is that the output itself can leak information about the input. For example, if Graph 1 is malicious and is able to repeat this protocol many times with Graph 2, it can slowly reconstruct Graph 2's input by adaptively providing different inputs each time. For the purposes of this paper, we assume Graph 1 will not do this, because it is semi-honest, and further Graph 2 would not entertain so many executions of the protocol.

As an artifact of our protocol, Graph 1 also learns the intermediate values to compute the number of common neighbours: local1 + local2 + crossover1 + crossover2 - overlap. This extra information does allow a malicious Graph 1 to reconstruct Graph 2 with fewer queries, but in Sect. 3.3 we show that the impact of the leakage is immaterial. This can be prevented with heavier cryptography (Sect. 4.1). In addition, Graph 2 can force Graph 1 to compute the wrong result only if it behaves maliciously. In conclusion, our threat model provides reasonable privacy protection while being lightweight enough to be practical, and we suggest it represents a useful compromise for many real-world applications.

2.3   Building Blocks from Cryptography

Private set intersection (PSI) is a two-party cryptographic protocol that allows two entities, each with a set of data, to learn the intersection of their data without either learning any information about data that is outside the intersection [13]. After a detailed investigation of PSI variants and other related primitives, we

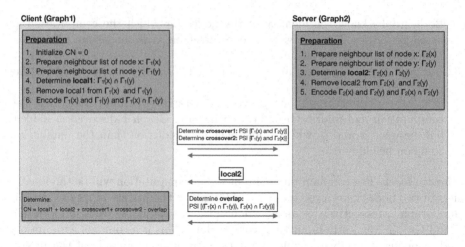

Fig. 2. Overview of the proposed PSI-based solution. PSI is called three times in the protocol for determining crossover1, crossover2 and overlap. PSI itself is described in Fig. 3

choose [9] as the core scheme to deploy for our link prediction. Our scenario requires a scheme that calculates only the cardinality (sometimes called PSI-CA) of the intersection of the two sets in an efficient and scalable way with minimum information leakage with no third party's assistance. A security model for semi-honest adversaries is sufficient, and we leave additional (stronger) security guarantees for future work. A summary of relevant cryptographic primitives is given in Table 2 and we provide more details of each primitive in the full version of the paper[1].

2.4 Proposed Protocol

We use PSI scheme proposed in [9] to perform distributed link prediction between two graph databases. Figure 2 shows the interactive protocol between Graph 1 and Graph 2. Graph 1 wants to learn the common neighbour index to determine whether to suggest a link between the nodes x and y. Both Graph 1 and Graph 2 locally determine the neighbour sets of x and y (local1 and local2, respectively). In order to determine crossover1, crossover2, and overlap, Graph 1 and Graph 2 run three separate PSI protocols among themselves. Each PSI leaks a certain amount of information and we discuss this partial information leak in Sect. 3.3. At the end of the protocol, Graph 1 learns the exact cardinality of common neighbours of nodes x and y on the joint graph. Figure 3 shows the details of the PSI protocol for calculating crossover1 (the calculations for crossover2 and overlap are also the same). It is an interactive protocol between Graph 1 and Graph 2, with offline and online stages. At the offline stage, Graph 1 masks its set and Graph 2 masks its set and shuffles it. During the online stage, Graph 2

---
[1] Full paper.

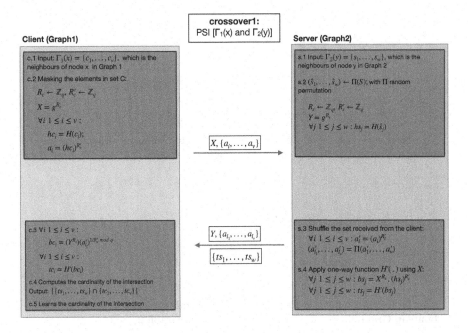

Fig. 3. PSI protocol for determining crossover1 (adapted from [9])

receives the masked set of Graph 1, masks it with its own randomness and shuffles it. When Graph 1 receives the sets, it removes the randomness and determines the intersection of two sets. PSI is described in the multiplicative subgroup $\mathbb{G}_q$ of $\mathbb{Z}_p^*$, where p and q are large primes, $q \mid p - 1$ and $g \in \mathbb{G}_q$ is the generator. $|p| = 1024$ bits and $|q| = 160$ bits. This is for experimental purposes only, these parameters should be at least doubled in length to meet the current, accepted security level[2]. H and H′ are hash functions that are modeled as random oracles.

3   Evaluation

3.1   Performance

We implemented the proposed distributed link prediction algorithm and evaluated it considering different aspects. We used the implementation of PSI defined in [9] where q and p are 160 and 1024 bits, respectively. We ran our experiments on macOS High Sierra, 2.3 GHz Intel Core i5, 8 GB RAM, and 256 GB hard disk. We ran each experiment for 20 times and reported the average.

We used the Flickr dataset in our experiments and using the SALab tool[3], we generated two graphs based on Flickr. Node and edge similarities are set to 0.5. Graph 1 and Graph 2 has 37377 and 37374 nodes; 1886280 and 1900553 edges

---

[2] NIST Special Publication 800-131A Revision 2.
[3] GitHub: SALab.

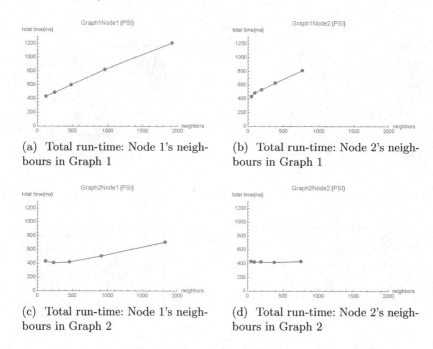

(a) Total run-time: Node 1's neighbours in Graph 1

(b) Total run-time: Node 2's neighbours in Graph 1

(c) Total run-time: Node 1's neighbours in Graph 2

(d) Total run-time: Node 2's neighbours in Graph 2

Fig. 4. Total run-time (in milliseconds) of common neighbour on joint graph according to varying sizes of neighbours for Node 1 and Node 2.

respectively. We picked two random nodes, determined their neighbour sets in each graph and ran our experiments using them. In Graph 1, node 1 has 120 neighbours; 48 for node 2 in graph 1; 114 for node 1 in graph 2; and 47 for node 2 in graph 2. Figure 4 shows the total run-time of the common neighbour protocol on the joint graph if we vary the size of neighbours for Node 1 and Node 2 in both graphs.

3.2   Utility of the Protocol

We illustrate the additional common neighbour information gained by a graph when it collaborates with a second graph. In our first experiment, we created two graphs with the same Barabasi-Albert Distribution where 22 edges are added at each step. Both graphs contain 4039 nodes. Average number of common neighbours for each pair is 0.9 in Graph 1. When we consider the merged graph of two networks, average number of common neighbours for each pair increases to 3.3. This shows that distributed link prediction provides significantly more accurate results (compared to local link prediction) and is worth pursuing.

In our second experiment, we created two graphs with the same number of nodes. Both Graph 1 and Graph 2 have 200 nodes. Graph 1 is created with Barabasi-Albert Distribution, where 22 edges are added at each step. Graph 2 is also created in the same setting and, we computed the average number of

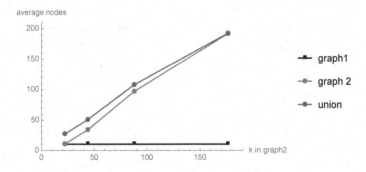

Fig. 5. The change in the average number of common neighbours of two pairs according to connectedness of Graph2. k is the number of edges added at each step in Barabasi-Albert distribution. As k increases in Graph 2, Graph 1 benefits more and more from performing the protocol with Graph 2.

neighbours of each pair in the union and in Graph 2, with increasing values of k. In this setting, as Graph 2 becomes more connected, it benefits less from the distributed link prediction, as the connectedness of Graph 2 becomes more similar to the union. This is shown in Fig. 5.

3.3 Security

The privacy and integrity of our proposed solution is largely subsumed by the security of the underlying PSI protocol [9]. This protocol is shown to be secure under the decisional Diffie-Hellman problem in an appropriate group with semi-honest adversaries. The security proof is in the random oracle model. We make three sequential calls to the protocol. While (universal) composability of the PSI protocol is left by the authors for future work, there is no obvious issue with running the protocol multiple times. For safety, Graph 1 can wait for the first PSI to finish before starting the second one. The PSI protocol leaks (an upper-bound) on the size of each party's graph, and its output is the cardinality of the intersection. Our protocol, with the three PSI calls, leaks the cardinality of four intermediary values (local2, crossover1, crossover2, and overlap) in computing the common neighbours. We now quantify the impact of this leakage on what Graph 1 can learn about Graph 2 beyond the number of common neighbours.

Leakage of Partial Information. In our setting, there are three different categories of threats to privacy: identity disclosure, link disclosure, and attribute disclosure. As PSI does not leak the nodes in the set intersection, we do not learn about the identities or the attributes related to the nodes. In PSI [9], the cardinality of intersection leaks information about the possible combination of nodes in the intersection set. Graph 1, who learns the size of the intersection set, can compute these combinations (which corresponds to link disclosure). The only time Graph 1 learns the identity of a node (which means that the node is

Graph 1	
Vertex	**Neighbour set**
1	{2,6,7,9,10}
2	{3,8}
3	{2,6,7,8,9,10}
4	{8,9}
5	{6,7,10}
6	{2,3,4,5,8,10}
7	{3,5,10}
8	{2,3,4,6,9}
9	{1,3,4,8}
10	{3,5,7}

Graph 2	
Vertex	**Neighbour set**
1	{4,5,9,10}
2	{5,6,7,9}
3	{8,9,10}
4	{1,9}
5	{1,2,6,7}
6	{2,5,6,7,9,10}
7	{2,5,6,9,10}
8	{3,9}
9	{1,2,3,4,6,7,8}
10	{1,3,6,7}

Fig. 6. Sample graphs with 10 nodes. We refer to this sample graph in Sect. 2.1 to explain how common neighbours are computed among two parties and in Sect. 3.3 to quantify the partial information leak.

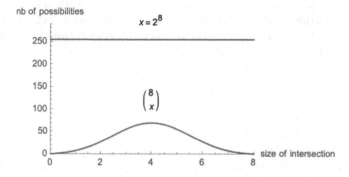

Fig. 7. Number of possible combinations of intersection set according to cardinality of intersection.

in the set that Graph 2 owns) is when Graph 1 has only one node in its set and the cardinality of the intersection it receives as the result of the PSI protocol is 1. Consider the case where Node 1 in Graph 1 has only the node 7 in the set, in Fig. 1. When Graph 1 learns that Crossover2 is 1, it can infer that 7 is connected to Node 6 in Graph 2. Therefore, Graph 1 learns the identity of one of the nodes in the neighbour set of Node 6 in Graph 2 and consequently, the link between 7 and Node 6.

We refer to the graphs in Fig. 6 in order to illustrate what type of information is leaked during the PSI protocol run between Graph 1 and Graph 2, each having 10 nodes. Graph 1 wants to utilize the graph structure of Graph 2 to decide whether to recommend a link between nodes 1 and 6. At the beginning of the protocol, Graph 2 sends the size of the common neighbours of node 1 and node 6 (which corresponds to local2 and its size is 3) to Graph 1. Hence, Graph 1 learns that there are $\binom{8}{3}$ possibilities for local2 as opposed to 2^8 (we choose from

8 nodes as we assume that 1 and 6 are not neighbours in both of the graphs). When we look at the end cases: (i) if the size of intersection is 0, Graph 1 does not learn any extra information (for node 1, there are 2^8 possibilities with the condition that for each possibility, node 1 and node 6 do not have any nodes in the intersection); and (ii) if the size of the intersection is 8, Graph 1 learns that nodes 1 and 6 are connected to all of the 8 nodes. Figure 7 illustrates the number of possibilities learned by Graph 1 for each size of the intersection. It also shows that even at the worst case, there is still a lot of information that is not learned by Graph 1.

For a graph generated using the Flickr data set that has 37377 nodes, the average number of neighbours of a node is 50. So, for two nodes with average number of neighbours, there are $\binom{37377}{50}$ possibilities for their intersection, which is a very large number.

4   Discussion

4.1   Strengthening the Privacy

Here, we discuss a solution based on additively homomorphic encryption (*e.g.,* exponential Elgamal or Paillier) that hides all partial information such that Graph 1 learns only the cardinality. At the beginning of the protocol which is shown in Fig. 8, Graph 1 determines the neighbour sets of nodes x and y, determines local1 and removes local1 from these sets. It encrypts each element in these sets and the cardinality of local1. Graph 2 performs the same steps for local2. In order to determine crossover1, an encrypted matrix is created: each encrypted element in the neighbour set of node x at Graph 1 is compared against all of the encrypted elements in the neighbour set of node y at Graph 2. The same is done for crossover2 between the neighbour set of y at Graph 1 and the neighbour set of node x at Graph 2. In order to compare two encrypted values, we adapt the protocol proposed in [15]. The comparison function takes two encrypted values and the output is either the encryption of 0 if these encrypted values are different or the encryption of 1 otherwise. The sum over all the elements in the matrix is determined using homomorphic addition both for crossover1 and crossover2. Overlap, which is the intersection of crossover1 and crossover2, is also determined in a similar way using privacy-preserving integer comparison. The final common neighbours cardinality (CN), which is encrypted, is determined as CN= local1 + local2 + crossover1 + crossover2 - overlap. Even though this approach strengthens privacy, it is significantly more costly compared our proposed solution based on PSI. We think for most applications, the efficiency is a larger concern than the partial leakage from our protocol, but it is possible that entities might prefer complete privacy for very sensitive data.

4.2   Complexity

Our protocol's complexity is linear in the sizes of the neighbour set of the nodes. In this paper, we discuss the setting for performing distributed link prediction

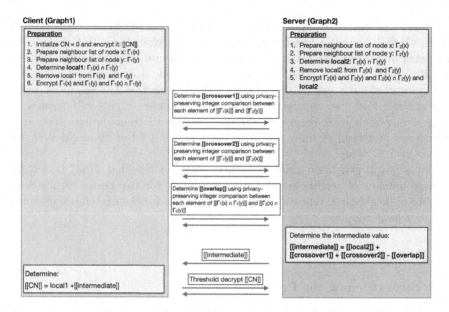

Fig. 8. Overview of the solution with stronger privacy. Note that $[[\Gamma_1(x)]]$ means that each element in the neighbour set of node x in Graph 1 is encrypted.

between two particular nodes in two networks. A network may want to expand this computation for every possible pair in its graph. The complexity depends on the size (which affects the number of possible pairs) and the density of the network (the sizes of neighbour sets affects PSI run-time). PSI runs in linear time complexity. Our protocol is for a specific pair of nodes. The number of pairs in a graph with n nodes is n^2, so running our protocol (or any protocol based on PSI) one an entire graph will require running a linear time operation on a quadratic number of nodes: thus, cubic time complexity in the worst-case. Reductions in this complexity (*e.g.,* based on heuristics for prioritizing which nodes to look at) is an interesting future work.

5 Concluding Remarks

For better accuracy, link prediction can be performed on merged graphs belonging to different parties. This leads to privacy concerns as parties do not want to reveal sensitive data related to their network structures. Therefore, in this work, we proposed a PSI-based, privacy preserving distributed link prediction scheme among two graph databases. In our current proposed scheme, Graph 2 learns among which nodes Graph 1 is computing the common neighbours metric. As a future work, a scheme that allows Graph 2 to hide the identities of these nodes from Graph 1 can be proposed. We might also explore if more recent PSI proposals [5,16] produce faster results.

Acknowledgements. We thank the reviewers who helped to improve our paper. J. Clark acknowledges support for this research project from the National Sciences and Engineering Research Council (NSERC), Raymond Chabot Grant Thornton, and Catallaxy Industrial Research Chair in Blockchain Technologies and NSERC through a Discovery Grant. E. Ayday acknowledges that research reported in this paper was partly supported by the National Science Foundation (NSF) under grant number NSF CCF 2200255 and Cisco Research University Funding grant number 2800379. M. Namazi acknowledges that this work was partially funded by the Spanish Government through grant RTI2018-095094-B-C22.

References

1. Anagreh, M., Laud, P., Vainikko, E.: Parallel privacy-preserving shortest path algorithms. Cryptography **5**(4), 27 (2021)
2. Boshrooyeh, S.T., Küpçü, A.: Inonymous: anonymous invitation-based system. In: Garcia-Alfaro, J., Navarro-Arribas, G., Hartenstein, H., Herrera-Joancomartí, J. (eds.) ESORICS/DPM/CBT -2017. LNCS, vol. 10436, pp. 219–235. Springer, Cham (2017). https://doi.org/10.1007/978-3-319-67816-0_13
3. Boshrooyeh, S.T., Küpçü, A., Özkasap, Ö.: Anonyma: anonymous invitation-only registration in malicious adversarial model. Cryptology ePrint Archive (2019)
4. Brickell, J., Shmatikov, V.: Privacy-preserving graph algorithms in the semi-honest model. In: Roy, B. (ed.) ASIACRYPT 2005. LNCS, vol. 3788, pp. 236–252. Springer, Heidelberg (2005). https://doi.org/10.1007/11593447_13
5. Chandran, N., Gupta, D., Shah, A.: Circuit-psi with linear complexity via relaxed batch OPPRF. Cryptology ePrint Archive (2021)
6. Chen, C., Cui, J., Liu, G., Wu, J., Wang, L.: Survey and open problems in privacy preserving knowledge graph: merging, query, representation, completion and applications. arXiv preprint arXiv:2011.10180 (2020)
7. Chen, H., Huang, Z., Laine, K., Rindal, P.: Labeled psi from fully homomorphic encryption with malicious security. In: Proceedings of the 2018 ACM SIGSAC Conference on Computer and Communications Security, pp. 1223–1237 (2018)
8. Chen, H., Laine, K., Rindal, P.: Fast private set intersection from homomorphic encryption. In: Proceedings of the 2017 ACM SIGSAC Conference on Computer and Communications Security, pp. 1243–1255 (2017)
9. De Cristofaro, E., Gasti, P., Tsudik, G.: Fast and private computation of cardinality of set intersection and union. In: Pieprzyk, J., Sadeghi, A.-R., Manulis, M. (eds.) CANS 2012. LNCS, vol. 7712, pp. 218–231. Springer, Heidelberg (2012). https://doi.org/10.1007/978-3-642-35404-5_17
10. Dong, Y., et al.: Link prediction and recommendation across heterogeneous social networks. In: 2012 IEEE 12th International Conference on Data Mining (ICDM), pp. 181–190. IEEE (2012)
11. Dong, Y., Zhang, J., Tang, J., Chawla, N.V., Wang, B.: CoupledLP: link prediction in coupled networks. In: Proceedings of the 21th ACM SIGKDD International Conference on Knowledge Discovery and Data Mining, pp. 199–208. ACM (2015)
12. Duong, T., Phan, D.H., Trieu, N.: Catalic: delegated PSI cardinality with applications to contact tracing. In: Moriai, S., Wang, H. (eds.) ASIACRYPT 2020. LNCS, vol. 12493, pp. 870–899. Springer, Cham (2020). https://doi.org/10.1007/978-3-030-64840-4_29

13. Freedman, M.J., Nissim, K., Pinkas, B.: Efficient private matching and set inter-section. In: Cachin, C., Camenisch, J.L. (eds.) EUROCRYPT 2004. LNCS, vol. 3027, pp. 1–19. Springer, Heidelberg (2004). https://doi.org/10.1007/978-3-540-24676-3_1

14. He, X., Vaidya, J., Shafiq, B., Adam, N., Terzi, E., Grandison, T.: Efficient privacy-preserving link discovery. In: Theeramunkong, T., Kijsirikul, B., Cercone, N., Ho, T.-B. (eds.) PAKDD 2009. LNCS (LNAI), vol. 5476, pp. 16–27. Springer, Heidelberg (2009). https://doi.org/10.1007/978-3-642-01307-2_5

15. Hubaux, J.P., et al.: Privacy-preserving computation of disease risk by using genomic, clinical, and environmental data. In: Proceedings of USENIX Security Workshop on Health Information Technologies (HealthTech 2013), number EPFL-CONF-187118 (2013)

16. Karakoç, F., Küpçü, A.: Linear complexity private set intersection for secure two-party protocols. In: Krenn, S., Shulman, H., Vaudenay, S. (eds.) CANS 2020. LNCS, vol. 12579, pp. 409–429. Springer, Cham (2020). https://doi.org/10.1007/978-3-030-65411-5_20

17. Leicht, E.A., Holme, P., Newman, M.E.: Vertex similarity in networks. Phys. Rev. E **73**(2), 026120 (2006)

18. Liben-Nowell, D., Kleinberg, J.: The link-prediction problem for social networks. J. Am. Soc. Inform. Sci. Technol. **58**(7), 1019–1031 (2007)

19. Liu, W., Lü, L.: Link prediction based on local random walk. EPL (Europhys. Lett.) **89**(5), 58007 (2010)

20. Pinkas, B., Schneider, T., Tkachenko, O., Yanai, A.: Efficient circuit-based PSI with linear communication. In: Ishai, Y., Rijmen, V. (eds.) EUROCRYPT 2019. LNCS, vol. 11478, pp. 122–153. Springer, Cham (2019). https://doi.org/10.1007/978-3-030-17659-4_5

21. Tang, J., Lou, T., Kleinberg, J., Wu, S.: Transfer learning to infer social ties across heterogeneous networks. ACM Trans. Inf. Syst. (TOIS) **34**(2), 1–43 (2016)

22. Wu, X., Ying, X., Liu, K., Chen, L.: A survey of privacy-preservation of graphs and social networks. In: Aggarwal, C., Wang, H. (eds.) Managing and Mining Graph Data. ADBS, vol. 40, pp. 421–453. Springer, Boston (2010). https://doi.org/10.1007/978-1-4419-6045-0_14

23. Xu, Z., Zhou, F., Li, Y., Xu, J., Wang, Q.: Privacy-preserving subgraph matching protocol for two parties. Int. J. Found. Comput. Sci. **30**(04), 571–588 (2019)

24. Yu, K., Chu, W.: Gaussian process models for link analysis and transfer learning. In: Advances in Neural Information Processing Systems, pp. 1657–1664 (2008)

25. Zhang, J., Yu, P.S., Zhou, Z.H.: Meta-path based multi-network collective link prediction. In: Proceedings of the 20th ACM SIGKDD International Conference on Knowledge Discovery and Data Mining, pp. 1286–1295. ACM (2014)

DPM Workshop: Regulation, Artificial Intelligence, and Formal Verification

An Email a Day Could Give Your Health Data Away

Christof Lange, Thomas Chang, Maximilian Fiedler, and Ronald Petrlic$^{(\boxtimes)}$

Nuremberg Institute of Technology, Nürnberg, Germany
`ronald.petrlic@th-nuernberg.de`

Abstract. Are doctors allowed to communicate with their patients via email? The GDPR sets the bar high for securing health data: either an end-to-end-encryption (E2EE) or a guaranteed transport encryption needs to be used. As E2EE (with PGP or S/MIME) is not widely used in practice, only a guaranteed transport encryption comes into question. But are doctors' email servers properly configured and provide such strong security guarantees? As we found out in a large-scale investigation of German medical institutions, this is not the case at all. Only a very small minority of email servers provides state-of-the-art security. In all other cases, communication between doctors and patients via email is not secure and, thus, not permitted with regards to the GDPR.

Keywords: Email security · Opportunistic transport encryption · GDPR

1 Introduction

"Emails are like postcards; everybody can read them"—this analogy is often used by people when talking about email security. Looking at email security in more detail, one can see that this analogy is not very suitable, though. There are mechanisms (e.g., transport encryption) in place that guarantee confidentiality and authenticity to a certain extent, as we will point out in the next section. However, guarantees "to a certain extent" do not always suffice in practice. There are cases where we want true guarantees that the emails we send cannot be read or forged by any unauthorized third parties; one might think of communication with doctors, for example. End-to-end encryption (E2EE)—and signatures—with PGP or S/MIME can provide such guarantees. However, E2EE has still not found its breakthrough in practice for securing emails—leaving people with a certain feeling of unease when sending emails with sensitive content without any further protective measures (having the postcard analogy in mind). People can just not estimate whether their email will be sent in a secure way to the proper destination or not; chances are good[1], but there is no guarantee.

---

[1] Google regularly publishes numbers that show that around 90% of all emails sent and received via Google Mail are protected with transport encryption: https://transparencyreport.google.com/safer-email/overview.

© The Author(s), under exclusive license to Springer Nature Switzerland AG 2023
J. Garcia-Alfaro et al. (Eds.): DPM 2022/CBT 2022, LNCS 13619, pp. 53–68, 2023.
https://doi.org/10.1007/978-3-031-25734-6_4

Coming back to our communication with doctors[2] example from above, we should not only ask ourselves whether such communication via "unencrypted" email (i.e., without E2EE) is a good idea, but whether such communication is allowed at all. Since May 2018, the General Data Protection Regulation (GDPR) is applied in Europe, raising the bar in terms of *security* for controllers. According to *Article 32 GDPR*:

> Controllers shall implement appropriate technical and organisational measures to ensure a level of security appropriate to the risk—taking into account the state of the art, the costs of implementation and the nature, scope, context and purposes of processing as well as the risk of varying likelihood and severity for the rights and freedoms of natural persons.

In our example, with respect to the nature, scope and context of the transmission of sensitive medical data via email and, thus, (potentially) high likelihood and severity for the rights and freedoms of patients (if their medical data gets disclosed), one can see that proper technical measures need to be set in place to ensure a level of security appropriate to the potential high risk. What would be such proper technical measures in our scenario? The solution seems to be clear: E2EE, being a state of the art measure with low costs of implementation. And yet, practically none of the medical institutions[3] have the ability to communicate with E2EE (with their patients). Even if medical institutions would have the ability, there would be few patients with whom they could communicate in a secure way, as most patients also do not have E2EE facility set up on their devices. [18] Despite all of that, email communication between medical institutions and patients is taking place (without E2EE), be it to set up appointments, send examination results and blood values, sick notes, covid test results, and so forth.

Not only since the application of the GDPR do data protection authorities (DPAs) argue with controllers (companies, medical institutions, public authorities,...) whether they need to employ E2EE in order to communicate with their customers, patients, citizens, etc. [25] In March 2020, the German DPAs[4] published a guideline for controllers[5], in which they state in detail which kind of technical measures need to be taken by the controllers (according to the risk of the communication—based on the sensitivity of the data) in order to be on the safe side (and not risk fines). Controllers that *intend to receive emails with high risk* or that *send emails with high risk* need to take (one of) the following technical measures:

- provide public key for E2EE; send emails with E2EE
- provide the facility for a "qualified" transport encryption

---

[2] In the rest of the paper, we use the more general term medical institution, which also covers clinics and medical care centers.

[3] The same is true for other businesses and authorities as well.

[4] In Germany, other than in other European countries, there are 18 DPAs in toal.

[5] https://www.datenschutzkonferenz-online.de/media/oh/20200526_orientierungshilf e_e_mail_verschluesselung.pdf.

A qualified transport encryption according to the German DPAs means that TLS 1.2 (with secure cipher suites and perfect forward secrecy) or TLS 1.3 is used and that DANE is employed.

Summing up, we can conclude the following:

– Medical institutions have websites where they state their email addresses (and, thus, *intend* to receive emails with high risk—as emails containing sensitive medical data always impose a high risk),
– Medical institutions communicate with their patients via email (during covid pandemic time, covid test results were sent without any further protection mechanisms via email, for example),
– E2EE is generally not employed in email communication between medical institutions and patients.

Medical institutions would therefore need to make sure that their email servers are configured according to the requirements of the DPAs, i.e., support a qualified transport encryption. Otherwise, the medical institutions would put their patients' medical data at risk (when communicating via email) and furthermore risk high fines by DPAs.

In this paper, we investigate whether medical institutions in Germany adhere to the requirements by the DPAs with regard to secure email communication.

2 Background

This section describes relevant parts of the underlying principles of email communication.

2.1 SMTP Protocol

SMTP is a plaintext protocol originally defined in 1980 as part of a system for asynchronous email communication [7]. SMTP is used to transport the email from the sender's email client to the sender's email server and from the sender's email server to the receiver's email server. To finally collect the emails from the server, the receiver needs to request the mails using IMAP or POP.

Since it was first defined, the protocol has received multiple extensions, like CHUNKING for large messages [16], AUTH for user authentication [13] or STARTTLS for TLS transport encryption [14,15] and many more.

2.2 Opportunistic Transport Encryption

For many years, data security and privacy protection was not a big concern and emails were sent completely without any security measures.

The first step in this direction was E2EE using tools like PGP [10]. PGP (and also S/MIME [3]) enables senders to encrypt their emails at their side and decryption is only possible for the legitimate receiver (with the proper private key); neither eavesdroppers nor the involved email servers can read the contents.

This approach requires additional efforts for both sides of the communication (e.g., in our scenario: for patients and doctors), because they have to actively exchange their public keys.

The next step towards more privacy (more precisely, confidentiality) was transport encryption for the SMTP protocol using the previously mentioned STARTTLS extension [14]. Up until the STARTTLS command is issued by the sender, the communication is still sent over plaintext. The STARTTLS message then initiates a TLS Handshake where a common TLS version is negotiated and session keys are generated using public key cryptography. All of the following communication in this session is then encrypted.

This way of establishing an encrypted communication channel is easy to attack for a man in the middle (MITM), though. An eavesdropper with the ability to modify the communication could simply strip the STARTTLS capability from the EHLO response and therefore enforce plain text communication.

2.3   DNS-Based Authentication of Named Entities

To mitigate this so-called downgrade attack, a technology called DANE can be used. It uses DNSSEC and a special DNS record type, called TLSA, to prove the authenticity of a mailserver. A domain owner needs to enable DNSSEC for their domain and create a TLSA entry, which stores either a signed TLS certificate, a public key or a hash value of one of these. When a mail transfer agent (MTA) wants to forward an email to this server, it firt checks if the contents of the TLSA record match with the contents of the certificate provided by the server during the STARTTLS initiation. This way, DNS is used as a trusted communication channel to prove the authenticity of the certificate used for the mail transport. DANE therefore makes it impossible for an MITM to just replace the certificate in transmission. This implicitly prevents a downgrade attack, since a mailserver with a valid TLSA record always has to support STARTTLS encryption. An additional security advantage of DANE is that the owner of the domain can specify a trust anchor of his choice and is not bound by official certification authorities.

3   Related Work

Durumeric, et al. [21] examined the coverage of STARTTLS in Gmail Inbound traffic between January 2014 and April 2015, recording an increase from 52% to 80% coverage within one year (mainly due to the start of support by Yahoo and Hotmail). Zhu, et al. [26] measured a low DANE support between 0.05% (for .com-domains) and 0.23% (for .net-domains) from March 2013 to October 2014.

Foster, et al. [22] compared the TLS support of the top 22 email providers in 2013 and 74 web services of the Alexa Top 100 list that send emails as part of their service. They found that the percentage of users that use email providers with TLS support increased from 52% in 2014 to 89% in 2015. The TLS support of email-sending web services is generally lower and varies between categories, being the highest for financial institutions (67%) and lowest for news and dating sites (0%).

This increasing trend can also be observed in a DANE study [23] where domains worldwide (50% from Germany) have been tracked between 2014 and 2020. The study concludes with a result of 96.4% secure domains regarding STARTTLS (ranging from 97.6% having at least one TLS-secure MX record and 94.3% exclusively having secure MX records). The authors also report a valid DANE support for 17.6% of domains.

Lee, et al. [24] further examined the regional differences in DANE support by using data from OpenINTEL [9]. By comparing international top-level-domains (.com and .org) with country-top-level domains (.se and .nl) between October 2017 and October 2019, they found a higher DANE support for region-specific email servers (38.2% for .se and 9.8% for .nl) than for international ones (0.6% for .com and 0.73% for .org). Despite the generally low coverage of DANE support, they could observe an increasing trend in DANE support over these two years.

3.1 Our Contribution

In this paper, we present further analysis regarding email security as of June 2022. Particularly, we examine the security of email servers of medical institutions in Germany by measuring the used TLS versions and the coverage of DANE support among the used email providers.

4 Methodology

This section describes our methodology for performing a security analysis of email servers used by medical institutions.

4.1 Dataset Generation

Our analysis is based on domains of German medical institutions as of May 2022. We developed a python web crawler that extracts registered profile information of medical institutions from *jameda.de*, an independent medical appointment booking platform.

To extract these profiles, combinations of all available German cities and medical subject areas are queried. Many profiles contain a link to individual websites, which are further scanned for email addresses using regular expressions.

All information is compiled by the crawler into a dataset with the following structure:

- list of profiles containing:
  - name of responsible doctor
  - medical subject area
  - extracted email addresses
  - link to individual website and imprint section

- list of all email addresses
- list of all domains
- list of websites that could not be scanned automatically

Some websites may contain multiple email addresses, including contact details of medical associations, website building services and data protection officers. In order to eliminate non-medical email addresses, we performed a cleanup: each email address has to contain a part of the doctor's name or the medical institution's website URL in order to be seen as valid.

There were some cases in which no matches could be found and manual verification was necessary.

With this approach, we gathered a total of 3772 email addresses (4414 before cleanup) and 2938 domains (3382 before cleanup).

However, it is also possible that the crawler also collects email addresses that are not visible to humans due to styling and formatting. Because of this, the dataset could contain some outdated email addresses which are no longer used.

4.2   Security Analysis

The first step towards analyzing the email server's security configuration is to extract the domain from the email address and retrieve the respective MX and A records of the responsible SMTP server(s). Then a TLS version test and a check for DANE support is performed for each individual SMTP server.

DNS Records. The developed software uses the tool dig for performing DNS queries [4]. We use the Google DNS as DNS server, which can be reached under the IP 8.8.8.8 [6]. It supports DNSSEC, which means that we can determine if it is a validated response by looking at the AD flag [5]. This is important for the DANE analysis. Through trial and error, we found that if too many requests are made, not all of them will be answered. For this reason we implemented a rate limit of 10 queries per second. The following steps are conducted to get the MX records and corresponding A records:

1. The domain name is extracted from the email address. Then all domain names are deduplicated which results in a list of distinct domains.
2. For each domain, all MX records are queried and saved. Note that we do not check whether implicit MX is used, which is why not all email servers may be covered [12]. In addition, it is stored whether the response was validated by DNSSEC (for DANE analysis).
3. For each MX record, all A records are queried and saved.

The result is a data structure in which all MX records are stored for each domain. Each MX record itself has one or more A record entries.

To increase reliability of mailing, there can be multiple SMTP servers for a domain. This can be due to multiple MX records or multihomed hosts (multiple A records for one MX record). The order in which the SMTP servers are contacted depends on the preference values of the MX records and the order of the A records. If there are multiple MX records, the sender tries to contact the host with the smallest preference value first. The A records are processed in the order in which the entries were provided by the DNS resolver.

One consideration was whether it is necessary to test each individual SMTP server or if it is sufficient to test the first SMTP server from the MX record with the lowest preference value (highest priority). If an SMTP server is not reachable, then the sender selects the next one in the ordered list (but there may be an installation-specific limit for connection attempts) [12]. When a domain offers multiple SMTP servers, but not all of them offer the same level of security, an attacker can take advantage of this fact. He blocks the SMTP connection attempts to the secure SMTP servers and, thus, the sender connects to the insecure email servers. Because of this, we decided to test each email server individually and verify if *all* SMTP servers from a domain implement a security feature.

TLS Version Scan. Our goal is to determine whether an email server offers encryption via STARTTLS and if so, which TLS versions are supported.

For this purpose, the open-source tool testssl.sh was chosen because it is actively developed and has a high popularity [17]. The tool is supplied with each unique combination of MX record and IP address from the DNS lookup done before. With our configuration, it connects to the server on port 25 and performs the SMTP protocol. It is tested, whether STARTTLS is offered at all. If so, the availability of SSLv2, SSLv3, TLS 1.0, TLS 1.1, TLS 1.2 and TLS 1.3 is determined.

DANE Scan. The next step is to analyze if an email server supports DANE.

For a secure implementation of DANE, (1) DNSSEC must be enabled (for the retrieval of the MX, A and TLSA records), (2) a TLSA entry must be published, and (3) STARTTLS must be offered with a correct certificate chain [19,24].

Whether DNSSEC is available for querying the MX records is included in the data from the DNS queries. To check the remaining conditions, we employ the open source program gotls [11]. The tool receives the MX record and DNS server as input. In this case the Google DNS server is passed. The domain of our server is used as the hostname for the EHLO command.

First, all TLSA entries are queried. Through the use of DNSSEC, it must be ensured that the response is authentic. Then the A entries are queried and a connection with the individual SMTP server(s) is established. The tool checks if the presented certificate matches the data from the TLSA entry. From the console log it is possible to extract whether DANE is available and correctly implemented for a particular SMTP server.

4.3   Execution

The runtime of our program[6] on a server with 2 vCores is approximately 2 h for the dataset described in Sect. 4.1. Parallelization allows multiple servers to be tested simultaneously.

To avoid spam, some email servers have blocked requests from dynamic IP addresses. Therefore we run our program on a server with a static IP address. Furthermore, an rDNS record is entered in the DNS, which points to our server.

5   Evaluation

In this section, we present the results of our email server analysis. We analyzed 2938 different domains. Recall that there may be multiple SMTP servers for one domain. For 2836 domains (which are used by 2806 medical institutions) there is at least one valid test result for an SMTP server. For the further analysis, only those domains are used.

A detailed breakdown of the dataset is shown in Table 1.

Table 1. For the majority of domains we were able to obtain test results

Status	Domains
No MX Records	77 (2.6%)
No valid test results (e.g. connection problems, blocklist)	25 (0.9%)
Valid test results (for at least one SMTP server)	2836 (96.5%)

5.1   TLS Deployment - Domains

A test is performed to determine whether STARTTLS is supported and if so, which TLS versions are offered.

Highest Possible TLS Version. First we check the maximum TLS version supported by *at least one* SMTP server under a domain (the maximum TLS version of the strongest member of the group). However, there is no guarantee that a patient can reach the SMTP server(s) with the high TLS version (for example, because an attacker blocks the connection). Therefore, we also examine the maximum TLS version that *all* SMTP servers of a domain support (the maximum TLS version of the weakest member of the group).

2712 domains (95.6%) have the same highest TLS version for each SMTP server. There are differences for 124 domains (4.4%): Here the maximum TLS version for at least one SMTP server is different.

---

[6] The sourcecode for the project is available at https://git.informatik.fh-nuernberg. de/email-research/medical-institution-email-check.

The analysis for *all* SMTP servers shows that 59.6% of the domains use TLS version 1.3 and 39.8% use TLS version 1.2. The TLS versions SSLv2 to TLS 1.1, which are considered insecure and are not state-of-the-art anymore, are used by 0.1% of the domains. No encryption is possible for 0.5% of the domains. Table 2 shows detailed results.

Table 2. The majority of domains (99.5%) offers encryption with STARTTLS

Highest possible TLS Version	Domains (at least one SMTP server)	Domains (all SMTP servers)
No STARTTLS	9 (0.3%)	13 (0.5%)
SSLv2	0 (0%)	0 (0%)
SSLv3	0 (0%)	0 (0%)
TLS 1	0 (0%)	2 (0.1%)
TLS 1.1	0 (0%)	0 (0%)
TLS 1.2	1012 (35.7%)	1130 (39.8%)
TLS 1.3	1815 (64%)	1691 (59.6%)

Lowest Possible TLS Version. The lowest TLS version of a domain is the minimum TLS version that *at least one* SMTP server under that domain supports (from the weakest member of the group, the minimum TLS version). This is the worst case (from an encryption point of view) where the email is still accepted by the receiving end with transport encryption.

2796 domains (98.6%) have the same minimum TLS version for all SMTP servers. For 40 domains (1.4%), at least one SMTP server offers a different minimum TLS version.

We find that 72.3% of domains accept emails with the deprecated versions SSLv2 to TLS 1.1. 27.7% of domains require at least TLS version 1.2 for email transport. Table 3 shows detailed results.

5.2   DANE Deployment - Domains

First, we take a look at the domains where *at least one* SMTP server offers DANE. From a security perspective, this is not recommended. An attacker could block the connections to the email servers with DANE support and force a connection to insecure email servers. Therefore, we also check how many domains offer DANE for *all* SMTP servers. We find that 25 (0.9%) domains provide DANE for *at least one* SMTP server and 25 (0.9%) domains offer DANE for *all* SMTP servers (see Table 4). The fact that each of the domains supports DANE for all SMTP servers guarantees that the patient can take advantage of the security features.

Table 3. 2041 (72.3%) domains allow encrypted email sending with the deprecated TLS versions SSLv2 to TLS 1.1

Lowest possible TLS Version	Domains (at least one SMTP server)	Domains (all SMTP servers)
SSLv2	2 (0.1%)	1 (0%)
SSLv3	23 (0.8%)	19 (0.7%)
TLS 1	1845 (65.4%)	1823 (64.5%)
TLS 1.1	171 (6.1%)	172 (6.1%)
TLS 1.2	782 (27.7%)	812 (28.7%)
TLS 1.3	0 (0%)	0 (0%)

For DANE, according to RFC 7671, at least TLS 1.0 must be supported, and TLS 1.2 or higher should be supported [20]. In our dataset, all domains that support DANE for all SMTP servers use at least TLS 1.2.

Of the 25 domains that support DANE, 4 are from major German email providers ("web.de", "gmx.de", "gmx.net" and "posteo.de")[7]. The rest are, according to the name, own domains of the medical institutions. The email infrastructure of the latter domains is provided by 6 providers (see Sect. 5.3 for details on identifying the email infrastructure provider). In 14 out of 21 (60%) cases, this is "one.com". The remaining 7 domains (40%) are distributed among 5 other providers.

The 25 domains are used by 81 medical institutions that offer at least one email address that supports DANE. 22 of the domains are used by 66 medical institutions, of which all email addresses support DANE. Of the latter, 47 facilities use email addresses from major providers ("gmx.de/net" and "web.de") and 19 have their own domain.

Table 4. Only a small percentage of domains (0.9%) supports DANE

Status	Domains (at least one SMTP server)	Domains (all SMTP servers)
DANE Ok	25 (0.9%)	25 (0.9%)
DANE Not Ok	2.811 (99.1%)	2.811 (99.1%)

5.3 Email Infrastructure Provider Analysis

If a medical facility decides to accept emails through its own domain, email server management can be outsourced to an external provider. These providers

---

[7] web.de and GMX actually are part of the same company called "1 & 1 Mail & Media GmbH". Web.de and GMX are very popular freemailing services in Germany; there exist paid premium services as well, though.

can provide the email infrastructure for many domains. This means that the security level of all managed domains depends on what the provider offers.

We investigate which providers manage the most domains for our dataset and check which TLS versions are offered and whether DANE is supported.

Extracting Providers from MX Records. In our dataset, the MX records are used to determine the providers. We found that the naming of the hosts of a provider differs only on the subdomain level. For example, a provider has the MX records *mail1.myprovider.de* and *mail2.myprovider.de*. For the analysis, the two MX records are combined into one provider named *myprovider.de*. All domains that have **.myprovider.de* (star as wildcard) as MX record are counted as managed domains of the provider *myprovider.de*. Note that not all providers may be captured correctly using this method, as the naming of MX records may differ.

It can be stated that only 6 providers (out of total 789) manage over 50% of domains[8]. A change in security measures at these providers could have a major impact on the security level of many domains.

TLS Deployment - Providers. We only analyze the 6 top providers in more detail.

When looking at the SMTP servers per provider, we find that all servers offer the same maximum TLS version. For the minimum TLS version, this only applies to 5 of the 6 providers: kasserver.com has servers in our dataset that offer TLS 1.0 as well as ones that offer TLS 1.1 or TLS 1.2 as the minimum version.

All providers offer the latest TLS versions 1.2 and 1.3. However, at the same time 4 out of 6 providers still support the deprecated version TLS 1.0. The other 2 providers only allow encrypted receiving with at least the secure TLS version 1.2. Table 5 shows the detailed results.

DANE Deployment - Providers. To check whether a provider supports DANE, its MX records and the associated SMTP servers are considered. The difference to the domain DANE analysis is that it is not checked whether DNSSEC is also activated for querying the MX records. It is therefore possible that a provider enables DANE, but the domain owner has not enabled DNSSEC (e.g. missing DS entry in the parent zone).

None of the top providers supports DANE and, thus, leaving the email communication of their customers (in our scenario: medical institutions) with their users (here: patients) insecure.

Microsoft as a Service Provider. We were surprised that 249 medical institutions use email services provided by Microsoft, because Microsoft has long been in the focus of criticism of German data protection authorities—justified or not.

[8] Since one provider can manage multiple domains (MX records of two providers on one domain) it is actually the sum of the managed domains of all providers.

Table 5. Six providers handle the mail transport for over 50% of the domains

Provider	Domains	Min. TLS version	Max. TLS version	DANE
kundenserver.de	397 (13.6%)	TLS 1	TLS 1.3	No
rzone.de	373 (12.8%)	TLS 1.2	TLS 1.3	No
outlook.com	239 (8.2%)	TLS 1.2	TLS 1.2	No
kasserver.com	237 (8.1%)	TLS 1 (TLS 1.2)	TLS 1.3	No
ispgateway.de	163 (5.6%)	TLS 1	TLS 1.2	No
ionos.de	131 (4.5%)	TLS 1	TLS 1.3	No

We first suspected that the medical institutions made use of a free outlook.com account, which would have been definitely a problem in terms of privacy protection. One must know that Microsoft offers both private ("consumer") and business email services.

Microsoft differentiates between private and business customers both in terms of the *Service Agreements* and in terms of the *Privacy Policies*—and this differentiation is also relevant for the email service, and, thus, our scenario.

As an example, Microsoft states in its service agreements for private customers[9] that the provided services are only intended to be used for private and non-commercial usage. Medical institutions that use a (free) private email service from Microsoft might violate the service agreements[10]. Moreover, and this is the more critical part: Microsoft states in its privacy policy for private customers[11] that *personal data are used for*:

- Development and improvement of products
- Personalization of Microsoft products and provision of recommendations
- Targeted advertisement

To sum it up, Microsoft could use all the personal data (in our scenario: medical data of medical institutions' patients) sent and received via email through a medical institution's private customer email account as test data for product development, for feeding recommender systems and for advertisement purposes.

Medical institutions, as controllers according to the GDPR, shall only use processors that provide *sufficient guarantees* to implement appropriate technical and organisational measures according to Art. 28 GDPR. A private email service provided by Microsoft definitely does not provide sufficient guarantees and must not be used by medical institutions for communication with patients.[12]

---

[9] https://www.microsoft.com/en-us/servicesagreement.

[10] And due to an absence of privacy guarantees for private accounts, such medical institutions might violate another term in the service agreement: The Code of Conducts requires: "Don't engage in activity that violates the privacy of others.".

[11] https://privacy.microsoft.com/de-de/privacystatement.

[12] It should be noted that this might not only be the case for Microsoft but for other freemail services (like web.de or GMX) as well; we did not check their service agreements and privacy protection policies in detail, though.

We thus needed to find a way to check whether a Microsoft email address is based on a private or business account. We can make a distinction between three different variants:

(1) As a private customer, an account can be created at outlook.com, whereupon an email address is created which ends with outlook.com. Depending on the country, other top level domains are also possible, for example outlook.de. The service outlook.com has been renamed several times over the years, which is why there are still a number of "legacy" domains[13] [8]. If such an email address is used, the private plan is used.
(2) Both private and business customers can use their own (paid) domain with the underlying email infrastructure provided by Microsoft [1,8]. This can be recognized by the fact that the MX record of the domain points to a Microsoft email server.
(3) Business customers are provided with an email address that ends with onmicrosoft.com [2]. In this case, a business plan is used.

Table 6 shows the breakdown of our analysis.

Table 6. Breakdown of the adoption of Microsoft's email services. A medical facility is included in a category if at least one email address from the facility meets the criterion.

Variant	Medical institutions
(1) private outlook.com address	9 (0.3%)
(2) Microsoft email service with own domain	240 (8.6%)
(3) Microsoft business email account	0 (0%)

Especially variant 2 was of special interest for us, as most medical institutions use this variant and we could not directly derive from the data whether those email addresses are based on a private or business account. We then analyzed the MX records in more detail and noticed that they ended either with "mail.protection.outlook.com", "msv1.mail.outlook.com" or "mail.eo.outlook.com". In the next step, we needed to find out whether private or business accounts are provided with such records. We therefore created different Microsoft email accounts: private and business accounts, which we all linked to our own paid domain. We found that private email accounts get an MX record ending with "pamx1.hotmail.com" and business accounts get an MX record ending with "mail.protection.outlook.com". Help pages on the internet indicate that the other MX records were previously used for the business offer. Thus, we are quite sure that the 240 medical institutions that use a Microsoft email service

---

[13] We used outlook.com, outlook.de, live.com, live.de, msn.de, msn.com, hotmail.com, hotmail.de for the analysis.

with their own domain use a business account with proper guarantees in terms of security and privacy protection and these cases are not as problematic as they first seemed to be.[14]

6 Conclusion

In this paper we investigated the state of email security of German medical institutions. For this purpose, we built a dataset of email addresses from a medical portal and analyzed the corresponding email servers. We can conclude that (1) the support of STARTTLS is high (99.5% of domains). Furthermore, we can state that (2) 99.5% of the domains support the current TLS versions 1.2 and 1.3. The availability of DANE (3) is very low with 0.9% of the domains, however. In addition, we derived from the MX records which provider manages the email infrastructure of a domain. We can see (4) that only few providers (0.6%) manage more than 50% of the domains. The top providers all enable current TLS versions, but DANE is not supported by any of them. If the providers would implement state-of-the-art security properly, all of their customers' email communication would be secured at once.[15]

Only 25 of 2836 analyzed domains of medical institutions (used by 66 different medical institutions) are fully protected with DANE, thus meeting the requirements of the German data protection authorities for high risk email communication.[16] All the other medical institutions must not exchange medical data via email, unless they employ further technical measures like E2EE.

Medical institutions do not need to operate their email servers themselves—they can make use of processors. However, what many forget: the medical institutions still stay the responsible controllers (in terms of the GDPR). If email providers are chosen that do not provide state-of-the-art security, medical institutions risk GDPR fines from data protection authorities.

We will regularly repeat our investigation in the future and provide the results at https://www.mail-sicherheit.jetzt.

References

1. Alle Microsoft 365-Pläne vergleichen | Microsoft. https://www.microsoft.com/de-de/microsoft-365/business/compare-all-microsoft-365-business-products?market=de. Accessed 14 June 2022

---

[14] Rather, those email accounts will soon be protected with DANE, as Microsoft announced a DANE roll-out for 2022: https://techcommunity.microsoft.com/t5/exchange-team-blog/releasing-outbound-smtp-dane-with-dnssec/ba-p/3100920.

[15] It is a good sign that Microsoft started DANE roll-out for Exchange Online in early 2022: https://techcommunity.microsoft.com/t5/exchange-team-blog/releasing-outbound-smtp-dane-with-dnssec/ba-p/3100920.

[16] However, 47 of these medical institutions employ a gmx or web.de address and it is not clear whether it is a freemail or a business account.

2. Change your Microsoft 365 email address to use your custom domain. https:// docs.microsoft.com/en-us/microsoft-365/admin/email/change-email-address? view=o365-worldwide. Accessed 14 June 2022

3. Cryptographic Message Syntax (CMS). https://datatracker.ietf.org/doc/html/ rfc3369. First CMS RFC that mentions S/MIME. Accessed 15 June 2022

4. dig(1) - OpenBSD manual pages. https://man.openbsd.org/dig.1. Accessed 18 June 2022

5. Google Online Security Blog: Google Public DNS Now Supports DNSSEC Validation. https://security.googleblog.com/2013/03/google-public-dns-now-supports-dnssec.html. Accessed 19 June 2022

6. Google Public DNS. https://developers.google.com/speed/public-dns. Accessed 15 Apr 2022

7. Mail Transfer Protocol. https://datatracker.ietf.org/doc/html/rfc772. Original Mail Transfer Protocol RFC. Accessed 15 June 2022

8. Microsoft 365 Single Kaufen - Premium-Office-Paket | Microsoft. https://www. microsoft.com/de-de/microsoft-365/p/microsoft-365-single/cfq7ttc0k5bf?rtc=1& activetab=pivot:overviewtab. Accessed 14 June 2022

9. OpenINTEL. https://www.openintel.nl/. Accessed 24 Mai 2022

10. PGP Message Exchange Formats. https://datatracker.ietf.org/doc/html/rfc1991. First PGP RFC. Accessed 15 June 2022

11. shuque/gotls: Diagnostic tool to perform DANE & PKIX authentication of a TLS server. https://github.com/shuque/gotls. Accessed 18 June 2022

12. Simple Mail Transfer Protocol. https://datatracker.ietf.org/doc/html/rfc5321. Accessed 18 Apr 2022

13. SMTP Service Extension for Authentication. https://datatracker.ietf.org/doc/ html/rfc4954. sMTP Auth Extension RFC. Accessed 15 June 2022

14. SMTP Service Extension for Secure SMTP over TLS. https://datatracker.ietf.org/ doc/html/rfc2487. Original SMTP STARTTLS Extension RFC. Accessed 15 June 2022

15. SMTP Service Extension for Secure SMTP over Transport Layer Security. https:// datatracker.ietf.org/doc/html/rfc3207. Updated SMTP STARTTLS Extension RFC. Accessed 15 June 2022

16. SMTP Service Extensions for Transmission of Large and Binary MIME Messages. https://datatracker.ietf.org/doc/html/rfc1830. sMTP Chunking Extension RFC. Accessed 15 June 2022

17. Testing TLS/SSL encryption. https://testssl.sh/. Accessed 15 Apr 2022

18. Braun, S., Oostveen, A.M.: Encryption for the masses? An analysis of PGP key usage. Mediatization Stud. (2) (2018)

19. Dukhovni, V., Hardaker, W.: SMTP security via opportunistic DNS-based authentication of named entities (DANE) transport layer security (TLS). RFC 7672, IETF (2015)

20. Dukhovni, V., Hardaker, W.: The DNS-based authentication of named entities. DANE) protocol: updates and operational guidance. Technical report (2015)

21. Durumeric, Z., et al.: Neither snow nor rain nor MITM... an empirical analysis of email delivery security. In: Proceedings of the 2015 Internet Measurement Conference, pp. 27–39 (2015)

22. Foster, I.D., Larson, J., Masich, M., Snoeren, A.C., Savage, S., Levchenko, K.: Security by any other name: On the effectiveness of provider based email security. In: Proceedings of the 22nd ACM SIGSAC Conference on Computer and Communications Security, pp. 450–464 (2015)

23. Kambourakis, G., Gil, G.D., Sanchez, I.: What email servers can tell to Johnny: an empirical study of provider-to-provider email security. IEEE Access **8**, 130066–130081 (2020)
24. Lee, H., Gireesh, A., van Rijswijk-Deij, R., Chung, T., et al.: A longitudinal and comprehensive study of the DANE ecosystem in email. In: 29th USENIX Security Symposium (USENIX Security 2020) (2020)
25. Petrlic, R.: The general data protection regulation: from a data protection authority's (technical) perspective. IEEE Secur. Priv. **17**(6), 31–36 (2019). https://doi.org/10.1109/MSEC.2019.2935701
26. Zhu, L., Wessels, D., Mankin, A., Heidemann, J.: Measuring DANE TLSA deployment. In: Steiner, M., Barlet-Ros, P., Bonaventure, O. (eds.) TMA 2015. LNCS, vol. 9053, pp. 219–232. Springer, Cham (2015). https://doi.org/10.1007/978-3-319-17172-2_15

Explanation of Black Box AI for GDPR Related Privacy Using Isabelle

Florian Kammüller[1,2(✉)]

[1] Middlesex University London, London, UK
`f.kammueller@mdx.ac.uk`
[2] Technische Universität Berlin, Berlin, Germany

Abstract. In this paper, we present a methodology for constructing explanations for AI classification algorithms. The methodology consists of constructing a model of the context of the application in the Isabelle Infrastructure framework (IIIf) and an algorithm that allows to extract a precise logical rule that specifies the behaviour of the black box algorithm thus allowing to explain it. The explanation is given within the rich logical model of the IIIf. It is thus suitable for human audiences. We illustrate this and validate the methodology on the application example of credit card scoring with special relation to the right of explanation as given by the GDPR.

1 Introduction

Artificial intelligence (AI) uses various methods of machine learning to solve problems automatically. Some of the used methods, for example linear regression or decision trees are amenable to human understanding. However, other very successful ones, for example deep learning methods and convolutional neural networks (CNN), are black boxes for humans: it is not clear from the outside how the machine intelligence arrives at decisions. In critical applications, however, it is absolutely necessary that humans can understand what is going on and why.

We provide a method for explanation using the expressive Higher Order logic of the interactive theorem prover Isabelle. The Isabelle Infrastructure framework (IIIf) provides rich contexts for actors, infrastructures and policies to enable explanations of black box machine learning decisions to humans. This can be particularly relevant for privacy critical application. Black box algorithms are trained on data sets whose classification may have human biases but those are hidden in the opaqueness of the learning algorithm. Explanation is necessary to shed light into this. We propose a process of precondition refinement to arrive at logical rules for explanation using counterfactuals for iterating the refinement process. We illustrate and validate the proposed methodology by an example of credit scoring. There private information is used in the automated decision process of credit scoring guided by a black box AI algorithm. The GDPR grants a right of explanation. We show how our approach using attack trees and an expressive logical rule for explanation serves the main purposes of GDPR explanation. All Isabelle sources are available [14].

© The Author(s), under exclusive license to Springer Nature Switzerland AG 2023
J. Garcia-Alfaro et al. (Eds.): DPM 2022/CBT 2022, LNCS 13619, pp. 69–84, 2023.
https://doi.org/10.1007/978-3-031-25734-6_5

2   Background and Related Work

2.1   Explanation

Bau et al's article "Explaining Explanation [...]" [5] gives a good overview of the techniques used for explainable AI (XAI). The more recent work [1] provides a critical analysis of current literature on the field of XAI providing some challenges primarily featuring the post-hoc explanation of black box machine learning like CNN and Deep Learning and providing human comprehensible explanations. Belle and Papantonis [2] also give a very comprehensive survey of current explanation approaches including very accessible illustrations of their use on human centric examples.

Pieters distinguishes the main incentives of explanation as transparency (for the user) and justification [23]. Explanation trees may be used to visualize the relation of explanation goals and their subgoals according to Pieters providing "a tree in which the goals and subgoals of an explanation are ordered systematically" [23]. This work is a very strong motivation to our approach to explainability because explanation trees have much in common with attack trees. An attack tree makes an attack more transparent by a step by step process that can be characterized as "attack tree refinement" [7]. Ultimately, the attack tree refinement leads to a fully expanded explanation that can be automatically verified on the model as is shown in the Isabelle Insider framework [8,10]. Thus similar to an explanation tree, a sub-tree of an attack tree "explains" the attack expressed by the parent node.

2.2   GDPR, Explanation and IIIf

The GDPR explicitly mentions a right of explanation. Wachter et al. [25] investigate the use of counterfactuals for the explanation of automated decisions. They argue that counterfactuals are in themselves sufficient to provide explanations. We challenge their approach (see Sect. 5.1). Nevertheless, we also adopt the use of counterfactuals but only as a means to construct a general explanation as a logical rule. However, Wachter et al. also give a very detailed analysis of where explanation is mentioned in the GDPR [25]. They clearly identify the purposes of an individual who would want to claim an explanation against a data controller based on the GDPR. Explanations serve three main purposes [25, Section 5].

- *Understand decisions*: provide transparency of the scope of automated decisions and reasons.
- *Contest decisions*: provide the means to challenge a decision.
- *Alter future decisions*: provide help to adapt future behaviour to receive the preferred outcome.

We will show that the logical method of explanation we provide serves all three purposes (see Sect. 4.3).

In terms of logical modeling and analysis, it is worth mentioning that the IIIf has been used for GDPR relevant applications. In fact, [9] evaluates IoT scenarios with respect to GDPR related privacy. This work shows that the IIIf can be applied to provide *privacy by design* – one of the major principles stipulated by the GDPR. However, this early application of IIIf in the context of the GDPR can be seen as a formal experiment inspired by the concepts propagated by the GDPR and to advocate the use of formal verification to support GDPR compliance checking of IoT architectures. What the current work achieves is much closer to actual applications of the GDPR in law practice. It is thus more relevant to the application of the GDPR as a law to privacy related societal issues. This is illustrated as well by the case study we present in this paper where the explanation that our logical method IIIf provides can serve as a basis for challenging a decision made by a data controller using an AI based black box decision algorithm.

2.3   Isabelle Infrastructure Framework (IIIf)

Attack trees are fully embedded as "first-class citizens" into the logic in the Isabelle Insider and Infrastructure framework (IIIf). It is thus possible to provide a formal semantics for valid attacks based on Kripke structures and the temporal logic CTL as well as to derive an efficient decision procedure. Code is generated in the programming languages Scala for deciding the validity of attack trees.

The Isabelle Infrastructure framework (IIIf) is implemented as an instance of Higher Order Logic in the interactive generic theorem prover Isabelle/HOL [22]. The framework enables formalizing and proving of systems with physical and logical components, actors and policies. It has been designed for the analysis of insider threats. However, the implemented theory of the temporal logic CTL combined with Kripke structures and its generic notion of state transitions are a perfect match to be combined with attack trees into a process for formal security engineering [4] including an accompanying framework [11]. In the current paper, we show that the IIIf can also be used for explaining AI decisions made by black box algorithms. We provide here a very brief overview of the main features of the IIIf.

Kripke Structures, CTL and Attack Trees. A number of case studies have contributed to shape the Isabelle framework into a general framework for the state-based security analysis of infrastructures with policies and actors. Temporal logic and Kripke structures are deeply embedded into Isabelle's Higher Order logic thereby enabling meta-theoretical proofs about the foundations: for example, equivalence between attack trees and CTL statements have been established [8] providing sound foundations for applications. This foundation provides a generic notion of state transition on which attack trees and temporal logic can be used to express properties for applications. The logical concepts and related notions thus provided for sound application modeling are:

– Kripke structures and state transitions:
   A generic state transition relation is $\rightarrow$; Kripke structures over a set of states t reachable by $\rightarrow$ from an initial state set I can be constructed by the `Kripke` constructor as

```
Kripke {t. ∃ i ∈ I. i →* t} I
```

– CTL statements:
We can use the Computation Tree Logic (CTL) to specify dependability properties as

```
K ⊢ EF s
```

This formula states that in Kripke structure K there is a path (E) on which the property s (given as the set of states in which the property is true) will eventually (F) hold.

– Attack trees:
attack trees are defined as a recursive datatype in Isabelle having three constructors: $\oplus_\vee$ creates or-trees and $\oplus_\wedge$ creates and-trees. And-attack trees $l\oplus_\wedge^s$ and or-attack trees $l\oplus_\vee^s$ consist of a list of sub-attacks which are themselves recursively given as attack trees. The third constructor takes as input a pair of state sets constructing a base attack step between two state sets. For example, for the sets I and s this is written as $\mathcal{N}_{(I,s)}$. As a further example, a two step and-attack leading from state set I via si to s is expressed as

$$\vdash [\mathcal{N}_{(I,si)}, \mathcal{N}_{(si,s)}]\oplus_\wedge^{(I,s)}$$

– Attack tree refinement, validity and adequacy:
Attack trees can be constructed also by a refinement process but this differs from the system refinement presented in the paper [12]. An abstract attack tree may be refined by spelling out the attack steps until a valid attack is reached:
⊢A :: (σ:: state) attree).
The validity is defined constructively so that code can be generated from it. Adequacy with respect to a formal semantics in CTL is proved and can be used to facilitate actual application verification.

The IIIf has a wide range of applications ranging from Insider threats in auction protocols [17] and airplane policies [16], security and privacy of IoT healthcare systems, for example, [9,11], the Quantum Key Distribution protocol [10], Inter-blockchain protocols [19], the Corona-Warn App [12,18], and awareness in social networks and unintentional insiders [15].

The potentials of using the IIIf for explanation (for AI and security) has already been presented in an earlier paper but at the level of position paper only [13] while the current paper provides a feasible methodology, an implementation of explanation within the IIIf illustrating it on an application to a relevant case study in the context of GDPR related privacy. Online sources are available [14].

3   Case Study of Credit Scoring

In this section, we give a brief introduction to credit scoring and its relevant factors to motivate the case study that is used to illustrate how IIIf is applied to it to provide a basis for explanation.

3.1   Credit Scoring

Credit scores are ranks assigned to people to allow quantifying their "financial fitness" [3]. These scores are used by banks as well as credit institutes to decide whether a client may receive a credit card or more importantly whether a potential lender may receive a mortgage. It also influences the interest rate you may receive which can lead to disadvantaging poorer people. According to Internet publications [3,6] the research supporting the actual credit scoring "has come from ClearScore.com" [3]. An interactive map provided by this company allows to easily check credit scores as is illustrated in Fig. 1. An open question is how such credit scores are created as they rely on private data. As Bull writes [3]: "A higher income does not automatically lead to a higher credit score. For example, residents in Kensington and Chelsea are among the capital's highest average earners at £131,000 a year but they rank in the middle of the credit score table." Nevertheless, it is quite obvious that such scores are used by credit institutes. It seems rather likely that also AI based decision making procedures are applied within financial institutions. In order to clarify such opaque relations logical modeling can help as it remodels the actual context of the original data collection and thus may show up any biases used. In the next section, we present a simple example to illustrate how the credit scoring scenario can be represented as an infrastructure model in IIIf.

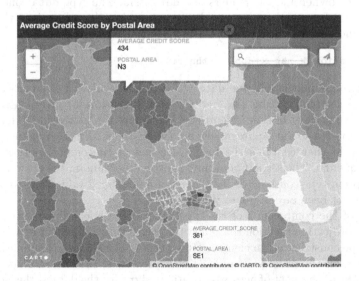

Fig. 1. Interactive map illustrates how credit scores differ in London districts [6].

3.2   Model in IIIf

The Isabelle Infrastructure framework supports the representation of infrastructures as graphs with actors and policies attached to nodes. These infrastructures are the *states* of a Kripke structure describing the credit scoring scenario. The behaviour is defined by a transition relation on states. This transition between states is triggered by non-parameterized actions put, eval, move, and get executed by actors. Actors are given by an abstract type actor and a function Actor that creates elements of that type from identities (of type string written ''s'' in Isabelle). Actors reside at locations of an infrastructure graph of type igraph constructed by its constructor Lgraph.

```
datatype igraph =
        Lgraph (location × location)set
               location ⇒ identity set
               identity ⇒ (dlm × data) set
               data ⇒ bool
               (identity × bool option)set
```

For the current application to the credit scoring scenario, this graph contains the actual location graph of type (location × location)set given by a set of location pairs, and a function of type location ⇒ identity set that assigns the actors to their current location. The third component of the datatype igraph is of type identity ⇒(dlm ×data) set. It assigns security labeled data to actors. The label type is called dlm as a reference to the decentralized label model by Myers and Liskov who inspired it [21]. It is a pair of type actor ×actor set defining the owner and the readers of a data item. The type data contains the private data of users. For our example, we use the location, the salary, their date of birth and ethnicity.[1]

```
data = location × nat × dob × ethnicity
```

The fourth component of type data ⇒ bool is the black box function: effectively a table that contains the credit approval decision for given data inputs. The final component of type (identity ×bool option)set records that a user has requested a credit approval by uploading their identity together with a boolean field that contains the future decision of the credit approval to the set of requests. The second boolean component containing the answer is lifted by the option type constructor that enables an undefined value None to flag that there has not been any response yet.

Each of the components of the type constructor is equipped with a corresponding projection function that allows to access this component in an instance of this type constructor (an element of this type). These projection functions are named gra for the set of pairs of location representing the infrastructure graph, agra for the assignment of actors to locations, dgra for the data at that location, bb for the black box, and requests for the pairs of request and approval decision of actors of requesting credits.

We omit some standard constructions for infrastructure assembly and the policy definition from local policies (see for example [12]). A generic state transition relation over Kripke structures is defined together with logic and decision

---

[1] The latter two type definitions are omitted for brevity.

procedures for IIIf. This is then instantiated to concrete applications of the IIIf – like in the current credit scoring example – by defining the rules for the state transition relation over a defined infrastructure type – as given by the above `igraph`. This state transition relation then implements the behaviour for credit scoring systems by explaining how actions executed by actors change the infrastructure state. The execution of actions is conditional on enabledness as defined by the local policies and other conditions of the context. For credit scoring systems, we consider here the actions `put` representing that a client requests a credit approval and `eval` where an entitled client (presumably a credit institute) executes a requested credit application.

In the precondition of the rule for a `put` action, the actor `a` residing at location `l` in the infrastructure graph `G` (given by the predicate `Actor a @`$_G$` l`) who is enabled to put a request, uploads their data to the `requests` `G` field into the infrastructure graph `G`. A potential credit institute `Actor c` can see a new request since now there is a new pair `(a, None)` in the requests set where the second component of this pair is flagged by the `None` constructor of the option type as "unprocessed" while the first element is the requesting actor's identity `a`.

```
put: G = graphI I ⟹ Actor a @_G l ⟹ Actor c ∈ actors G ⟹
     enables I l (Actor a) put ⟹
  I' = Infrastructure
          (Lgraph (gra G)(agra G)(dgra G)(bb G)
                  (insert (a, None)(requests G)))
          (delta I)
⟹ I → I'
```

The action `eval` allows evaluation of a request filed by actor `a` by a (presumable) credit institute `c` given that `c` is contained in the readers set of the `dlm` label `lb` that is given as the second element of the first element of the data item `dgra G a`. Also `c` needs to be enabled to evaluate requests by the local policy. Given these prerequisites, the actual evaluation is done by applying the black box function to the data item `d` and recording the outcome in the second component of the corresponding pair for `a` in the `requests` set.

```
eval: G = graphI I ⟹ Actor a @_G l ⟹ l ∈ nodes G ⟹
          Actor c ∈ actors G ⟹ (a, None) ∈ requests G ⟹
          (lb,d) = dgra G a ⟹ Actor c ∈ snd lb ⟹
          enables I l (Actor c) eval ⟹
  I' = Infrastructure
          (Lgraph (gra G)(agra G)(dgra G)(bb G)
                  (insert (a, Some((bb G) d))(requests G - {(a, None)})))
          (delta I)
⟹ I → I'
```

We omit the state transition rules for the actions `get` and `move`. They will be illustrated in the evaluation of the example below. For details of their definitions see the online sources [14].

The above infrastructure Kripke model for credit scoring formalises credit scoring scenarios enabling reasoning in general about all instances. To simulate concrete example scenarios, we can use the generic nature of the IIIf with its polymorphic Kripke structure and state transition. Defining a locale [20] named CreditScoring allows fixing some concrete values for the actors, locations, and local policies and inherits all general definitions and properties of infrastructures from the framework. For simplicity we consider just two actors Alice and Bob and a credit institute CI.

```
locale CreditScoring =
defines CreditScoring_actors = {''Alice'', ''Bob'', ''CI''}
```

The locale allows to initialize a concrete igraph with these and other values. Moreover it serves to illustrate the explanation process that we are going to present next.

4   Precondition Refinement Process (PCR Cycle)

In this section, we define a Precondition Refinement process (PCR cycle) which is a cyclic method to derive a general logical characterization of what the black box mechanism decides within any given state of the world. A possible world is described in the IIIf as a Kripke state comprising actors, policies and infrastructures including any features necessary to specify the context of a human centric scenario. After defining the process, we continue by illustrating its use on the previously introduced credit scoring system.

4.1   Definition of PCR Cycle

In contrast to the RR-cycle [12], we do not refine a system specification instead we refine the precondition of an explanation rule using the dynamic behaviour of an infrastructure system. But similar to the RR-cycle, we use attack trees to find "failure states", that is, states in which a desirable outcome is not given. These failure states allow us to find counterfactuals, which are local rules for specific instances for which the desirable outcome is achieved. The preconditions of these local rules guide the refinement of a general precondition. The refinement of the precondition is repeated until it yields a general rule for explanation. The starting point for this cyclic process of precondition refinement is an attack tree, i.e. a proof of a temporal property of the form $M \vdash EF \neg DO$ showing that "failure" states in the model M can be reached that do not fulfill the *desirable outcome (DO)*. This DO is comparable to what the "global policy" is in the RR-cycle [12]. The failure state can be used to define a *counterfactual*, essentially given as an additional precondition that would have provided an alternative path to a state fulfilling the DO property. Besides helping to guide the refinement by counterfactuals, the DO also provides the termination condition of the cyclic precondition refinement process. Since the DO property is the positive classification of the AI algorithm given as a black box, the process yields a general explanation rule that gives a precise logical description how the DO property can be achieved.

This is in a nutshell the working of the PCR cycle. In what follows we provide its high level yet detailed algorithmic description including the formal definitions of the core concepts used. However, before we come to that we need to introduce how we formalise counterfactuals.

Counterfactuals. A counterfactual is best explained by example. We give one that fits into the context of our case study: "if the client would have a monthly salary of 40K, he would have got the loan approval". Intuitively, counterfactuals try to illustrate facts in the current state of the world by showing alternative hypothetical developments of the world that feature the opposite case of the fact. It is not a coincidence that our explicit world model of Kripke structures and state transitions lends itself so naturally to modeling counterfactuals.

However, apart from modeling the different possible worlds and their evolution, we also need a metric on them. As Wachter observes "the concept of the "closest possible world" or the smallest change to the world that can be made to obtain a desirable outcome, is key throughout the discussion of counterfactuals" [25]. We use the step-relation between possible states (worlds) to define a unique notion of "closest" between three states. Intuitively, it formalises the closest predecessor s of two possible states s' and s'' by stipulating that any other state s_0 that is also a predecessor (with respect to $\to^*$) to states s' and s'' must already be a predecessor to s.

Definition 1 (Closest State). *A state s is closest (predecessor) to s',s'' with respect to step-relation $\to^*$ iff*

closest s s' s'' $\equiv$ s $\to^*$ s' $\wedge$ s $\to^*$ s'' $\wedge$
$\forall$ s_0. s_0 $\to^*$ s' $\wedge$ s_0 $\to^*$ s' $\Rightarrow$ s_0 $\to^*$ s

This definition is used for defining counterfactuals with respect to a desirable outcome DO by simply stating that for a state s with ¬ DO s there must be an alternative trace leading to another possible world s'' with DO s'' such that they are connected by a closest state s'. Using the definition of closest we can define this simply as the set of states for which such a closest predecessor exists.

Definition 2 (Counterfactuals). *Counterfactuals for a state s with respect to a desirable property DO are the states s'' that fulfill DO and have a closest predecessor s'.*

counterfactuals s DO $\equiv$ {s''. DO s'' $\wedge$
($\exists$ s'. (s' $\to^*$ s'') $\wedge$ closest s' s s'')}

We will see the application of these concepts in the following algorithm.

PCR Cycle Algorithm

1. Using attack tree analysis in the CTL logic of the IIIf we *find the initial starting condition of the PCR*. The variable B is an element of a datatype for which we seek explanation (in the example it is actors).

   M ⊢ EF { s ∈ states M. ¬ DO(B, s) }.

   This formula states that there exists a path (E) on which eventually (F) a state s will be reached in which the desirable outcome is not true for B. The path corresponds to an attack tree (by adequacy [8]) designating failure states s.

2. *Find the (initial or refined) precondition using a counterfactual.*

   That is, for a state s in the set of failure states identified in the previous step
   (a) Find states s' and s'' such that closest s' s s'', that is, s' →* s and s' →* s''. In addition, DO(B,s'') must hold.
   (b) Identify the precondition pc_i leading to the state s'' where DO holds, that is, find an additional predicate Δ_i with Δ_i(B, s') and use it to extend the previous predicate pc_i to $pc_{i+1} := pc_i \wedge \Delta_i$.

3. *Generalisation.*
   Use again attack tree analysis in the CTL logic of the IIIf to check whether the following formula is true on the entire datatype of B: it is globally true (AG) that if the precondition pc_i holds, there is a path on which eventually (EF) the desirable outcome DO holds.[2]

   ∀ A. M ⊢ AG {s ∈ states M. pc_i (A, s) ⟶ EF {s. DO(A, s)}}

   (a) If the check is negative, we get an attack tree, that is, IIIf provides an explanation tree for
   M ⊢ EF { s ∈ states M. pc_i(A,s) ∧ ¬ DO(A, s) }
   and a set of failure states s with pc_i(A,s) and the desirable outcome is not true: ¬DO(A,s).

   In this case, *go to step 2. and repeat* with the new set of failure states in order to find new counterfactuals and refine the predicate.
   (b) If the check is positive, we have *reached the termination condition* yielding a precondition pc_n such that for all A:
   M ⊢ AG { s ∈ states M. pc_n (A, s) ⟶ EF {s. DO(A, s)} }

Note, that the analysis in Step 3 might potentially reveal a new variable as part of Δ_i over another datatype (locations in the example). This is not a problem as it will eventually lead to tease out the entire set of parameters that the black box decision procedure uses. We did not attempt to formalise it explicitly into the above algorithm description to keep the exposition easier understandable.

---

[2] Note, that the interleaving of the CTL-operators AG and EF with logical operators, like implication ⟶ is only possible since we use a Higher Order logic embedding of CTL.

4.2   Applying the PCR Cycle to Credit Scoring Case Study

We now demonstrate the PCR algorithm on our case study introduced in Sect. 3.
We consider the scenario, where Bob gets an evaluation by the credit institute
CI and it is not approved. Bob wants to understand why this is the case and
requests an explanation. The experts in the credit institute cannot give this
explanation as they have used a black box machine learning system bb. Now,
the IIIf and the PCR algorithm can be used by modeling the scenario and using
the bb system as a black box, that is, requesting only its classification output
(verdict) for any given inputs.[3] The desirable outcome DO in an infrastructure
state s is given by the pair that a filed having a True as second component
(lifted by Some).

DO(a,s) ≡ (a, Some(True)) ∈ requests s

We show the run of the algorithm by going through its steps 1..3 for the application additionally ornating the numbers with $\alpha, \beta, \ldots$ to indicate the round of
the algorithm.

α.1 For actor Bob, we use CTL modelchecking in the IIIf to verify the formula

        Credit_Kripke ⊢
              EF { s ∈ states Credit_Kripke. ¬ DO(''Bob'', s) }.

From this proof, the IIIf allows applying Completeness and Correctness
results of CTL [8] to derive the following attack tree.

⊢ $[\mathcal{N}_{(I,c)}, \mathcal{N}_{(c,cc)}] \oplus_{\wedge}^{(I,cc)}$

The attack tree corresponds to a path leading from the initial state I to the
failure state CC where Bob's approval field in requests CC gets evaluated
by the credit company I as negative "False". The evaluation steps are:
I → C : Bob puts in a credit request; this is represented by a put action. So,
        the state C has (''Bob'', None) ∈ requests C.
C → CC : the credit institute CI evaluates the request represented as an eval
        action with the result of the evaluation left in requests CC. So, the
        state CC has (''Bob'', Some(False)) ∈ requests CC.
To derive the final failure state CC, the credit institute has applied the bb
function as Some((bb C) d) which evaluates Bob's request as Some(False)
(see rule eval in Sect. 3.2).
α.2 Next, the PCR algorithm finds an initial precondition that yields the desirable outcome in a closest state using counterfactuals. The closest state is
given as Ca which differs from C in that Bob has a higher salary of 40K as
opposed to 35K as in C. The state Ca is reachable: Bob first applies for a

---

[3] It is important to note that we request really only input output pairs and not
a mathematical description of the black box. This is in contrast to the stronger
assumptions made in the literature, for example [25] (see also the discussion in
Sect. 5.1).

promotion via the action get. From the state Ca, Bob puts in the credit application leading to CCa, before the credit institute CI evaluates leading to CCCa. We see that now with the increased salary of 40K, Bob receives a credit approval.

$\alpha.3$ The next step of the PCR algorithm is generalisation. We want to investigate whether the salary of 40K is a sufficient precondition in general (for all actors) to explain why the bb algorithm approves the credit. When we try to prove according to Step 3 that this is the case, the attack tree analysis proves the opposite.

```
M ⊢ EF { s ∈ states M.  pc_i(''Alice'',s) ∧ ¬ DO(''Alice'', s) }
```

It turns out that Alice who already has a salary of 40K doesn't get the credit approval. She lives, however, in London's district SE1 unlike Bob who lives in N3. Following thus Step 3.(a) we need to go to another iteration and go back to Step 2. to refine the precondition by counterfactuals.

$\beta.2$ In this β-run, we now have the state s where Alice doesn't get the approval. According to Step 2.(a), we find a counterfactual state as the one in which Alice first moves to N3. The new precondition now is created by adding the additional Δ_0 as A $@_s$ N3.

```
pc_{i+1} (A, s) := salary A s >= 40K ∧ A @_s N3
```

$\beta.3$ Going to Step 3 again in this β-run, now the proof of the generalisation succeeds.

```
∀ A. M ⊢ AG {s ∈ states M. pc_{i+1} (A, s) ⟶ EF {s. DO(A, s)}}
```

4.3   Discussion

With respect to the explanation, the algorithm finishes with the precondition

```
pc_{i+1} (A, s) := salary A s >= 40K ∧ A @_s N3
```

for any A of type actor. Although we terminated the algorithm there, we could have entered another cycle by extending the list of parameters of the precondition adding the location. The generalisation in Step 3 would have triggered the new cycle with providing a precise precondition Δ to specify which locations are sufficient for a desirable outcome. For the sake of conciseness of the exposition, we omit this additional round. But we nevertheless want to discuss it here as it sheds an interesting light onto the evaluation in particular with respect to the GDPR relevance.

It turns out that often there is a bias in the data that has been used to train the black box algorithm. For our case study, we deliberately used such an example to show its potential use for the logical explanation we provide. Since we give a general rule that formally describes and explains the decision process based on actual features of the context of the world. Here, the full run of the PCR algorithm would reveal that for postcodes of London areas in which predominantly black population lives, the salary has to be higher to gain credit approval. While our example is synthesized, biases like this are known to be implicit in data sets because of the data workers who provided the training data classifications. A very important contribution of our explicit logical model is thus to reveal such biases that are implicit in black box AI algorithms for data evaluation.

How now is this relevant for the GDPR discussion of rights of explanation? The three purposes of explanation that have been identified by Wachter et al. [25] (see Sect. 2.2) with respect to the GDPR are all met by our explanation algorithm.

– *Understand decisions*: the explicit model of context in IIIf contains the rules of the state transition providing the details of each step. The attack trees that produce the traces leading to failure states thus give detailed explanations how the decisions have been arrived at. The algorithm finally produces a general logical rule containing the precondition that explains precisely within the detailed application context what are the relevant facts for decisions.
– *Contest decisions*: the attack trees are explanation trees showing how the decision has been made. The general rule with the precondition provides a means for contesting a decision as it allows to check the decision criteria and reveal potential biases.
– *Alter Future Decisions*: the general rule and its precise precondition allow to read out what are the criteria that can be used as a guideline to alter future decisions. Moreover, the IIIf Kripke model can be explicitly used to simulate the outcome of behaviour by simulating actions of the state transition rules to arrive at favorable states.

5   Related Work and Conclusions

5.1   Related Work

Vigano and Magazzeni [24] argue that explainability is not only needed for AI but as well for security. They use the notion of *XSec* or *Explainable Security* and provide a research agenda for explainability in security centered around the "Six Ws" of XSec: Who? What? Where? When? Why? And hoW? Our point of view is quite similar to Vigano's and Magazzeni's but we emphasize the technical side of explanation using interactive theorem proving and the Isabelle Infrastructure framework, while they focus on differentiating the notion of explanation from different aspects, for example, stake holders, system view, and abstraction levels. Their paper is a position paper that produces a range of research questions illustrating them on examples and showing up potential avenues for future research while we address a very specific way of providing a solution for explanation using automated reasoning with IIIf.

Relevant for the application of the IIIf to the task of explanation is (a) that attack trees resemble explanation trees and (b) that developing a system using attack trees using the RR-cycle resembles the process of generalizing local rules by precondition refinement. Belle and Papantonis [2] already describe how to infer local explanations from counterfactuals using quantitative information. A local explanation corresponds to a rule. "Robustness" of the rule means that similar instances will get the same outcome – a starting point for developing more general rules. Their approach strongly inspired our development of the PCR cycle because – in analogy to using attack trees as a trigger for the RR-cycle – counterfactuals are now used to guide the development of general "robust" rules. Nevertheless our work provides a precise process of precondition refinement within Isabelle as well as a framework that extends the IIIf to support explanation within rich human centric models.

Wachter et al. [25] is a paper that strongly inspired our work. We used their analysis of explanation and the GDPR as requirements for our analysis and validation of the PCR cycle. However, there are a number of differences. Wachter advocates strongly the use of counterfactuals as fully sufficient for the explanation of black box decision procedures. Nevertheless, they use a function f_w [25, p. 854] as explicit input to their optimiser that allows the computation of counterfactuals at any given data points. Thus it is not really a black box algorithm they assume. Consequently, in their demonstration example [25, Appendix A], they easily outperform a very simple explanation method like LIME that uses linear regression. Another difference to our work is that they only consider quantitative functions, like salary. Context features, like location, ethnicity, etc., that are central to our logical method of building a complete rule explanation are not represented.

5.2   Conclusions

In this paper, we have shown how the RR-cycle of the IIIf can be adapted to provide a method for iteratively extracting an explanation by interleaving attack tree analysis with precondition refinement. This precondition refinement (PCR) cycle finally yields a general rule that describes the decision taken by a black box algorithm produced by AI. Since it is a logical rule within a rich context of an infrastructure model of the application scenario, it provides transparency, We argue that the three purposes of the right of explanation of the GDPR of understanding, contesting and altering a decision given by an automated AI decision procedure are supported by the PCR cycle.

The PCR cycle only needs to slightly adapt the RR-cycle by implementing an algorithm to define a methodology for interleaving attack tree analysis with a step by step refinement of a precondition using counterfactuals. Responsible for the ease of this adaptation is the first class representation of attack trees in the IIIf. That is, the existing Correctness and Completeness result of attack trees with respect to the CTL logic defined over Kripke structures allows changing between attack trees and CTL EF formulas. Thus attack trees can be reused as explanation trees because they explain how failure states are reached. This in turn allows the construction of counterfactuals that guide the refinement of the precondition. This paper has validated the algorithm of the PCR cycle by a case study of credit scoring. Further work should address to what extent finding the counterfactuals and thereby the refined precondition can be automated.

References

1. Arrieta, A.B., et al.: Explainable artificial intelligence (XAI): concepts, taxonomies, opportunities and challenges toward responsible AI. Inf. Fusion **58**, 82–115 (2020)
2. Belle, V., Papantonis, I.: Principles and practice of explainable machine learning. CoRR, abs/2009.11698 (2020)
3. Bull, S.: London boroughs mapped and ranked by residents' credit scores - how money-savvy is your area? Accessed 22 July 2022
4. CHIST-ERA. Success: Secure accessibility for the internet of things (2016). http://www.chistera.eu/projects/success
5. Gilpin, L.H., Bau, D., Yuan, B.Z., Bajwa, A., Specter, M.A., Kagal, L.: Explaining explanations: an approach to evaluating interpretability of machine learning. CoRR, abs/1806.00069 (2018)
6. T. is Money. How well do your neighbours manage their money? Interactive map reveals average credit scores by postcode. https://www.thisismoney.co.uk/money/cardsloans/article-3273996/How-neighbours-manage-money-Interactive-map-reveals-average-credit-scores-postcode.html. Accessed 22 July 2022
7. Kammüller, F.: A proof calculus for attack trees in Isabelle. In: Garcia-Alfaro, J., Navarro-Arribas, G., Hartenstein, H., Herrera-Joancomartí, J. (eds.) ESORICS/DPM/CBT 2017. LNCS, vol. 10436, pp. 3–18. Springer, Cham (2017). https://doi.org/10.1007/978-3-319-67816-0_1
8. Kammüller, F.: Attack trees in Isabelle. In: Naccache, D., et al. (eds.) ICICS 2018. LNCS, vol. 11149, pp. 611–628. Springer, Cham (2018). https://doi.org/10.1007/978-3-030-01950-1_36
9. Kammüller, F.: Formal modeling and analysis of data protection for GDPR compliance of IoT healthcare systems. In: IEEE Systems, Man and Cybernetics, SMC 2018. IEEE (2018)
10. Kammüller, F.: Attack trees in Isabelle extended with probabilities for quantum cryptography. Comput. Secur. **87** (2019)
11. Kammüller, F.: Combining secure system design with risk assessment for IoT healthcare systems. In: Workshop on Security, Privacy, and Trust in the IoT, SPTIoT 2019, co-located with IEEE PerCom. IEEE (2019)
12. Kammüller, F.: Dependability engineering in Isabelle (2021). arXiv preprint, http://arxiv.org/abs/2112.04374
13. Kammüller, F.: Explanation by automated reasoning using the Isabelle infrastructure framework (2021). arXiv preprint, http://arxiv.org/abs/2112.14809
14. Kammüller, F.: Isabelle Insider and Infrastructure framework with Kripke strutures, CTL, attack trees, security refinement, and examples including IoT, GDPR, QKD, social networks, and credit scoring (2022). https://github.com/flokam/IsabelleAT
15. Kammüller, F., Alvarado, C.M.: Exploring rationality of self awareness in social networking for logical modeling of unintentional insiders (2021). arXiv preprint, http://arxiv.org/abs/2111.15425

16. Kammüller, F., Kerber, M.: Applying the Isabelle insider framework to airplane security. Sci. Comput. Program. **206** (2021)
17. Kammüller, F., Kerber, M., Probst, C.: Insider threats for auctions: Formal modeling, proof, and certified code. J. Wirel. Mob. Netw. Ubiquit. Comput. Dependable Appl. (JoWUA) **8**(1) (2017)
18. Kammüller, F., Lutz, B.: Modeling and analyzing the corona-virus warning app with the Isabelle infrastructure framework. In: Garcia-Alfaro, J., Navarro-Arribas, G., Herrera-Joancomarti, J. (eds.) DPM/CBT 2020. LNCS, vol. 12484, pp. 128–144. Springer, Cham (2020). https://doi.org/10.1007/978-3-030-66172-4_8
19. Kammüller, F., Nestmann, U.: Inter-blockchain protocols with the Isabelle infrastructure framework. In: Formal Methods for Blockchain, 2nd International Workshop, co-located with CAV 2020, Open Access Series in Informatics. Dagstuhl Publishing (2020, to appear)
20. Kammüller, F., Wenzel, M., Paulson, L.C.: Locales a sectioning concept for Isabelle. In: Bertot, Y., Dowek, G., Théry, L., Hirschowitz, A., Paulin, C. (eds.) TPHOLs 1999. LNCS, vol. 1690, pp. 149–165. Springer, Heidelberg (1999). https://doi.org/10.1007/3-540-48256-3_11
21. Myers, A.C., Liskov, B.: Complete, safe information flow with decentralized labels. In: Proceedings of the IEEE Symposium on Security and Privacy. IEEE (1999)
22. Nipkow, T., Wenzel, M., Paulson, L.C. (eds.): Isabelle/HOL – A Proof Assistant for Higher-Order Logic. LNCS, vol. 2283. Springer, Heidelberg (2002). https://doi.org/10.1007/3-540-45949-9
23. Pieters, W.: Explanation and trust: what to tell the user in security and AI? Ethics Inf. Technol. **13**(1), 53–64 (2011)
24. Viganó, L., Magazzeni, D.: Explainable security. In: IEEE European Symposium on Security and Privacy Workshops, EuroS&PW. IEEE (2020)
25. Wachter, S., Mittelstadt, B., Russell, C.: Counterfactual explanations without opening the black box: automated decisions and the GDPR. Harvard J. Law Technol. **31**(2) (2018)

Secure Internet Exams Despite Coercion

Mohammadamin Rakeei[1], Rosario Giustolisi[2(✉)], and Gabriele Lenzini[1]

[1] SnT, University of Luxembourg, Esch-sur-Alzette, Luxembourg
{amin.rakeei,gabriele.lenzini}@uni.lu
[2] Department of Computer Science, IT University of Copenhagen,
Copenhagen, Denmark
rosg@itu.dk

Abstract. We study coercion-resistance for online exams. We propose two new properties, Anonymous Submission and Single-Blindness which preserve the anonymity of the links between tests, test takers, and examiners even when the parties coerce one another into revealing secrets. The properties are relevant: not even Remark!, a secure exam protocol that satisfies anonymous marking and anonymous examiners, results to be coercion resistant. Then, we propose a coercion-resistance protocol which satisfies, in addition to known anonymity properties, the two novel properties we have introduced. We prove our claims formally in ProVerif. The paper has also another contribution: it describes an attack (and a fix) to an exponentiation mixnet that Remark! uses to ensure unlinkability. We use the secure version of the mixnet in our new protocol.

Keywords: Coercion-resistance · Formal verification · Exponentiation mixnet · Security flaws · Security protocol design · Proverif

1 Introduction

One of the most tangible consequences of the Corona virus pandemic in education has been that academic institutions moved exams to the Internet. The migration to an online format did aggravate the problem of fraud, which is now a concern for all institutions worldwide (Watson and Sottile 2010).

Cheating at exams, *i.e.,* taking advantage of the process for one's own benefit, is a practice as old as the establishment of exams, and it is unsurprising that candidates try to cheat; However, the use of Information and Communication Technologies (ICT) in exams makes it easier and more appealing even for the authorities to temper with the exam processes. Authorities have been found to increase the grades in order to boost their university national ranking[1]; More recently, a famous legal firm has been fined 100M $ because hundreds of auditors at the firm cheated at ethics tests required to keep their professional license[2].

---

[1] Valerie Strauss, "Remember the Atlanta schools' cheating scandal? It is not over", 1 February 2022, Washington Post, accessed on 2022/06.

[2] Tory Newmyer, "Ernst & Young hit with a 100 million fine over cheating on ethics tests", 28 June 2022, Washington Post, accessed 2022/07.

© The Author(s), under exclusive license to Springer Nature Switzerland AG 2023
J. Garcia-Alfaro et al. (Eds.): DPM 2022/CBT 2022, LNCS 13619, pp. 85–100, 2023.
https://doi.org/10.1007/978-3-031-25734-6_6

With electronic exams (or e-exams), the implementation of traditional anti-cheating mitigation actions is harder and less scalable than in traditional pencil-and-paper exams. Frauds perpetrated by attacking the underline communication infrastructure are subtle and hard-to-detect. The use of ICT in exams, and the migration of them them online, may compromise the quality of education assessment unless we can provide exam protocols that are *secure by-design*.

Security in e-exam is not a new topic. Previous research, shows that is possible to formally express and study properties such as anonymous marking, question secrecy, and mark integrity (Giustolisi 2018); that e-exam protocols can preserve privacy despite curious authorities (Bella et al. 2017); and that e-exams can be designed to be *verifiable* (Dreier et al. 2014), and *privacy-preserving verifiable* (Giustolisi et al. 2017).

Contribution. This work contributes to the state of the art in e-exam security, in several ways. First, it studies two new properties meant to capture *coercion resistance*, a property never studied in e-exams. The new properties are called *Anonymous Submission* and *Single-Blindness*. The former, expresses that examiners cannot get to know the link between candidates (*i.e.,* test takers) and the tests that they had submitted, even if examiners force the candidates to reveal their secrets (*i.e.,* private keys); the latter, says that candidates cannot learn the link between examiners and the tests that the examiners had marked, even if they compel examiners to reveal their secrets.

Anonymous Submission and *Single-Blindness* are novel, although they may resemble to *Anonymous Marking* (marks remain secret until notification) and *Anonymous Examiner* (test takers ignore the identities of examiners). To answer the question, we select a state-of-the-art secure exam protocol, Remark! (Giustolisi et al. 2014), which uses the exponentiation mixnet proposed by Haenni-Spycher (Haenni and Spycher 2011) to preserve anonymity and unlinkability, and that satisfies *Anonymous Marking* and *Anonymous Examiner* even if candidates and examiners can collude. Under collusion, Remark! does not satisfy *Anonymous Submission* and *Single-Blindness*, supporting that *Anonymous Submission* and *Single-Blindness* are unprecedented.

Besides, we propose a new *coercion-resistant exam protocol*, which we call Coercion-Resistant Electronic Exam (C-Rex). It satisfies *Anonymous Submission* and *Single-Blindness* under coercion, and we prove this statement formally using Proverif (Blanchet 2001), a model checker. We also verify that C-Rex satisfies the other security properties already met by Remark!.

This work has another orthogonal, but not less important, contribution. We discover that by injecting specific messages into the *mixnet* used by Remark!—the Haenni-Spycher's exponentiation mixnet—an attacker can break unlinkability. An immediate consequence is that, in Remark!, various anonymity properties no longer hold, including *Anonymous Marking* and *Anonymous Examiner*. We discuss how to secure the exponentiation mixnet so that to restore *Anonymous Marking* and *Anonymous Examiner* in Remark!. We believe that our fix also improves the security of Haenni-Spycher's mixnet in other domains than the online assessment, a statement that will be investigated in future work.

2   Related Work

Although a discussion about security in e-exams has recently gained attention, the topic is not new and has been researched before. For a fairly extensive list of requirements for e-exams, we refer the reader to (Giustolisi 2018); for a brief account, we recall that security requirements for e-exams have been informally expressed in (Weippl 2005; Furnell et al. 1998), while (Dreier et al. 2014) defines a formal framework in the applied π-calculus to specify and analyze authentication and privacy in e-exams; in addition, the authors define and show how to prove a set of verifiability properties for exams (Dreier et al. 2015). In a similar domain, that of computer-supported collaborative work, (Foley and Jacob 1995) formalizes confidentiality, proposing exams as a case study.

In the state-of-the-art, we find not only works that describe properties for secure and private assessment, but also proposals for new security protocols for computer-assisted exams. (Castella-Roca et al. 2006) designs a protocol that meets authentication and privacy properties in the presence of a fully trusted exam manager. (Bella et al. 2014) proposes an e-exam, which considers a corrupted examiner, but assumes an honest-but-curious anonymiser. This assumption was later removed in (Bella et al. 2017).

(Huszti and Pethö 2010) tackles on-line exams and discusses an Internet-based exam protocol with few trust requirements on principals. (Giustolisi et al. 2014) describes *Remark!*, another Internet-based exam protocol that ensures authentication and conditional anonymity requirements with minimal trust assumptions; this is the protocol we refer to here as use case.

The interest in e-exams is not limited to researchers. Many institutions for language proficiency tests, for example the Educational Testing Service (ETS)[3], or organizations for personnel selection, for instance Pearson[4] or the EU EPSO[5], offer computer-assisted and online testing.

Some related protocols have been proposed in the area of conference management systems. Our proposed properties can be seen as double-blind review properties, typically requested in the submission of conference papers. (Kanav et al. 2014) introduced *CoCon*, a formally verified implementation of a conference management system that guarantees confidentiality. Arapinis *et al.* introduced and formally analysed *ConfiChair*, a cryptographic protocol that addresses secrecy and privacy risks coming from a *malicious-but-cautious* cloud. Their work has been extended to support any cloud-based system that assumes honest managers, such as the public tender management and recruitment process (Arapinis et al. 2013). All such works do not mention or consider coercion resistance, a class of properties that, instead, we study here for e-exams.

---

[3] https://www.ets.org/.

[4] https://www.pearsonassessments.com/.

[5] https://epso.europa.eu/.

3   Background

Exam procedures differ one another in the details, but they all share the same organization and information flow at a certain level of abstraction. They are generally organized in four distinct phases: *Registration, Examination, Marking*, and *Notification*. Several roles are involved: *candidates*, the test takers; *question committee*, which prepares the exam questions; *examiners*, those who mark the tests; and *exam authorities*, a set of potentially distinct agents that help *e.g.,* distribute the test to students, assign examiners, and notify marks.

3.1   Security Properties of an e-Exam

An e-exam protocol is expected to guarantee specific security properties. The ones this work refers to are: (i) *Test Answer Authentication* (only tests submitted by eligible candidates are collected); (ii) *Examiner Authentication* (only authenticated examiners are allowed to marking tests); (iii) *Mark Privacy* (the marks given to a candidate's test remain unknown to the other candidates); (iv) *Anonymous Marking* (examiners do not learn the owner of a test they are marking, until after the markings are notified); (v) *Anonymous Examiner* (candidates do not learn the identity of the examiners who marked their tests). To this list, we study *Anonymous Submission* and *Single-Blindness* (see Sect. 3).

3.2   Coercion Resistant e-Exams

Since no one studied coercion-resistance *in e-exams* (the property has been studied extensively but in other domain, for instance, e-voting), we propose our interpretation. In layman terms, it means that an exam protocol should preserve privacy between examinees and examiners even when they force one another into revealing secrets the lead to de-anonymization, such as, private keys.

The threat is not negligible considering that e-exams are used not only for university grading but also, for instance, in national and international educational assessments like for instance, the PISA[6]; the PIAAC[7]; the various Tests for English as a Foreign Language required to get US VISA and studentships. Here, the benefits at stake are higher and so are the incentives to stress the procedure for one's own profit.

To address coercion resistance, we propose two additional security requirements for e-exams, *Anonymous Submission* and *Single-Blindness. Anonymous Submission* states that an examiner cannot learn which answer is submitted by which candidate. At first glance, it sounds similar to *Anonymous Marking*, as both aim to achieve unlinkability between the identity of a candidate and the answer that she submitted. The difference is that the definition of *Anonymous Submission* is based on the indistinguishability of the answers submitted by

---

[6] The Programme for International Student Assessment.
[7] Programme for the International Assessment of Adult Competencies.

two known candidates, while the definition of *Anonymous Marking* is based on the indistinguishability of the candidates' identities who submitted two known answers. As shall we see in Sect. 5.1, this is a key difference that allows us to model coercion in an e-exam by starting from the definition of *Anonymous Submission*. The property is relevant when an examiner tries to coerce candidates to reveal their private keys, or the answers they submitted.

Single-Blindness ensures that no candidate can learn which mark has been assigned by an examiner. This property recalls *Anonymous Examiner*, as they both aim to achieve unlinkability between the identity of an examiner and the mark he provided. However, while the definition of *Anonymous Examiner* is based on the indistinguishability of the examiners' identities who provided a mark for two known tests, *Single-Blindness* is based on the indistinguishability of the marks provided by two known examiners. Here, the main difference is that *Single-Blindness* does not consider the tests at all. The property is relevant when a candidate attempts to compel an examiner to reveal a private key to get access to the marks he has reported to the exam authority.

4   Use Case and a Relevant Attack on Mixnet

We are interested to verify whether our new properties are novel and relevant, and not other properties renamed. Thus, we pick a state-of-the-art exam protocol Remark! (Giustolisi et al. 2014)—an internet-based exam that preserves all the properties listed in the previous section, including *Anonymous Marking* and *Anonymous Examiner* and study our new properties against it. In Remark!'s threat model, all parties are malicious and can collude. It seems a good choice to start with to explore resilience against coercion.

4.1   Remark! in a Nutshell

It is organized into four phases: at *Registration* private/public keys and pseudo-identities are generated and distributed to candidates and examiners using an exponentiation mixnet; during *Examination*, questions are anonymously distributed (relying on a bulletin board) to candidates; the exam authority receives the answers submitted by the candidates; at *Marking* the æanonymously distributes the tests to examiners; at *Notification*, the exam authority records the marks and notifies the candidates their results. Dreier *et al.* in (Dreier et al. 2014) formally proved that Remark! satisfied *Test Answer Authentication, Mark Privacy, Anonymous Marking* and *Anonymous Examiner*.

Remark! relies on the Haenni-Spycher's exponentiation mixnet (Haenni and Spycher 2011) to generate pseudo-identities for examiners and candidates.

Haenni-Spycher's Exponentiation Mixnet. (Haenni and Spycher 2011) proposed a structure called *verifiable shuffling mixnet* or *exponentiation mixnet*, and designed an e-voting protocol based on it. The aim of the mixnet is to generate a list of pseudonyms from a list of public keys in a way that only the owner of a public key can find the corresponding pseudonym in the output list. This mixnet construction is used in Remark! to output a list of pseudo-public keys (pseudonyms) from an input list of public keys, while preserving unlinkability between input and output lists. To do so, the exam authority sends the list of eligible candidates' and examiners' public keys to the mixnet. Upon receiving the list of public keys the mixnet generates the output list as depicted in Fig. 1. In this structure, $PK_i = g^{SK_i}$, $\overline{PK}_i = h_C{}^{SK_i}$, $\bar{r}_k = \prod_{i=1}^{k} r_i$ and $\bar{\pi}_k = \pi_k \circ \cdots \circ \pi_1$, where SK_i, r_k and π_k are, respectively, the private key of party i_{th}, the secret element of the mixnet k_{th}, and the secret permutation of the mixnet k_{th}. For a more detailed description, see (Haenni and Spycher 2011).

	mix_1	mix_2		mix_m	
$C_1\ PK_1$	$PK_{\bar{\pi}_1(1)}^{\bar{r}_1}$	$PK_{\bar{\pi}_2(1)}^{\bar{r}_2}$	$\cdots$	$PK_{\bar{\pi}_m(1)}^{\bar{r}_m}$	$= \overline{PK}_1$
$C_2\ PK_1$	$PK_{\bar{\pi}_1(2)}^{\bar{r}_1}$	$PK_{\bar{\pi}_2(2)}^{\bar{r}_2}$	$\cdots$	$PK_{\bar{\pi}_m(2)}^{\bar{r}_m}$	$= \overline{PK}_2$
$\vdots$ $\vdots$	$\vdots$	$\vdots$		$\vdots$	
$C_n\ PK_n$	$PK_{\bar{\pi}_1(n)}^{\bar{r}_1}$	$PK_{\bar{\pi}_2(n)}^{\bar{r}_2}$	$\cdots$	$PK_{\bar{\pi}_m(n)}^{\bar{r}}$	$= \overline{PK}_n$
g	$g^{\bar{r}_1}$	$g^{\bar{r}_2}$	$\cdots$	$g^{\bar{r}_m}$	$= h_C$

Fig. 1. Using exponentiation mixnet to generate pseudonyms. All the terms within the box are published on the bulletin board.

4.2   Intermezzo: An Attack and a Fix on Remark!'s Mixnet

Before proceeding further, we have to comment on a finding that we discovered while reflecting on the role of the mixnet in preserving anonymity and unlikability. It is a new attack against the implementation of Haenni-Spycher's mixnet used in Remark! that compromises anonymity and unlinkability, and which we have to fix before proceeding further.

The attack allows an attacker to link any public key to its corresponding pseudonym. Let $L = \{g^{t_1}, \ldots, g^{t_n}\}$ be a list of n values where g is the generator of a multiplicative subgroup G_q of prime order q and $t_i \in Z_q$, $1 \leq i \leq n$.

Let us assume that E is a party that receives L and is requested to send it to the mixnet. We show that a malicious E is capable of deanonymizing an arbitrary element of L by adding an additional input to the list. E first chooses a random number $s \in Z_q$ and computes g^s. Then, she selects the pseudonym she wants to deanonymize, say $g^{t_i} \in L$, it inserts $g^{t_i} \cdot g^s$ into L,and sends L to the mixnet. The mixnet returns $L' = \{L'_1, \ldots, L'_{n+1}\} = \{g^{t_1 \cdot r}, \ldots, g^{t_n \cdot r}, (g^{t_i} \cdot g^s)^r\}$ as output and publicly publishes g^r. Now, E computes $(g^r)^s$ and searches in L' for the element $g^{rs} \cdot L_j$. That element is the pseudonym that links to t_i.

The attack exploits the fact that $g^{rs} \cdot g^{t_i \cdot r} = (g^{t_i} \cdot g^s)^r$. It lets E learn $L'_j = g^{t_i \cdot r}$ which is the corresponding output for the chosen input g^{t_i} without E knowing the secret element t_i. If E runs it for each element, in $O(n^2)$ time, he can learn all the n links between L and L'.

It is worth to stress that if the mixnet has a procedure to check the eligibility of the input public keys run by E, the attack is possible if E is untrustworthy, which is usually a health assumption (*i.e.*, better not to have trusted parties): E can violate this check and inputs a manipulated public key. If we assume that the mixnet has no eligibility check feature for inputs, then the attack can even be done by any external attacker who only knows a member from L.

The attack mentioned above is independent of the system in which the mixnet is used. Any protocol that relies on the Haenni-Spycher's exponentiation mixnet is vulnerable to this injection attack. In Remark!, exam authority can launch this attack to learn the link between public keys and their associated pseudonyms that violates *Anonymous Marking* and *Anonymous Examiner*.

4.3 A Mixnet Resilient to Injection Attacks

To secure the mixnet against our linkability attack, one possible solution is to prevent the injection of biased public keys into the mixnet. We propose an *Injection-Resistant Exponentiation Mixnet* setup based on Haenni-Spycher's mixnet, where the input public keys should be accompanied by their Zero Knowledge Proofs of Knowledge (ZKPKs) for their corresponding private keys. The rest of the structure remains unchanged.

With this simple fix, the mixnet only accepts a public key that is associated with a verified ZKPK and aborts otherwise.

5 Security Formal Analysis

Having fixed the mixnet construction, a question remains open: does Remark! with the stronger mixnet (for reference, we call it Injection-Resistant Exponentiation Mixnet (IRemix)) satisfy *Anonymous Submission* and *Single-Blindness* even if we assume that the parties can coerce one another? If that were true, *Anonymous Submission* and *Single-Blindness* could be simply achieved by ensuring unlinkability. We could even suspect that *Anonymous Submission* and *Single-Blindness* are implied by *Anonymous Marking* and *Anonymous Examiner*. Fortunately, this is not the case, as we argue later in this section, after we set up the formal framework where we perform our security analysis.

Formalizing e-Exams. Since we aim at a formal verification, we need to model an e-exam protocol in a formal language. We choose the applied π-calculus (Abadi and Fournet 2001) for the task, and we refer to the strategy advanced by Dreier *et al.* . in (Dreier et al. 2014), which we remind here.

Definition 1 (E-exam protocol) *(Dreier et al. 2014). An e-exam protocol is a tuple $(C, E, Q, A_1, \dots, A_l, \tilde{n}_p)$, where C is the process executed by the candidates, E is the process executed by the examiners, Q is the process executed by the question commitee, A_i's are the processes executed by the authorities, and $\tilde{n}_p$ is the set of private channel names.*

Note that all candidates and all examiners execute the same process, but with different variable values, *e.g.*, keys, identities, and answers.

Definition 2 (E-exam instance) *(Dreier et al. 2014). An e-exam instance is a closed process $EP = \nu\tilde{n}.(C\sigma_{id_1}\sigma_{a_1}| \ldots |C\sigma_{id_j}\sigma_{a_j}|E\sigma_{id'_1}\sigma_{m_1}| \ldots |E\sigma_{id'_k}\sigma_{m_k}|Q\sigma_q|A_1\sigma_{dist}| \ldots |A_l)$, where $\tilde{n}$ is the set of all restricted names, which includes the set of the protocol's private channels; $C\sigma_{id_i}\sigma_{a_i}$'s are the processes run by the candidates, the substitutions σ_{id_i} and σ_{a_i} specify the identity and the answers of the ith candidate respectively; $E\sigma_{id'_i}\sigma_{m_i}$'s are the processes run by the examiners, the substitution $\sigma_{id'_i}$ specifies the ith e xaminer's identity, and σ_{m_i} specifies for each possible question and answer pair the corresponding mark; Q is the process run by the question committee, the substitution σ_q specifies the exam questions; the A_i's are the processes run by the exam authorities, the substitution σ_{dist} determines which answers will be submitted to which examiners for grading. Without loss of generality, we assume that A_1 is in charge of distributing the copies to the examiners.*

Definition 2 does not specify whether the examiners are machines or humans. For the purpose of our model this distinction is not necessary; it is sufficient that an examiner attributes a mark to a given answer.

Note that Q and A_1 could coincide if for instance there is only one authority A, in that case we can write simply $A\sigma_q\sigma_{dist}$ instead of $Q\sigma_q|A_1\sigma_{dist}$.

Model Checking and Equational Theories. We use ProVerif (Blanchet 2001) for the analysis of e-exam protocols. ProVerif allows one to analyze reachability and equivalence-based properties in the symbolic attacker model. We chose ProVerif mainly because it has been extensively used to analyze exam protocols (Giustolisi 2018), hence we could easily check formerly defined security properties for exams. ProVerif is also one of the few tools that allows for automated analysis of privacy properties using observational equivalence; therefore, we can check *Anonymous Submission* and *Single-Blindness* in our protocol automatically. The input language of ProVerif is the applied π-calculus (Abadi and Fournet 2001), which the tool automatically translates to Horn clauses. Cryptographic primitives can be modeled by means of equational theories. An equational theory E describes the equations that hold on terms built from the signature. Terms are related by an equivalence relation $=$ induced by E. For instance, the equation $dec(enc(m, pk(k)), k) = m$ models an asymmetric encryption scheme. The term m is the message, the term k is the secret key, the function $pk(k)$ models the public key, the term enc models the encryption function, and the term dec models the decryption function. The list of all equational theories used to model the Remark! protocol can be found in (Dreier et al. 2014).

5.1   Threat Model and Formalization of the New Properties

We let the attacker read all public data on the bulletin board and impersonate misbehaving parties, including an unbounded number of dishonest examiners when checking *Anonymous Submission*, and an unbounded number of dishonest

candidates when checking *Single-Blindness*. In addition, we check both properties under a coercion scenario, meaning that the coerced candidate (resp. examiner) reveals their secrets before notification.

Privacy properties can be modeled as observational equivalence properties.
To model *Anonymous Submission*, we consider two honest candidates and an
unbounded number of dishonest examiners; to model *Single-Blindness*, we consider two honest examiners and an unbounded number of dishonest candidates.
We check both *Anonymous Submission* and *Single-Blindness* considering an honest exam authority. We also check *Anonymous Marking* and *Anonymous Examiner* considering a dishonest exam authority.

First, we check whether *Anonymous Submission* holds in our protocol: specifically, that even if two honest candidates swap their answers in two different runs
of the protocol then the attacker cannot distinguish the two resulting systems.

Definition 3 (Anonymous Submission). *An exam protocol ensures Anonymous Submission if any exam process EP, any two candidates id_1 and id_2, and
any two answers a_1 and a_2.*

$$EP_{\{id_1,id_2\}}[C\sigma_{id_1}\sigma_{a_1}|C\sigma_{id_2}\sigma_{a_2}]|_{\mathtt{marked}} \approx_l EP_{\{id_1,id_2\}}[C\sigma_{id_1}\sigma_{a_2}|C\sigma_{id_2}\sigma_{a_1}]|_{\mathtt{marked}}$$

The difference between *Anonymous Submission* and *Anonymous Marking*
is that the latter considers two honest candidates who swap their secret keys
in two different runs. While both properties aim at hiding the link between
candidate's key and answer, the definition of *Anonymous Submission* crucially
enables a definition of coercion-resistance. To model this, we additionally let the
candidates publish their answers and their secret keys on the public channel,
and verify that *Anonymous Submission* still holds:

$$EP_{\{id_1,id_2\}}[C\sigma_{id_1}\sigma_{a_1}|C\sigma_{id_2}\sigma_{a_2}]|_{\mathtt{marked}} \approx_l EP_{\{id_1,id_2\}}[C'|C\sigma_{id_2}\sigma_{a_1}]|_{\mathtt{marked}}$$

where C' is a process such that $C'^{\backslash\mathsf{out}(chc,\cdot)} \approx_l C\sigma_{id_1}\sigma_{a_2}$, i.e. C' is the process
that acts like one submitting answer a_2, but pretends to cooperate with the
attacker by revealing their secrets trough channel chc.

Then, we check whether *Single-Blindness* holds in our protocol. We check
that if two honest examiners swap their marks in two different runs of the protocol, then the attacker cannot distinguish the two resulting systems.

Definition 4 (Single-Blindness). *An exam protocol ensures Single-Blindness
if for any exam process EP, any two examiners id_1 and id_2, any two marks m_1
and m_2*

$$EP_{\{id_1,id_2\}}[E\sigma_{id_1}\sigma_{m_1}|E\sigma_{id_2}\sigma_{m_2}] \approx_l EP_{\{id_1,id_2\}}[E\sigma_{id_1}\sigma_{m_2}|E\sigma_{id_2}\sigma_{m_1}]$$

As for *Anonymous Submission*, we also check that *Single-Blindness* holds
under examiner coercion. We let the examiners publish their marks and secret
keys on the public channel:

$$EP_{\{id_1,id_2\}}[E\sigma_{id_1}\sigma_{m_1}|E\sigma_{id_2}\sigma_{m_2} \approx_l EP_{\{id_1,id_2\}}[E'|E\sigma_{id_2}\sigma_{m_1}]$$

where E' is a process such that $E'^{\backslash\mathsf{out}(chc,\cdot)} \approx_l E\sigma_{id_1}\sigma_{m_2}$.

The difference between *Single-Blindness* and *Anonymous Examiner* is that the latter considers two honest examiners who swap their keys in two different runs. While both properties aim at hiding the link between key and mark, the definition of *Single-Blindness* enables the definition of coercion-resistance.

Security Findings. Under the only threat of collusion, ProVerif proves that both properties holds in Remark!. However, under coercion threats, it finds attacks.

Anonymous Submission does not hold under candidate coercion, because the exam authority publishes on the bulletin board the answer of a candidate along with their pseudo public keys (see step 6 in (Giustolisi et al. 2014)). ProVerif shows an attack trace in which a coercer, who knows the secret key of a coerced candidate, finds out the candidate's answer by retrieving their pseudo public key from the output of the exp. mixnet (see step 1 in (Giustolisi et al. 2014)).

Single-Blindness does not hold under examiner coercion either, because, at notification, the mark and the answer are signed with the examiner's pseudo signing key (see step 8 in (Giustolisi et al. 2014)). ProVerif shows an attack trace in which a coercer, finds out which answers have been marked by a coerced examiner by retrieving their pseudo signing key from the output of the exp. mixnet (see step 2 in (Giustolisi et al. 2014)). Table 1 summarizes the findings.

6   A Secure Coercion Resistant Exam Protocol

We now present our new protocol, C-Rex, whose goal is to guarantee all the properties outlined above. C-Rex has four main phases *Registration*, *Examination*, *Marking*, and *Notification* and one additional phase which is run before the exam begins. We assume that each test consists of at least two questions. We also assume that there is an append-only bulletin board (BB), which records data concerning examiners, candidates and exam authority. The bulletin board is used to publish public parameters and is also needed for verifiability guarantees. Moreover, we assume that each principal has a pair of Elgamal public/private key which used in an Elgamal cryptosystem (ElGamal 1985). The five phases of C-Rex are depicted in Fig. 2 and are as follows:

Pre-Assignment: Let us assume n candidates and m examiners. Before starting the exam, the exam authority forms $A = \{1, \ldots, n\}$ and then partitions A into d subsets as $A_P = \{A_{P_1}, \ldots, A_{P_d}\}$, and labels them as $P = \{P_1, \ldots, P_d\}$. The exam authority sends A_P and P to each examiner through a secure channel. The examiners sign the partitions and send them back to exam authority, which distributes the signatures among all examiners so that each examiner can check if they have received the same message as the others.

Registration: This phase is as the registration phase in Remark!, but with the IRemix explained in Sect. 4. In this phase, we create pseudo public keys (pseudonyms) as outputs from a list of public keys as inputs while preserving the unlinkability between input and output lists. exam authority sends the list of public keys of eligible candidates and examiners and the list of corresponding *Zero-Knowledge Proofs of Knowledge* (ZKPKs) of those keys to the mixnet.

Each candidate and examiner, during the authorization and eligibility checks, provides the ZKPK of their keys. When receiving the list of public keys *accompanied by their ZKPKs*, the mixnet checks the proofs and generates the output list in the same fashion as in Fig. 1.

Testing: The exam authority signs and encrypts the questions with the candidate's pseudonym and posts them on the bulletin board. The candidate decrypts the test, checks the signature, and answers the questions. Then she sends $[Sign_{SK_C,h_C}(quest, ans, \overline{PK}_C)]_{PK_A}$ where SK_A, PK_A, $quest$, ans and $\overline{PK}_C$ are the private key of exam authority, the public key of exam authority, the answers, and the candidate pseudonym, respectively. Furthermore, exam authority sends the candidate $[Sign_{SK_A}H(quest, ans, \overline{PK}_C, \alpha)]_{PK_A}$ where H and α are a secure hash function and a random value generated by exam authority.

Marking: In this phase, we introduce a new technique called *Shuffled Answers* to assign the collected tests to the examiners in a way that guarantees *Anonymous Submission* and *Single-Blindness* also in case of coercion. The idea behind this technique is that when the *Marking* phase starts, each examiner receives a test where each (*question, answer*) pair belongs to a random candidate. After collecting the tests from the candidates, exam authority forms a matrix named T, which consists of all candidates' (*question, answer*) pairs. Then it chooses a secure permutation matrix named Π and applies it to T to form a new matrix T^π, that is $\Pi(T) = T^\pi$. The following transform mathematically expresses the shuffling procedure. Here, if we assume k questions and n candidates, $(q, a)_{(i,j)}$ is the answer of candidate j to question i.

$$T = \begin{bmatrix} (q,a)_{1,1} & \cdots & (q,a)_{1,n} \\ \vdots & & \vdots \\ (q,a)_{k,1} & \cdots & (q,a)_{k,n} \end{bmatrix} \xrightarrow{\Pi} \begin{bmatrix} (q,a)_{(1,\pi_1^1)} & \cdots & (q,a)_{(1,\pi_n^1)} \\ \vdots & & \vdots \\ (q,a)_{(k,\pi_1^k)} & \cdots & (q,a)_{(k,\pi_n^k)} \end{bmatrix} = T^\pi$$

Let us define T and T^π as sets of n vectors $T = [V_1, \ldots, V_n]$ and $T^\pi = [V_1^\pi, \ldots, V_n^\pi]$, respectively. V_j, $1 \le j \le n$ shows the test of candidate j, while V_j^π, $1 \le j \le n$ represents a new test whose each question belongs to a random author. exam authority signs T^π with its private key and publishes it on the bulletin board in front of its public key. Then exam authority randomly assigns each examiner a member of P and posts this assignment on the bulletin board. Therefore, each examiner sees a label in front of their pseudonym on the bulletin board that means which subset they should mark. Let us name P_E the label assigned to the examiner E. E grades the corresponding assigned vectors and, for each, sends the message $[Sign_{SK_E,h_E}(M_j^\pi, A_{P_E})]_{PK_A}$ to exam authority where M_j^π is the vector of marks associated with V_j^π and $j \in A_{P_E}$.

Notification: Let $S_j^\pi = Sign_{SK_E,h_E}(M_j^\pi, A_{P_E})$. When the exam authority receives all messages from all examiners, first it checks if the examiners marked the correct assigned subsets, and then it constructs two $S^\pi = [S_1^\pi, \ldots, S_n^\pi]$ and $M^\pi = [M_1^\pi, \ldots, M_n^\pi]$ matrices. Then, it applies the inverse permutation Π^{-1} to these matrices and generates $S = [S_1, \ldots, S_n]$ and $M = [M_1, \ldots, M_n]$, respectively. M is the matrix of final marks and each column of it, which means M_j, is a vector showing the marks for the jth candidate's test. S represents a notification matrix which includes the marks signed by the eligible examiners. The exam authority signs and encrypts each column of S with the pseudonym of the corresponding candidate and then posts the output on the bulletin board. Finally, the mixnet servers reveal their secret exponents that are used to anonymize the candidates. The anonymity of the candidate is revoked, and the exam authority can register the marks and reveal the secret element α at the end of the exam.

Let us now assume that the coercer has asked a candidate to reveal her private key and her submitted test. The coerced candidate first looks at T^π and, from each row, picks an arbitrary pair of *(question,answer)*. Then, she reveals her real private key, as well as the set of *(question,answer)* pairs chosen. We claim that the coercer cannot distinguish whether the candidate has demonstrated her real test or a fake one. Instead, let us assume an examiner E_j, $1 \leq j \leq d$ who is coerced by a candidate and is supposed to mark the tests labeled $P_r \in P$. In addition to P_r, E_j marks $P_{r'}$ where $P_{r'} \in P$ and $r \neq r'$. Now, if the coercer asks E_j to reveal her secret keys, E_j pretends that she has marked only the tests labeled $P_{r'}$. Our assertion is that the coercer cannot distinguish whether E_j lies about her assigned partition.

Security Formal Analysis. ProVerif proves that our protocol meets both *Anonymous Submission* and *Single-Blindness*, including the coercion alternatives. Our protocol resists the attack on candidate coercion seen in Remark! because the exam authority re-randomizes the pseudo public key of the candidate. Single-Blindness is proved also under examiner coercion because, differently from Remark!, a coerced examiner can lie to a coercer by claiming that the examiner is marking a different partition of tests.

In addition to *Anonymous Submission* and *Single-Blindness*, we prove in ProVerif that our protocol meets all the original properties meet by Remark!, namely, anonymous marking, anonymous examiner, test answer authentication and examiner authentication. Table 1 summarizes the findings.

Table 1. Synthesis of the findings of the formal analysis under different threats.

Properties	Remark! (with IRemix)	C-Rex	Threat model
Answer Authentication	✓	✓	Dishonest E
Examiner Authentication	✓	✓	Dishonest C
Mark Privacy	✓	✓	Dishonest (C^*, E^*)
Anonymous Marking	✓	✓	Collusion (EA, E)
Anonymous Examiner	✓	✓	Collusion (EA, C)
Anonymous Submission	✓	✓	Dishonest E
Single-Blindness	✓	✓	Dishonest C
Anonymous Submission	✗	✓	Coercion (E)
Single-Blindness	✗	✓	Coercion (C)

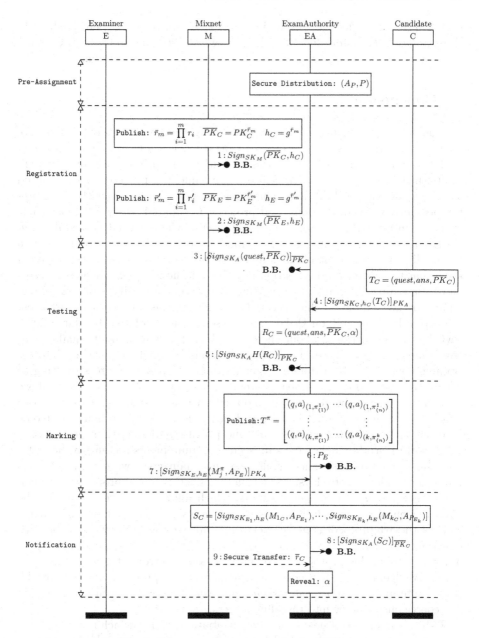

Fig. 2. The message sequence chart of C-Rex

Table 1 highlights the dishonest parties in our analysis. For *Mark Privacy*, C^* and E^* are, respectively, all candidates and examiners except the candidate and examiner concerned. Collusion is possible when at least two parties misbehave. Therefore, *Anonymous Marking* and *Anonymous Examiner* are discussed in the collusion threat model with respectively *EA* & *E*, and *EA* & *C* being dishonest. *Anonymous Submission* and *Single-Blindness* are studied under both coercion and non-coercion scenarios. The ProVerif codes are accessible online[8].

7   Conclusion

The use of online exams, which peaked during the pandemic, raises issues of security and privacy, since it is easier to cheat when exams are held in remote.

In certain sectors, like in e-voting, security and privacy are already well-established subjects of research. Various academic and industrial collaboration activities have been established, which now support the sectors with ideas, prototypes, forums for discussions, and projects. Compared to e-voting, electronic exams seem underrepresented. One could discuss whether what is at stake in e-voting, aka one important cog in the democracy process, is more important than the quality of assessment of skills and knowledge of people, but recent events show that the government attention to a fair and honest assessment is not second to anything. At the time of writing, giant companies like Ernst & Young, admitted their employees had cheated on ethics exams, an act that cost them a fine of a hundred million USD[9]. This episode is not isolated. In March 2022, PwC has been sanctioned about one million USD for "having faulty quality control standards that allowed more than 1,200 professionals to cheat on internal training courses"[10]. In a different domain, many universities are struggling to achieve robust online assessment systems, where at stake is the trust that we have in the general reward strategy of our educational systems. It is clear that to adhere to a code of conduct is not a sufficient guarantee for an honest outcome and that we need better, more secure, and private by-design exam protocols.

This work studies a class of exam security requirements missing in the state-of-the-art: coercion resistance. Following this main goal, we obtained several important achievements. First, we formally defined two new properties, *Anonymous Submission* and *Single-Blindness*, which allow one to reason about the phenomenon of coercion in online exams. Thanks to this effort, we find that a state-of-the-art protocol is not coercion resistant in the sense we describe with our properties. Coercion resistance requires a different approach, and we propose a new cryptographic protocol Coercion-Resistant Electronic Exam (C-Rex). To our knowledge, it is the first coercion-resistant e-exam protocol: unlike Remark!, it guarantees *Anonymous Submission* and *Single-Blindness* even if the parties can coerce one another into revealing secrets.

C-Rex implements a new secure exponentiation mixnet which is also an original, although orthogonal, contribution of this work. In fact, while investigating the security of a state-of-the-art e-exam protocol, Remark!, we found an linkability attack on the Haenni-Spycher's mixnet, the main building block of

---

[8] C-Rex Code Repository.

[9] *id. at* 2.

[10] Soyoung Ho, "Canada for Widespread Employee Cheating on Internal Tests", Thomson Reuters, 2 March 2022, last access 2022/07.

Remark!. The attack completely breaks the claimed unlinkability property of this mixnet. The new injection-resistant exponentiation mixnet which we propose, called Injection-Resistant Exponentiation Mixnet (IRemix), is fully based on the structure of Haenni-Spycherbut add an important steps requiring ZKPKs which, we prove informally, works as a countermeasure against the attack. Formally verifying the security of IRemix remains an important further work. Furthermore, in the *Pre-Assignment* phase, we proposed a simple protocol which assures that all parties have received the same set of partitions. It is desirable for future research to formally verify this protocol.

Future studies could also investigate the security of the systems that used Haenni-Spycher's mixnet as an identity mixer, against the linkability attack that we have found. The first one could be Haenni-Spycher's e-voting protocol (Haenni and Spycher 2011), which seems, but we need to corroborate this statement, vulnerable to this attack if the election authority is dishonest. Other schemes that might be prone to the attack are (Dubuis et al. 2013), (Locher and Haenni 2014), (Ryan 2016), and (Haenni and Koenig 2013). Since our formal verification of the C-Rex protocol in this work are about authentication and privacy properties, another direction for future research is investigating the verifiability guarantees of C-Rex.

Acknowledgement. Rakeei and Lenzini's research is supported by the ANR and FNR international project INTER/AN/20/14926102 - "Secure and Verifiable Electronic Testing and Assessment Systems" (SEVERITAS). Giustolisi is supported by the Villum Foundation, within the project "Enabling User Accountable Mechanisms in Decision Systems".

References

Abadi, M., Fournet, C.: Mobile values, new names, and secure communication. ACM Sigplan Not. **36**(3), 104–115 (2001)

Arapinis, M., Bursuc, S., Ryan, M.: Privacy-supporting cloud computing by in-browser key translation. J. Comput. Secur. **21**(6), 847–880 (2013)

Bella, G., Giustolisi, R., Lenzini, G.: Secure exams despite malicious management. In: PST 2014, pp. 274–281. IEEE (2014)

Bella, G., Giustolisi, R., Lenzini, G., Ryan, P.Y.: Trustworthy exams without trusted parties. Comput. Secur. **67**, 291–307 (2017)

Blanchet, B.: An efficient cryptographic protocol verifier based on prolog rules. In: CSFW 2001, pp. 82–96. IEEE (2001)

Castella-Roca, J., Herrera-Joancomarti, J., Dorca-Josa, A.: A secure e-exam management system. In: ARES 2006. IEEE (2006)

Dreier, J., Giustolisi, R., Kassem, A., Lafourcade, P., Lenzini, G.: A framework for analyzing verifiability in traditional and electronic exams. In: Lopez, J., Wu, Y. (eds.) ISPEC 2015. LNCS, vol. 9065, pp. 514–529. Springer, Cham (2015). https://doi.org/10.1007/978-3-319-17533-1_35

Dreier, J., Giustolisi, R., Kassem, A., Lafourcade, P., Lenzini, G., Ryan, P.Y.A.: Formal analysis of electronic exams. In: SECRYPT 2014. SciTePress (2014)

Dubuis, E., et al.: Verifizierbare internet-wahlen an schweizer hochschulen mit univote. INFORMATIK 2013 (2013)

ElGamal, T.: A public key cryptosystem and a signature scheme based on discrete logarithms. IEEE Trans. Inf. Theor **31**(4), 469–472 (1985)

Foley, S.N., Jacob, J.L.: Specifying security for computer supported collaborative working. J. Comput. Secur. **3**, 233–253 (1995)

Furnell, S., et al.: A security framework for online distance learning and training. Internet Res. **8**(3), 236–242 (1998)

Giustolisi, R.: Modelling and Verification of Secure Exams. Information Security and Cryptography, Springer, Germany (2018)

Giustolisi, R., Iovino, V., Lenzini, G.: Privacy-preserving verifiability - A case for an electronic exam protocol. In: SECRYPT. SciTePress (2017)

Giustolisi, R., Lenzini, G., Ryan, P.Y.A.: Remark!: a secure protocol for remote exams. In: Christianson, B., Malcolm, J., Matyáš, V., Švenda, P., Stajano, F., Anderson, J. (eds.) Security Protocols 2014. LNCS, vol. 8809, pp. 38–48. Springer, Cham (2014). https://doi.org/10.1007/978-3-319-12400-1_5

Haenni, R., Koenig, R.E.: A generic approach to prevent board flooding attacks in coercion-resistant electronic voting schemes. Comput. Secur. **33**, 59–69 (2013)

Haenni, R., Spycher, O.: Secure internet voting on limited devices with anonymized {DSA} public keys. In: EVT/WOTE (2011)

Huszti, A., Pethö, A.: A secure electronic exam system. Publicationes Math. Debrecen **77**(3–4), 299–312 (2010)

Kanav, S., Lammich, P., Popescu, A.: A conference management system with verified document confidentiality. In: Biere, A., Bloem, R. (eds.) CAV 2014. LNCS, vol. 8559, pp. 167–183. Springer, Cham (2014). https://doi.org/10.1007/978-3-319-08867-9_11

Locher, P., Haenni, R.: A lightweight implementation of a shuffle proof for electronic voting systems. Informatik 2014 (2014)

Ryan, P.Y.A.: Crypto santa. In: Ryan, P.Y.A., Naccache, D., Quisquater, J.-J. (eds.) The New Codebreakers. LNCS, vol. 9100, pp. 543–549. Springer, Heidelberg (2016). https://doi.org/10.1007/978-3-662-49301-4_33

Watson, G. R., Sottile, J.: Cheating in the Digital Age: Do Students Cheat More in Online Courses? Online Journal of Distance Learning Administration (2010)

Weippl, E.: Security in E-learning, vol. 6 of Advances in Information Security. Springer, cham (2005)

DPM Workshop: Leakage Quantification and Applications

Privacy with Good Taste

A Case Study in Quantifying Privacy Risks in Genetic Scores

Raúl Pardo[1]([✉]), Willard Rafnsson[1], Gregor Steinhorn[2], Denis Lavrov[2],
Thomas Lumley[3], Christian W. Probst[2], Ilze Ziedins[3], and Andrzej Wąsowski[1]

[1] IT University of Copenhagen, Copenhagen, Denmark
raup@itu.dk
[2] Unitec Institute of Technology, Auckland, New Zealand
[3] University of Auckland, Auckland, New Zealand

Abstract. Analysis of genetic data opens up many opportunities for medical and scientific advances. The use of phenotypic information and polygenic risk scores to analyze genetic data is widespread. Most work on genetic privacy focuses on basic genetic data such as SNP values and specific genotypes. In this paper, we introduce a novel methodology to quantify and prevent privacy risks by focusing on polygenic scores and phenotypic information. Our methodology is based on the tool-supported privacy risk analysis method Privug. We demonstrate the use of Privug to assess privacy risks posed by disclosing a polygenic trait score for bitter taste receptors, encoded by TAS2R38 and TAS2R16, to a person's privacy in regards to their ethnicity. We provide an extensive privacy risks analysis of different programs for genetic data disclosure: taster phenotype, tasting polygenic score, and a polygenic score distorted with noise. Finally, we discuss the privacy/utility trade-offs of the polygenic score.

1 Introduction

Genetics strongly influence *phenotypes*, the observable traits of humans and other species. Since the successful sequencing of a human genome in 2003, many attempts have been made to develop new methods utilizing this vast information. Research focuses on understanding the association between phenotypic and genetic information (see, *e.g.*, [18,20] on taste reception genes). *Polygenic risk scores* are developed to summarize the effect of genes on phenotype, especially in medical applications [21]. They are typically defined as a weighted sum on genetic data related to a single phenotype trait. Unfortunately, the use of a genotype in a polygenic score could disclose information about other conditions it is associated with. For example, the Apolipoprotein E (ApoE) gene shows both strong correlation with cardiovascular disease risk and Alzheimer's disease risk [15].

Researchers have demonstrated privacy risks associated with genetic data [16]. For instance, an individual's genomic data can be used to find out predisposition to disease, *e.g.*, using the phenotypic information or polygenic scores mentioned above. A person's

Work partially supported by the Danish Villum Foundation through Villum Experiment project No. 00023028 and New Zealand Ministry of Business, Innovation and Employment – Hīkina Whakatutuki through Smart Ideas project No. UNIT1902.

ⓒ The Author(s), under exclusive license to Springer Nature Switzerland AG 2023
J. Garcia-Alfaro et al. (Eds.): DPM 2022/CBT 2022, LNCS 13619, pp. 103–119, 2023.
https://doi.org/10.1007/978-3-031-25734-6_7

genome is based on their ancestry, with the addition of any mutations acquired by that person or their ancestors [7]. As a consequence, disclosing genetic data poses privacy risks, not only for its owner, but also her relatives and ancestors [11]. On a population level (not necessarily for individuals), knowledge about an individual's ancestry allows to make predictions about their ethnicity. The distribution of genotypes for a population is based on ancestry, therefore genetic data correlates to the ethnicity of individuals (*e.g.*, [18]). This poses a privacy risk for individuals who may be subject to discrimination.

Most privacy risk analyses and anonymization mechanisms in genetics focus on basic genetic data—such as SNP values or specific genotypes [16]. These approaches have been proven to be very effective in anonymizing and quantifying different kinds of privacy risks such as reidentification, kin privacy, or health care privacy [5,7,9,14]. See Sect. 8 for a detailed discussion of related works.

In this paper, we propose to quantify and prevent privacy risks by focusing on polygenic scores and phenotypic information. To the best of our knowledge, this is the first work to explore this viewpoint to tackle genetic privacy. Our work does not aim to replace existing methods, but to complement them through this new lens. This work is motivated by the observation that genetic data is often disclosed in terms of phenotypic information and polygenic scores. So it is directly applicable to the way geneticists process and disclose information. We build on top of the privacy risk analysis method PRIVUG [17]. Given a disclosure program (*e.g.*, the program to compute a polygenic score), a probabilistic model of attacker knowledge and an output of the program, PRIVUG computes the attacker posterior knowledge that can be used to assess privacy risks. We demonstrate the use of PRIVUG to assess the privacy risks posed by disclosing a polygenic trait score for the TAS2R38 and TAS2R16 taste receptor genes. We quantify the risks to a person's privacy in regards to their ancestry and thereby derived their likely ethnicity. The data and programs in this case study are selected to enhance readability and to serve as a template to apply our methodology. The methodology we present can be applied to phenotypes and polygenic scores working on any kind of sensitive genetic data. In summary, our contributions are:

- A methodology to analyze privacy risks of phenotypic information and polygenic scores based on the PRIVUG method.
- A demonstration of the methodology on a real case study based on the TAS2R38 and TAS2R16 taste receptor genes and their correlation with ethnicity.
- An extensive privacy risks analysis of different programs for genetic data disclosure: taster phenotype, tasting polygenic score, and a polygenic score distorted with noise.
- An analysis of the trade-off between privacy and utility of the polygenic score.

The data and source code of all experiments are available at: https://github.com/itu-square/privug-genetic-privacy.

2   Background

Taster Genes. The *genotype* is the genetic description of an organism made up of the specific alleles of genes an individual has inherited. A *phenotype* is an observable trait of an organism, in our case, tasting bitterness or sourness. Several studies found correlations between TAS genotypes (a fragment of the entire genotype of humans) and the perception of chemical substances [2,4,6,18]. TAS2R38 is predominantly responsible for detecting bitterness [2,18] and TAS2R16 is associated with detecting sourness [4]. Together they define the taster phenotype explored in this study. A *haplotype* is (a part of) a genotype containing chromosomes from one parent only. In this paper, we focus on the pairs of haplotypes that compose the genotypes of TAS2R38 and TAS2R16. We do not consider more basic elements such as *alleles*. The haplotypes of TAS2R38 are PAV, AVI, AAV, AVV, PAI, PVI, AAI and PVV. The haplotypes of TAS2R16 are HAP-CD, HAP-A, HAP-B. Thus, a given individual has a pair of haplotypes for each TAS2R genotype.

Data Privacy Analysis with PRIVUG. PRIVUG is a tool-supported method to explore information leakage properties of data analytics programs [17]. PRIVUG assumes that a program transforms an input dataset into an output, which is subsequently disclosed to a third party called an *attacker*. PRIVUG does not require a dataset, but starts with a probabilistic model of the attacker's knowledge. The model is analyzed together with the program to study the risks of inference of sensitive information.

Let $\mathbb{I}$, $\mathbb{O}$ denote sets of inputs and outputs of a program. Let $\mathcal{D}(\mathbb{I})$ be a distribution over a set, in this case the set of inputs. We write $I \sim \mathcal{D}(\mathbb{I})$ to denote a random variable over the set of inputs. The PRIVUG method is divided in the following five steps:

Step 1: Attacker's Prior Knowledge. We model what the attacker knows about the input before observing the output of the program as a belief distribution. For a program that receives an integer ($\mathbb{I} \triangleq \mathbb{Z}$), this could be a distribution $\mathcal{U}(-10,10)$, a discrete uniform distribution on integers between -10 and 10, which models an attacker knowing *only* that the input is between -10 and 10 but not more. We write $p(I)$ for the probability distribution associated with the random variable I representing the input to the program.

Step 2: Interpret the Program. We run the program not on a concrete input data set from $\mathbb{I}$, but on the belief distribution representing the attacker's knowledge about the input. For example, the following program takes as input an integer and returns its value perturbed by a Laplacian distribution with mean 0 and scale 1:

```
def program(x: int): return x + stats.laplace.rvs()
```

We transform this program into a probabilistic one taking a distribution over inputs and run it on the attacker's knowledge distribution:

```
def program(x: Dist(int)): return x + stats.laplace.rvs()
```

where `Dist(int)` denotes a distribution over integers ($\mathcal{D}(\mathbb{Z})$). The attacker's knowledge together with the program define the joint distribution over inputs and outputs: $p(I, O)$.

Step 3: Observation. Optionally, we can assume that the output of the program, or some information about it, has been disclosed to the attacker (otherwise we reason about all possible input data sets). For instance, assume that the attacker learned that the output of the program was greater than 7. Adding this observation amounts to conditioning the joint distribution, *e.g.*switching from $p(I, O)$ to $p(I, O \mid O > 7)$.

Step 4: Posterior. We approximate the joint distribution using standard Markov Chain Monte Carlo (MCMC) methods. In this paper, we use the PyMC3 [19] library.

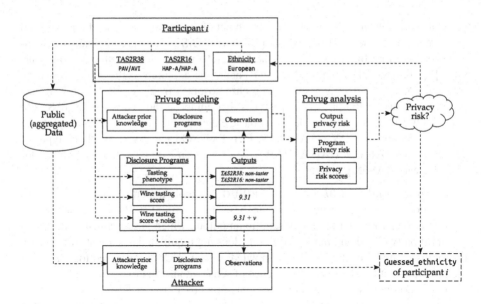

Fig. 1. The case study overview.

Step 5: Posterior Analysis. We query the inferred distribution to study the posterior knowledge of the attacker. To this end, we can query for probabilities and compute summary statistics of the distributions (mean, variance, etc.), and standard leakage measures such as entropy, KL-divergence, mutual information, and Bayes vulnerability [1].

3   The Case Study

A data analyst wants to disclose data about the ability of study participants to taste wine. Such data is commonly released [2,4,6,18]. To compute the tasting information, the analyst uses the information about the taste receptor genes TAS2R38 and TAS2R16. Figure 1 includes an example of data for a single participant in the box labeled *Participant i*, including haplotype pairs PAV/AVI for TAS2R38 and HAP-A/HAP-A for TAS2R16. The analyst considers the following three options of disclosing the data.

1. Taster/non-taster binary Phenotype. This program labels participants as *taster*, who can taste bitterness and sourness (having relevant haplotypes of TAS2R38 and TAS2R16), or *non-taster*. For Participant i the output of this program is *non-taster* on both accounts.

2. Wine tasting score/polygenic score. Combines TAS2R38 and TAS2R16 haplotype pairs to compute a genetic trait score. The polygenic score is based on biochemical tests, published in [2], to determine the response of TAS2R38 haplotypes to bitter substances, and the presence TAS2R16 taster haplotypes. The larger the score, the better the wine tasting abilities of the participant. For Participant i the program output is 9.31.

Table 1. TAS2R38 and TAS2R16 haplotype probability for each ethnicity, $p(H^{r38}|E)$ and $p(H^{r16}|E)$, respectively [18,20]

	TAS2R38								TAS2R16		
	PAV	AVI	AAV	AVV	PAI	PVI	AAI	PVV	HAP-CD	HAP-A	HAP-B
African	.5076	.4270	.0248	.0032	.0018	.0007	.0339	.0010	.1511	.8355	.0133
Asian	.5076	.3518	.0061	.0008	.0000	.0015	.1322	.0000	.0011	.6309	.3679
European	.6451	.3531	.0000	.0017	.0000	.0000	.0000	.0000	.0000	.6810	.3189
American	.4566	.4922	.0356	.0049	.0032	.0003	.0055	.0017	.0000	.8105	.1894

3. Wine tasting score with noise. This program adds noise to the output of the previous one with the goal of decreasing privacy risks. For Participant i, it outputs 9.31 plus a random perturbation ν drawn from a Normal distribution with mean 0 and standard deviation σ. The value of σ determines the amount of noise. In Sect. 7 we evaluate the impact of different values of σ on privacy risks and utility.

The first two disclosure programs are standard methods to aggregate and share genetic data. They are not designed with privacy protection in mind. The last method attempts to enhance privacy by adding random noise to the wine tasting score.

In this case study, the ethnicity of participants is considered sensitive information. Note that our programs do not use ethnicity as input. Still, their output could be used to learn about ethnicity using a linking attack. Genetic information is correlated with ethnicity, and, in this case, the attacker may conclude that Participant i has European ethnicity.

We consider an information-theoretical attacker that has access to: i) publicly available aggregated data correlating TAS2R38, TAS2R16 and ethnicity [2,4,6,18], in particular Table 1; ii) the source of the disclosure program; and iii) the program output released by the data analyst. This is depicted in Fig. 1 as lines connecting those elements to the attacker model at the bottom. The goal of the attacker is to infer the ethnicity of a study participant. There are no bounds on the computational resources available to the attacker.

Our objective is to apply the PRIVUG method to reason about this case, to expose privacy risks involved in releasing genetic data, as well as to encourage geneticists to consider PRIVUG (and similar tools) as an aid in decision making.

4   Modeling

In the following, we use $\mathbb{H}$ to denote the set of TAS2R38 *haplotypes*: PAV, AVI, AA, etc. (second row in Table 1). We use $\mathbb{E}$ to denote the set of *ethnicities* (first column in Table 1). We use H and E to denote the corresponding random variables. We consider an attacker who, *a priori*, makes no assumptions about the ethnicity of the participant. In other words, before observing the output of the program, the attacker considers all ethnicities in Table 1 to be equally likely. For convenience, we map each ethnicity to an element in $\mathbb{N}_0$. The prior is uniform over the ethnicities, i.e. $E \sim \mathcal{U}(0,3)$.

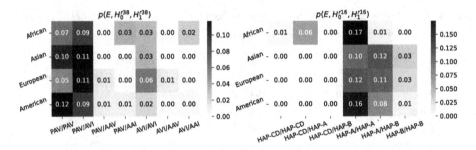

Fig. 2. Priors on ethnicity, and haplotype pairs. Left: TAS2R38. Right: TAS2R16.

For the taste receptor haplotypes we consider an attacker informed by publicly available population genetics studies [18,20] containing information about the correlation between ethnicity, TAS2R38, and TAS2R16. Given an ethnicity E, we use $r38_E$ and $r16_E$ to refer to vectors composed by columns 2–9 and columns 10–12 in row E of in Table 1, respectively, so we have that $H^{r38} \sim Cat(r38_E)$ and $H^{r16} \sim Cat(r16_E)$, where, for example, $Cat(r38_E)$ is a categorical (discrete) distribution defined by vector $r38_E$. Here again, each haplotype value is mapped to an element in $\mathbb{N}_0$.

Figure 2 shows the joint distributions of ethnicity and haplotype pairs representing the beliefs of the attacker. For instance, the top-left cell (left graph) shows that the probability of African ethnicity and the haplotype pair PAV/PAV is 0.07. For TAS2R38, this prior assigns high probability to haplotype pairs PAV/PAV and PAV/AVI—as [18] established that PAV and AVI are common haplotypes in all tested populations. For TAS2R16, the haplotype pairs HAP-A/HAP-A and HAP-A/HAP-B are most likely, due to the common occurrence of HAP-A [20].

We now investigate and compare the privacy risks of the three disclosure programs from the previous section. All these work on pairs of haplotypes: we use (H_0^{r38}, H_1^{r38}) to refer to each TAS2R38 haplotype and (H_0^{r16}, H_1^{r16}) for TAS2R16.

Taster/Non-taster Binary Phenotype. We consider a disclosure program that maps TAS2R38 and TAS2R16 to binary phenotypes: *taster*, *non-taster*. For TAS2R38, the haplotype pair AVI/AVI corresponds to the non-taster phenotype, and the remaining haplotype pairs to taster. For TAS2R16, the haplotype pair HAP-CD/HAP-CD corresponds to the non-taster phenotype, and the remaining haplotype pairs to taster:

$$Ph_{nt}^{r38} \triangleq \bigwedge_{i \in \{0,1\}} H_i^{r38} = AVI \qquad Ph_{nt}^{r16} \triangleq \bigwedge_{i \in \{0,1\}} H_i^{r16} = HAP\text{-}CD$$

Figure 3 shows their Python implementations. Both programs take a haplotype pair and return a Boolean stating whether the pair corresponds to a non-taster.

Wine Tasting Score/Polygenic Score. The polygenic score is a linear combination of genotype weights and haplotype weights:

$$L_{gs} \triangleq \alpha_{r38} \cdot gt_{r38}(H_0^{r38}, H_1^{r38}) + \alpha_{r16} \cdot gt_{r16}(H_0^{r16}, H_1^{r16})$$

The function $>_j : \mathbb{H} \times \mathbb{H} \rightarrow \mathbb{R}$ is the genotype weights; it assigns a score modeling the impact on tasting ability of a pair of haplotypes. The coefficient $\alpha_j \in \mathbb{R}$ is the gene

```
def non_taster_TAS2R16(h1,h2): return h1==HAP-CD and h2==HAP-CD
def non_taster_TAS2R38(h1,h2): return h1==AVI and h2==AVI
```

Fig. 3. Taster disclosure program for TAS2R16 (line 1) and for TAS2R38 (line 2)

```
def linear_gs(r38_h1,r38_h2,r16_h1,r16_h2):
    l_gs = α_r38*gt_38(r38_h1,r38_h2) + α_r16*gt_16(r16_h1,r16_h2)
    return round(l_gs,2)
```

Fig. 4. Wine tasting linear polygenetic score disclosure program

```
def noisy_linear_gs(r38_h1,r38_h2,r16_h1,r16_h2):
    nl_gs = linear_gs(r38_h1,r38_h2,r16_h1,r16_h2) + np.random.normal(0,σ)
    return round(nl_gs,2)
```

Fig. 5. Wine tasting linear polygenetic score disclosure program with random noise

weight; it assigns a score modeling the influence of the gene on the tasting score. We set the weight values based on the biochemical test [2], for the response of TAS2R38 to bitter substances, and the presence TAS2R16 taster haplotypes. Figure 4 shows Python code for the polygenic score. The implementation rounds the value to 2 decimal points. This is how polygenic scores are normally disclosed (and perceived by the attacker).

Wine Tasting Score with Random Noise. Here we consider a polygenic score aimed at reducing privacy risks. We use a normal distribution with mean 0 and different values of standard deviation to generate random noise:

$$\nu \sim \mathcal{N}(0,\sigma) \qquad\qquad NL_{gs} \triangleq L_{gs} + \nu$$

Figure 5 shows a Python implementation. The function np.random.normal(0,σ) uses the NumPy [10] library to sample from a normal distribution with mean 0 and standard deviation σ. We do not fix the value of σ, to study the effect of increasing values in Sect. 7.

5 Privacy Risk Metrics

Output privacy risk. We evaluate the privacy risk associated with disclosing a concrete output of the disclosure method. To this end, we look at the posterior distribution of ethnicity given a concrete program output. Let O denote a random variable modeling the output of any of the programs in Sect. 4, we compute

$$p(E \mid O = v) \text{ for a concrete output } v \text{ in the domain of } O.$$

If the probability for an ethnicity is high, then it means that the attacker can learn with high probability the ethnicity of the individual. Output privacy is useful when a data analyst is trying to decide whether or not to disclose a program output. For instance, in the taster phenotype program for TAS2R38, suppose that $p(E = \text{African} \mid Ph^{r38} =$

$taster) = 1$. Now consider a data analyst that after running the program obtains *taster*. Then, releasing that output also discloses the individual's African ethnicity.

Program Privacy Risk. To evaluate the overall privacy risks of a program, we use a metric that accounts for the probability of each output, $p(O)$. Note that output privacy measures risks disregarding how likely the output is. Naturally, combining output privacy with the probability of the output yields the joint distribution of ethnicities and outputs,

$$p(E \mid O)p(O) = p(E, O).$$

Program privacy is useful for data analysts assessing risks before computing a concrete output. High values indicate both a high risk of leaking the individual's ethnicity and that it is likely that the leak may occur. Suppose that, for the taster TAS2R38 phenotype program, we have that $p(E = \text{American}, Ph^{r38} = taster) = 0.8$. That is, if the program outputs taster and the ethnicity of the individual is American with probability 0.8, indepent of the input. Intuitively, this program has high privacy risks for Americans. Ideally, the program should distribute probability among ethnicities and outputs uniformly.

Privacy Risk Scores. These scores aim to summarize the output and program privacy risks into a single score (real value). We use two privacy risk metrics to summarize privacy risks into a score: *maximum output privacy* and *Bayes vulnerability* [1].

Maximum Output Privacy. This metric summarizes the results of output privacy risks. It reports the maximum output privacy for all possible program outputs. That is,

$$\max_{e \in E, o \in O} p(E = e | O = o)$$

Maximum output privacy is a *pessimistic* upper bound on privacy risks, as it is pessimistic because it does not take into account the probability of the output. A program may have large maximum output privacy for an output that is very unlikely. Recall the example above where $p(E = \text{African} \mid Ph^{r38} = taster) = 1$ and $P(Ph^{r38} = taster) = 0.01$. Here the maximum output privacy equals 1. Note that we do not need to explore other outputs; as 1 is the maximum output privacy risk. This metric does not indicate what/how many outputs or ethnicities produce the maximum output privacy. However, since maximum output privacy is an upper bound on privacy risks, a low value of output privacy does indicate low risks for all outputs.

Bayes Vulnerability. This metric summarizes program privacy risks. Bayes vulnerability [1] measures the *expected probability of correctly guessing the ethnicity by observing the output of the program.* Bayes vulnerability is defined as

$$V = \sum_{o \in O} \max_{e \in E} p(E = e, O = o).$$

A high value of Bayes vulnerability implies high privacy risks. Bayes vulnerability does not indicate what ethnicity is at risk or what output causes the leak. Bayes vulnerability is especially useful when comparing disclosure programs. The joint distribution (program privacy risk) may consist of a large number of ethnicity/output pairs, making it

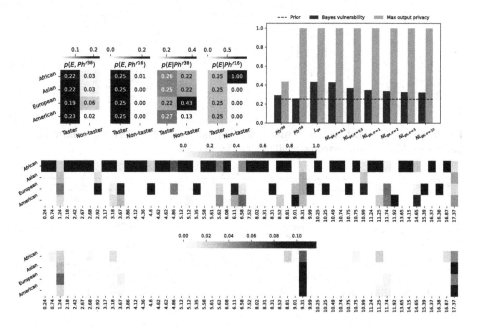

Fig. 6. Top-left: Program privacy risks of binary phenotype program (first two histograms), and output privacy risk of binary phenotype program (3rd and 4th histograms). Top-right: Privacy risk scores results for all disclosure programs. Middle: Output privacy risk of polygenic scores. Bottom: Program privacy risk of polygenic score.

tedious to compare among several programs. Furthermore, Bayes vulnerability can be used as a first indicator of privacy risks. In case Bayes vulnerability is high, then the joint distribution may be explored to find the ethnicities at high risk.

6   Utility Metrics

Absolute Difference. We consider the absolute difference of the wine tasting score (real output) and the wine tasting score with noise (distorted output), *i.e.*, $|L_{gs} - NL_{gs}|$. A value of 0 indicates perfect utility, the larger the value the worse the utility. Since our analysis estimates distributions $p(L_{gs})$ and $p(NL_{gs})$, we actually analyze the distribution of the absolute difference, $p(|L_{gs} - NL_{gs}|)$.

Error Bound Probability. As for privacy risk metrics, now we define a score that summarizes utility. Specifically, we consider the probability that the absolute difference is within a bound δ, formally, $p(|L_{gs} - NL_{gs}| < \delta)$. The value δ defines the amount of error that the analyst considers acceptable. For this paper, we (arbitrarily) set to study $\delta \in \{0.1, 0.5, 1\}$, but our analysis can be applied for any δ. High error bound probability indicates high utility, with 1 being perfect utility and 0 worst utility.

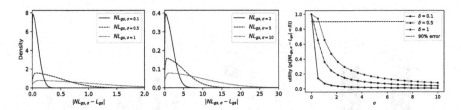

Fig. 7. Utility results. Left, center: Distribution of absolute distance between noisy and real polygenic score. Right: Error bound probability for different σ and δ.

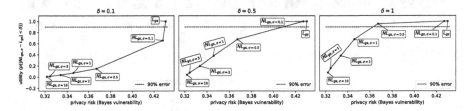

Fig. 8. Utility/privacy trade-off for all polygenic scores for different error bounds.

7 Analysis and Results

In this section, we discuss: i) the quality of the inferred posterior distribution; ii) privacy risks of each disclosure program using the privacy risk metrics presented in Sect. 5; and iii) the utility evaluation for the disclosure programs adding random noise.

7.1 Posterior Inference

To estimate the joint posterior distribution, we use a Metropolis-within-Gibbs sampler optimized for Categorical variables [3, 19]. The model in Sect. 4 is composed of ethnicity and haplotype variables which are in a nominal (categorical) scale. We generate 100k samples with a burn-in period of 50k samples. The resulting posterior distribution shows good sampling/convergence diagnosis [3]: Estimated Sample Size (ESS) of at least 50k, a Markov Chain Standard Error (MCSE) below 0.15, and $\hat{R}$ of 1.0 for all parameters. This diagnosis indicates that the inferred posterior has converged and it is accurate.

7.2 Output Privacy Risk

Binary Tasting Phenotype. The last two heatmaps in Fig. 6 (top-left) show the output privacy results for the tasting phenotype program, for TAS2R38 and TAS2R16, respectively. We observe that the non-taster output carries higher privacy risks in both cases. For TAS2R16, it implies completely giving away the ethnicity of the individual. Interestingly, the taster output is (mostly) uniformly distributed among ethnicities. This means that in both cases it is safe to publish that the individual is a taster.

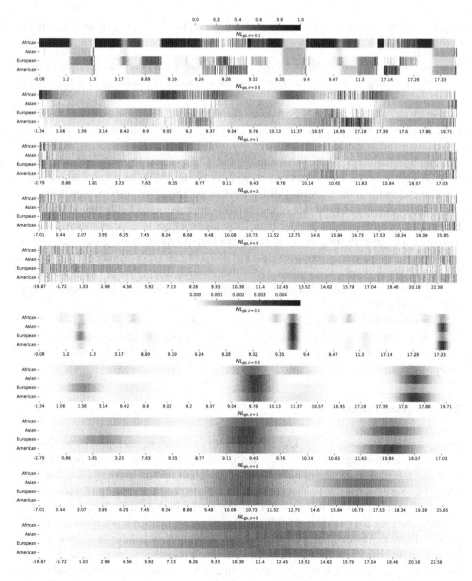

Fig. 9. Output privacy risk (top) and program privacy risks (bottom) for polygenic scores with random noise for increasing σ.

Wine Tasting Score. Figure 6 (middle) shows the output privacy risk of the wine tasting score. For more than half of the possible outputs, the African ethnicity is at high risk, *i.e.*, output privacy risk close to 1. European is the second most vulnerable ethnicity. The American ethnicity shows high risk only for 3 possible outputs. The Asian ethnicity shows low risk for all outputs. For the outputs 9.31 and 17.37 the output privacy risk of each ethnicity is very close to 0.25 (the same as in the prior). This means that the attacker would not learn much by observing this output. For data analysts interested in output privacy risk, we recommend to only disclose the output if it equals 9.31 or 17.31.

Wine Tasting Score with Random Noise. Figure 9 (top) shows the output privacy results of the wine tasting score with random noise for an increasing noise level σ from 0.1 to 5.

For $\sigma = 0.1$, Africans and Europeans have higher output privacy risk. Due to the large number of outputs, now we discuss ranges of possible outputs. A gray homogeneous color indicates that risk is distributed uniformly across ethnicities. We observe this effect in the range $(9.35, 9.40)$ and around 17.33. These intervals are close to the low risk values in the wine tasting score without noise. Values of σ equal to 0.5 and 1 increase the width of the uniformly distributed areas. This effect also reduces the size of solid black ranges, meaning that output privacy improves, especially for Africans and Europeans. For values of σ greater than 1 the above effect is more pronounced. As σ increases, a large uniform gray range (with low output privacy risks) covers most of the spectrum of output values. For $\sigma = 2$ and $\sigma = 5$, outputs (approximately) in the range $(9.5, 11.5)$ show good output privacy. We also observe that, in these cases, the border regions (low and high output values) show high contrast indicating high output privacy risks for some ethnicities.

Our results indicate that for $0 < \sigma < 1$ outputs in the regions close to 9.31 and 17.37 have low output privacy risk. For $1 < \sigma \leq 5$, outputs in the range $(9.5, 11.5)$ show low output privacy risks. As expected, the larger σ the higher the privacy, but we compromise its utility. We discuss this in Sect. 7.5.

7.3   Program Privacy Risk

Binary Tasting Phenotype. For TAS2R16 (Fig. 6, 2nd heatmap in top-left), we observe that *taster* has the highest probability and is uniformly distributed across ethnicities. This indicates (almost) complete absence of program privacy risks. Recall that *non-taster* has very high output privacy (Sect. 7.2). Now program privacy reveals that the non-taster output has very low probability; only 0.01. (Probability values do not add up to 1 because they are rounded.) TAS2R38 (Fig. 6, 1st heatmap in top-left) shows similar results: Taster is a more likely output than non-taster, and probability is distributed uniformly across ethnicities for taster. We observe that for tasters, Europeans have slightly lower program privacy risk than the other ethnicities. However, when the output is non-taster, Europeans have double the program privacy risks compared to other ethnicities; with this scenario occurring with probability 0.06. This is inline with the high output privacy risks for Europeans and this program output, but program privacy shows that this case is unlikely.

To sum up, both binary tasting genotype programs have low program privacy risks, with TAS2R16 offering better protection than TAS2R38.

Wine Tasting Score. Figure 6 (bottom) shows the program privacy risks for the wine tasting score. We observe that only outputs 1.24, 9.31 and 17.37 have non-negligible probability. This is useful information, as output privacy allocated high privacy risks for Africans, but now we discover that those outputs are very unlikely. In fact, within the high probability outputs, Africans show the lowest risk of all ethnicities. Interestingly, the outputs with non-negligible probability coincide with some of those having low output privacy risks, *i.e.,* 9.31 and 17.37. As for output 1.24, although it does not exhibit high program privacy risks, the probability for Europeans is higher than for others.

All in all, the wine tasting score shows a good level of program privacy risks. Probability is mostly distributed across ethnicities for all likely outputs. However, this distribution is less uniform than for the binary tasting phenotype. This is expected as the polygenic score contains genetic information about TAS2R38 *and* TAS2R16. On the contrary, the phenotype programs work on either TAS2R38 or TAS2R16.

Wine Tasting Score with Noise. Figure 9 (bottom) shows the results of program privacy risks for the wine tasting score with random noise. Each row displays the results for a value of σ, starting from $\sigma = 0.1$ up to $\sigma = 5$.

In the first 3 rows ($0.1 \leq \sigma \leq 1$), we observe 3 distinct high probability regions. Note that these coincide with the high probability outputs in the program privacy risks for the wine tasting score without noise: 1.24, 9.31 and 17.37. Similarly to the score w/o noise, program privacy reveals that most of the high risk outputs for Africans are unlikely events. Also, program privacy is (mostly) uniformly distributed across ethnicities for the high probability outputs. With higher program privacy risk for: i) Europeans in outputs around 1.24, Asian and Europeans; ii) Europeans and Asians in outputs around 9.31; and iii) Asians and Americans for outputs around 17.37. Nevertheless, these results are positive, as there is no ethnicity with significantly higher risks. For the last 2 rows ($2 \leq \sigma \leq 5$), the 3 regions above merge into a single high probability region centered around 10. Program privacy risks across ethnicities become more uniform as σ grows. This is displayed as a uniform gray tone across ethnicities. This is a clear indication of low program privacy risks. As mentioned earlier, these results must be considered together with utility metrics. We discuss utility in Sect. 7.5.

To sum up, random noise improves the program privacy of the wine tasting score, especially for large values of σ where privacy risks are uniformly distributed across ethnicities. It is unclear, however, how it compares with the binary phenotype programs. The following section, that discusses the results of program privacy scores, will allow us to effectively compare all disclosure programs.

7.4 Privacy Risk Scores

Maximum Output Privacy. Figure 6 (top-right, light gray columns) shows the maximum output privacy risk for all disclosure programs. We observe that all programs except for Ph^{r38} have max. output privacy risk 1. This is because they have at least one output for which output privacy risk equals 1. As discussed earlier, this metric is quite pessimistic: we saw in the program privacy results that most of the outputs with high output privacy are very unlikely. Nevertheless, maximum output privacy serves as a good upper bound on risk. Here we can see that Ph^{r38} is close to 0.4. This means that, no matter the output, output privacy risks will never be above this value. This may be a sufficient level of privacy, taking into account that 0.25 is the prior probability for each ethnicity.

Bayes Vulnerability. Figure 6 (top-right, dark gray columns) shows the Bayes vulnerability results for all disclosure programs. Recall that Bayes vulnerability measures the expected probability of learning ethnicity by observing the output. This metric scales the risk in each output by the probability of the output. As a consequence, we observe lower risk levels when compared with maximum output privacy. Interestingly, Ph^{r16} has a lower risk score than Ph^{r38} (as opposed to what we observed in maximum output privacy). This is because the output with high output privacy risk in Ph^{r16} is very unlikely. As expected, the wine tasting score without noise has the largest Bayes vulnerability; as it encapsulates the most information. The results show that the effect of noise reduces the risk, but not substantially. None of the levels of noise we analyzed show lower privacy risks than the binary tasting phenotype programs. However, the maximum Bayes vulnerability is ≈ 0.42, which is not a very high value.

There is no universal value for perfect Bayes vulnerability. Companies/institutions may fix values for Bayes vulnerabilities based on their privacy requirements. For illustrative purposes, we (arbitrarily) set on a value no more than 0.35 Bayes vulnerability, *i.e.*, at most 0.1 more than the prior. Then, only the tasting phenotype programs and wine tasting score with random noise and $\sigma \geq 0.5$ are considered privacy preserving.

7.5 Utility

Absolute Distance Distribution. Figure 7 (left,center) shows the absolute distance distribution between the wine tasting score with and without noise for different values of σ. The results are split into two figures to better appreciate the High Density Interval (HDI) of the distributions; note the difference range values for x and y axes. For $0.1 \leq \sigma \leq 1$ (left plot), all distributions have their mode close to 0 and the HDI ends around 1 (or 1.5 for $\sigma = 1$). This indicates a small introduced error. For the right plot ($\sigma > 1$), the mode is close to 0 as well, but the HDIs are much wider: The HDI ends at 5 for $\sigma = 2$, at 10 for $\sigma = 5$ and at 15 for $\sigma = 10$.

The extent to which the error in the linear score is admissible is problem dependent. However, this analysis shows the large amount of distortion that values of $\sigma > 0.5$ introduce. Fixing a maximum level of error would be helpful in deciding what programs have acceptable error. The next metric explores this.

Error Bound Probability. Figure 7 (right) shows the error bound probability results for increasing value of σ in the wine tasting score program with noise for error bound values $\delta \in \{0.1, 0.5, 1\}$. We consider these values acceptable given the scale of the wine tasting score. However, the value of δ is application dependent, and our method can be used with any value of δ. The plots show the 90% probability boundary, which we consider sufficient confidence. Stronger requirements can be set, e.g., 95% or even 100%.

For all δ values, we observe a sharp exponential decay in utility as σ increases. For $\delta = 0.1$, utility decays below 20% even for $\sigma = 0.5$. For $\sigma > 0.1$, we observe worse utility: with values very close to 0. This indicates that *only* values of σ close to 0.1 are acceptable. Increasing the error bound to $\delta = 0.5$ yields better utility. Yet no value $\sigma > 0.1$ meets our requirements. It is only for $\delta = 1$ that $\sigma = 0.5$ meets our utility requirements. As for the other cases, no value $\sigma > 0.5$ has acceptable utility.

Adding noise decreases privacy, but it is not a panacea. The results in this section show that we can only add a small amount of noise, if we want to preserve utility.

Privacy/Utility Trade-off. We conclude by putting together the privacy and utility scores. Figure 8 plots the error bound probability (utility) and Bayes vulnerability (privacy). We analyze different levels of δ, as before.

For $\delta = 0.1$ (left in Fig. 8), we observe that no level of noise meets the utility requirements. Only L_{gs} (wine tasting score w/o noise) is above the 90% line. NL_{gs} with $\sigma = 0.5$ shows a utility level around 60% with almost the same Bayes vulnerability. In other words, we gain no privacy and deteriorate utility to an unacceptable degree (for $\delta = 0.1$). Reducing the utility requirements to $\delta = 0.5$ (center in Fig. 8) includes $\sigma = 0.1$ as an acceptable program. But, again, we gain almost no privacy protection. Finally, for $\delta = 1$, NL_{gs} with $\sigma = 0.5$ meets the utility requirements. In this case, Bayes vulnerability is reduced by 0.06 (from 0.43 to 0.37). This privacy score is still far from the prior (*i.e.,* 0.25), but it is a significant improvement.

Data analysts may use these results to make an informed decision on the programs to disclose the wine tasting score. Given our results and privacy/utility requirements we set forth, the best choice would be NL_{gs} with $\sigma = 0.5$. That said, the most valuable takeaway is the analysis process and privacy/utility information we described.

8   Related Work

There exists a wide spectrum of research on genetic privacy [16]. Below we cover the most relevant work in the context of this paper.

Cai *et al.* [5] develop a re-identification attack based on Genome-Wide Association Studies (GWAS). These studies are applied to human genomic data to understand disease associations. The presented algorithm scales well for realistic GWAS datasets. They show that the number of re-identified individuals grows with number of released genotypes. Gymrek *et al.* [7] demonstrate re-identification risks by combining haplotype information with demographics such as age and state. In particular, they analyze the probability of re-identifying US males. Our work focuses on privacy risks associated to phenotypes and polygenic scores instead of working directly on genotypes. Also, we focus on the problem of inferring sensitive data (ethnicity) as opposed to re-identification.

Gürsoy *et al.* [8] study the probability of inferring *sensitive* phenotypes, *i.e.*, phenotypes the victim wants to keep secret. They consider an attacker with access to public studies on the correlation between genotypes and sensitive phenotypes. Given the genotype of a victim, they compute the probability of learning the sensitive phenotypes. The authors propose a data sanitation protocol for genotypes that minimizes the probability of learning sensitive phenotypes. Similarly, Harmancie and Gerstein [9] study privacy risks on genomic deletions on signal profiles. Genomic deletions may enable attacker to infer sensitive phenotypes via public statistics on the correlation between deletions and phenotypes. The authors propose an anonymization method based on removing dips in signal profiles. These works tackle the problem of inferring sensitive phenotypes from genotype data. Instead, we quantify and protect against inferring sensitive data from public polygenic scores or phenotypes.

Humbert *et al.* [11,13] propose a probabilistic model to infer Single Nucleotide Polymorphism (SNP) values. They use an inference algorithm (belief propagation or Bayesian inference) to estimate the distribution of unknown SNP values from information about observed SNPs, genomic data of family members, familial relationships, etc. The authors also define health privacy scores based on SNP values. Anonymization is performed by masking specific SNPs. They further propose an optimization algorithm that determines the SNP to mask to minimize risks in the aforementioned model [12]. In this context, Humbert *et al.* [14] have developed a tool for communicating and raising aware of kin privacy to lay users. These works focus on SNP information to quantify privacy risks, we instead target polygenic scores and phenotypes.

9   Conclusion

Polygenic risk scores are typically defined as a weighted sum on genetic data related to a single phenotype trait. They are used to summarize the effect of genes on phenotypes, both to inform the individual patient and to anonymize results for publication. As discussed above, any disclosure of genetic data including polygenic scores is associated with the risk of re-identifying individuals or to find out a predisposition to a disease.

In this paper, we have introduced an approach to quantify and prevent privacy risks by focusing on polygenic scores and phenotypic information. We believe that this is the first work to explore this viewpoint to tackle genetic privacy. Building on top of the privacy risk analysis method PRIVUG [17], we compute the attacker posterior knowledge from a program to compute the polygenic risk score, a probabilistic model of attacker knowledge about the individuals covered and populations, and an output of the program.

Our approach aims at supporting existing methods with a novel way to measure the risk of privacy violations. We have demonstrated its application on a polygenic trait score for the TAS2R38 and TAS2R16 taste receptor genes. We have shown how to quantify the risks for a person's privacy in regards to their ancestry and thereby derived their likely ethnicity. While the data and programs in this case study were selected to enhance readability, our methodology can be applied to phenotypes and polygenic scores working on any kind of sensitive genetic data.

References

1. Alvim, M.S., et al.: The Science of Quantitative Information FlowInformation Security and Cryptography. Springer, Cham (2020)
2. Behrens, M., et al.: Genetic, functional, and phenotypic diversity in TAS2R38-mediated bitter taste perception. Chem. Senses **38**, 475–484 (2013)
3. Brooks, S., Gelman, A., Jones, G., Meng, X.L.: Handbook of Markov Chain Monte Carlo. CRC, Boca Raton (2011)
4. Bufe, B., et al.: The human TAS2R16 receptor mediates bitter taste in response to β-glucopyranosides. Nat. Genet. **32**(3), 397–401 (2002)
5. Cai, R., et al.: Deterministic identification of specific individuals from GWAS results. Bioinform. **31**(11), 1701–1707 (2015)
6. Carrai, M., et al.: Association between taste receptor (TAS) genes and the perception of wine characteristics. Sci. Rep. **7**(1), 1–7 (2017)

7. Gymrek, M., McGuire, A.L., Golan, D., Halperin, E., Erlich, Y.: Identifying personal genomes by surname inference. Science **339**(6117), 321–324 (2013)
8. Gürsoy, G., et al.: Data sanitization to reduce private information leakage from functional genomics. Cell **183**, 905–917 (2020)
9. Harmanci, A., Gerstein, M.: Analysis of sensitive information leakage in functional genomics signal profiles through genomic deletions. Nat. Commun. **9**(1), 1–10 (2018)
10. Harris, C.R., et al.: Array programming with NumPy. Nature **585**(7825), 357–362 (2020)
11. Humbert, M., Ayday, E., Hubaux, J., Telenti, A.: Addressing the concerns of the lacks family: quantification of kin genomic privacy. In: CCS, pp. 1141–1152. ACM (2013)
12. Humbert, M., Ayday, E., Hubaux, J., Telenti, A.: Reconciling utility with privacy in genomics. In: Workshop on Privacy in the Electronic Society, WPES, pp. 11–20. ACM (2014)
13. Humbert, M., Ayday, E., Hubaux, J., Telenti, A.: Quantifying interdependent risks in genomic privacy. ACM Trans. Priv. Secur. **20**(1), 3:1–3:31 (2017)
14. Humbert, M., Didier, D., Mauro, C., Kévin, H.: KGP meter: communicating kin genomic privacy to the masses. In: EuroS&P. IEEE (2022)
15. Lumsden, A.L., et al.: Apolipoprotein E (APOE) genotype-associated disease risks: a phenome-wide, registry-based, case-control study utilising the UK biobank. EBioMedicine **59**, 102549 (2020)
16. Naveed, M., et al.: Privacy in the genomic era. ACM Comput. Surv. **48**(1), 6:1–6:44 (2015)
17. Pardo, R., Rafnsson, W., Probst, C.W., Wąsowski, A.: Privug: using probabilistic programming for quantifying leakage in privacy risk analysis. In: Bertino, E., Shulman, H., Waidner, M. (eds.) ESORICS 2021. LNCS, vol. 12973, pp. 417–438. Springer, Cham (2021). https://doi.org/10.1007/978-3-030-88428-4_21
18. Risso, D.S., et al.: Global diversity in the TAS2R38 bitter taste receptor: revisiting a classic evolutionary proposal. Sci. Rep. **6**(1), 1–9 (2016)
19. Salvatier, J., Wiecki, T.V., Fonnesbeck, C.: Probabilistic programming in Python using PyMC3. PeerJ Comput. Sci. **2**, e55 (2016)
20. Soranzo, N., et al.: Positive selection on a high-sensitivity allele of the human bitter-taste receptor TAS2R16. Curr. Biol. **15**(14), 1257–1265 (2005)
21. Torkamani, A., Wineinger, N.E., Topol, E.J.: The personal and clinical utility of polygenic risk scores. Nat. Rev. Genet. **19**(9), 581–590 (2018)

A Parallel Privacy-Preserving Shortest Path Protocol from a Path Algebra Problem

Mohammad Anagreh[1] and Peeter Laud[2]([✉])

[1] Institute of Computer Science, Tartu University,
Narva mnt. 18, 51009 Tartu, Estonia
mohammad.anagreh@ut.ee
[2] Cybernetica AS, Narva mnt. 20, 51009 Tartu, Estonia
peeter.laud@cyber.ee

Abstract. In this paper, we present a secure multiparty computation (SMC) protocol for single-source shortest distances (SSSD) in undirected graphs, where the location of edges is public, but their length is private. The protocol works in the Arithmetic Black Box (ABB) model on top of the separator tree of the graph, achieving good time complexity if the subgraphs of the graph have small separators (which is the case for e.g. planar graphs); the achievable parallelism is significantly higher than that of classical SSSD algorithms implemented on top of an ABB.

We implement our protocol on top of the Sharemind MPC platform, and perform extensive benchmarking over different network environments. We compare our algorithm against the baseline picked from classical algorithms—privacy-preserving Bellman-Ford algorithm (with public edges).

Keywords: Secure multiparty computation · Path algebra · Semiring framework · Single-instruction-multiple-data · Bellman-Ford · Sharemind

1 Introduction

Graph algorithms are the foundation of many computer science applications such as navigation systems, community detection, supply chain networks [32,38,39], hyperspectral imaging [35], and sparse linear solvers. Privacy-preserving parallel algorithms are needed to expedite the processing of large private data sets for graph algorithms and meet high-end computational demands. Constructing real-world privacy applications based on secure multiparty computation is challenging due to the round complexity of the computation parties of SMC protocol [11,23, 24]. The round complexity problem of SMC protocol can be solved using parallel computing [10,14].

Single-Instruction-Multiple-Data (SIMD) a principle for parallel computations [19]. Recently, SIMD principles have been used to reduce the round

© The Author(s), under exclusive license to Springer Nature Switzerland AG 2023
J. Garcia-Alfaro et al. (Eds.): DPM 2022/CBT 2022, LNCS 13619, pp. 120–135, 2023.
https://doi.org/10.1007/978-3-031-25734-6_8

complexities in many privacy-preserving graph algorithms, including minimum spanning tree [4,25] and shortest path [2,3,5]. These privacy-preserving graph protocols are constructed on top of SMC protocols, and they are capable to process sizeable private data sets, where both the location and length of edges are private. The construction of these protocols follows the classical graph algorithms [15], storing the intermediate values privately, invoking SMC protocols for the computational steps in these algorithms, and attempting to parallelize the computations as much as possible.

In this paper we show that certain other SSSD algorithms may be even more suitable for conversion into SMC protocols. Considering the *Parallel RAM* (PRAM) model of execution, Pan and Reif [29,31] proposed a parallel algorithm for the Algebraic Path Computation (APC). Their algorithm assumes the availability of the *separator tree* of the graph and computes a recursive factorization of the graph's adjacency matrix on its basis [31], with the number of steps and the parallel complexity depending on the height of the tree and the size of separators. We also assume that the separator tree is among the public inputs for the SMC protocol, and show how to privately execute Pan and Reif's algorithm. Our empirical evaluation shows that for graphs with "good" separator trees, including planar graphs, our protocol may be up to two orders of magnitude faster than protocols based on classical SSSD algorithms.

The availability of the separator tree implies that the locations of the edges of the graph have to be public (this is accounted for in our empirical comparisons), only their lengths are private. Privately computing SSSD in this setting can still be relevant for a number of applications. E.g. private SSSD in city streets with public layouts has been tackled using either SMC [37] or differential privacy [34]. However, SMC protocols based on classical SSSD algorithms either do not benefit from the public end-points of edges at all [17], or benefit only slightly [6].

Our Contributions. In this paper, we present the following:

- The first privacy-preserving parallel computation protocol of algebraic shortest path. The protocol uses the sparse representation of an (adjacency) matrix, where the locations of edges are public, while their lengths are private. We propose suitable data structures and normalizations for this task.
- Implementations (on top of the Sharemind MPC platform [7,8]) of the algebraic shortest path protocol, and an optimized privacy-preserving Bellman-Ford protocol, with public locations and private lengths of edges. Benchmarking results for both implementations for various sizes of graphs, and different network environments.

2   Preliminaries

2.1   Secure Multiparty Computation

Secure multiparty computation (SMC) is a cryptographic technique, allowing a number of parties each give input to a pre-agreed functionality F, and learn the input meant for this party, such that each party (or a *tolerable* coalition of parties) will learn nothing besides their own input and output. There exist a number of different approaches for constructing SMC protocols, including garbled circuits [40], homomorphic encryption [16,21], or secret sharing [12,20], and offering security either against passive or active adversaries. These approaches typically include steps for entering a value into the computation in a privacy-preserving manner, for performing simple arithmetic operations (e.g. addition and multiplication in a finite field or ring) with private values present in the computation, and for opening a private value to a party upon the agreement of sufficiently many other parties. These steps, that constitute protocols by themselves, can be combined relatively freely. Hence, if the functionality F has been presented as an arithmetic circuit, then these protocols for input/output and arithmetic operations can be combined to yield a protocol for F.

Availability of such compositions leads to the typical abstraction of SMC in privacy-preserving applications—the *Arithmetic Black Box* (ABB) [16,26]. An ABB is an ideal functionality in the *Universal Composability* [13] framework. This framework considers a set $\mathcal{T}$ of interacting Turing machines [22], executing a protocol Π. Beside the set of machines $\mathcal{T}$, there is also another Turing machine—the *adversary* that can interfere with Π by sending to machines in $\mathcal{T}$ certain commands that have been defined in the adversarial API's of these machines. The set of the machines also includes the *environment* that interacts with machines in $\mathcal{T}$ and the adversary over a well-defined API. Given two sets of machines $\mathcal{T}$ and $\mathcal{T}'$ implementing the same API towards the environment, we say that $\mathcal{T}$ is *at least as secure as* $\mathcal{T}'$, if for any possible adversary $\mathbf{A}$ targeting $\mathcal{T}$ (i.e. its adversarial API), there exists an adversary $\mathbf{S}$ targeting $\mathcal{T}'$, such that the environment cannot distinguish whether it is executing with $\mathcal{T}$ and $\mathbf{A}$, or with $\mathcal{T}'$ and $\mathbf{S}$. This notion is composable: if additionally $\mathcal{T} = \mathcal{T}_0 \cup \{\Xi\}$ for a Turing machine Ξ, and a set of machines $\mathcal{U}$ is at last as secure as $\{\Xi\}$, then $\mathcal{T}_0 \cup \mathcal{U}$ is at least as secure as $\mathcal{T}'$. Often, we say that Ξ is the ideal functionality for the corresponding real functionality $\mathcal{U}$ that implements it.

The ABB functionality is represented by a Turing machine $\mathcal{F}_{ABB}$ that allows the environment representing all parties of a multiparty application to perform private computations. If one of the parties sends the command (store, v) to the ABB, where v is a value from one of the rings that the ABB supports, then it creates a new *handle* h, stores the pair (h, v), and sends h back to all parties. If all (or sufficiently many) parties send the command (perform, $op, h_1, \ldots, h_k$) to the ABB, where op is one of the supported operations and $h_1, \ldots, h_k$ are existing handles, then the ABB looks up the stored pairs $(h_1, v_1), \ldots, (h_k, v_k)$, computes $v = op(v_1, \ldots, v_k)$, creates a new handle h, stores (h, v), and sends h back to all parties. If all (or sufficiently many) parties send the command (declassify, h), then ABB looks up (h, v) and sends v back to all parties. A secure application that makes use of the ABB remains secure if $\mathcal{F}_{ABB}$ is replaced with a set of Turing machines that securely implement the ABB, i.e. run secure multiparty computation protocols. Note that if we want to compute a function F with the help of an ABB, and if the ABB only declassifies the end result of F, then the resulting protocol is trivially private [26].

In the following, a value v stored in the ABB and accessed through a handle is denoted by $[\![v]\!]$. Similarly, $[\![\boldsymbol{v}]\!]$ denotes a vector of values, and $[\![\mathbf{V}]\!]$ a matrix of values stored in the ABB. We use the notation $[\![u]\!] + [\![v]\!]$ [resp. $\min([\![u]\!], [\![v]\!])$] to denote that the addition [resp. minimum] operation is being invoked on the values $[\![u]\!]$ and $[\![v]\!]$; the result of this operation is again stored in the ABB. We extend this notation pointwise to vectors and matrices.

The *cost* of the operations of the ABB depends on the implementation of $\mathcal{F}_{ABB}$. If Sharemind has been used as the implementation, then the addition is a free operation (i.e. it requires no communication between parties), and minimum requires a constant amount of bits to be exchanged in a constant number of rounds. Hence the bandwidth cost of $\min([\![u]\!], [\![v]\!])$ is linear in the length of $\boldsymbol{u}$ and $\boldsymbol{v}$, while the round complexity is logarithmic in their length. In the following descriptions of algorithms built on top of the ABB, we have to be explicit in stating, which operations can or cannot be performed in parallel. For loops, we write **forall** to denote that all iterations take place in parallel; we write **for** to state that the loop is sequential.

2.2 Graphs, Separators, Semirings, and Algebra Path Problem

A *graph* $G = (V, E)$ is a mathematical structure consisting of a set V of *vertices* that are connected by *edges* from a set $E \subseteq V \times V$. The edges between vertices may have *lengths* assigned to them; these are given by a function $w : E \to \mathbb{Z}$. A graph may be directed or undirected; in the latter case, E is symmetric. If $V' \subseteq V$, then we let $G[V']$ denote the *induced subgraph* $(V', E \cap V' \times V')$.

A graph $G = (V, E)$ can be represented in computer memory in different ways. The *dense* representation of G is the *adjacency matrix*—a $|V| \times |V|$ matrix over $\mathbb{Z} \cup \{\infty\}$, where the entry at u-th row and v-th column is $w(u, v)$. On the other hand, the *adjacency list representation* gives for each vertex $u \in V$ the list of pairs $(v_1, w_1), \dots, (v_k, w_k)$, where $(u, v_1), \dots, (u, v_k)$ are all edges in G that start in u, and $w_i = w(u, v_i)$; we call such representations *sparse*. If $|E| \ll |V|^2$, then sparse representation takes up less space than dense representation and the algorithms working on sparse representation may be faster [9].

We call a graph (actually, an infinite family of graphs) *sparse* if its number of edges is *proportional* to its number of vertices, $|E| = O(|V|)$; otherwise we call it *dense*. A graph is *planar* if it can be drawn a plane without crossing the edges outside vertices. If G is planar, then $|E| \leq 3|V| - 6$ according to Euler's formula for the number of vertices, edges and faces of its drawing [36].

A *separation* of the graph $G = (V, E)$ is a partition of its vertices $V = V_1 \dot\cup S \dot\cup V_2$, such that any path from a vertex in V_1 to a vertex in V_2 must pass through a vertex in S (called a *separator*). It is known [27] that planar graphs have separations where $|S| = O(\sqrt{|V|})$ and $|V_1|, |V_2| \leq 2|V|/3$. A *separator tree* of G is either a single node containing $(\emptyset, V, \emptyset)$; or the root node (V_1, S, V_2) for some separation of G, and its two subtrees—separator trees for $G[V_1 \cup S]$ and $G[V_2 \cup S]$. Planar graphs thus have separator trees of height $O(\log |V|)$.

A *(commutative) semiring* is an algebraic structure S with two binary operations $\oplus$ and $\otimes$, where both are associative and commutative, have unit elements

$\textcircled{0}$ and $\textcircled{1}$, where $\otimes$ distributes over $\oplus$, and where $a \otimes \textcircled{0} = \textcircled{0}$ for all $a \in S$. We overload $\oplus$ and $\otimes$ to also denote addition and multiplication of matrices with elements from S; the multiplication may also be denoted by juxtaposition. Given matrices $\mathbf{A} \in S^{n \times n}$ and $\mathbf{X} \in S^{m \times n}$, the *algebra path problem* is to find a matrix $\mathbf{Y} \in S^{m \times n}$, such that $\mathbf{Y} = \mathbf{X} \oplus \mathbf{YA}$. Let $\mathbf{I} \in S^{n \times n}$ be the identity matrix. If $\mathbf{A}$ has a *quasi-inverse*, i.e. a matrix $\mathbf{A}^* \in S^{n \times n}$, such that $\mathbf{I} \oplus \mathbf{AA}^* = \mathbf{I} \oplus \mathbf{A}^*\mathbf{A} = \mathbf{A}^*$, then $\mathbf{Y} = \mathbf{XA}^*$ is a possible solution to the algebra path problem.

Algebra path problem generalizes a number of graph-theoretic tasks. Let $G = (V, E)$ be a graph and let $t \in V$, and let $S = \mathbb{N} \cup \{\infty\}$, $\oplus$ be the minimum, $\otimes$ be the addition, $\textcircled{0} = \infty$, $\textcircled{1} = 0$, $n = |V|$, $m = 1$, $\mathbf{A}$ be the adjacency matrix of G, and $\boldsymbol{x} = \mathbf{X} \in S^{1 \times n}$ be the t-th unit vector (i.e. $v_t = \textcircled{1} = 0$ and $v_j = \textcircled{0} = \infty$ for $j \neq t$). Then $\boldsymbol{y} = \mathbf{Y}$ is the vector of shortest distances from the t-th vertex [28]. Other instantiations of the semiring and $\mathbf{X}$ give solutions to other problems [30].

Having the semiring instantiated as in the previous paragraph, the quasi-inverse of $\mathbf{A} \in S^{n \times n}$ is defined; it is equal to $(\mathbf{I} \oplus \mathbf{A})^n$. If $\mathbf{A}$ is the adjacency matrix of some graph, then $\mathbf{A}^*$ is the matrix of shortest distances between the vertices of the same graph. Hence any all-pairs shortest distance (APSD) algorithm is suitable for computing $\mathbf{A}^*$; but it would be inefficient to use for the SSSD problem, particularly when $\mathbf{A}$ is a sparse(ly represented) matrix.

Given $\boldsymbol{x}$ and symmetric $\mathbf{A}$, Pan and Reif [30], proposed the following algorithm for computing $\boldsymbol{x} \otimes \mathbf{A}^*$ without ever materializing $\mathbf{A}^*$. Let $d \in \mathbb{N}$ and pick numbers $n = n_0 > n_1 > \cdots > n_d > 0$. Let $\mathbf{P} \in S^{n \times n}$ be a permutation matrix. Define matrix $\mathbf{A}_0 = \mathbf{PAP}^T$ (i.e. we permute the rows and columns of $\mathbf{A}$ in the same manner; this corresponds to reordering the vertices of G) and define the matrices $\mathbf{X}_h, \mathbf{Y}_h, \mathbf{Z}_h, \mathbf{A}_{h+1}$ (for $h \in \{0, \ldots, d-1\}$) by

$$\begin{bmatrix} \mathbf{X}_h & \mathbf{Y}_h^T \\ \mathbf{Y}_h & \mathbf{Z}_h \end{bmatrix} := \mathbf{A}_h \mathbf{A}_{h+1} := \mathbf{Z}_h \oplus \mathbf{Y}_h \mathbf{X}_h^* \mathbf{Y}_h^T \tag{1}$$

where $\mathbf{Z}_h, \mathbf{A}_{h+1} \in S^{n_{h+1} \times n_{h+1}}$; this also defines the sizes of $\mathbf{X}_h$ and $\mathbf{Y}_h$. Letting $\mathbf{I}$ and $\mathbf{O}$ denote identity and zero matrices of appropriate sizes, one can verify that the following identity holds:

$$\mathbf{A}_h^* = \begin{bmatrix} \mathbf{I} & \mathbf{X}_h^* \otimes \mathbf{Y}_h^T \\ \mathbf{O} & \mathbf{I} \end{bmatrix} \otimes \begin{bmatrix} \mathbf{X}_h^* & \mathbf{O} \\ \mathbf{O} & \mathbf{A}_{h+1}^* \end{bmatrix} \otimes \begin{bmatrix} \mathbf{I} & \mathbf{O} \\ \mathbf{Y}_h \otimes \mathbf{X}_h^* & \mathbf{I} \end{bmatrix}. \tag{2}$$

We thus have an algorithm to compute $\boldsymbol{y} = \boldsymbol{x} \otimes \mathbf{A}^*$. Let $\boldsymbol{x}_{\mathrm{P}} = \boldsymbol{x} \otimes \mathbf{P}^T$. Let $h = 0$. Extract $\mathbf{X}_h, \mathbf{Y}_h, \mathbf{Z}_h$ from $\mathbf{A}_h$ and compute $\mathbf{X}_h^*$ (using any APSD algorithm), $\mathbf{Q}_h = \mathbf{Y}_h \otimes \mathbf{X}_h^*$ and $\mathbf{A}_{h+1}$. Note that $\mathbf{X}_h^* \otimes \mathbf{Y}_h^T = \mathbf{Q}_h^T$. Multiply $\boldsymbol{x}_{\mathrm{P}}$ with the first matrix in (2), then the result with the second matrix, and then the result with the third matrix, thus defining $\boldsymbol{y}_{\mathrm{P}} = \boldsymbol{x}_{\mathrm{P}} \otimes \mathbf{A}_0^*$. Finally remove the permutation, computing $\boldsymbol{y} = \boldsymbol{y}_{\mathrm{P}} \otimes (\mathbf{P}^T)^{-1}$. All computations are done with sparse matrices. Importantly, multiplication with the second matrix in (2) splits the current vector into two parts, where the left part is multiplied with $\mathbf{X}_h^*$, and the right part with $\mathbf{A}_{h+1}^*$ through a *recursive call*. The recursion stops by computing $\mathbf{A}_d^*$ directly (using any APSD algorithm).

Pan and Reif [30] show that if the choice of $\mathbf{P}$ and $n_0, \ldots, n_d$ is informed by a separator tree $\mathbf{T}$ of G with height $d = O(\log n)$ and separators of size $O(\sqrt{n})$, then, depending on how $\mathbf{X}_h^*$ and $\mathbf{A}_d^*$ are computed, the described algorithm requires either $O(\log^3 n)$ parallel time and $O(n^{3/2} \log n)$ work, or $O(\sqrt{n} \log n)$ parallel time and $O(n^{3/2})$ work. The time estimate follows directly from the parallel time complexity of the matrix operations, multiplied by the depth of the recursion. The work estimate follows from careful counting of elements in the sparse representations of matrices [31].

Pan and Reif [31, Sec. 7] describe, what kind of information is extracted from the separator tree $\mathbf{T}$. We refer to them for details, but let us describe the result. The main outcome is a list $\mathcal{L} = (\mathcal{L}_0, \ldots, \mathcal{L}_d)$ of lists of lists of vertices of G, such that each $i \in V$ occurs in $\mathcal{L}$ exactly once. The permutation matrix $\mathbf{P}$ must reorder the vertices so, that they appear in the same order as in flattened $\mathcal{L}$. For $h \in \{0, \ldots, d\}$, the number n_h is equal to the number of vertices in $(\mathcal{L}_h, \mathcal{L}_{h+1}, \ldots, \mathcal{L}_d)$. Let $L = (L_0, \ldots, L_d)$, where each L_h is the list of lengths of elements of $\mathcal{L}_h$ (note that elements of $\mathcal{L}_h$ are lists of vertices). In (1), $\mathbf{X}_h$ is going to be a block-diagonal matrix with the block sizes listed in L_h; this is used in the computation of $\mathbf{X}_h^*$.

3   Privacy-Preserving Algebraic Shortest Path Protocol

This section presents the privacy-preserving version of the algorithm decsribed above. We present the used data structures, the auxiliary functionalities, and the main computation.

Data Structures. We mostly use the sparse representation of matrices. The representation $\langle\!\langle \mathbf{A} \rangle\!\rangle$ for a matrix $\mathbf{A} \in S^{m \times n}$ where we do not hide the position of non-$\circledcirc$ *cells*, but we hide the contents of these cells, is a triple $\langle\!\langle \mathbf{A} \rangle\!\rangle = \langle m, n, \mathcal{C} \rangle$, where $\mathcal{C}$ is the list of cells of the matrix that may contain an element different from $\circledcirc$. Each cell is again a triple $(i, j, [\![v]\!])$, where $i \in \{0, \ldots, m-1\}$ and $j \in \{0, \ldots, n-1\}$ are the coordinates of that cell, and $v \in S = \mathbb{N} \cup \{\infty\}$ is the value in it. The value v is stored privately in the ABB. In our implementation on top of Sharemind, we represent elements of S as 64-bit integers (representing ∞ as a large number). In the following, we use the standard list constructors, destructors, and combinators—NIL, cons, length, head, tail, ++ (concatenation)— to express algorithms working with lists. We write $\mathcal{C}[k]$ for the k-th element of the list (starting with 0).

We allow the same coordinates (i, j) to occur several times in $\mathcal{C}$. We define that the triple $\langle m, n, \mathcal{C} \rangle$ represents a $m \times n$ matrix, where the cell at coordinates (i, j) contains the value $\min\{v \mid (i, j, [\![v]\!]) \in \mathcal{C}\}$.

We also make use of the dense representation $[\![\mathbf{V}]\!]$ of (small) matrices. It is simply a matrix of elements of S stored in the ABB.

Auxiliary Functions. We have a relatively large set of helper functions for decomposing and combining matrices, as well as normalizing and converting between different representations. We list them below and shortly describe how they work.

getMin($[\![v]\!], \imath$) takes a private vector of values, and an equal-length public vector of *indicators*. The indicator vector consists of segments of equal values. If there are k such segments of length $l_1, \ldots, l_k$ (with $|v| = \sum_j l_j$), then the output of getMin is a private vector of k values, where the j-th element is the minimum among the elements of v at the positions corresponding to the j-th segment of equal values in $\imath$. The implementation of getMin is straightforward, we can divide $[\![v]\!]$ into k segments according to the values in $\imath$, and then call min from the ABB for all segments in parallel. Sharemind does not directly support such parallel invocation for segments of different length, but it is still possible to design getMin to run in SIMD fashion, doing $O(|v|)$ work and requiring $O(\log \max_j l_j)$ rounds.

$\mathsf{norm}_1(\langle m, n, \mathcal{C}\rangle)$ takes a sparsely represented matrix. It returns the same matrix, having sorted elements $(i, j, [\![v]\!])$ of $\mathcal{C}$ by (i, j). It does not invoke any MPC protocols.

$\mathsf{norm}_2(\langle m, n, \mathcal{C}\rangle)$ first invokes norm_1 on its input, and then removes the duplicate occurrences of the same cell from $\mathcal{C}$. It does the latter by invoking getMin.

getSlice($\langle m, n, \mathcal{C}\rangle, u, l, m', n'$) returns the $m' \times n'$-sized submatrix of $\langle m, n, \mathcal{C}\rangle$, whose upper corner is in the cell (u, l) of the input matrix. Its output is $\langle m', n', \mathcal{C}'\rangle$, where $\mathcal{C}'$ is the list of elements $(i - u, j - l, [\![v]\!])$, where $(i, j, [\![v]\!]) \in \mathcal{C}$, $u \leq i < u + m'$, and $l \leq j < l + n'$.

overlay($\langle m, n, \mathcal{C}\rangle, u, l, m', n'$), where $m' \geq m + u$ and $n' \geq n + l$, outputs $\langle m', n', \mathcal{C}'\rangle$, where $\mathcal{C}'$ is the list of elements $(i + u, j + l, [\![v]\!])$, where $(i, j, [\![v]\!]) \in \mathcal{C}$. I.e. overlay creates a $m' \times n'$-sized supermatrix of the original matrix, where the upper left corner of the original matrix is at position (u, l), and the rest of the matrix is filled with $\textcircled{0} = \infty$.

overlap($\langle m, n, \mathcal{C}_1\rangle, \ldots, \langle m, n, \mathcal{C}_k\rangle$) returns $\langle m, n, \mathcal{C}_1 +\!\!+ \cdots +\!\!+ \mathcal{C}_k\rangle$.

transpose($\langle m, n, \mathcal{C}\rangle$) returns $\langle n, m, \mathcal{C}'\rangle$, where the elements of $\mathcal{C}'$ are the elements of $\mathcal{C}$ with their first two components swapped.

identity(n) returns the $n \times n$ identity matrix, represented sparsely.

sparse-to-dense($\langle m, n, \mathcal{C}\rangle$) returns the dense representation of its argument (which has to be normalized). It initializes a $m \times n$ array of values $[\![\infty]\!]$, and copies the elements of $\mathcal{C}$ to their places.

dense-to-sparse($[\![\mathbf{V}]\!]$) returns the sparse representation of its argument. It returns $\langle m, n, \mathcal{C}\rangle$, where m and n are dimensions of $\mathbf{V}$, and $\mathcal{C}$ is a list of length mn, containing one element for each cell of $[\![\mathbf{V}]\!]$.

Major Functions. These include the addition and multiplication of matrices, and the computation of quasi-inverses of block-diagonal matrices. The first of them—pointwise minimum—is simple: if $\langle\!\langle \mathbf{M}\rangle\!\rangle$ and $\langle\!\langle \mathbf{N}\rangle\!\rangle$ have the same dimensions, then $\langle\!\langle \mathbf{M}\rangle\!\rangle \oplus \langle\!\langle \mathbf{N}\rangle\!\rangle = \mathsf{norm}_2(\mathsf{overlap}(\langle\!\langle \mathbf{M}\rangle\!\rangle, \langle\!\langle \mathbf{N}\rangle\!\rangle))$.

The multiplication protocol for sparse matrices, given in Algorithm 1, is also unsurprising. An interesting detail is the transposition (and normalization) of the first matrix before the actual multiplication. In this way, the values of both x_1 and x_2 are non-decreasing during the loop. In our implementation we optimize the inner loop by running only through the segment of $\mathcal{D}$, where $x_2 = x_1$.

Algorithm 1: Matrix multiplication over the semiring $\mathbb{N} \cup \{\infty\}$

Data: Matrices $\langle\!\langle \mathbf{M} \rangle\!\rangle = \langle m, n, \mathcal{C} \rangle$ and $\langle\!\langle \mathbf{N} \rangle\!\rangle = \langle n, k, \mathcal{D} \rangle$

Result: Matrix $\langle\!\langle \mathbf{M} \rangle\!\rangle \otimes \langle\!\langle \mathbf{N} \rangle\!\rangle$

1 **begin**

2      $\langle n, m, \mathcal{C}' \rangle \leftarrow \mathsf{norm}_1(\mathsf{transpose}(\langle\!\langle \mathbf{M} \rangle\!\rangle))$

3      $\mathcal{E} \leftarrow \mathsf{NIL}$

4   **for** $i \leftarrow 0$ *to* $\mathsf{length}(\mathcal{C}') - 1$ **do**

5          $(x_1, y_1, [\![v_1]\!]) \leftarrow \mathcal{C}'[i]$

6   **for** $j \leftarrow 0$ *to* $\mathsf{length}(\mathcal{D}) - 1$ **do**

7              $(x_2, y_2, [\![v_2]\!]) \leftarrow \mathcal{D}[j]$

8   **if** $x_1 = x_2$ **then** $\mathcal{E} \leftarrow \mathsf{cons}((y_1, y_2, [\![v_1]\!] + [\![v_2]\!]), \mathcal{E})$

9   **return** $\mathsf{norm}_2(\langle m, k, \mathcal{E} \rangle)$

Algorithm 2: Quasi-inverse of a block-diagonal matrix

Data: Matrix $\langle\!\langle \mathbf{M} \rangle\!\rangle = \langle n, n, \mathcal{C} \rangle$, list of block-sizes $\boldsymbol{B}$

Requires: $\mathcal{C}$ contains no cells outside the blocks defined by $\boldsymbol{B}$

Result: Matrix $\langle\!\langle \mathbf{M} \rangle\!\rangle^*$

1 **begin**

2   **forall** $i \in \{0, ..., \mathsf{length}(\boldsymbol{B}) - 1\}$ **do**

3          $\langle\!\langle \mathbf{A}_i \rangle\!\rangle \leftarrow \mathsf{getSlice}(\langle\!\langle \mathbf{M} \rangle\!\rangle, \sum_{j=0}^{i-1} B[j], \sum_{j=0}^{i-1} B[j], B[i], B[i])$

4          $\langle\!\langle \mathbf{B}_i \rangle\!\rangle \leftarrow \mathsf{dense\text{-}to\text{-}sparse}(\mathsf{FloydWarshall}(\mathsf{sparse\text{-}to\text{-}dense}(\langle\!\langle \mathbf{A}_i \rangle\!\rangle)))$

5          $\langle\!\langle \mathbf{C}_i \rangle\!\rangle \leftarrow \mathsf{overlay}(\langle\!\langle \mathbf{B}_i \rangle\!\rangle, \sum_{j=0}^{i-1} B[j], \sum_{j=0}^{i-1} B[j], n, n)$

6   **return** $\mathsf{overlay}(\langle\!\langle \mathbf{C}_0 \rangle\!\rangle, ..., \langle\!\langle \mathbf{C}_{\mathsf{length}(\boldsymbol{B})-1} \rangle\!\rangle)$

The only non-local operation in Algorithm 1 is the final norm_2. The addition in line 8 is performed locally by the parties running the protocols implementing the ABB. Both the round complexity and the number of non-free operations of Algorithm 1 depend on the cells included in $\mathcal{C}$ and $\mathcal{D}$.

Algorithm 2 for quasi-inverse of $\langle\!\langle \mathbf{M} \rangle\!\rangle$ finds the quasi-inverse of each block of $\mathbf{M}$, and then combines the blocks. The input to Algorithm 2 is a list of sizes of the blocks on the main diagonal of $\mathbf{M}$; the sum of elements of $\boldsymbol{B}$ has to be n. We use the Floyd-Warshall APSD algorithm [18] for computing the quasi-inverse of a single block. We have adapted our privacy-preserving implementation [2, Alg. 8] to compute the APSD for several (adjacency) matrices at the same time, such that the round complexity of Algorithm 2 is $O(\max \boldsymbol{B})$, while the number of non-free operations is $O(\sum_i (B[i])^3)$. Our experiments [2] show that despite greater round complexity, Floyd-Warshall is faster than repeated squaring.

Main Computation. The computation corresponding to the multiplication $\boldsymbol{x} \otimes \mathbf{A}^*$ according to (2) is given in Algorithm 3. It takes as inputs the sparse matrix representations of both $\mathbf{A}$ and $\boldsymbol{x}$, where we think of the latter as a matrix with a single row. The multiplication operation also takes as input a list $\boldsymbol{L}$ of lists of

---

Algorithm 3: Main loop of the algebra path computation

Data: Symmetric matrix $\langle\!\langle \mathbf{A} \rangle\!\rangle$ of size $n \times n$, non-empty list of lists of lengths L,
vector $\langle\!\langle \boldsymbol{x} \rangle\!\rangle$ of length n

Result: Vector $\langle\!\langle \boldsymbol{y} \rangle\!\rangle = \langle\!\langle \boldsymbol{x} \rangle\!\rangle \otimes \langle\!\langle \mathbf{A} \rangle\!\rangle^*$

1 **Function** *Algebraic-paths*$(n, \langle\!\langle \mathbf{A} \rangle\!\rangle, L, \langle\!\langle \boldsymbol{x} \rangle\!\rangle)$ **is**

2     $B \leftarrow \mathsf{head}(L); \; L' \leftarrow \mathsf{tail}(L); \; s \leftarrow \sum B$

3   **if** $L' = \mathsf{NIL}$ **then**

4         $\lfloor$ **return** $\langle\!\langle \boldsymbol{x} \rangle\!\rangle \otimes \mathsf{quasi\text{-}inverse}(\langle\!\langle \mathbf{A} \rangle\!\rangle, B)$

5     $\langle\!\langle \mathbf{X}^{\mathrm{ast}} \rangle\!\rangle \leftarrow \mathsf{quasi\text{-}inverse}(\mathsf{getSlice}(\langle\!\langle \mathbf{A} \rangle\!\rangle, 0, 0, s, s), B)$

6     $\langle\!\langle \mathbf{Y} \rangle\!\rangle \leftarrow \mathsf{getSlice}(\langle\!\langle \mathbf{A} \rangle\!\rangle, s, 0, n - s, s)$

7     $\langle\!\langle \mathbf{Z} \rangle\!\rangle \leftarrow \mathsf{getSlice}(\langle\!\langle \mathbf{A} \rangle\!\rangle, s, s, n - s, n - s)$

8     $\langle\!\langle \mathbf{Q} \rangle\!\rangle \leftarrow \langle\!\langle \mathbf{Y} \rangle\!\rangle \otimes \langle\!\langle \mathbf{X}^{\mathrm{ast}} \rangle\!\rangle$

9     $\langle\!\langle \mathbf{A}' \rangle\!\rangle \leftarrow \langle\!\langle \mathbf{Z} \rangle\!\rangle \oplus \langle\!\langle \mathbf{Q} \rangle\!\rangle \otimes \mathsf{transpose}(\langle\!\langle \mathbf{Y} \rangle\!\rangle)$

10    $\langle\!\langle \boldsymbol{z} \rangle\!\rangle \leftarrow \langle\!\langle \boldsymbol{x} \rangle\!\rangle \otimes \mathsf{overlap}(\mathsf{identity}(n), \mathsf{overlay}(\mathsf{transpose}(\langle\!\langle \mathbf{Q} \rangle\!\rangle)), 0, s, n, n))$

11    $\langle\!\langle \boldsymbol{z}_{\mathrm{L}} \rangle\!\rangle \leftarrow \mathsf{getSlice}(\langle\!\langle \boldsymbol{z} \rangle\!\rangle, 0, 0, 1, s)$

12    $\langle\!\langle \boldsymbol{z}_{\mathrm{R}} \rangle\!\rangle \leftarrow \mathsf{getSlice}(\langle\!\langle \boldsymbol{z} \rangle\!\rangle, 0, s, 1, n - s)$

13    $\langle\!\langle \boldsymbol{w}_{\mathrm{L}} \rangle\!\rangle \leftarrow \langle\!\langle \boldsymbol{z}_{\mathrm{L}} \rangle\!\rangle \otimes \langle\!\langle \mathbf{X}^{\mathrm{ast}} \rangle\!\rangle$

14    $\langle\!\langle \boldsymbol{w}_{\mathrm{R}} \rangle\!\rangle \leftarrow$ *Algebraic-paths*$(n - s, \langle\!\langle \mathbf{A}' \rangle\!\rangle, L', \langle\!\langle \boldsymbol{z}_{\mathrm{R}} \rangle\!\rangle)$

15    $\langle\!\langle \boldsymbol{w} \rangle\!\rangle \leftarrow \mathsf{overlap}(\mathsf{overlay}(\langle\!\langle \boldsymbol{w}_{\mathrm{L}} \rangle\!\rangle, 0, 0, 1, n), \mathsf{overlay}(\langle\!\langle \boldsymbol{w}_{\mathrm{R}} \rangle\!\rangle, 0, s, 1, n))$

16    $\lfloor$ **return** $\langle\!\langle \boldsymbol{w} \rangle\!\rangle \otimes \mathsf{overlap}(\mathsf{identity}(n), \mathsf{overlay}(\langle\!\langle \mathbf{Q} \rangle\!\rangle, s, 0, n, n))$

---

block-sizes; it is formed on the basis of the separator tree of the graph having the adjacency matrix $\mathbf{A}$ (described at the end of Sect. 2.2), its length is $d + 1$.

Algorithm 3 closely follows (1)–(2). The current length of L describes the current depth of the recursion; length 1 (checked in line 3) indicates the base. Otherwise, $\langle\!\langle \mathbf{A} \rangle\!\rangle$ is the reprensetation of one of the matrices $\mathbf{A}_h$. We start by decomposing $\mathbf{A}_h$ into $\mathbf{X}_h$ (and find its quasi-inverse, using the list of lengths in the first element of L), $\mathbf{Y}_h$ and $\mathbf{Z}_h$, compute $\mathbf{Q}_h$ and $\mathbf{A}_{h+1}$, multiply $\langle\!\langle \boldsymbol{x} \rangle\!\rangle$ with the first matrix in (2). We will then split the resulting vector $\boldsymbol{z}$ into two parts of lengths s and $n - s$, and multiply the left half with $\mathbf{X}_h^*$. We now recursively call Algorithm 3 with the right half of $\boldsymbol{z}$, with $\mathbf{A}_{h+1}$, and with the list of lists of lengths missing the first element. We complete the computation by concatenating the two vectors, and multiplying it with the third matrix in (2). The round complexity, and the number of invoked ABB operations follow directly from Pan and Reif's analysis [31].

In order to compute the distances from a vertex t of an undirected graph $G = (V, E)$ with public locations, but private lengths of edges, we have to perform more steps before and after invoking Algorithm 3, but all these steps are public. Starting from the sparsely represented adjacency matrix $\langle\!\langle \mathbf{A} \rangle\!\rangle$ of G, we have to find the separator tree of G, permute the vertices of G (giving us the matrix $\langle\!\langle \mathbf{A}_0 \rangle\!\rangle$), and create the list L. We have to create the vector $\langle\!\langle \boldsymbol{x} \rangle\!\rangle$ as a unit vector, where we have the value ① $= 0$ only at the position corresponding to the location of vertex t after the permutation. After calling Algorithm 3 with $\langle\!\langle \mathbf{A}_0 \rangle\!\rangle$, L and $\langle\!\langle \boldsymbol{x} \rangle\!\rangle$, we have to apply the inverse permutation to the resulting vector $\langle\!\langle \boldsymbol{y} \rangle\!\rangle$.

4   Security and Privacy of Protocols

The privacy-preserving APC protocol is built on top of a universally composable ABB. It receives its private inputs through the handles to values stored in the ABB, and returns its private outputs in the same fashion. The protocol contains no declassify-operations. Hence, as discussed in Sect. 2.1, it inherits the same security properties against various adversaries as the underlying secure computation protocol set. In particular, if the ABB is implemented by the Sharemind MPC platform, then the resulting APC protocol is a three-party protocol, working with public locations but secret-shared lengths of edges, and provides information-theoretic security against an adversary passively corrupting at most one of the parties.

5   Empirical Evaluation

5.1   Privacy-Preserving Bellman-Ford with Public Edges

We want to compare the APC protocol with protocols based on classical SSSD algorithms, where the locations of edges are public, but their lengths are private. We see that Dijkstra's algorithm cannot benefit from public location of edges, because the order in which it relaxes the vertices depends on the lengths of the edges, thus the random permutation of vertices that could hide that order [1] would make the locations of edges private again. Hence we think that it is fair to compare the new protocol against a protocol based on the Bellman-Ford (BF) algorithm.

Such privacy-preserving algorithm is given in Algorithm 4. We see that at each iteration of the main loop, it defines $\llbracket a \rrbracket$ as the current distance of the start vertex of each edge from s. Vector $\llbracket b \rrbracket$ will then record the current distance of the end vertex of each edge, when the last step is made over this edge. The same getMin operation as in Sect. 3 is used to find the minimum distance for each vertex. We see that the number of non-free operations executed by Algorithm 4 is $O(mn)$, while its round complexity is $O(n \log D)$, where D is the maximum in-degree of a vertex.

5.2   Setup of Benchmarking

We have implemented the APC and BF algorithm on the Sharemind MPC platform, using the SecreC language [33] offered by this platform. The benchmarking took place on three servers with 12-core 3 GHz CPUs with Hyper-Threading running Linux, and 48 GB of RAM, connected by an Ethernet 1 Gbps LAN. The local computations in Sharemind MPC are single-threaded, and there is no support for performing computations and network operations at the same time.

We want to measure the performance in different network environments, corresponding to LAN and WAN deployments. We throttle the connections between the servers in order to simulate these environments. In our experiments, we consider "HBLL", "HBHL" and "LBHL" settings. Here HB (high-bandwidth) means

---

Algorithm 4: Bellman-Ford based SSSD algorithm with public edge locations

Data: Number of vertices and edges n and m
Data: Vectors (of length m) of starting and ending vertices, and lengths of edges: $\boldsymbol{S}$, $\boldsymbol{T}$, and $[\![\boldsymbol{W}]\!]$
Data: starting vertex $s \in \{0, \ldots, n-1\}$
Requires: $\boldsymbol{T}$ is sorted
Requires: There is a loop edge with length 0 at each vertex
Result: Vector of distances $[\![\boldsymbol{D}]\!]$ from vertex s

1 **begin**
2   $\quad [\![\boldsymbol{D}]\!] \leftarrow \infty$; $[\![D[s]]\!] \leftarrow 0$
3   $\quad$ **for** $i \leftarrow 0$ *to* $n-1$ **do**
4   $\quad\quad$ **forall** $j \in \{0, \ldots, m-1\}$ **do** $[\![a[j]]\!] \leftarrow [\![D[S[j]]]\!]$;
5   $\quad\quad [\![\boldsymbol{b}]\!] \leftarrow [\![\boldsymbol{a}]\!] + [\![\boldsymbol{W}]\!]$
6   $\quad\quad [\![\boldsymbol{D}]\!] \leftarrow \mathsf{getMin}([\![\boldsymbol{b}]\!], \boldsymbol{T})$
7   $\quad$ **return** $[\![\boldsymbol{D}]\!]$

---

1 Gbps and LB (low-bandwidth) 100 Mbps link speed between servers. Also, LL (low-latency) means no added delay for the messages sent between the servers, while HL (high-latency) means additional 40 ms delay.

The performance of the APC algorithm is highly dependent on the locations of edges. As we are most interested in the performance of the algorithms on planar graphs, and as we want to focus on optimizing the privacy-preserving computations, not the computation of the separator tree, we have selected *grid graphs* as the family of graphs on which we have performed benchmarking. The $R \times C$ grid graph has RC vertices that can be thought as being placed in a $R \times C$ grid. Each vertex is connected with 4 of its closest neighbours (less for vertices at the edges of the grid); the number of (undirected) edges is $(2RC - R - C)$. Grid graphs have easy-to-compute separators of size $\min(R, C)$ that split their set of vertices into two roughly equal parts; the height of the resulting separator tree is $\approx \log R + \log C$. In the following we let $G(N)$ denote the $N \times N$ grid graph.

5.3 Measuring the Performance of Algebraic Path Computation

We report the running times and the bandwidth consumption (per computing server) for grid graphs $G(N)$ for different values of N, on Sharemind cluster for the HBLL network environment in Table 1. The times correspond to the execution of Algorithm 3; we have not measured the time it takes to construct the separator tree, the lists $\mathcal{L}$ and $\boldsymbol{L}$, or to permute the matrices and vectors.

The largest grid graph that we ran our implementation on, was $G(600)$. This graph has 360 k vertices and $\approx$1.4 M (directed) edges. We are not aware of any previous executions of privacy-preserving SSSD on graphs of similar size, no matter if the locations of edges are private or not, or what the actual shape of

Table 1. Running time (in seconds) and bandwidth consumption of privacy-preserving algebraic path computation protocol for graphs $G(N)$

N	Bandwidth	Time
5	0.16 MB	0.1
9	0.30 MB	0.3
17	2.31 MB	1.2
33	27.3 MB	8.2
50	90.3 MB	30.1

N	Bandwidth	Time
65	366 MB	66.4
100	874 MB	244
129	1972 MB	522
150	3136 MB	838

N	Bandwidth	Time
200	7792 MB	2029
257	16.4 GB	4280
513	138.3 GB	35341
600	224.6 GB	58082

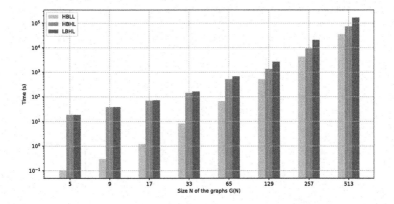

Fig. 1. Performance of algebraic path computation protocol on graphs with given numbers of vertices in different network environments

the graph is. We see that the running time for such a graph was a bit over 16 h, which may be practical for certain settings.

In Fig. 1, we compare the running time of privacy-preserving Algebraic path computation protocol on graphs of different sizes in different network environments. We see that for small graphs, the performance only depends on the latency of the network. Only for graphs with 1000 or more vertices ($N = 33$) does the available bandwidth start having an effect.

5.4 Comparison of APC and BF Protocols

The running times of both privacy-preserving SSSD protocols that use public edges—Bellman-Ford and Algebraic path computation—for the sparse representation of the graphs are illustrated in Table 2. The experiments also show average bandwidths in different network environments. The running times of all graphs in different network environments for Algebraic path computation are lower than the running times of the Bellman-Ford protocol. Similarly, the bandwidth consumption in Algebraic path computation is smaller than bandwidth in Bellman-Ford protocol.

Table 2. Benchmarking results (bandwidth for a single computing server) for Bellman-Ford and Algebraic path protocol in different network environments, for grid graphs $G(N)$

N	Bellman-Ford				Algebraic path computation				Speed-up		
	Bandwidth	Running time (s)			Bandwidth	Running time (s)			BF vs. APC		
		HBLL	HBHL	LBHL		HBLL	HBHL	LBHL	HBLL	HBHL	LBHL
5	0.4 MB	0.33	33.3	33.3	0.09 MB	0.1	18.2	18.2	3.3x	1.8x	1.8X
9	2.64 MB	2.74	108	108	0.28 MB	0.3	38.0	38.0	9.1x	2.8x	2.8x
17	22.3 MB	18.4	388	399	2.33 MB	1.2	69.4	71.4	15.3x	5.6x	5.6x
33	324 MB	214	1509	1684	24.1 MB	8.2	146	165	26.1x	10.3x	10.2
65	4.4 GB	819	6542	9205	273 MB	66.4	522	670	12.3x	12.5x	13.7x
129	173 GB	13395	36835	81346	2005 MB	522	1355	2669	25.6x	27.1x	30.5x
257	2.86 TB	203428	521491	1154261	17.2 GB	4280	9182	20276	47.5x	56.8x	56.9x
513	37.3 TB	3092314	7147049	17883699	144 GB	35341	73215	166643	87.4x	97.6x	107.3x

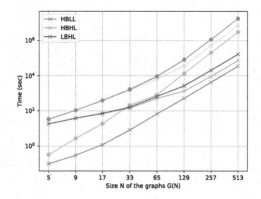

Fig. 2. Performance (time in seconds) of Bellman-Ford Version 3 and Algebraic path computation protocols on graphs of different sizes in different network environments (red: HBLL, green: HBHL, blue: LBHL, light: Bellman-Ford, dark: Algebraic path computation) (Color figure online)

In Table 2, the execution times of the Bellman-Ford protocol on larger graphs have been estimated: we benchmarked the larger examples by running only a few iterations of the main loop in Algorithm 4, measured the running time of a single iteration, and then multiplied with the total number of iterations.

We depict the running times also in Fig. 2, presenting the comparison of Algebraic path computation and Bellman-Ford protocol for different network environments. We see that despite the simple structure of Bellman-Ford, Algebraic path computation is still faster also in high-latency environments.

6   Conclusion and Future Work

We have shown that designers of privacy-preserving applications working with data in graph form and needing to find the distances between vertices should look beyond the classical SSSD algorithms when selecting the protocol for shortest paths' computation on top of a SMC framework. Even though many of the Parallel RAM algorithms proposed for SSSD have components that are not easily converted into parallel privacy-preserving protocols (e.g. the spawning and scheduling of tasks based on private data), there may be algorithms that process data sufficiently uniformly in order to serve as basis of SMC protocols.

We have shown how APC may be used to compute SSSD in privacy-preserving manner. It gives us efficient protocols, compared to classical SSSD algorithms. The same semiring framework may be instantiated in different ways, and be used for solving other graph problems, e.g. finding the minimum spanning trees or solving the all-pairs shortest distance problem. These algorithms may be converted into SMC protocols exactly as we have done here, with the only possible slight difference arising from the scalar $\otimes$-operation no longer being free.

In this paper, we have presented a protocol for undirected graphs. The APC algorithm is equally well applicable to directed graphs [31, Remark 6.1], and this change can also be implemented on top of an ABB.

In this paper, we have required the locations of edges to be public. We believe that a protocol with private locations is possible. This would not significantly change the subroutines. Still the matrix multiplication may become more expensive due to the need to run through both loops in Algorithm 1, and quasi-inverse will become more expensive due to the need to consider a central stripe of diagonals, instead of just the blocks on the main diagonal. There may be more changes to the main computation, as we no longer know the sizes of matrices; hence padding may be necessary. Also, the main computation would receive the list of lists of block-sizes as a private parameter, too.

Computing that list of lists of block-sizes privately is likely an even more complex problem. We are not aware of efficient parallel RAM algorithms for computing the separator tree, that could be easily converted to run on top of a SMC framework.

Acknowledgements. This research received funding from the European Regional Development Fund through the Estonian Centre of Excellence in ICT Research-EXCITE.

References

1. Aly, A., Cleemput, S.: An improved protocol for securely solving the shortest path problem and its application to combinatorial auctions. Cryptology ePrint Archive, Paper 2017/971 (2017)
2. Anagreh, M., Laud, P., Vainikko, E.: Parallel privacy-preserving shortest path algorithms. Cryptography **5**(4), 27 (2021)
3. Anagreh, M., Laud, P., Vainikko, E.: Privacy-preserving parallel computation of shortest path algorithms with low round complexity. In: Mori, P., Lenzini, G., Furnell, S. (eds.) Proceedings of the 8th International Conference on Information Systems Security and Privacy, ICISSP 2022, Online Streaming, 9–11 February 2022, pp. 37–47. SCITEPRESS (2022)

4. Anagreh, M., Vainikko, E., Laud, P.: Parallel privacy-preserving computation of minimum spanning trees. In: Mori, P., Lenzini, G., Furnell, S. (eds.) Proceedings of the 7th International Conference on Information Systems Security and Privacy, ICISSP 2021, Online Streaming, 11–13 February 2021, pp. 181–190. SCITEPRESS (2021)

5. Anagreh, M., Vainikko, E., Laud, P.: Parallel privacy-preserving shortest paths by radius-stepping. In: 2021 29th Euromicro International Conference on Parallel, Distributed and Network-Based Processing (PDP), pp. 276–280. IEEE (2021)

6. Bellman, R.: On a routing problem. Q. Appl. Math. **16**(1), 87–90 (1958)

7. Bogdanov, D., Laur, S., Willemson, J.: Sharemind: a framework for fast privacy-preserving computations. In: Jajodia, S., Lopez, J. (eds.) ESORICS 2008. LNCS, vol. 5283, pp. 192–206. Springer, Heidelberg (2008). https://doi.org/10.1007/978-3-540-88313-5_13

8. Bogdanov, D., Niitsoo, M., Toft, T., Willemson, J.: High-performance secure multiparty computation for data mining applications. Int. J. Inf. Secur. **11**(6), 403–418 (2012)

9. Bollobás, B.: Modern Graph Theory, Graduate Texts in Mathematics, vol. 184. Springer Science & Business Media, Berlin, Heidelberg (1998). https://doi.org/10.1007/978-1-4612-0619-4

10. Boyle, E., Chung, K.-M., Pass, R.: Large-scale secure computation: multi-party computation for (parallel) RAM programs. In: Gennaro, R., Robshaw, M. (eds.) CRYPTO 2015. LNCS, vol. 9216, pp. 742–762. Springer, Heidelberg (2015). https://doi.org/10.1007/978-3-662-48000-7_36

11. Boyle, E., Jain, A., Prabhakaran, M., Yu, C.H.: The bottleneck complexity of secure multiparty computation. In: 45th International Colloquium on Automata, Languages, and Programming (ICALP 2018). Schloss Dagstuhl-Leibniz-Zentrum fuer Informatik (2018)

12. Burkhart, M., Strasser, M., Many, D., Dimitropoulos, X.: SEPIA: privacy-preserving aggregation of multi-domain network events and statistics. In: 19th USENIX Security Symposium (USENIX Security 10) (2010)

13. Canetti, R.: Universally composable security: a new paradigm for cryptographic protocols. In: Proceedings 42nd IEEE Symposium on Foundations of Computer Science, pp. 136–145. IEEE (2001)

14. Cohen, R., Coretti, S., Garay, J., Zikas, V.: Round-preserving parallel composition of probabilistic-termination cryptographic protocols. J. Cryptol. **34**(2), 1–57 (2021)

15. Cormen, T.H., Leiserson, C.E., Rivest, R.L., Stein, C.: Introduction to Algorithms. MIT Press, Cambridge (2022)

16. Damgård, I., Nielsen, J.B.: Universally composable efficient multiparty computation from threshold homomorphic encryption. In: Boneh, D. (ed.) CRYPTO 2003. LNCS, vol. 2729, pp. 247–264. Springer, Heidelberg (2003). https://doi.org/10.1007/978-3-540-45146-4_15

17. Dijkstra, E.W.: A note on two problems in connexion with graphs. Numer. Math. **1**(1), 269–271 (1959)

18. Floyd, R.W.: Algorithm 97: shortest path. Commun. ACM **5**(6), 345 (1962)

19. Flynn, M.J.: Very high-speed computing systems. Proc. IEEE **54**(12), 1901–1909 (1966)

20. Gennaro, R., Rabin, M.O., Rabin, T.: Simplified VSS and fast-track multiparty computations with applications to threshold cryptography. In: Proceedings of the Seventeenth Annual ACM Symposium on Principles of Distributed Computing, pp. 101–111 (1998)

21. Henecka, W., Kögl, S., Sadeghi, A.R., Schneider, T., Wehrenberg, I.: Tasty: tool for automating secure two-party computations. In: Proceedings of the 17th ACM Conference on Computer and Communications Security, pp. 451–462 (2010)
22. Hodges, A.: Alan Turing: The Enigma. Princeton University Press, Princeton (2014)
23. Katz, J., Koo, C.-Y.: Round-efficient secure computation in point-to-point networks. In: Naor, M. (ed.) EUROCRYPT 2007. LNCS, vol. 4515, pp. 311–328. Springer, Heidelberg (2007). https://doi.org/10.1007/978-3-540-72540-4_18
24. Katz, J., Ostrovsky, R., Smith, A.: Round efficiency of multi-party computation with a dishonest majority. In: Biham, E. (ed.) EUROCRYPT 2003. LNCS, vol. 2656, pp. 578–595. Springer, Heidelberg (2003). https://doi.org/10.1007/3-540-39200-9_36
25. Laud, P.: Parallel oblivious array access for secure multiparty computation and privacy-preserving minimum spanning trees. Proc. Priv. Enhanc. Technol. 2015(2), 188–205 (2015)
26. Laud, P.: Stateful abstractions of secure multiparty computation. Appl. Secur. Multiparty Comput. Cryptol. Inf. Secur. 13, 26–42 (2015)
27. Lipton, R.J., Tarjan, R.E.: A separator theorem for planar graphs. SIAM J. Appl. Math. 36(2), 177–189 (1979)
28. Mohri, M.: Semiring frameworks and algorithms for shortest-distance problems. J. Autom. Lang. Comb. 7(3), 321–350 (2002)
29. Pan, V., Reif, J.: The parallel computation of minimum cost paths in graphs by stream contraction. Inf. Process. Lett. 40(2), 79–83 (1991)
30. Pan, V., Reif, J.: Fast and efficient solution of path algebra problems. J. Comput. Syst. Sci. 38(3), 494–510 (1989)
31. Pan, V., Reif, J.: Fast and efficient parallel solution of sparse linear systems. SIAM J. Comput. 22(6), 1227–1250 (1993)
32. Pinto, A., Carloni, L.P., Sangiovanni-Vincentelli, A.L.: Efficient synthesis of networks on chip. In: Proceedings 21st International Conference on Computer Design, pp. 146–150. IEEE (2003)
33. Randmets, J.: Programming Languages for Secure Multi-party Computation Application Development. Ph.D. thesis, Tartu University (2017)
34. Sealfon, A.: Shortest paths and distances with differential privacy. In: Proceedings of the 35th ACM SIGMOD-SIGACT-SIGAI Symposium on Principles of Database Systems, pp. 29–41 (2016)
35. Tarabalka, Y., Chanussot, J., Benediktsson, J.A.: Segmentation and classification of hyperspectral images using watershed transformation. Pattern Recogn. 43(7), 2367–2379 (2010)
36. West, D.B., et al.: Introduction to Graph Theory, vol. 2. Prentice Hall, Upper Saddle River (2001)
37. Wu, D.J., Zimmerman, J., Planul, J., Mitchell, J.C.: Privacy-preserving shortest path computation. arXiv preprint arXiv:1601.02281 (2016)
38. Yamada, T.: A mini-max spanning forest approach to the political districting problem. Int. J. Syst. Sci. 40(5), 471–477 (2009)
39. Yamada, T., Takahashi, H., Kataoka, S.: A heuristic algorithm for the mini-max spanning forest problem. Eur. J. Oper. Res. 91(3), 565–572 (1996)
40. Yao, A.C.: Protocols for secure computations. In: 23rd Annual Symposium on Foundations of Computer Science (SFCS 1982), pp. 160–164. IEEE (1982)

A Blockchain-Based Architecture to Manage User Privacy Preferences on Smart Shared Spaces Privately

Charles V. Neu[1]([✉]), Joel Gibson[1], Roben C. Lunardi[2], Natalie Leesakul[1], and Charles Morisset[1]

[1] Newcastle University, School of Computing, Newcastle upon Tyne NE4 5TG, UK
{charles.neu,j.c.gibson1,natalie.leesakul,
charles.morisset}@newcastle.ac.uk
[2] Federal Institute of Rio Grande do Sul (IFRS), Porto Alegre, Brazil
roben.lunardi@restinga.ifrs.edu.br

Abstract. Smart shared spaces, such as smart buildings, represent a fast-growing market and can benefit from several sensors that generate data which can be used to improve automatisation, increase efficiency in energy management, and optimise occupant's comfort. Equally, the smart shared spaces pose many privacy challenges as they are equipped with sensors that can potentially be used to gather data about occupants that they may or may not feel comfortable disclosing, for example, details of their daily routine or occupancy reports of their office. Due to these challenges, it can lead to the opposite results to the optimisation of occupant's comfort as occupants may not want to use the space due to the privacy concerns. Therefore, it is important to allow the occupants to inform their privacy settings so they feel more confident knowing that their privacy preferences are being respected. We recognise that in some spaces (e.g., shared workplaces) occupants may feel uncomfortable disclosing their preferences if their anonymity is not respected due to the lack of transparency about who can control that data. Thus, this work focuses on a decentralised system based on the SITA privacy model to provide occupants of shared spaces a way to specify and manage their privacy preferences anonymously. We propose a blockchain solution through smart contracts to control how the privacy settings are shared, ensuring that the users have full control of these records. Moreover, it allows traceability over the user's preferences data usage. Our evaluation shows that the system performs well in regard to time and usability and it can be linked to different smart building management systems. Consequently, this work demonstrates data protection in practice as it puts in place an appropriate technical and organisational measure to safeguard the individual's privacy by increasing transparency and accountability of smart building data management in accordance to the data protection by design and default approach under the General Data Protection Regulations (GDPR).

Keywords: Privacy preferences · Smart spaces · Blockchain · Smart buildings · Smart contracts · Data protections

© The Author(s), under exclusive license to Springer Nature Switzerland AG 2023
J. Garcia-Alfaro et al. (Eds.): DPM 2022/CBT 2022, LNCS 13619, pp. 136–150, 2023.
https://doi.org/10.1007/978-3-031-25734-6_9

1   Introduction

Many in academia and industry have stressed the growing concern around maintaining user privacy in an increasingly data-driven society [7]. Thus, enabling users to manage their privacy preferences and correctly specify how they would like their data to be used is an important issue [18].

Smart buildings are one of the areas where such concerns for privacy are being raised [3]. In particular, due to the increasing concern about personal data breaches [9]. Smart buildings are a fast-growing market and their growing prevalence means more data is being collected about people whether they know it or not [17]. Privacy preferences management can be done using a privacy policy, such as P3P, which is centralised as presented by Pappachan et al. [17]. This raises many privacy concerns, particularly regarding the disclosure of data that a user may not feel comfortable disclosing [17]. A wide variety of sensors and systems found in smart buildings [14] could be used to track the location or behaviours of a person, including smartphone usage, occupancy detection, CO_2 monitoring, light level monitoring, temperature monitoring, and smart-meter readings [10,20,21].

Therefore, the objective of this work is to address such privacy concerns surrounding smart buildings by building a system which enables users to easily specify their privacy preferences and share them with smart building systems. This allows users to have a fine-grained control over their privacy within these smart buildings and put the control back in their hands regarding what data is collected about them. These privacy preferences will also be kept private to alleviate any fears users may have of being discriminated against because of their choices. For example, an employee working in a smart building may not feel comfortable with regular occupancy readings of their office but may feel too intimidated by their employer to set their preferences as such. Preferences are thus kept private and the intention is that when preferences are shared with smart building management systems they are simply used to ensure data collected by sensors within the smart building respect these preferences. Consequently, this system demonstrates data protections in practice. In accordance to the General Data Protection Regulation, Article 25 outlines the requirement of data protection by design and default, concerning the implementation of data protection principles in an effective manner and "to integrate the necessary safeguards into the processing in order to meet the requirements of this Regulation and protect the rights of data subjects" [6]. Building occupants are the data subjects in this regard. On that account, the adoption of this proposed system acts as a safeguard to ensure that the rights of data subjects are respected in the smart shared space by improving transparency of data collection and informing individuals of the data being collected by the smart buildings. Moreover, as the system is enabled by smart contracts, it improves transparency in data processing [1] as well as allowing building occupants to select the privacy preferences to limit the purpose of processing. However, further analysis of the GDPR principles [6] and the data subject rights in relation to smart buildings is beyond the scope of this paper. This proposed work is only intended to illustrate the use of smart contracts to improve privacy and individual's control over their personal data, highlighting the application of individuals rights and principles under the GDPR in a form of technical and organisational measures.

In this work, we investigate the usage of a public blockchain to manage user's privacy preferences in smart building environments. The proposed solution allows users to store and manage their privacy preferences through smart contracts to ensure decentralisation, authenticity, integrity and trust on the use of information. This solution follows the GDPR principles of lawfulness, fairness, and transparency of process and purpose limitation. It also respects the rights to be informed and to restrict processing as the system places control over personal information in the hands of the data subjects. Our solution allows users to set different privacy preferences for each smart building or sharing a specific set of privacy preferences to different rooms within the same smart building. Consequently, users can delete or remove a set of privacy preferences, though the costs (based on the current exchange rate for Ethers) might not be compatible with the recurrent modifications on these preferences yet. It would, therefore, suit a model where users register their preferences only once or another solution could be using a private blockchain for privacy preferences. However, further evaluation is required.

The remainder of this work is as follows. Section 2 provides a background on recent works about privacy in smart spaces, as well as, recent contributions of blockchain to privacy concerns. Section 3 presents our proposed solution to manage user's privacy preferences using a blockchain-based solution through smart contracts. An experimental evaluation is presented in Sect. 4 considering the public blockchain Ethereum. Finally, Sect. 5 concludes this work and indicates future work directions.

2   Background and Related Work

2.1   Privacy in Smart Spaces

An increasing number of spaces are becoming so called 'smart' by using a plethora of sensors that continuously collect data [13]. Such spaces usually have a management system that captures a digital representation of a dynamically evolving space at any point in time for different purposes, for example, occupant's comfort, safety, and management automatising. However, such representation could lead to the modelling of patterns that might reveal people's activities which could disclose data that people might not feel comfortable disclosing. For example, it could reveal their location at different times, their current activities, or when and whom they spend time with [19]. Thus, privacy concerns are rising in such spaces. Previous research already addresses [16,19] concerns about the privacy preferences of smart spaces occupants, regarding what data they feel comfortable sharing, how and with whom.

Smart buildings are socio-technical systems that connect building systems, IoT technology, and occupants [9]. Several sensors that collect and handle building data are highly influenced by the presence of building occupants; these could be used to monitor and track their location and activities. Therefore, occupant's privacy concerns are rising where stringent data protection legislation (e.g., GDPR) plays an important role in regulating the smart built environments. Harper *et al.* [9] present a study conducted amongst occupants of a state-of-the-art commercial smart building to understand their privacy concerns and preferences. Their results show that most of the occupants are concerned and called for more transparency in the data collection process.

Bugeja *et al.* [2] discuss that the heterogeneous, dynamic, and Internet-connected nature of smart spaces environments adds several privacy concerns as personal data is more accessible. According to the authors, this accessibility alongside the rising risks of data security and privacy breaches makes smart home security and privacy a critical topic that needs more research. Thus, their research presents an overview of the privacy and security challenges directed towards smart homes including the evaluations on constraints and challenges of existing solutions.

A study on the privacy concerns and preferences of the occupants of smart buildings when used as their workplace is presented by Harper *et al.* [8] based on online questionnaires to map the opinion of participants who were residents of a real-world smart building, as well as, non-residents. Their research concludes that both smart building residents and non-residents care about privacy over data collection in smart buildings, especially regarding sensors in the building that collect data about them as that could lead to monitoring and tracking at work. Also, they discuss that more transparency is required throughout the whole cycle of data collection, storage, processing, usage and beyond. The authors conclude their paper by indicating that current approaches for getting the consent of smart building occupants are not efficient regarding privacy preferences and data collection.

Therefore, it is important to follow a structured model to handle data in such spaces; for example, SITA [16] is a conceptual privacy model that divides location privacy into four dimensions: Spatial, Identity, Temporal, and Activity. Each of the dimensions are divided into five levels each of these having their own interpretation of privacy in form of a privacy method referred to as a strategy, and the values of these levels can be changed individually in each dimension. The aim of SITA is to be an intuitive and easily implemented model where it overcomes other existing location privacy solutions that usually are binary privacy or constrained to either identity, temporal, or spatial data. The authors claim that SITA is a complete model providing that all existing privacy methods can be described using SITA and that the model can be applied to all types of location based services. However, such privacy preferences should be set and handled properly as they could be considered as sensitive user data and therefore should be managed privately and securely.

2.2   Blockchain-Based Technology to Improve Privacy

Blockchain is a technology that aims to address some of the challenges regarding securely and properly storing and handling personal and sensitive data. Despite its initial concept applied to the financial domain where it keeps a public ledger, changes are constantly made to fit it to other applications, making it suitable for different domains [15].

Researches have been published regarding the adoption of blockchain to protect personal data. Zyskind *et al.* [23] discuss the implementation of decentralising privacy using blockchain to protect personal data, addressing that privacy concerns are arising due to the increasing amount of user data stored by both public and private companies. Their proposal combines blockchain with non-blockchain technologies to produce a system looking to overcome some common privacy issues. Firstly, it ensures that users have ownership over their own data. With a centralised database, the service in control of the database has full ownership and unlimited access to the data. Blockchain's decentralised nature places ownership back into the user's hands, and they get to delegate access permissions to services as they see fit. This is a crucial part of what our system looks to achieve as well, giving the user control of their privacy preferences and who they share them with. Secondly, it embraces data transparency and auditability. With a centralised database it can be unclear what data is being collected about the user, how it is being used, and by who. Blockchain is transparent by nature, with transaction logs being open for everyone to view. This makes it easily visible who is accessing data, when they accessed it, and how. This is the core value of the system proposed in our work - to make it clearly visible and traceable of who is accessing and using a user's privacy preferences including any changes made to them. This reinforces how blockchain can help to protect personal data, and thus why it is being used in this proposed system.

A blockchain-based approach for matching desired and real privacy settings of social network users is presented by Lax *et al.* [11]. This demonstrates the ability for blockchain's decentralised nature to place control back into the hands of users. Taking an example of privacy settings on social media, what stops a social media platform from manipulating your privacy settings for their own gain? They store your settings, and if such settings were altered, it would not be possible to prove who did it. Perhaps you changed them and simply forgot? The auditability of blockchain places the full control of settings back in the hands of the user where the settings can only be managed by the users and allows for traceability when changes are made. Therefore, the paper by Lax et al. presents a model for interaction between a social media and a user via a smart contract which inspired the model produced for the proposed work in this paper.

In a different approach, Li *et al.* [12] proposed a scheme to allow privacy preservation but also the possibility to reward the privacy data shared by the user. To do this, they used a smart contract approach to provide incentives for data sharing. The solution was implemented using a deniable ring signature and Monero blockchain. This system has similarities with what is proposed in our paper, but they focus on incentives and payments to use user data and not necessarily to manage privacy preferences.

Given this background, these works show that blockchain and decentralisation can help protect the privacy of users and give them control of their own data, but such technology has not yet to be used in smart spaces, like smart buildings. Hence, this paper presents a system that aims to apply blockchain to preserve privacy in smart shared spaces as it represents a growing market with serious implications on user privacy and trust. Moreover, the proposed system supports the movement of Industry 5.0 [4] which complements the existing Industry 4.0 [5] paradigm. Industry 5.0 attempts to capture the value of new technologies, providing prosperity beyond jobs and growth, while respecting planetary boundaries. The movement places wellbeing of the industry workers at the centre of the production process including improving the workers comfort and respecting privacy preferences.

3   Privacy Preferences Management Through Smart Contracts

This section presents our blockchain-based system to manage user privacy preferences in smart shared spaces according to the SITA model. SITA is considered the most appropriate model for our system as it allows five different privacy levels on four dimensions, allowing the user to easily chose several different privacy preferences that can be adapted to different smart shared spaces (for example, smart shared offices) and therefore was adopted in this work.

The overall system model is explained including the detailed descriptions of the system's functionality. Figure 1 shows the overall system model. It breaks down the system into four key parts, and two parties that will use it. The key parts are the DApp UI, JavaScript methods, the smart contract, and the blockchain itself. The two parties are the ordinary user who defines and manages their privacy preferences using the DApp, and the smart building control system which interacts directly with the smart contract to retrieve the privacy preferences shared by its occupants.

The smart contract handles all interaction with data stored on the blockchain, whether that is retrieving preferences, storing or modifying preferences, or managing access to preferences. As mentioned above smart building control systems will interact with this contract directly by calling the relevant commands. The access of preferences by smart building systems is controlled by the users and owners of those preferences. Users can manage a list of 'approved addresses' which are allowed to retrieve their preferences from the blockchain. The smart contract will allow only these approved blockchain addresses to retrieve a user's preferences, ensuring that the user has full control over who can access them. Consequently, users can manage as many different sets of preferences as they want, each with its own secret key. Thus, for example, users can define and manage some privacy preferences under one key which can be shared with a certain smart space, and under another key they manage different preferences which could be shared with another smart space. This allows the users to share different preferences with different smart spaces. Regular users do not directly interact with the contract, instead they make inputs via the DApp UI, and JavaScript methods work as an intermediary calling the necessary commands on behalf of the user.

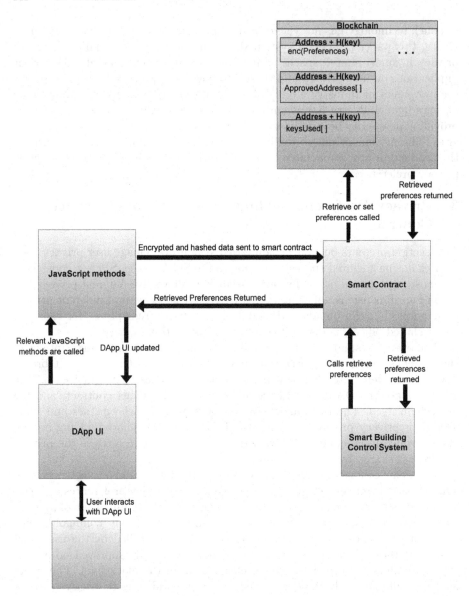

Fig. 1. Overall system overview

3.1   Smart Contract Design

The smart contract in the system retrieves and modifies data stored on the blockchain. Although this mostly involves the encrypted privacy preferences of users, the lists of approved addresses are also included as discussed above. The smart contract is divided into a list of features which in this case refers to individual functions.

The following functions are required features for a smart contract:

- **Set Preferences:** Used to store a set of privacy preferences on the blockchain. It is called both the first time a set of preferences are stored, as well as when modifying already existing preferences. Preferences are stored in a mapping (dictionary) in which the key is the combination of the user's address and the hash of the secret key, and the value stored is the encrypted privacy preferences of the user.
- **Get Preferences:** Used to retrieve the preferences of any user, but only approved addresses will be successful and have the encrypted preferences returned. It takes a user's address and secret key hash as parameters, which in combination should produce a mapping key like in the Set Preferences Function. The address that called the function ($msg.sender$) will be checked to see if it is an approved address for these preferences, and the encrypted preferences will be returned only if it is.
- **Delete Preferences:** Allows the user to delete a certain set of privacy preferences. It is a self-explanatory function, which can only be called by the user to delete preferences of their own.
- **Delete All Preferences Function:** Allows the user to delete all preferences stored under every one of their keys. It could be used, for example, if the user has forgotten their secret key and wishes to prevent their privacy preferences from being accessed.
- **Add Approved Address Function:** Adds an approved address for a certain key, to allow that address to retrieve the preferences stored under the key. This is how the user can manage who they share their preferences with.
- **Remove Approved Address Function:** Removes an approved address for a certain key, preventing that address from being able to retrieve those preferences anymore.

3.2 JavaScript Methods Design

The JavaScript methods implemented act as an intermediary between the DApp and the smart contract, responsible for calling the contract functions set out above on behalf of the user. The main methods are:

- **Encrypt Preferences:** The system requires the preferences to be encrypted to overcome blockchain's transparency. If the setPreferences contract function was called with unencrypted preferences, the user's preferences would be available to anyone viewing the transaction logs on the blockchain. This would compromise the privacy of the user's preferences, hence the preferences must be encrypted. Thus, a symmetric encryption scheme (AES) was chosen as users will need to share the encryption key with smart spaces management systems.
Once returned, the preferences will be decrypted with the same key allowing them to be read and used by a smart building system.

– **Decryption Function:** As privacy preferences are stored encrypted on the blockchain, when retrieved they will still be encrypted. Hence, a decryption function is necessary so the preferences can be read. This function will simply AES decrypt the encrypted preferences to return the original plaintext preferences. This function will be called after preferences are retrieved.
– **Generate Key Function:** Produces an AES-256[1] key used to encrypt preferences, which will also be hashed for use as part of the composite key in the smart contract. This function is required to enable AES encryption and decryption, and thus is just as necessary.
– **Hash Key Function:** Encrypted preferences are stored on the blockchain under a composite key which includes the hash of the secret key. Therefore, a function to perform this hashing is necessary.
  Thus, to hash the key we feed in the secret key as a parameter and receive its hash in return. In our implementations, SHA-3[2], the most secure hashing standard for the time was chosen.

3.3 DApp Design

Design of the DApp required identifying the necessary UI features to allow the user to manage their privacy preferences. This means the UI needed to provide a way for the user to do all the things the smart contract offers from getting and setting preferences, to adding and removing approved addresses. Figure 2 shows the DApp UI Wireframe that was implemented, and illustrates the main features.

The main features of the DApp UI are:

– Your Account: Displays the blockchain address the user is signed into via MetaMask[3]
– Secret Key Input Box: An input box for the secret key. User can type in an existing key, or have a new key generated to fill the box.
– Retrieve Button: Calls the smart contract getPreferences function with the user's address and hash of the secret key in the input box. Successful retrieval will have the preferences form filled with the retrieved preferences, and the approved addresses drop-down filled with all approved addresses for those preferences.
– Get New Key Button: Calls the genKey JavaScript function to generate a new AES key, which will fill the secret key input box.
– Delete These Preferences Button: Calls the smart contract deletePreferences function with the user's address and hash of the secret key from the input box.
– Preferences Form: Features one drop-down selection box for each SITA dimension, allowing the user to define their chosen level for each dimension.

---

[1] https://nvlpubs.nist.gov/nistpubs/fips/nist.fips.197.pdf.
[2] https://csrc.nist.gov/publications/detail/fips/202/final.
[3] MetaMask extension is available at https://metamask.io.

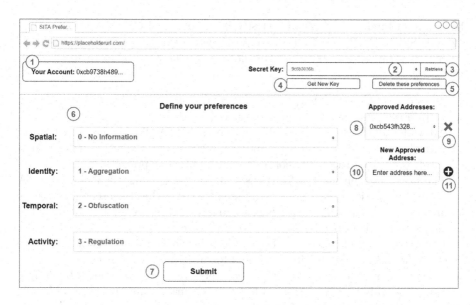

Fig. 2. DApp UI Wireframe

- Submit Button: Calls the smart contract setPreferences function from the user's address, with the preferences from the form encrypted, and the secret key from the input box hashed.
- Approved Addresses Drop-down: Drop-down selection displaying all the approved addresses for this preferences set. This selection can be used to choose an approved address to delete by pressing the cross (approved address remove button).
- Approved Address Remove Button: Calls the smart contract removeApprovedAddress function on the selected approved address.
- New Approved Address Input Box: Input box for new approved addresses.
- Approved Address Add Button: Calls the smart contract addApprovedAddress function on the approved address in the input box.

4   Experimental Evaluation

We evaluated the whole system based on its usability and performance regarding correctness, financial cost and time to perform each kind of transaction (insert, modify and delete preferences, add and remove approved addresses that can retrieve the user's privacy preferences) and usability. A basic documentation and all the source code is available at a GitHub repository[4].

The smart contract is deployed to a test Ethereum blockchain using Ganache, and the DApp is hosted locally on localhost:3000 using NPM on a hardware

---

[4] https://github.com/cvncodes/DPM2022.

based on an Intel Core i7-8565U @1.80 GHz processor, BC501 NVMe SK hynix 128 GB SSD disk, 16 GB DDR4 and Windows 10 Pro as operating system.

The following is a walkthrough of the system, showing the main steps to use the proposed solution.

1. A user accesses the DApp through their web browser, signing in using the MetaMask extension to confirm their credentials.
2. After the login, the system will retrieve the SITA dimensions on the form with the retrieved preferences if any are stored for that key. This information is retrieved from the smart contract that stores user preferences.
3. The user can then use the form (seen in Fig. 2) to define their desired SITA levels. Encryption is necessary in this step to ensure that the user's preferences are not visible in transaction logs when making *setPreferences* calls to the smart contract, thus ensuring they stay private.
4. Using the *setPreferences* method stores the encrypted preferences on the blockchain, both for the first time and for updating preferences.
5. The user can then specify who else can retrieve these preferences by adding approved addresses (*addAprovedAddress*), ensuring only approved addresses can retrieve a user's privacy preferences.
6. Approved addresses (e.g., smart buildings) would then call the contract *getPreferences* method through the console, retrieving the user's preferences.
7. If a user wants to prevent an address from retrieving their preferences again, they could remove them from the approved addresses (*removedApprovedAddress*).
8. Alternatively, the user could delete the preferences set altogether (*deletePreferences*).

As the system uses Ethereum there is a cost associated with actions that need to write to the blockchain, including setting, modifying, and deleting preferences, as well as adding and removing approved addresses. This entails the vast majority of actions that a user would carry out when using the system cost Ether.

Table 1 shows that the latency to insert new transaction (run a method in the smart contract) is approximately 1s. These results can vary considering the amount of gas used as incentive to the miners [22]. Additionally, the cost to perform the methods in the smart contract vary from 0.0014 Ethers (setPreferences, modifying an existing preferences set) to 0.0126 Ethers (deleteAllPreferences, considering 3 stored keys). Considering that 1 Ether is equivalent to US$1169.19[5] these means that to create a user privacy preferences set (setPreferences for the first time) would cost approx. US$5.85. While to modify existing preferences and to allow an address to access preferences would cost approx. US$1.64 and US$2.92, respectively. Finally, to delete preferences or to delete all preferences (considering 3 keys) it would cost approx. US$5.38 and US$14.73, respectively.

---

[5] Exchange Rate from July 11, 2022 at 1AM availabe at https://coinmarketcap.com/.

Table 1. Transactions cost and Latency

Contract function	Cost (ETH)	Time (ms)
setPreferences (First time)	0.005	1100
setPreferences (Modifying)	0.0014	1090
addApprovedAddress	0.0025	1090
removedApprovedAddress	0.0019	1094
deletePreferences	0.0046	1100
deleteAllPreferences (1 Key)	0.0046	1100
deleteAllPreferences (2 Keys)	0.0085	1175
deleteAllPreferences (3 Keys)	0.0126	1205

Smart contract costs certainly raise an important question of who is responsible for the payment. Having this system deployed to the main net is certainly an option and the system could be extended to record transaction costs so that smart building systems can reimburse their users. This, however, relies on those in charge of the smart building management systems accepting these extra costs.

In the case that users would bear the costs of managing their preferences, they could be discouraged from managing accurate preferences due to the costs associated, in particular, deleting existing preferences.

Alternatively, the smart contract could be deployed on a private or semi-private blockchain. This would require smart buildings to host their own blockchain where they deploy the contract and allow users of the smart building to register and manage their preferences. Such a solution would allow the waiving of any transaction fees, eliminating any concerns regarding transaction costs. This would unfortunately come at the cost of the transferability available within the base system. With smart buildings running their own blockchain networks, users would no longer be able to easily share their preferences between smart buildings like the base system offers. There may also be some concerns regarding how decentralised the system actually is if the blockchain is hosted by the smart building that will use the preferences.

Another possible alternative would be a consortium solution, such as, a blockchain that has its control shared by different entities or institutions that will share the infrastructure costs. For example, universities, governmental institutions and other organisations could maintain enough active nodes to keep the decentralisation, but with a reduced cost to the user of the solution. This would allow users to share their privacy preferences in different buildings or facilities.

5   Final Considerations and Future Work

Due to the popularisation of smart shared spaces, they are equipped with several sensors to better manage that spaces and provide services, such as better comfort to the occupants; however, this also poses many privacy concerns and data protections challenges as occupants may not know what data are being collected, they may feel less confident or uncomfortable staying in such spaces. These challenges are potential drawbacks to the use of smart shared spaces along with the compliance to data protection regulations. Therefore, this proposed work contributes to the data protection by design and by default approach in smart buildings to ensure that privacy and the individuals' rights over their personal data are respected and protected in such space through the data management system. This work shows that it is possible to use blockchain to allow users to store and manage their privacy preferences privately. With the proposed system, smart space occupants can set and modify their privacy preferences according to the SITA privacy model dimensions and levels, as well as, define with whom those preferences are shared with.

A system has been developed as a prototype and evaluated through a test case. The results show that the usage of a public blockchain is promising regarding its functionality and usability, handling user's privacy preferences properly according to time and hardware usage, as well as, providing a way to allow users to handle their privacy preferences privately. However, using a public blockchain can also be a problem due its significant financial costs to deploy and run smart contracts. We recognise that the system's operations should cost users as little as possible to encourage them to correctly specify and update their privacy preferences without concern for the cost. An alternative is the adoption of a consortium blockchain solution to reduce the operation costs, without centralising the control to a single organisation. Another alternative, could be such a system being financially supported by an organisation, e.g., a city council.

As future work, developing an API is to be considered to provide an easy way to connect this project to smart building management systems so that it can work according to its occupants privacy preferences. This would include adding events to the smart contract to alert the smart building system when preferences they are using have been updated. Furthermore, the system presented in this work could be hosted in a webserver to be used as a tool to collect user privacy preferences to evaluate its usability in real world by real potential users.

Acknowledgement. This work has been supported by the PETRAS National Centre of Excellence for IoT Systems Cybersecurity, which has been funded by the UK EPSRC under grant number EP/S035362/1. Roben C. Lunardi is funded by IFRS.

References

1. Alharby, M., Castagna Lunardi, R., Aldweesh, A., van Moorsel, A.: Data-driven model-based analysis of the ethereum verifier's dilemma. In: 2020 50th Annual IEEE/IFIP International Conference on Dependable Systems and Networks (DSN), pp. 209–220 (2020). https://doi.org/10.1109/DSN48063.2020.00038
2. Bugeja, J., Jacobsson, A., Davidsson, P.: On privacy and security challenges in smart connected homes. In: 2016 European Intelligence and Security Informatics Conference (EISIC), pp. 172–175 (2016). https://doi.org/10.1109/EISIC.2016.044

3. Cejka, S., Knorr, F., Kintzler, F.: Privacy issues in smart buildings by examples in smart metering. In: 25th International Conference on Electricity Distribution (CIRED) (2019)
4. European Commission, D.G.f.R., Innovation, Renda, A.S.S.S.T.D.e.a.: Industry 5.0, a transformative vision for europe: governing systemic transformations towards a sustainable industry. Publications Office of the European Union (2022). https://data.europa.eu/doi/10.2777/17322
5. European Parliament, Directorate-General for Internal Policies of the Union, G.F.: Industry 4.0, European parliament. Publications Office (2017). https://data.europa.eu/doi/10.2861/085601
6. European Union (EU): Regulation (EU) 2016/679 of the European parliament and of the council of 27 April 2016 on the protection of natural persons with regard to the processing of personal data and on the free movement of such data, and repealing directive 95/46/ec (general data protection regulation) (2016). https://eur-lex.europa.eu/eli/reg/2016/679/oj
7. G. Zyskind, O.N., Pentland, A.S.: Decentralizing privacy: using blockchain to protect personal data. In: 2015 IEEE CS Security and Privacy Workshops, pp. 180–184 (2015). https://doi.org/10.1109/SPW.2015.27
8. Harper, S., Mehrnezhad, M., Mace, J.: On privacy and security challenges in smart connected homes. In: 2016 European Intelligence and Security Informatics Conference (EISIC), pp. 172–175 (2016). https://doi.org/10.1109/EISIC.2016.044
9. Harper, S., Mehrnezhad, M., Mace, J.C.: User privacy concerns and preferences in smart buildings. In: Groß, T., Viganò, L. (eds.) STAST 2020. LNCS, vol. 12812, pp. 85–106. Springer, Cham (2021). https://doi.org/10.1007/978-3-030-79318-0_5
10. Khalil, N., Benhaddou, D., Gnawali, O., Subhlok, J.: Nonintrusive occupant identification by sensing body shape and movement. In: Proceedings of the 3rd ACM International Conference on Systems for Energy-Efficient Built Environments, pp. 1–10. Association for Computing Machinery, New York, NY, USA (2016). https://doi.org/10.1145/2993422.2993429
11. Lax, G., Russo, A., Fascì, L.S.: A blockchain-based approach for matching desired and real privacy settings of social network users. Inf. Sci. **557**, 220–235 (2021). https://doi.org/10.1016/j.ins.2021.01.004, https://www.sciencedirect.com/science/article/pii/S0020025521000050
12. Li, T., Wang, H., He, D., Yu, J.: Blockchain-based privacy-preserving and rewarding private data sharing for IoT. IEEE Internet Things J. **14**(8), 1–12 (2022). https://doi.org/10.1109/JIOT.2022.3147925
13. Lunardi, R.C., Alharby, M., Nunes, H.C., Dong, C., Zorzo, A.F., van Moorsel, A.: Context-based consensus for appendable-block blockchains. In: 2020 IEEE International Conference on Blockchain (Blockchain), pp. 401–408 (2020)
14. Lunardi, R.C., Michelin, R.A., Neu, C.V., Zorzo, A.F.: Distributed access control on IoT ledger-based architecture. In: 2018 IEEE/IFIP Network Operations and Management Symposium (NOMS), pp. 1–7 (2018)
15. Lunardi, R.C., Michelin, R.A., Neu, C.V., Nunes, H.C., Zorzo, A.F., Kanhere, S.S.: Impact of consensus on appendable-block blockchain for IoT. In: 16th EAI International Conference on Mobile and Ubiquitous Systems: Computing, Networking and Services (MobiQuitous), pp. 228–237. Association for Computing Machinery (2019)
16. Andersen, M.S., Kjærgaard, M.B., Grønbæk, K.: The SITA principle for location privacy - conceptual model and architecture. In: International Conference on Privacy and Security in Mobile Systems (PRISMS), pp. 1–8 (2013). https://doi.org/10.1109/PRISMS.2013.6927184

17. Pappachan, P., et al.: Towards privacy-aware smart buildings: capturing, communicating, and enforcing privacy policies and preferences. In: IEEE 37th International Conference on Distributed Computing Systems Workshops (ICDCSW), pp. 193–198 (2017). https://doi.org/10.1109/ICDCSW.2017.52

18. Rudolph, M., Polst, S., Doerr, J.: Enabling users to specify correct privacy requirements. In: Knauss, E., Goedicke, M. (eds.) REFSQ 2019. LNCS, vol. 11412, pp. 39–54. Springer, Cham (2019). https://doi.org/10.1007/978-3-030-15538-4_3

19. Schomakers, EM., L.C.Z.M.: All of me? users' preferences for privacy-preserving data markets and the importance of anonymity. Electron Markets **30**, 649–655 (2020). https://doi.org/10.1007/s12525-020-00404-9, https://link.springer.com/article/10.1007/s12525-020-00404-9

20. Stellios, I., Mokos, K., Kotzanikolaou, P.: Assessing vulnerabilities and IoT-enabled attacks on smart lighting systems. In: Katsikas, S., et al. (eds.) ESORICS 2021. LNCS, vol. 13106, pp. 199–217. Springer, Cham (2022). https://doi.org/10.1007/978-3-030-95484-0_13

21. Včelák, J., Vodička, A., Maška, M., Mrňa, J.: Smart building monitoring from structure to indoor environment. In: 2017 Smart City Symposium Prague (SCSP), pp. 1–5 (2017). https://doi.org/10.1109/SCSP.2017.7973859

22. Zhang, L., Lee, B., Ye, Y., Qiao, Y.: Evaluation of ethereum end-to-end transaction latency. In: 2021 11th IFIP International Conference on New Technologies, Mobility and Security (NTMS), pp. 1–5 (2021). https://doi.org/10.1109/NTMS49979.2021.9432676

23. Zyskind, G., Nathan, O., Pentland, A.S.: Decentralizing privacy: using blockchain to protect personal data. In: Proceedings - 2015 IEEE Security and Privacy Workshops, SPW 2015, pp. 180–184 (2015)

No Salvation from Trackers: Privacy Analysis of Religious Websites and Mobile Apps

Nayanamana Samarasinghe[(✉)], Pranay Kapoor, Mohammad Mannan, and Amr Youssef

Concordia University, Montreal, Canada
{n_samara,p_apoo,mmannan,youssef}@ciise.concordia.ca

Abstract. Many religious communities are going online to save costs and reach a large audience to spread their religious beliefs. Since the COVID-19 pandemic, such online transitions have accelerated, primarily to maintain the existence and continuity of religious communities. However, online religious services (e.g., websites and mobile apps) open the door to privacy and security issues that result from tracking and leakage of personal/sensitive information. While web privacy in popular sites (e.g., commercial and social media sites) is widely studied, privacy and security issues of religious online services have not been systematically studied. In this paper, we perform privacy and security measurements in religious websites and Android apps: 62,373 unique websites and 1454 Android apps, pertaining to major religions (e.g., Christianity, Buddhism, Islam, Hinduism). We identified the use of commercial trackers on religious websites—e.g., 32% of religious websites and 78% of religious Android apps host Google trackers. Session replay services (*FullStory, Yandex, Inspectlet, Lucky Orange*) on 198 religious sites sent sensitive information to third parties. Religious sites (14) and apps (7) sent sensitive information in clear text. Besides privacy issues, we also identify sites with potential security issues: 19 religious sites were vulnerable to various security issues; and 69 religious websites and 29 Android apps were flagged by VirusTotal as malicious. We hope our findings will raise awareness of privacy and security issues in online religious services.

1 Introduction

With the advancement of technology, significant changes are made as to how religious practices are conducted during the last couple of decades [1]. The early online churches simply used websites with static pages (e.g., scriptorium pages of religious texts) to share information with an increased audience. Gradually, these websites started to include dynamic content hosting various interactive services (e.g., chat and messaging services, podcasts, videos of sermons, interactive worship). Also, with the proliferation of mobile devices, religious services were offered through mobile apps [2]. The recent COVID-19 pandemic has also resulted in offering religious services through online social media platforms (e.g.,

© The Author(s), under exclusive license to Springer Nature Switzerland AG 2023
J. Garcia-Alfaro et al. (Eds.): DPM 2022/CBT 2022, LNCS 13619, pp. 151–166, 2023.
https://doi.org/10.1007/978-3-031-25734-6_10

Facebook Live, YouTube) [3], and religious faiths in the United States have strengthened due to the pandemic [4]; 57% of the adults in the United States who attended religious services at least monthly, are now watching religious services online due to the pandemic [4]; churches supplement their revenue using virtual offering (e.g., donation) services. Unfortunately, various third parties included on religious online services to support various functionalities, are used to track users [5], and engage in privacy violations [6] leaking sensitive information; a prayer app (*Muslim Pro*) that eases the practicing of daily rituals prescribed in Islam, has leaked user location data to a broker (*X Mode*), which in turn had sold the same information to its contractors (including US military contractors) [7]; another prayer app (*pray.com*) sold the prayers of a grieving user who suffered a tragedy [8]. Also, while the possible influences from artificial intelligence (AI) technology on religious online services is still an under-studied area, potential exposures of highly confidential conversations relating to spiritual needs of users through chatbots (included on religious online services) will impact the privacy of users. In addition, security issues in religious online services can expose sensitive information of users; the Vatican site was hacked and compromised (in 2020) [9] with the aim of stealing sensitive information.

Past studies primarily discussed the evolution of digital religious communities from traditional religious institutions. Campbell [10] studied Internet trends and their implications on religious practices (including social and cultural shifts) and challenges related to online religious networks. The author observed that studying the religious practices of Internet users leads to a more refined understanding of the complex interactions with online services. Campbell et al. [2] provided a methodological approach to study religious-oriented mobile apps available on iTunes app store. The authors reviewed 451 religious app functions and their use, and group those apps into 11 categories.

In this work, we perform a large scale web privacy measurement of religious websites and Android apps. To the best of our knowledge, this is the first measurement study on privacy/security of religious online services, performed on a global scale. For the web privacy measurements, we use 62,373 websites collected from the *URL Classification* [11] source, after filtering out false positives (i.e., non-religious sites) using VirusTotal [12] website categorizations. Thereafter, we crawl the extracted religious websites using OpenWPM [13] web privacy measurement framework. We analyze the instrumented tracking metrics (third party scripts/cookies, fingerprinting APIs) using the instrumented data saved to the OpenWPM database. We identify religious websites that use session replay services, by inspecting the traffic sent by potential sites including session replay services with *HTTP Toolkit* [14]. In addition, we examine religious sites that send personal information to external parties using the chatbot functionality. We look for leaked personal/sensitive information (e.g., name, email address, address, prayer requests, confessions, user's location provided for searches) from religious websites that use HTTP or configured to use session replay. To find potential TLS vulnerabilities and weaknesses, we collect and analyze TLS certificates of 45,004 religious websites. In order to find other vulnerabilities in religious websites (e.g., Cross Site Scripting, SQL Injection, Path Traversal), we scan 11,888 religious websites using the *Wapiti* scanner. We also collect religious Android apps, and leverage MobSF [15], LiteRadar [16], and mitmproxy (with Google UI/Application Exerciser Monkey), to perform static and dynamic analysis techniques (using a Pixel 6 phone). However, we limit the security evaluation of religious online services due to possible legal and ethical issues. We also use VirusTotal [12] to identify religious sites, Android APKs and included third party domains hosting scripts/cookies that are malicious.

Contributions and Notable Findings

1. We develop a framework to collect religious websites and Android apps by eliminating false positives from given external source(s), and a test methodology to evaluate the privacy and security exposures from these religious websites.
2. 198/62,373 (0.3%) religious websites include session replay services—e.g., *FullStory* (*fullstory.com*), *Inspectlet* (*inspectlet.com*), *Luckyorange* (*luckyorange.com*), *Yandex* (*yandex.com*). We observed that users' personal/sensitive information is sent from the analyzed religious websites to session replay services (*FullStory, Yandex, Inspectlet*). Such shared sensitive information includes name, phone number, address, email address, message/comment, prayer request, location searches, login information, donation information, and keywords used in site searches.
3. 19/11,888 religious websites were found to be vulnerable—SQL Injection (9), Reflected Cross Site Scripting (7), Server Side Request Forgery (2), Path Traversal (1). The Path Traversal attack (on *christcc.org*) exposes several local files under /etc directory (e.g., /etc/password).
4. 7/1454 religious Android apps leaked sensitive information (e.g., user credentials, API key, phone number) from unprotected Firebase endpoints. In addition, 2 apps (*cdff.mobileapp, com.avrpt.teachingsofswamidayananda*) sent user credentials/device information over HTTP.
5. 17,418/62,373 (27.9%) and 3569/62,373 (5.7%) of religious sites include commercial tracking scripts and cookies, respectively. These trackers embed analytic and other third party services (e.g., social media plugins) on religious websites. Google dominates in tracking on both religious sites (32%) and apps (78%). There were tracking cookies that expire after a long period of time (including 4 tracking cookies by center.io on 4 religious sites that expire in year 9999). In addition, 1351/1454 (93%) of religious Android apps included tracking SDKs.
6. 69/62,373 religious websites were flagged as malicious at least by 5 security engines used by VirusTotal (e.g., *samenleesbijbel.nl, csiholytrinitychurch.com*). We also observed 12 malicious domains set tracking scripts/cookies on religious sites. Additionally, 29/1454 (2%) religious Android apps were flagged by VirusTotal by at least one security engine; *islamictech.slfgo* religious Android app was flagged by 10 security engines in VirusTotal.
7. 14/24 religious websites that use HTTP, sent personal/sensitive information (name, email address, phone number, address, message, prayer request, confession, date of birth, password).

We disclosed our findings on security vulnerabilities of the 10 websites and 9 Android apps to the corresponding admins/developers. We also notified Google about *islamictech.slfgo*.

2   Related Work

Web Privacy Measurements. There are various privacy measurement studies that are performed in the past. Englehardt et al. [17] implemented OpenWPM, a fully automated web privacy measurement framework. Using OpenWPM, Englehardt et al. [17] performed a web privacy measurement of the top-1M Alexa popular sites (mostly commercial sites), and found Google and Facebook dominates in tracking. Samarasinghe et al. [18] measured tracking on 150,244 government websites and 1166 Android apps, and found commercial trackers on those online services (mostly Google trackers), although it was unexpected to have trackers on government sites that are funded by the taxpayers. Hoy et al. [19] studied 102 church websites in the United States and found that they collect personal identifying information. The confidential information that are entered to church guest books and prayer requests, were leaked from corresponding church websites. We studied tracking on religious websites and found a larger proportion of those sites with Google trackers (32%, 19,772 out of 62,373 websites). In addition, we found 22 websites leak sensitive information of users (e.g., name, address, email, donation amount, prayer requests) to session recording services.

Privacy Analysis of Mobile Apps. Several past studies analyzed privacy and security issues in mobile apps. For example, Binns et al. [20] studied 959,000 apps from US and UK Google Play stores, and found that third party tracking follows a long tail distribution dominated by Google (87.75%). Nguyen et al. [21] performed a large-scale measurement on Android apps to understand violation of General Data Protection Regulation (GDPR) explicit consent. They found 28.8% (24,838/86,163) of apps sent data to ad-related domains without explicit user consent. Several recent studies (e.g., [22]) analyzed COVID-19 tracing apps, and highlighted privacy and surveillance risks in these apps. In contrast, we study privacy and security issues of 1454 religious Android apps and found Google specific tracking SDKs in a large proportion (78%, 1132 out of 1454) of them.

Analysis of SSL/TLS Certificates Used in Online Services. Felt et al., [23] measured the HTTPS adoption on the web, and found the number of top websites (from HTTPWatch Global, Alexa top-1M, Google top-100) that use HTTPS (by default) doubled between early 2016 and 2017. Alabduljabbar et al. [24] investigated the potential vulnerabilities (SSL/TLS) in free content websites (FCW) and premium websites. The authors found 17% and 12% of free websites have invalid and expired certificates, respectively. The authors also found more FCWs (38%) use ECDSA signature algorithm compared to premium websites (20%). We analyze TLS certificates of 45,004 religious websites and found 92.9% and 7.1% of HTTPS sites use RSA and ECDSA signature algorithms, respectively.

3   Methodology

In this section, we provide details of our website and apps collection methodology. Then, we elaborate our privacy analysis and measurement techniques; see Fig. 1 for an overview of our methodology.

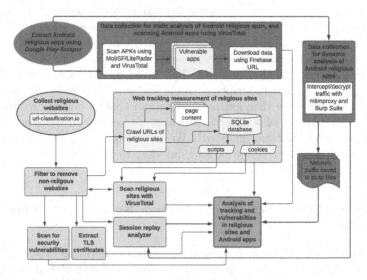

Fig. 1. Overview of our methodology.

3.1   Collecting Religious Websites and Android Apps

Religious Websites. We acquired a list of 583,784 websites (on April 26, 2022) from *URL Classification* [11] that are categorized as *Religion*; 448,646 (out of 583,784, 76.9%) are classified into multiple categories (including *Religion*). *URL Classification* provides a confidence rank for classified categories of each website, and with manual inspection, we find websites ranked 50 and above are likely religious sites; 202,968 (out of 583,784, 34.8%) websites are ranked 50 and above. To ensure, false positives are eliminated, we scan the 202,968 websites with VirusTotal [12], and filter 62,373 (out of 583,784, 10.7%) websites that are flagged as *Religion* by at least one security engine included in VirusTotal.

Religious Android Apps. We feed unique keywords related to major religions (i.e., Christianity, Islam, Hinduism, Buddhism) to *Google-Play-Scraper* [25], that crawls and extracts 2512 Android apps matching those search keywords from Google Play Store. We eliminate false positives by manual inspection, and finally select 1454 apps for our analysis.

3.2   Web Privacy Measurements

We configure OpenWPM [13] web privacy measurement framework to run with 10 parallel browser instances in headless mode. We configure OpenWPM instrumentations for HTTP requests/responses, JavaScript, cookies, DNS requests and callbacks. JavaScipt instrumentation also collects passive fingerprinting APIs included in religious websites. To mimic a new request, and to avoid any influence from past browsing history, for each URL visit, we clear the browser profile after each visit to a website. We use a physical machine (connected to our university network) running Ubuntu server 20.4 LTS, 64 GB RAM, 1TB SSD, AMD Ryzen Threadripper 2950X 16-Core Processor for our measurements between May 1, 2022 - May 7, 2022. A total of 62,373 religious sites were successfully crawled. We also configure OpenWPM to save the site content to a *LevelDB* [26] database. The instrumented tracking metrics extracted from OpenWPM are saved to an SQLite database for further analysis. The saved information in the database contains both stateful (i.e., scripts/cookies) and stateless (fingerprinting) forms of tracking metrics. We then extract scripts and cookies hosted on third-party domains (i.e., domains of scripts/cookies that do not match the domain of the religious site that they are included). We use *EasyPrivacy* [27] filtering rules that block third party trackers in religious sites to identify known third party tracking scripts/cookies.

3.3 Session Replay Scripts and Chatbot Services in Religious Websites

We identify a list of known session replay scripts offering session replay services [28]—*FullStory* (fs.js), *Inspectlet* (inspectlet.js), *Lucky Orange* (core/lo.js), *Yandex* (watch.js, tag.js). Then we extract the religious websites (198 out of 62,373, 0.32%) that include those scripts, from the *javascript* table of OpenWPM SQLite database. Thereafter, we inspect these 198 sites manually, to identify possible personal/sensitive information leaked during user interactions with the religious websites (e.g., while submitting messages and prayer requests, donating to religious institutions). During the interactions with these websites, we use crafted data (e.g., name, email, date of birth, messages, amount for donations), but do not submit the form, as input information is sent to remote servers, after each keystroke during user input. Personal information is also sent during interactions with chatbots in religious websites. We manually inspect the network traffic using *HTTP Toolkit* [14] to identify information sent over the network.

3.4 Security Issues in Religious Websites

Potential security issues in religious websites can cause privacy issues. In this section, we discuss security issues in the analyzed religious websites.

Malicious Religious Websites. In order to determine if the religious websites and included third party domains (hosting scripts/cookies) are malicious, we scan all 62,373 religious websites, and included 1906 third party tracking domains using VirusTotal. Note that, at least in some cases, VirusTotal engines[1] may

---

[1] https://tinyurl.com/2p8ynsfj (we exclude CRDF and Quttera for their unreliable results as we observed).

misclassify or delay in updating domain categorization labels [29]. We report domains that are flagged by at least 5 security engines as malicious.

HTTP/HTTPS Traffic and TLS Certificates Used in Religious Websites. We use *PyOpenSSL* [30] to collect the TLS certificates (in X509 format) of the analyzed religious websites. Then we extract various information of the collected certificates—i.e., validity duration, common name, issuer information (e.g., issuer name, issuer country, issuer organization), signature algorithm, public key size (for RSA only). We identify the protocol used in each web request (i.e., HTTP, HTTPS). We also analyze the collected information, to determine whether any of the religious websites send personal/sensitive information over plain HTTP, or the associated certificates used in religious websites expose users to risks.

Other Security Issues in Religious Websites. We randomly selected 11,888 religious websites (out of 62,373), and scanned them using the *Wapiti* [31] scanner to find other security issues (e.g., Cross Site Scripting, Server Side Request Forgery, SQL Injection). *Wapiti* crawls the web pages of a given website, and looks for scripts and forms in web pages where it can inject payloads to identify vulnerabilities. We configured *Wapiti* to use 15 s as *max-attack-time* and *max-scan-time*, and scan up to a depth of 5 levels from the base URL.

3.5   Android App Analysis

Tracking SDK Detection. We perform static analysis, using LiteRadar [16] by feeding APK files of each of the religious Android apps. The output from this process includes the tracking SDKs included in religious Android apps, the use of tracking SDKs, and requested permissions (including dangerous permissions such as camera, contacts, microphone, SMS, storage, and location).

Misconfigured Firebase Database. Many Android apps, including religious apps, use Google Firebase [32] (a widely used data store for mobile apps) to manage their backend infrastructure. However, due to possible misconfiguration, Android apps connected to Firebase database can be vulnerable. Exposed data from Firebase vulnerabilities includes personally identifiable information (PII) and plain text passwords. We leverage MobSF [15] to extract URLs of unprotected Firebase endpoints for each APK file, which contains potential vulnerabilities; we then download the exposed data from the Firebase datastore URL[2] and check for apparent sensitive and PII items, including: user identifiers, passwords, email addresses, and phone numbers. However, for ethical/legal considerations, we do not validate the leaked information (e.g., login to an app using the leaked user credentials). Then we remove the downloaded datastore.

Dynamic Analysis. We use a rooted Pixel 6 mobile phone with Android 12, to proxy traffic from newly installed apps via mitmproxy [33]. To avoid collecting

---

[2] The URL is of the form <*Firebase project name*>.*firebaseio.com/.json* (e.g., https://catholic-connect-213606.firebaseio.com/.json).

traffic from other apps, we uninstall all other apps, except those apps required for basic functionalities (e.g., Camera, Google Play Store). A mitmproxy root certificate is installed on the phone. We also install mitmproxy on a separate desktop machine to collect and decrypt HTTPS traffic. Both the desktop machine and phone are connected to the same Wi-Fi network. We use adb [34] to automate the installation, launch, and uninstallation of the apps. We also use Monkey [35] with 5000 events (e.g., touch, slide, swipe, click) for each app; login to app UI is not supported (if prompted). The network traffic is captured and stored in pcap files. We use the captured network traffic to determine sensitive information (e.g., device identifiers sent to trackers, leaked hardcoded user/admin credentials and API keys) sent to external entities. We close mitmproxy and uninstall the installed religious app before moving to the next app.

Session Replay from Android Apps. We leverage the dynamic analysis to inspect third party domains included in apps, to identify those known session replay services (e.g., Yandex, Hotjar, MouseFlow, UXCam) to which apps send HTTP requests. For this exercise, we use Burp Suite [36] to identify apps that send sensitive information to corresponding session replay services.

Malicious Domains and Apps. We scan the APK files of 1454 religious Android apps with VirusTotal. We also scan 1539 domains included in apps (as found in the network traffic) with VirusTotal.

3.6   Ethical Considerations and Limitations

We do not use the sensitive information (e.g., user identifiers and passwords) extracted from static and dynamic analyses of Android apps for any intrusive validations that may have an impact to the privacy of users. In addition, we did not retain any data from exposed Firebase databases. The *Wapiti* black-box scanner we use to find vulnerabilities in religious websites, limits the scope of the scan only to the web page (e.g., add/remove query parameters).

EasyPrivacy [27] filtering rules that we use are not comprehensive enough to identify all possible tracking scripts/cookies set on religious sites (especially country specific trackers). We also resorted to use manual steps in verifying false positives/negatives of religious websites and Android apps, which are not trivial to automate (e.g., inspection of sensitive information relayed from session replay services to third parties). Android apps with obfuscated code may have impacted our static analysis, but not so on our dynamic analysis. Random clicks triggered from the UI automation that use monkeyrunner, may not precisely target the specific targeted areas on the UI.

4   Results: Religious Websites

4.1   Session Replay and Chatbot Services

With session replay services that are included in websites, a user's session is replayed through the browser and sent to a remote third party; information replayed includes user interactions on a website, such as typed inputs, mouse movements, clicks, page visits, tapping and scrolling events. During this process, user's sensitive information can be exposed to third-party servers that host session replay scripts. We identified four session replay services on the analyzed religious sites (62,373): *FullStory* (4), *Inspectlet* (5), *Lucky Orange* (1), *Yandex* (187). The Lucky Orange session replay service was included only on one analyzed religious site (*discoverquran.com*), and we found session replaying on this site was disabled by the site owner. FullStory was used (e.g., in *fbckahoka.org*, *emmausdenver.com*) to replay requests for religious material and prayer requests by users. Inspectlet was used to replay meta-information (e.g., page title, browser information, dependent resources of websites requested) of religious sites (e.g., *gbcga.com*, *afci.com.au*) browsed by users, which can be leveraged for fingerprinting. We found personal information (e.g., name, email, phone, message, address, login ID), donation details (e.g., donation amount), prayer requests and keywords used during site searches being replayed to Yandex session replay services from 19 religious sites; see Table 1.

Furthermore, AI-based chatbots are being included in religious websites to emulate personal human conversations. Exposure of these conversations to adversaries may divulge personal information of users. We observed chatbots of two religious sites shared personal conversation to third parties: *chertzumc.com* transmitted user conversations in base64 format to an external domain (*chat.amy.us*), and *immersivehistory.com* sent user conversations as is, over a websocket to a third party domain (*socket.tidio.co*).

4.2   Religious Sites with Security Issues

The *Wapiti* scanner identified security issues in 19 (out of 11,888) religious websites—SQL Injection (9), Reflected Cross Site Scripting (7), Server Side Request Forgery (2), Path Traversal (1); see Table 2 for examples of security issues in religious websites. *Christcc.org* is vulnerable to the Path Traversal attack that exposes the local /etc/passwd file. Although, user passwords are not revealed from the /etc/passwd file, the content (e.g., full names, list of system users indicating software installed on the host) of it can be used for reconnaissance and social engineering efforts, which may eventually lead to reverse shells and local privilege escalations. The potential Reflected Cross Site Scripting attacks that can be launched by some websites (e.g., *abccolumbia.org*, *christcc.org*, *cogsabbath.org*), are proof of the attacker's ability to execute much more harmful attacks (e.g., steal credentials, hijack user accounts, exfiltrate sensitive information) on users. The same applies to religious websites (e.g., *abccolumbia.org*, *aoffcc.com*, *welfarebc.com*) subjected to SQL Injection vulnerability, where the consequences from such attacks (e.g., unauthorized viewing of user data, removal of data from database tables, attacker gaining database administrative rights) are far reaching. We also scanned religious Android apps pertaining to these religious websites (for security issues) using *Wapiti*, and found *com.subsplashconsulting.s_R858KV* (CCC

Table 1. Use cases for information leakage with session replay services (SRS) on religious sites.

Leakage type	Religious site	SRS	Leaked information
Personal information	glorygod.ru, aglow.org.uk, novizavet.ru, standrews.ru, slovo-istini.com, zhslovo.ru, sda-spb.ru	Yandex	Name, phone number, email, address/city, message
	nehemiah.ru	Yandex	Location entered to search for the closest church
	mbs.ru, belchurch.org	Yandex	Login ID
	solba.ru	Yandex	Email address used to subscribe for a newsletter
Request for religious material	fbckahoka.org	FullStory	Email address, sermon notes
Request for prayer	fbckahoka.org	FullStory	Full name, email, phone, prayer request
	solba.ru	Yandex	Name, message, donation amount of the prayer request for a patient (Corona and other diseases), and to succeed in studies/exams
Meta information of site requests	lifeteen.com	FullStory	links clicked by users (relating to various religious missions)
	gbcga.com	Inspectlet	Page title, URL browsed, browser information (i.e., browser type, version, webkit, user-agent).
	afci.com.au	Inspectlet	URL and dependencies (CSS, JavaScript) of the site browsed
	bengalipdfbooks.info	Yandex	Links clicked by users
Donation details	novizavet.ru	Yandex	First name, last name, donation amount
	rpconline.ru	Yandex	Donation amount, mode of payment (e.g., bank card)
Keywords uses for searches	new-church.ru, wolrus.org, sda-spb.ru, kateheo.ru	Yandex	Keywords used in site searches that may include sensitive information

Camp Hill, PA App) app that corresponds to *christcc.org* religious website, contains 2 endpoints (https://app.easytithe.com/AppAPI/api/account/churchInfo, https://app.easytithe.com/AppAPI/api/account/paymentList) that are vulnerable to SQL Injection.

4.3   Religious Sites Flagged as Malicious

We found 69 (out of 62,373, 0.1%) religious sites were flagged as malicious by VirusTotal (at least by 5 engines). We only considered sites that apparently were used for malicious purposes according to VirusTotal category labels and community comments, containing keywords including malware, compromised, infection, spyware, fraud, weapons, command and control, bot network and callhome. We also observed 12 malicious domains host tracking scripts/cookies on religious sites, as per VirusTotal (at least by 5 engines): *freecontent.date* (modifies files in Chrome extension folder) and *iclickcdn.com* (website redirected to malicious pages) were flagged as malicious by more than 10 engines. With *Retire.js* [37],

Table 2. Examples of security issues in religious websites.

Security issue	Website	Details of the security issue
Reflected Cross Site Scripting (XSS)	spiritofmedjugorje.org	This vulnerability is found via injection of parameter *ArticleSeq* (e.g., https://spiritofmedjugorje.org/index.php?ArticleSeq=%3C%2Fscript%3E%3CScRiPt%3Ealert%28%27wfj7hux5b6%27%29%3C%2FsCrIpT%3E)
SQL Injection	abccolumbia.org	Injection of parameter *media_id* (e.g., https://abccolumbia.org/video.php?media_id=10%27%20AND%2092%3D92%20AND%20%2714%27%3D%2714). The parameter value passed to *media_id* is decoded as *10' AND 92=92 AND '14'='14*
Path Traversal	christcc.org	Linux local files disclosure vulnerability via injection of parameter *path*—exposes /etc/passwd, /etc/group, /etc/hosts, /etc/host.conf, /etc/resolv.conf, /etc/profile, /etc/csh.login, /etc/fstab, /etc/networks, /etc/services files (e.g., https://christcc.org/vcf_download.php?path=%2Fetc%2Fpasswd)
Server Side Request Forgery (SSRF)	allsaintsphoenix.org	SSRF vulnerability via injection of parameter *url* (e.g., https://allsaintsphoenix.org/s/cdn/v1.0/i/m?url=http%3A%2F%2Fexternal.url%2Fpage&methods=resize%2C500%2C5000)

we found JavaScript sources (i.e., *bootstrap*, *jquery*, *swfobject*) included in 3 religious sites (*wierdapark-suid.co.za*, *divyabodhanam.org* and *divyabodhanam.org*) were using legacy script versions that are vulnerable to Cross Site Scripting.

4.4 Analysis of HTTP/HTTPS Traffic from Religious Websites

We analyze the HTTP/HTTPS traffic and characteristic of TLS certificates used in religious websites. We were able to extract 45,004 (72.2%, out of 62,349) websites that use HTTPS; 17,345 requests failed (e.g., because of timeout).

Use of HTTP in Religious Websites. We found 24 religious websites (out of 62,373, 0.04%) use plain HTTP for communication.

HTTP is not secure, and allow adversaries to listen to the traffic sent from these websites, and capture sensitive personal information. We found 14 out of 24 of religious websites that use HTTP, sent personal/sensitive information (first/last names, email address, phone number, address, message/comment, prayer request/confession, date of birth/age, password) of users over the clear; see Table 3 for top-5 religious websites that leak personal/sensitive information over HTTP.

Table 3. Top-5 religious websites with most leakages of personal/sensitive information over HTTP—DOB = Date of Birth, PR = Prayer Request

Website	Name	Email	Phone	Address	Message	DOB/Age	Password	PR/Confession
eliotchapel.org	✓	✓	✓	✓		✓	✓	
nbcog.net	✓	✓	✓	✓	✓			
therockchurchla.org	✓	✓	✓		✓			✓
walkatliberty.com	✓	✓			✓		✓	
catholicfamily.net	✓	✓				✓		✓

Validity Period of TLS Certificates. Popular browsers (e.g., Google Chrome) have announced in 2020, SSL/TLS certificates cannot be issued for more than 13 months (397 days) [38]. Larger validity periods make it tedious to roll out changes to cryptographic primitives of certificates (e.g., update to a stronger encryption algorithm) by certificate issuers, and to ensure the trust of an identity (i.e., website's domain). We found 590 (out of 45,004, 1.3%) of the religious websites that use HTTPS have a validity period between 24–28 months in the issued certificates; none of the certificate issuers of these certificates are free certificate authorities—e.g., *Sectigo Limited* (398), *GoDaddy.com, Inc.* (80), *Starfield Technologies, Inc.* (61), *DigiCert Inc* (27).

Analysis of Certificate Issuers. We observed that the top-5 certificate authorities that issue certificates for the analyzed religious websites are *Let's Encrypt* (29,357/45,004, 65.2%), *cPanel, Inc.* (4996, 11.1%), *Cloudflare, Inc.* (2945, 6.5%), *GoDaddy.com*, Inc. (2416, 5.4%), *DigiCert Inc* (1799, 4%). We also explored the country level distribution of TLS certificate issuing organizations, and found United States (42,618/45,004, 94.7%) and United Kingdom (1724, 3.8%) dominates in the distribution.

TLS Certificate Signature Analysis. We found 41,804 (out of 45,004, 92.9%) of HTTPS religious sites use RSA signature algorithms—i.e., *sha256 with RSA* (41,697), *sha384 with RSA* (106), *sha512 with RSA* (1); all RSA signature algorithms use a pubic key of at least 2048 bits. In addition, 3200 (out of 45,004, 7.1%) HTTPS religious websites use ECDSA (Elliptic Curve Digital Signature Algorithm) signature algorithm—i.e., *ecdsa with SHA256* (2966), *ecdsa with SHA384* (234). The ECDSA signature algorithm uses shorter keys for the same security level as in RSA with larger keys. Although ECDSA is a more efficient signature algorithm, recent studies found it is more vulnerable to attacks [24].

4.5 Third-Party Tracking Scripts

We found 27.9% (17,418/62,373) of religious websites had at least one known tracker on their landing pages, and a total of 359 unique known trackers. We observed popular non-commercial religious websites include commercial trackers on them—e.g., *churchofjesuschrist.org* (a top ranked religious website [39]) included third party scripts from 7 unique commercial tracking domains. The most common known commercial trackers on religious websites were *google-analytics.com* (12,653, 20.3% of websites), *googletagmanager.com* (7064,

Table 4. The top-10 known tracking cookies and their expiry periods (m = month, y = year).

Tracker	#Sites	Cookie expiry		
		1m-1y	1y-5y	> 5y
bidswitch.net	1165	1	1	–
adsrvr.org	686	–	690	–
rlcdn.com	517	4	513	–
id5-sync.com	454	390	–	–
demdex.net	201	402	–	–
statcounter.com	379	–	–	379
casalemedia.com	342	2	343	–
crwdcntrl.net	298	298	–	–
tapad.com	298	296	–	–
eyeota.net	271	–	3	–

11.3%) and *wp.com* (3713, 6%). Religious sites we analyzed, are often developed using WordPress and Squarespace website building services. The scripts included by the former are used for pixel tracking, while the latter use analytics to track users. In addition, the Facebook (*facebook.net*) social media plugin included in religious sites is used to collect information on users' browsing behaviors (e.g., websites and other apps visited), and share this information with other third parties. Furthermore, the PayPal plugin included in religious websites (for online donations) can also be used to track users.

4.6 Third-Party Tracking Cookies

We found 3569/62,373 (5.7%) websites set tracking cookies. The most number of cookies are set by *bidswitch.net* (1165/62,373, 1.9%), *adsrvr. org* (686/62,373, 1.1%) and *rlcdn.com* (514/62,373, 0.01). *Biblehub.com* and *biblegateway.com* are top ranked religious websites [39] that included cookies set by 42 and 16 tracking domains, respectively; a cookie set by *cpmstar.com* (an adware) on *biblehub.com* expires after 20 years. Cookies set by *statcounter.com* (used for web analytics) expires after 5 years; see Table 4. We also found tracking cookies set by center.io on 4 religious websites (*zionbaptistva.com, lavendervines.com, effect900.com, catholicfundraiser.net*) expire in year 9999.

5 Results: Religious Android Apps

Static Analysis Results: Tracking SDKs and Exposed Firebase Databases. With LibRadar, we found a total of 7398 tracking SDKs (203 unique) on 1454 religious Android apps. We also used LibRadar to check the usage types of these SDKs (e.g., *Google Mobile Services* is used as a development aid, *Google Analytics* is used for mobile analytics). Similar to religious websites, most tracking SDKs in apps were also from Google (1132/1454, 78%) and Facebook (205/1454, 14.1%). Note that Google tracking SDKs are also used for ad and mobile analytics. Although the collection of analytics can help provide a better user experience and improve protection (e.g., fraud detection [40]), it can also be effectively used for tracking/profiling. A notable example is the *com.prayapp* app that embedded 10 tracking SDKs (including Google and Facebook). The app collects personal information (e.g., location, app usage), and apparently, the app owners also purchase data (e.g., gender, age, ethnicity, religious affiliation) from third parties for better profiling [41]; they may also share personal information to third parties (e.g., advertisers) for commercial purposes.

We found 55 (3.8%, 1454) religious Android apps exposed their Firebase databases due to unprotected endpoints; 7 of these apps leaked sensitive information—e.g., user name, password, phone number, email, profile picture, chat details, API key, device type. However, we did not verify/use/store this info (deleted immediately after checking the data types). Notable examples: Vedic Library (*com.hinbook.library*)—an app that supports individual spiritual enhancement (100K+ installs), and Catholic Connect (*com.catholicconnect*)—a social media platform to build and collaborate between Catholic communities (10K+ installs).

Dynamic Analysis Results. Examples from what we observed from our dynamic analysis include a Christian dating chat app (*cdff.mobileapp*, 1M+ installs), that sent login information via HTTP to a domain owned by the same owner (*christiandatingforfree.com*). We also found *cdff.mobileapp* and *com.avrpt.teachingsofswamidayananda* sent device information (device ID, device model, device manufacturer, device operating system, screen resolution) over HTTP to *christiandatingforfree.com* and *avrpt.com* domains, respectively (both the apps and corresponding domains are owned by the same party). Such device data can be used to passively track users by fingerprinting their devices.

Session Replaying from Apps. We found that the UXCam session replay service collected users' location (i.e., GPS coordinates) from the *Tabella Catholic* app. Hotjar and MouseFlow collected fingerprinting information from *Muslim kids* (e.g., device model) and *Buddhist Sangam* (e.g., mouse events) apps, respectively.

Religious Apps and 3rd-Party Domains Flagged as Malicious. 29/1454 religious apps were flagged as malicious by VirusTotal: one app by 10 engines, eight apps by two engines and 20 apps flagged by one engine. *islamictech.slfgo* (50K+ installations) is flagged as malicious by 10 security engines. 8 apps included the *Android.WIN32.MobiDash.bm* [42] stealthy adware that usually displays ads when the mobile device screen is unlocked. 8 apps contained the *AdLibrary:Generisk* [43] malware that steals information (e.g., Facebook credentials). We also observed calls to two malicious 3rd-party domains by religious apps—*jainpanchang.in* and *orthodoxfacts.org* third party domains were included in *com.mosync.app_Jain_Panchang* (Jain Panchang) and *com.orthodoxfacts* (Orthodox Sayings) religious Android apps, respectively. Jain Panchang requires the *WRITE_SECURE_SETTINGS*[3] Android permission, allowing the app to read/write secure systems settings, which is not supposed to be used by third-party apps.

6   Conclusion

Online religious services raise concerns about user privacy. Information with deeply personal content shared by faith-based communities over online religious services are accessed by various third parties (via tracking scripts/cookies, session replay) that include commercial entities, governments (for surveillance purposes) [7]. As such, adherence to best practices is imperative to safeguard the privacy/security of users; developers need to be vigilant in including third party scripts/libraries in religious websites, and should do proper scanning before using such dependencies. Privacy regulations require personal data used to interact with religious websites to be protected; according to GDPR [44], personal data

---

[3] https://tinyurl.com/489ee9xu.

relating to religious beliefs are deemed sensitive. However, we observed religious online services do not fully comply with these regulations. Proliferation of privacy regulations should drive faith based organization to partner with trusted service providers that comply with industry standards/best practices. In addition, routine risk assessments, audits and inspections of the policies/procedures of religious online services should be carried out by the owners of these services.

Finally, we note that there are several privacy measurement studies [17,45–47] that looked into tracking/exposure of sensitive information from online services of different types (e.g., business, government). However, these measurements were done using different tools, environments, techniques and time intervals. Therefore, a naive comparison between the reported findings in these studies and ours is not meaningful, and we leave it as a future work to find a better comparison approach.

References

1. Campbell, H.: Introduction: The Rise of the Study of Digital Religion. Digital Religion, pp. 1–22 (2013)
2. Campbell, H.A., Altenhofen, B., Bellar, W., Cho, K.J.: There's a religious app for that! A framework for studying religious mobile applications. Mob. Media Commun. **2**(2), 154–172 (2014)
3. Pandemic Religion: Social media use during COVID-19 (2020). https://tinyurl.com/bdfbw3pk
4. Pew Research Center: Few Americans say their house of worship is open (2020). https://tinyurl.com/3ejcj7yr
5. Forbes: God is not the only one watching over your church's website (2014). https://tinyurl.com/5xx5wa5d
6. CNET: Religious apps with sinful permissions requests are more common than you think (2019). https://tinyurl.com/yckme9x3
7. Los Angeles Times: Muslims reel over a prayer app that sold user data (2020). https://tinyurl.com/4edmn96n
8. BuzzFeed News Nothing sacred: These apps reserve the right to sell your prayers (2022). https://tinyurl.com/3z6jz7wh
9. The Washington Post: Chinese state-backed hackers infiltrated vatican (2020). https://tinyurl.com/mpttxmc
10. Campbell, H.A.: Religion and the internet: a microcosm for studying internet trends and implications. New Media Soc. **15**(5), 680–694 (2013)
11. Keywords Standings Ltd.: URL Classification (2020). https://url-classification.io/
12. VirusTotal: VirusTotal (2021). https://www.virustotal.com
13. Princeton University: OpenWPM (2022). https://github.com/citp/OpenWPM
14. HTTP Toolkit: HTTP Toolkit (2022). https://httptoolkit.tech/
15. MobSF: MobSF (2022). https://tinyurl.com/mr2vwfr4
16. LiteRadar: LiteRadar (2020). https://github.com/pkumza/LiteRadar
17. Englehardt, S., Narayanan, A.: Online tracking: a 1-million-site measurement and analysis. In: ACM Conference on Computer and Communications Security (CCS 2016), Vienna, Austria (2016)
18. Samarasinghe, N., Adhikari, A., Mannan, M., Youssef, A.: Et tu, brute? Privacy analysis of government websites and mobile apps. In: TheWebConf 2022 (2022)

19. Hoy, M.G., Phelps, J.: Consumer privacy and security protection on church web sites: reasons for concern. J. Public Policy Mark. **22**(1), 58–70 (2003)
20. Binns, R., Lyngs, U., Van Kleek, M., Zhao, J., Libert, T., Shadbolt, N.: Third party tracking in the mobile ecosystem. In: ACM Conference on Web Science (WebSci 2018) (2018)
21. Nguyen, T.T., Backes, M., Marnau, N., Stock, B.: Share first, ask later (or never?)-studying violations of GDPR's explicit consent in Android apps. In: USENIX Security Symposium (USENIX Security 2021) (2021)
22. Cho, H., Ippolito, D., Yu, Y.W.: Contact tracing mobile apps for COVID-19: privacy considerations and related trade-offs. Preprint arXiv:2003.11511 (2020)
23. Felt, A.P., Barnes, R., King, A., Palmer, C., Bentzel, C., Tabriz, P.: Measuring HTTPS adoption on the web. In: USENIX Security Symposium (USENIX Security 2017) (2017)
24. Alabduljabbar, A., Ma, R., Choi, S., Jang, R., Chen, S., Mohaisen, D.: Understanding the security of free content websites by analyzing their SSL certificates: a comparative study. In: Workshop on Cybersecurity and Social Sciences (2022)
25. Google-Play-Scraper: Google-Play-Scraper (2022). https://tinyurl.com/pm75cxy2
26. LevelDB: LevelDB (2022). https://github.com/google/leveldb
27. EasyList: EasyList (2022). https://easylist.to/
28. Acar, G.: Script URL substrings used to detect the embeddings from the companies offering session replay services (2017). https://tinyurl.com/2rhnfbwz
29. Peng, P., Yang, L., Song, L., Wang, G.: Opening the blackbox of VirusTotal: analyzing online phishing scan engines. In: ACM Internet Measurement Conference (IMC 2019) (2019)
30. PyOpenSSL: PyOpenSSL (2022). https://pypi.org/project/pyOpenSSL/
31. Wapiti: Wapiti (2022). https://wapiti-scanner.github.io/
32. Google: Firebase (2021). https://firebase.google.com/
33. Mitmproxy: mitmproxy (2021). https://mitmproxy.org/
34. Google: Android Debug Bridge (ADB) (2020). https://tinyurl.com/2v2a28sc
35. Monkeyrunner: monkeyrunner (2020). https://tinyurl.com/yckz2hyb
36. PortSwigger: Burp Suite (2022). https://portswigger.net/burp
37. Retire.js: Retire.js (2022). https://retirejs.github.io/retire.js/
38. PKI Consortium: One Year Certs (2020). https://tinyurl.com/2p8y8eh4
39. Similarweb: Top Websites Ranking for Faith and Beliefs in the world. Online article (2022). https://tinyurl.com/2p9d43jk
40. OneSpan: Fraud Analytics (2021). https://tinyurl.com/muwn78j2
41. Foundation.mozilla.org: Pray.com (2022). https://tinyurl.com/2p8v5bep
42. Malwarebytes Labs: Android/Adware.MobiDash (2022). https://tinyurl.com/2p8kbcpk
43. 2-viruses.com: FlyTrap (2021). https://tinyurl.com/ma7hr3ma
44. European Commission: How is data on my religious beliefs/sexual orientation/health/political views protected (2022). https://tinyurl.com/5cj2fmpt
45. Han, C., et al.: The price is (not) right: comparing privacy in free and paid apps. Proc. Priv. Enhanc.g Techno. **2020**, 222–242 (2020)
46. Cassel, D., et al.: OmniCrawl: comprehensive measurement of web tracking with real desktop and mobile browsers. Proc. Priv. Enhancing Technol. **2022**(1), 227–252 (2022)
47. Samarasinghe, N., Mannan, M.: Towards a global perspective on web tracking. Comput. Secur. **87**, 101569 (2019)

CBT Workshop: Bitcoin, Lightning Network and Scalability

An Empirical Analysis of Running
a Bitcoin Minimal Wallet on an IoT Device

Mohsen Rahmanikivi[1]([envelope]) [iD], Cristina Pérez-Solà[1,3] [iD],
and Victor Garcia-Font[2,3] [iD]

[1] K-riptography and Information Security for Open Networks (KISON - IN3),
Universitat Oberta de Catalunya (UOC), Rambla del Poblenou, 156,
08018 Barcelona, Spain
`{mrahmanikivi,cperezsola}@uoc.edu`
[2] Universitat Rovira i Virgili (URV), Av. Països Catalans 26, 43007 Tarragona, Spain
`victor.garcia@urv.cat`
[3] CYBERCAT - Center for Cybersecurity Research of Catalonia, Barcelona, Spain
`http://www.cybercat.cat/`

Abstract. Integrating blockchain with IoT technology is a hot topic
in recent years. Some outstanding approaches propose to design new
blockchain platforms from scratch to adapt them to the special needs of
the resource-constrained devices of the IoT. On the other hand, integrating existing blockchain systems, like Bitcoin or Ethereum, would open
the door to extend and use a plethora of already successful applications
running on these systems. In this paper, we show the feasibility to interact with the Bitcoin blockchain with an IoT device. To this end, we
implement a minimal SPV wallet that we deploy on a microcontroller
unit from the STM32F4 family. Then, we empirically study the performance of this minimal wallet analyzing its key functionalities in terms of
execution time, memory usage, and network traffic. Beyond demonstrating the feasibility of integrating the most popular blockchain network
with the IoT, the results of this experiment show the most demanding
operations, which is a necessary first step to construct a wallet optimized
for the IoT.

Keywords: IoT · Blockchain · SPV wallet · Bitcoin

1 Introduction

In 2008, the author of [16], under the pseudonym, Satoshi Nakamoto, presented
Bitcoin as a peer-to-peer online payment system that works without a central
bank or administrator. Some months later, Nakamoto implemented an open-
source software version of the protocol and started running the first Bitcoin
node. Since then, thousands of users in the world have downloaded and installed
this software, creating a highly secure and decentralized payment infrastructure.

One of the most prominent innovations of Bitcoin is the blockchain, a data
structure to store the monetary transactions of the system, which is built collab-
oratively and stored in a distributed way on the network nodes. The blockchain

© The Author(s), under exclusive license to Springer Nature Switzerland AG 2023
J. Garcia-Alfaro et al. (Eds.): DPM 2022/CBT 2022, LNCS 13619, pp. 169–184, 2023.
https://doi.org/10.1007/978-3-031-25734-6_11

is considered to be immutable, secure, distributed, traceable, and scalable. Currently, there are many other proposals to build blockchain platforms beyond Bitcoin. Nonetheless, generally, they share several characteristics and have a similar architecture.

To send and receive monetary transactions in Bitcoin, users need wallet applications. These are basically used to manage keys, run cryptographic operations, and communicate with the Bitcoin network. Generally, the wallets are installed on laptop computers or mobile phone devices, and are operated by human users. However, with the advent of the Internet of Things (IoT), there is also the need to connect IoT devices to blockchain networks. These are normally computationally and memory-constrained instruments that, many times, are battery powered, and that are operated autonomously with minimal human interaction. Therefore, building wallet applications for the IoT has very different requirements than conventional wallets and, nowadays, represents a challenge.

Previous research works have focused on the design of new cryptocurrencies specially adapted to IoT requirements. However, in this paper, we question the need for such designs by evaluating to what extent IoT devices are able to interact with conventional public blockchains. Specifically, our goal is to design and implement a light minimal wallet for Bitcoin. The contributions of this paper are thus 1) to demonstrate that it is indeed possible to run a minimal Bitcoin wallet on a resource-constrained device, and 2) to measure the resources needed to perform different wallet functionalities. Additionally, our paper contributes to the discussion of whether special IoT specific blockchains are needed in order to be able to successfully use blockchain from IoT devices.

The rest of the paper is organized as follows. Section 2 presents the state of the art. Section 3 describes the operations and functionalities of a minimal wallet. Section 4 shows the performed experiment, describing the used board, the computed metrics, and discussing the results. Finally, Sect. 5 concludes the paper.

2   State of the Art

The Bitcoin network is made of nodes running a software called the Bitcoin client. Depending on the functionality that a node wants to carry on the network, the client can be deployed implementing some of the following four basic functions: wallet, miner, full blockchain database, and network routing [1, Chapter 8]. In this way, nodes are generally classified as full nodes, miners, or light nodes. Full nodes are responsible for downloading, verifying, and storing all blockchain blocks, from the genesis to the current block. They can also have wallet and mining functions, and can assist other nodes in updating their version of the blockchain, resending blocks, transactions, etc. Miners are responsible for receiving and verifying user transactions, and generating new blocks [1, Chapter 10]. Finally, lightweight nodes are designed to be installed on devices constrained in computational resources or storage capacity (e.g. mobile phones). The Simplified Payment Verification (SPV) protocol [1, Chapter 8] can be used by lightweight

clients to obtain and validate transactions of their interest. Instead of downloading all the data of all the blocks of the chain, SPV nodes only download the block
headers. A block header is a data structure that contains the basic information
to identify the block and guarantee the integrity of its transactions. Furthermore, each block header also includes the hash of the previously published block
header, creating, in this way, the chain of blocks. Since SPV nodes do not have
all the data of the system to validate transactions, they require the assistance
of, at least, one full node.

In this paper, we focus on the wallet component. A wallet [1, Chapter 5] is a
software that stores seeds (or the keys derived from seeds), provides key management, creates transactions, and verifies selected transactions. Also, a wallet can
gather the history of transactions related to a desired key. Since many wallets
are installed in mobile phones with a low storage and computational capacity,
they normally run the SPV process mentioned above and require the assistance
of another node.

Nevertheless, although mobile phone wallets are optimized to run in constrained environments, they are still not adequate for the IoT, since IoT requirements are much more strict than those for mobile devices. On the one hand, many
IoT elements are built just using microcontrollers that cannot run an operating
system, or computationally-reduced microprocessors running specially designed
operating systems including fewer functionalities, such as RTOS [26] or Con-
tiki [5]. On the other hand, the computational and storage restrictions of IoT
elements, and the fact that they are battery-powered in many cases, require
a higher degree of optimization for their applications. There are some works
that study, in a general way, the challenges and opportunities of implementing
blockchain in the IoT scenario, like [24]. Other works focus on creating IoT specific blockchain products, specially adapted to the needs of these systems. A
relevant project in this regard is IOTA [18].

However, the goal of this paper is to evaluate if IoT devices can interact
with conventional blockchain systems, like Bitcoin. Bitcoin is nowadays the most
important cryptocurrency by market capitalization [3], and implementing a minimal wallet compatible with IoT devices can enable many new applications. Some
research in this field has focused on creating bitcoin payment channels with IoT
elements [8,12]. Also, other researchers have studied the execution of Ethereum
transactions in IoT devices [9]. However, as far as we know, there are no papers
exhaustively evaluating the functionalities of a bitcoin wallet in an IoT device,
nor proposing the minimal wallet components for this type of environment.

We define the minimal wallet functionalities based on existing works mentioned above and we explain and clarify them in the next section.

3   A Minimal Bitcoin Wallet

A wallet is a software component used by the Bitcoin users to interact with the
Bitcoin network. Well-known Bitcoin wallets are Electrum, Exodus, or Trezor,
which allow users to manage keys, and create and receive several types of transactions. This research work has the goal to enable a minimal wallet that allows

IoT elements to interact with the Bitcoin network. For this, this minimal wallet has to connect to the network and be able to send, receive and validate basic transactions. Because of the limited resources IoT elements have, our design will be focused on implementing a lightweight wallet that does not store the full blockchain and validates transactions using the Simplified Payment Verification (SPV) protocol [15]. Moreover, since Pay-to-Public-Key-Hash (P2PKH) [1, Chapter 8] outputs are currently the most common UTXO type in Bitcoin [25], we focus our work on this kind of output. To enable these, the minimal wallet has to offer a set of functionalities (described in Sect. 3.1) and implement several operations, which we group into the following categories: K (key management), D (data structures), S (sign and verify), B (blockchain), and N (networking).

The key management category groups operations related to cryptographic keys, that is, the generation of the random seed value, the encoding of this seed for backup, the derivation of private and public keys from the seed, and the computation of addresses. Our minimal wallet follows BIPs 32 and 39 to generate keys and their backup. Bitcoin improvement proposal 39 (BIP39) [17] introduced the standard of mnemonic words which converts the seed into a series of 12 to 24 words to make a better way to store and back up the seed. Likewise, BIP32 [27] was proposed to avoid the creation of nondeterministic keys, a situation where keys are unrelated and nonrecoverable because each key is independently derived from a seed. Instead, BIP32 introduced hierarchical deterministic (HD) wallets, where keys are generated following a tree-based process. In this process, the seed is used to derive the root key of the tree. The root key can derive several child keys, each child can derive a series of grandchild keys, and so on.

The necessary sub-operations to fulfill key management following BIP39 and BIP32 are: K1 (create mnemonic words from random data), K2 (generate root private key from mnemonic words), K3 (derive child private key from root private key), K4 (generate child public key from child private key), K5 (generate address from child public key), and K6 (verify transaction belongs to the wallet).

The operations related to Data structures (D) are responsible for decoding received transactions to extract their basic components (e.g. inputs, outputs, etc.) and, also, preparing and encoding new transactions. This includes two sub-operations: D1 (encode transaction including prepare inputs, outputs, and transactions), and D2 (decode transaction).

The operations related to Signatures (S) employ the keys (generated by the Key management operations) to perform or verify the digital signature of a transaction (prepared by the Data structures operations). This includes two sub-operations: S1 (sign a transaction), and S2 (verify the signature of a transaction).

When receiving a transaction, the minimal wallet is responsible for verifying not only the signature but also the correct inclusion of the transaction in the blockchain. SPV clients validate transaction inclusion by requesting a Merkle proof from a full node. This Merkle proof allows the client to verify that a transaction is indeed included in a block using just the block header. Then, SPV clients also validate that the block header belongs to the main chain, by checking the previous hash pointers also found in the header. We have grouped these operations under the Blockchain (B) category. This includes two sub-operations: B1 (validate headers), and B2 (validate Merkle proof).

The operations related to Networking (N) include the following four sub-operations: N1 (download headers), N2 (send the transaction to the network), N3 (get transaction), and N4 (get Merkle proof).

3.1   Minimal Wallet Functionalities

With the operations from the previous section, a minimal wallet should perform the following functionalities shown in Fig. 1:

Bootstrap is a preprocessing functionality, performed once in the lifetime of the system, responsible for generating the necessary data required to perform other functionalities. During the Bootstrap, the wallet generates the BIP32 root private key and prepares it for backup following the BIP39 encoding.

Synchronization is another preprocessing functionality, performed in every startup of the system, responsible for updating the block header list with the current state of the blockchain. Therefore, to synchronize, the wallet downloads and validates the headers since the last header stored locally to the last header included in the blockchain.

Send is a functionality that transmits data (i.e. a transaction) to the blockchain. In a typical bitcoin payment, the UTXO(s) that the sender spends, generally, contains more BTC than the amount that he or she wants to pay. Thus, the sender creates what is known as the change address to send the difference between the intended value to transact and the actual value of the used outputs. For this, the wallet derives two keys (one for the change address, and another belonging to the output from which the funds are going to be redeemed). The latter is used for signing the transaction. When the keys are ready, the wallet creates a raw transaction, then signs it, and, finally, sends it to the network.

Receive obtains data from the blockchain to verify that received transactions from one address are valid. Here, the wallet sends a request to another node in the network specifying an address. The node responds by sending all the transactions that have as the recipient the given address[1]. Then, the wallet decodes each transaction and verifies: (1) if the transaction belongs to the wallet's keys, (2) the transaction signature, and (3) if the transaction belongs to the blockchain, validating the Merkle proof of the transaction in the block header where the transaction claims to be included.

3.2   Cryptographic and Codification Functions

The functionalities explained in the Sect. 3.1 require using some cryptographic and conversion functions. The most important of these functions are: hash functions (SHA256 and Double SHA256 [6], HMAC-SHA512 [11], RIPEMD160 [4]),

---

[1] For privacy reasons, the SPV client does not literally include its addresses on the request: it creates a Bloom filter that matches transactions of its interest, and sends the filter to the full node.

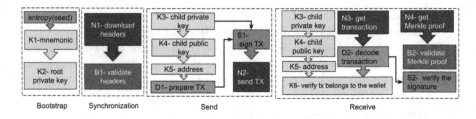

Fig. 1. The wallet functionalities.

Public-key cryptography (Elliptic curve version secp256k1 [13], and conversion (Base58 [21], Base16 [10]).

Table 1 describes the functions involved in each of the wallet functionalities. As the table shows, K1 uses SHA256 and Base10 to generate mnemonic words from random data (entropy). K2 generates the root private key executing the HMAC-SHA512 hash function 2048 times. K3 derives a child private key, using elliptic curve multiplication and HMAC-SHA512 in D iterations, where D is the generation depth (D = 1 for CHILD, D = 2 for a child(CHILD), D = 3 child(child(CHILD))), and so on). When the child private key is ready, K4 employs elliptic curve multiplication to make the child public key. Finally, K5 generates a legacy address (based on the P2PKH method) by executing HASH160, SHA256, and Base58. K6 compares the public key of the transaction with the list of the wallet keys, to check whether a transaction is paying to the wallet.

Data management operations do not require any cryptographic operations: D1 arranges and serializes data to prepare the transaction, and D2 parses the transaction to its components.

Regarding signature related operations, both S1 and S2 need to compute the hash of the transaction. This hash is used by S1 to compute the ECDSA signature and by S2 to verify that signature.

B1 validates the blockchain headers by computing its hash and comparing it with the previous block hash pointer in the next block. B2 checks the inclusion of the transaction in a confirmed block by validating a Merkle proof. This implies performing DoubleSHA256 N times, where N is log2 of the number of transactions in the block [1, Chapter 9].

4   Evaluation

In this work, we have implemented a minimal wallet, as described in the previous sections, for a basic IoT device to empirically demonstrate the feasibility of interacting with the Bitcoin network with this type of equipment and, also, to evaluate the cost of executing the basic functionalities and operations. A thorough analysis of this will allow us to optimize a minimal IoT Bitcoin wallet. Section 4.1 specifies the hardware used in this experiment, Sect. 4.2 describes the evaluation metrics, and Sect. 4.3 presents and discusses the results.

Table 1. Cryptographic functions required for each operation of the minimal wallet.

Op	Description	Functions	Conversion
K1	Mnemonic words	$1 \times SHA256$(CheckSum)	$1 \times Base10$
K2	Generate root private key	$2048 \times HMACSHA512$	$1 \times (Base16)^*$
K3	Derive child private key	$D \times EllipticCurveMultiplication$ $D \times HMACSHA512$	$1 \times (Base16)$
K4	Derive child public key	$1 \times EllipticCurveMultiplication$	$1 \times (Base16)$
K5	Generate address for P2PKH	$1 \times HASH160$ $1 \times SHA256$(CheckSum)	$1 \times Base58$
K6	Verify the transaction belongs to the wallet keys	–	–
D1	Prepare Transaction	–	–
D2	Decode transaction	–	–
S1	Sign The Transaction (Per P2PKH input)	$1 \times ECDSAsignature$ $1 \times DoubleSHA256$	–
S2	Verify the signature (Per P2PKH input)	$1 \times ECDSAverification$ $1 \times DoubleSHA256$	–
B1	Validate headers	$NumberOfHeaders \times$ DoubleSHA256	–
B2	Verify inclusion of transaction in the block	$N \times$ DoubleSHA256	–

* The base16 conversion is optional to make the result human-readable.

4.1 Hardware Description

Nowadays, IoT manufacturers produce a wide diversity of IoT devices according to market needs. This diversity materializes in significant differences in their resources and characteristics, such as in their processor, RAM, flash memory, sensors, connectivity, or power consumption.

The experimental part of this paper is made using an STM32f446RE microcontroller unit (MCU) with a 180 MHz ARM Cortex M4 CPU, 512 Kbytes of flash memory, and 128 Kbytes of SRAM. This MCU belongs to the STM32F4 series. Figure 2 shows the resources (CPU speed and RAM memory) available in different archetypal IoT devices, highlighting the board used for the experiments of this paper. Although this board can be considered a high-performance IoT device, as the figure shows, it is quite representative in the IoT space.

We use the ESP8266 (ESP-01) [14] wifi module for network communications. This module is able to operate in two different modes: with the AT command interface or using a native software development kit (SDK). On the one hand, the AT command interface allows an easy integration, but it is not optimized for speed nor efficiency, and has some limitations. On the other hand, the SDK includes driver libraries that can be used to implement embedded wifi solutions, which are more efficient than the AT command interface. As a first step, in this study, we used the AT command interface.

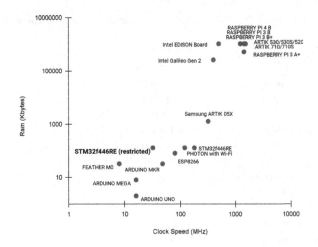

Fig. 2. Comparison of different IoT development boards [19].

4.2   Evaluation Metrics

This section describes the metrics used to evaluate the performance of the different functionalities and operations of a minimal wallet running on the IoT device detailed above. We focus on three different aspects: (1) execution time, (2) memory usage, and (3) network traffic.

Regarding (1) execution time, three considerations have to be made. First, although the CPU of the MCU is able to run at 180 MHz, the results included in this paper are computed with the speed restricted to 32 MHz. We conducted experiments with other clock speeds resulting in execution times proportional to the clock speed. We only show the results at 32 MHz, since they are more representative of a resource-constrained IoT scenario. Second, we measure time indirectly, through counting CPU cycles (and dividing them by the clock speed, $32 * 10^6$). Third, all measurements are made in bare metal mode (i.e. no operating system was loaded in the board).

Regarding (2), we measure the amount of used memory (both for SRAM and flash memory). To implement our code, we use the STM32CubeIDE 1.8.0 [22] integrated development environment (IDE) with its default configuration: arm-none-eabi-gcc [7] as the compiler for C language and arm-none-eabi-g++ [7] for C++ language. Additionally, we use the application programming interface (API) of the uBitcoin library [20], which is based on the Trezor wallet library [23].

Regarding (3), we measure the amount of sent and received data capturing the network traffic with Wireshark [2] in an external computer, running the Bitcoin Core to answer the requests of the minimal wallet in the microcontroller.

It is worth noting that some of the measurements are strongly dependent on many parameters, some of them influenced by external factors. For instance, synchronization time clearly depends on the time elapsed since the last synchronization and the network congestion, or the amount of traffic sent over the network depends on the transaction size (affected by the number of inputs, outputs, and the transaction type). To make the results more significant, we repeated each measurement ten times. In the next section, we show the average of these measures. The standard deviation was very low for all the measures, so we decided to not show it in the figures for the sake of readability. Moreover, we chose to depict the results for what can be considered the most common situations and discuss the worst case scenarios. With this regard, we used transactions with one input and two P2PKH outputs (one for the recipient and one for the change). As we have already mentioned, P2PKH outputs are nowadays the most common UTXO type in Bitcoin [25]. On the other hand, synchronization times are shown for clients who are 100 blocks away from the head of the blockchain (around 16 h without synchronization). Finally, transaction inclusion proofs are computed for blocks with 2000 transactions (which corresponds to the mean number of transactions per block in the last 200000 blocks).

4.3 Results

This section presents and discusses the measurements taken on execution time, memory usage, and network traffic, using the minimal wallet operations running in the hardware described in Sect. 4.1.

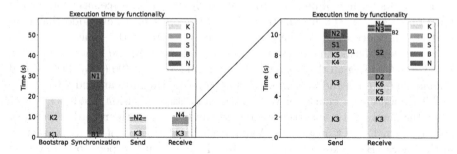

Fig. 3. Average time of 10 executions for each functionality, broken down by operations.

Execution Time. Figure 3 illustrates the execution time (in seconds) of each of the functionalities, broken down by individual operations. Downloading block headers for synchronizing the node (N1) is clearly the most time consuming operation. However, this result has to be taken with caution, since our implementation was not optimized for network transmissions: as we explained in Sect. 4.1, we use the AT command interface of the wifi module to send and receive data, and this interface is intended for rapid integration but it is not optimized for speed transmission.

Focusing on execution time, the most time consuming operation is definitely generating the master key from the entropy (K2), which requires 2048 iterations of HMAC-SHA512 and takes up to 19 s on average. Nonetheless, this operation is just required for bootstrapping the wallet (either when creating a new wallet or when recovering one from backup). In contrast, everyday functionalities such as sending and receiving transactions need around 11 s. Derivation of the child private key (K3) and signature validation (S2) are the most expensive cryptographic operations within these functionalities.

Taking into account the time spent deriving child private keys (K3), we could speed up the send and receive functionalities by precomputing the keys beforehand. The resulting keys could be stored and recovered whenever the wallet needs them. Additionally, since the receive functionality only needs to compute a receiving address, other key derivation paths could be used with the goal to avoid the computation of the child private key (K3)[2]. Likewise, the K3 operation executed in the send functionality to compute the change address could also be avoided (so just one execution of K3 would be needed). We leave the evaluation of these alternative paths as future work.

As we explained in Sect. 4, the results depicted in the figures correspond to common scenarios (i.e. synchronization is evaluated by a node which is 100 blocks behind, transactions have one input and two P2PKH outputs, and transaction inclusion proofs are computed for 2000 transaction blocks).

Furthermore, it is important to analyze the worst case scenario for certain functionalities. For synchronization, this corresponds to a new node that connects to the network and, therefore, it is only aware of the genesis block. In this case, considering the average results of synchronizing 100 headers shown in Fig. 3, downloading all the headers (N1) up until block 737700 (May 2022) would take up to 6.8 days and validating them (B1) would require around 2.6 h.

The worst case scenario for validating transaction inclusion in a block occurs when the number of transactions is maximum. Currently, the record is for block 367853, with 12239 transactions. Validating the Merkle proof for a transaction in this block (B2) takes 83 ms (just a 10% increase with respect to the average block).

Memory Usage. The board used for our experiments has three different types of memory: flash, SRAM, and micro SD memories. The first two are embedded in the board, and we have added an external micro SD extension in order to store user data. To understand memory usage results, it is important to note that the application code, constants, and initialized global variables are stored in the flash memory, whereas uninitialized global variables, addresses of initialized global variables, local variables (stack) and dynamic ones (heap) are stored in SRAM. User data such as keys, block headers, transactions and logs are stored in micro SD.

---

[2] BIP32 [27] Hierarchical Deterministic Wallets also allow to derive public child keys from their public parents directly, without first having to compute child private keys.

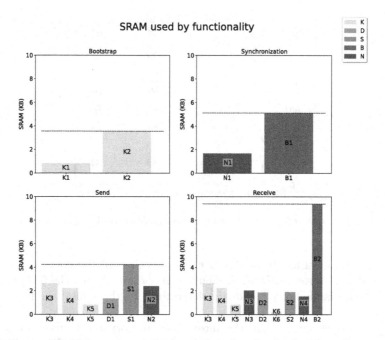

Fig. 4. Average SRAM memory used for each functionality, broken down by operations.

Figure 4 illustrates the SRAM used (in KB) for each of the functionalities, broken down by individual operations. Because operations are executed sequentially and they release their SRAM as soon as they finish, the SRAM used by each functionality is determined by the most SRAM-consuming operation in that functionality.

The most SRAM-consuming operation is validating Merkle proofs (B2) in the receive functionality, which needs 9.5 KB (this almost doubles the requirements of the next most demanding operation, header validation, B1). Therefore, all functionalities can be executed with less than 10 KB of RAM, with receive being the most demanding one. However, two considerations have to be taken into account.

First, it is worth mentioning the block headers that are downloaded (N1) and validated (B1) during synchronization are stored in a MicroSD memory. Therefore, they are not all kept in SRAM at the same time. This is the reason why synchronization does not have higher SRAM usage.

Second, the SRAM usage of the synchronization and receive functionalities is dominated by blockchain validation operations (validate headers, B1, and validate Merkle proof, B2, respectively). Meanwhile, cryptographic operations define the SRAM requirements for the bootstrap and send functionalities (generate root private key, K2, and signature generation, S1, respectively).

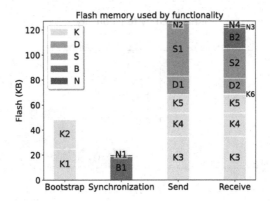

Fig. 5. Average flash memory used for each functionality, broken down by operations.

Flash memory usage is shown in Fig. 5. Because all the code to execute a functionality is stored in the flash memory at the same time, the flash memory used by each functionality is mostly[3] determined by the sum of the needs of its operations.

The two operations using the most flash memory are transaction signing (S1) and child private key derivation (K3), which need 42.5 KB and 35 KB of flash memory, respectively. Individual functionalities can be executed using less than 127 KB of flash memory. We have found significant differences between functionalities with respect to flash memory requirements. Both send and receive functionalities require more than 123 KB of flash memory, whereas bootstrap and synchronization require just 48 KB and 20 KB, respectively.

However, as explained before, key derivation operations (K3 and K4) could be precomputed beforehand, thus reducing flash memory usage for both the send and receive functionality.

Network Traffic. Figures 6 and 7 illustrate the amount of data transmitted through the network (in KB) for each of the functionalities. Figure 6 differentiates network traffic by direction: struck bars indicate sent data, whereas plain bars represent received data. Figure 7 displays the overhead introduced by sending data through the network: struck bars indicate the size of the data encoded for network transmission, whereas plain bars represent the amount of data transmitted through the network (i.e. taking into account datagram headers, json-RPC parameters, etc.).

To understand both direction and overhead in networking, it is important to note that although our minimal wallet implements the SPV protocol to validate transaction inclusion in blocks, it is connecting to a Bitcoin core RPC client to obtain blockchain data. This introduces some additional overhead in the communication, because of the json encoding of data. Moreover, it is also

---

[3] Although there is some code overlap between operations, our experimental data does not show significant differences.

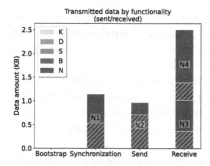

Fig. 6. Average data transmitted for each functionality, broken down by operations. Struck bars represent data sent.

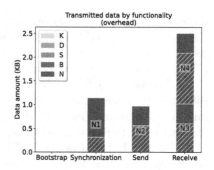

Fig. 7. Average data transmitted for each functionality, broken down by operations. Struck bars represent network overhead.

the reason why data is both sent and received for functionalities that may seem unidirectional.

In these plots, Synchronization is evaluated on just one single block (in contrast with the previous sections, where 100 blocks were taken into account). Within this context, synchronizing and sending a transaction requires around 1 KB of data transfer, and receiving it requires almost 2.5 KB. Reception indeed needs more transferred data, because both the transaction (N3) and its proof of inclusion into a block (N4) have to be transmitted. Moreover, note that the wallet has to be synchronized with the network in order to be able to validate new received transactions. On the contrary, a transaction can be sent with an outdated wallet (as long as it is aware of its current UTXOs).

We can appreciate that a considerable amount of data is sent over the network, even for functionalities that are intended to obtain data (i.e. synchronization obtains headers and receives a transaction and its proof of inclusion). The reason for this behavior is that requests for this data have to be sent, and since the amount of data received for each request is small, they represent a considerable proportion of the total traffic. On the other hand, a request to send a transaction to the network (N2) is answered with the hash of the transaction, so inbound traffic is also generated when sending.

The synchronization functionality is the one with the most overhead (both in proportion to the sent data and in absolute values). The reason is that two RPC calls are used to obtain each block header. On the contrary, all other operations require a single RPC call.

5   Conclusion

The integration of blockchain with IoT scenarios may open the door to the development of new applications and add security properties to existing solutions.

However, since IoT devices are usually resource-constrained, standard implementations of blockchain clients are not appropriate for these devices. To unveil the potential of blockchain for IoT, it is thus critical to evaluate to what extent IoT devices are able to run basic wallet functionalities.

In this paper, we have shown that it is indeed possible to execute a minimal Bitcoin SPV wallet in a resource-constrained device. Moreover, we have measured execution time, memory usage, and network data transmission of each of the wallet functionalities, and thus identified the most costly operations.

Using an STM32F4 family MCU without optimizations, we are able to fully synchronize a new SPV wallet in less than a week, and we are able to send and receive transactions in less than 11 s. Regarding the suitability of the STM32F4 to run our minimal Bitcoin wallet, SRAM requirements are more than fulfilled (functionalities can be executed using at most 10 KB from the 128 KB of SRAM available). On the contrary, flash memory management requires a thorough analysis and a better optimisation, since we should take into account that the wallet will not be the only executed application in a real case. In our experiment, individual functionalities can be executed using 127 KB of flash memory, so the whole wallet (without reusing code between functionalities) would need 319KB of the 512 KB of flash memory available on the board.

Taking into account all the metrics evaluated, we have not observed any single operation consuming significant amounts of resources for all the metrics. However, signature creation (S1), and derive child private key (K3) seem to have a significant impact in at least two of the three evaluated metrics.

Therefore, a first step to reduce the minimal resources needed to run a wallet should be to optimize these operations. The time needed to download headers (N1) is also notably high in our implementation, but we attribute it to the usage of the AT interface. Computing the root private key (K2) is also very costly. However, this operation is only executed once in the lifetime of the wallet and, therefore, execution time does not seem critical. In environments with really low memory capabilities, an alternative would be to precompute and load this key on the devices.

Yet our work is still a first step towards evaluating suitability of IoT devices to run wallet functions. On the one hand, our code and board configurations are still not fully optimized. On the other hand, IoT devices have, in many cases, more constrained capabilities than the board used in our experiments. Therefore, our most immediate future work is to optimize the code and evaluate its performance considering the heterogeneity of the IoT scenario, and empirically testing it on paradigmatic IoT devices with different capabilities, using different communication protocols (e.g. Zigbee, LoRa), boards, network configurations (e.g. multihop networks), security requirements, etc. Additionally, a natural extension of this work is to include layer 2 compatibility to our wallet and to extend it to other public blockchains such as Ethereum. Future work will also describe specific IoT scenarios, analyse their needs with respect to the use of blockchain systems, and study the feasibility of their interaction with established permissionless blockchains.

Acknowledgements. The authors acknowledge the funding of the Spanish Government through grants RTI2018-095094-B-C22 "CONSENT" and PID2021-125962OB-C31 "SECURING".

References

1. Antonopoulos, A.M.: Mastering Bitcoin: Programming the Open Blockchain, 2nd edn. O'Reilly Media, Inc. (2017). https://github.com/bitcoinbook/bitcoinbook. Accessed 17 June 2022
2. Bullock, J.: Introducing wireshark. In: Wireshark® for Security Professionals, pp. 1–18. Wiley (2017). https://doi.org/10.1002/9781119183457.ch1
3. Cryptocurrency market capitalizations. https://coinmarketcap.com/. Accessed 17 June 2022
4. Dobbertin, H., Bosselaers, A., Preneel, B.: RIPEMD-160: a strengthened version of RIPEMD. In: Gollmann, D. (ed.) FSE 1996. LNCS, vol. 1039, pp. 71–82. Springer, Heidelberg (1996). https://doi.org/10.1007/3-540-60865-6_44
5. Dunkels, A., Gronvall, B., Voigt, T.: Contiki-a lightweight and flexible operating system for tiny networked sensors. In: 29th Annual IEEE International Conference on Local Computer Networks, pp. 455–462. IEEE (2004)
6. Eastlake, D., Hansen, T.: US secure hash algorithms (SHA and HMAC-SHA). Technical report (2006). https://doi.org/10.17487/rfc4634
7. Gnu toolchain. https://developer.arm.com/downloads/-/gnu-rm. Accessed 17 June 2022
8. Hannon, C., Jin, D.: Bitcoin payment-channels for resource limited IoT devices. In: Proceedings of the International Conference on Omni-Layer Intelligent Systems, pp. 50–57 (2019)
9. Huh, S., Cho, S., Kim, S.: Managing IoT devices using blockchain platform. In: 19th International Conference on Advanced Communication Technology (ICACT), pp. 464–467. IEEE (2017)
10. Josefsson, S.: RFC3548: the base16, base32, and base64 data encodings. Technical report (2006). https://doi.org/10.17487/rfc4648
11. Krawczyk, H., Bellare, M., Canetti, R.: HMAC: keyed-hashing for message authentication. Technical report (1997). https://doi.org/10.17487/RFC2104
12. Kurt, A., Mercana, S., Erdin, E., Akkaya, K.: Enabling micro-payments on IoT devices using bitcoin lightning network. In: 2021 IEEE International Conference on Blockchain and Cryptocurrency (ICBC), pp. 1–3. IEEE (2021)
13. Menezes, A.J.: Elliptic Curve Public Key Cryptosystems, vol. 234. Springer, Heidelberg (1993). https://doi.org/10.1007/978-1-4615-3198-2
14. Mesquita, J., Guimarães, D., Pereira, C., Santos, F., Almeida, L.: Assessing the ESP8266 WiFi module for the internet of things. In: 2018 IEEE 23rd International Conference on Emerging Technologies and Factory Automation (ETFA), vol. 1, pp. 784–791. IEEE (2018)
15. Mike, H., Corallo, M.: BIP37: connection bloom filtering (2012). https://github.com/bitcoin/bips/blob/master/bip-0037.mediawiki. Accessed 17 June 2022
16. Nakamoto, S.: Bitcoin: a peer-to-peer electronic cash system. Decent. Bus. Rev. (2008)
17. Palatinus, M., Rusnak, P., Voisine, A., Bowe, S.: BIP39: mnemonic code for generating deterministic keys (2013). https://github.com/bitcoin/bips/blob/master/bip-0039.mediawiki. Accessed 17 June 2022

18. Silvano, W.F., Marcelino, R.: Iota tangle: a cryptocurrency to communicate internet-of-things data. Futur. Gener. Comput. Syst. **112**, 307–319 (2020)
19. Singh, D., Sandhu, A., Sharma Thakur, A., Priyank, N.: An overview of IoT hardware development platforms. Int. J. Emerg. Technol. **11**, 155–163 (2020)
20. Snigirev, S.: Micro-bitcoin. https://github.com/micro-bitcoin/uBitcoin. Accessed 17 June 2022
21. Sporny, M.: The base58 encoding scheme. https://tools.ietf.org/id/draft-msporny-base58-01.html. Accessed 17 June 2022
22. Stm32cubeide.   https://www.st.com/en/development-tools/stm32cubeide.html. Accessed 17 June 2022
23. Cryptocurrency wallet. https://github.com/trezor/trezor-wallet. Accessed 17 June 2022
24. Tseng, L., Yao, X., Otoum, S., Aloqaily, M., Jararweh, Y.: Blockchain-based database in an IoT environment: challenges, opportunities, and analysis. Clust. Comput. **23**(3), 2151–2165 (2020)
25. UTXO set repartition by output. https://txstats.com/dashboard/db/utxo-set-repartition-by-output-type. Accessed 06 June 2022
26. Walls, C.: RTOS services and facilities. In: Embedded RTOS Design, pp. 23–36. Elsevier (2021). https://doi.org/10.1016/b978-0-12-822851-7.00003-5
27. Wuille, P.: BIP32: hierarchical deterministic wallets (2012). https://github.com/bitcoin/bips/blob/master/bip-0032.mediawiki. Accessed 17 June 2022

The Ticket Price Matters in Sharding Blockchain

Geunwoo Kim[1]([✉]), Michael Franz[1], and Jong Kim[2]

[1] University of California, Irvine, USA
posgnu@gmail.com, franz@uci.edu
[2] Pohang University of Science and Technology, Pohang, South Korea
jkim@postech.ac.kr

Abstract. Sharding technology has been recognized to be a promising solution for blockchain scalability problems in recent years. For safety guarantees in each shard, mainly to prevent the single-shard takeover attack, sharding requires an identity establishment protocol in which participants have to pay a certain amount of resources (i.e., ticket price) to get a node and participate in the network. However, state-of-the-art sharding protocols overlook a non-democratic state of the real-world where every participant has a different amount of resources, termed a non-democratic environment. This oversight raises combined problems of security and scalability due to the design of the identity establishment protocol.

In this paper, we examine the effects of the non-democracy of blockchain networks in terms of the security and scalability of blockchain sharding and suggest formulae to quantitatively analyze the trade-off between security and scalability. Moreover, we conduct a numerical analysis by capturing four real-world resource distributions from renowned permissionless cryptocurrency networks. We re-evaluate the well-known sharding protocols through this numerical analysis and present the changed fault tolerance bounds and damage to scalability. The results show that the ticket price plays a leading role in tuning the effect of non-democracy. The main contribution of this paper is the proposal of new metrics for accessing the degree of security and scalability with regard to the ticket price in the identity establishment phase. Our discussion suggests further research on a more delicate ticket price control algorithm when designing a new sharding model for blockchain.

Keywords: Blockchain sharding · Scalability · Security

1 Introduction

A new kind of distributed system using blockchain has drawn tremendous attention in recent years from researchers as it has a huge success in cryptocurrency. Its decentralized but byzantine-resistant features enable it also to be adopted in various industrial use cases [26]. However, due to its limited performance

© The Author(s), under exclusive license to Springer Nature Switzerland AG 2023
J. Garcia-Alfaro et al. (Eds.): DPM 2022/CBT 2022, LNCS 13619, pp. 185–202, 2023.
https://doi.org/10.1007/978-3-031-25734-6_12

in terms of transactions per second (*e.g.*, 7 tx/s for Bitcoin [24] and 15 tx/s for Ethereum [5]), blockchain has a long way to go before it can be applied in practical usage for the public, considering that Visa supports 1,700 tx/s. To overcome this problem, sharding of blockchain is proposed for achieving horizontal scalability, *i.e.*, it can increase its performance in proportion to the number of participants. In the traditional blockchain, only a single network processes the entire transactions; thus, as the size of the network increases, the communication cost between validators and storage/computation overhead increase accordingly. On the contrary, sharding streamlines the transaction processing by splitting the network into a few small pieces of shard, and each shard processes the load in parallel. This allows participants to process and store only a part of the whole blockchain. Sharding is one good solution for scalability; however, it requires a strong theoretical foundation for dealing with the trade-off between security and scalability [12]. One of our major goals is to replenish the security research of sharding blockchain to better understand the trade-off between security and scalability.

Sharding is applied to permissionless and permissioned blockchains. We focus on applying sharding to the permissionless blockchain, which is more generally applicable and apt in terms of decentralization. Specifically, we explore problems that arise when participants establish their identities to get involved in the consensus of sharding blockchain. The recent research on sharding models [12,30] lacks a detailed study on this identity establishment process, which is vital for security. We, thus, argue that this paper is the first attempt to analyze the identity establishment protocol of sharding blockchain.

In the traditional blockchain, a single node can run with the participant's full resources (*e.g.*, computing power or stake). However, sharding blockchain requires participants to split their total resources and run with multiple nodes, each with a unit amount of resource, because it has to manage the safety of multiple shards independently. Unless every node has the same amount of voting power proportional to its resources, a single powerful participant can easily dominate one of the shards and surpass the intra-shard fault tolerance bound. This is the so-called single-shard takeover attack [2]. Most recent sharding blockchains [13,18,21,28,31] enforce that each node has a unit amount of resource to prevent this attack. The unit amount of resource is denoted as *ticket price* and every recent sharding blockchain model requires the *ticket price* for their identity establishment protocol except for a few variants which are not in the range of our discussion. We elaborate this in Sect. 2. Every participant pays for the tickets as much as its budget affords to maximize its incentive since the amount of incentive is proportional to what extent a validator contributes to the consensus. As a result, the total resource of each participant is fragmented, leaving some amount as a remainder which becomes redundant. We call the resources left after paying for the maximum number of tickets as *waste resource*, and we denote this phenomenon as *resource quantization*.

Under *resource quantization*, we found that the *ticket price* is instrumental in coordinating the trade-off between security and scalability. In sharding blockchain, participants who have bigger budgets run more nodes, and every

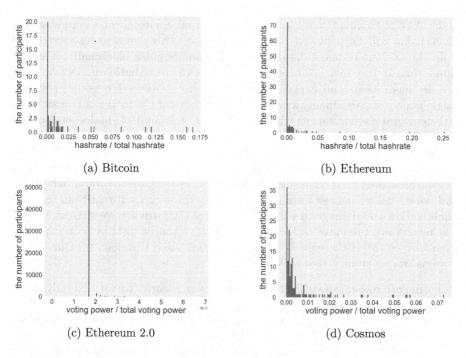

Fig. 1. Resource distributions of a few renowned blockchain networks. They are approximated by averaging the data collected during the period from Sep 04, 2021 to Dec 04, 2021.

participant will have a different amount of resources left in their wallets. Considering that nodes are randomly spread over shards, the participant having more than some amount of resources is most likely to have at least one node in each shard. This means that the participant might participate in every intra-shard consensus, the opposite of what the sharding technology intended. For this reason, the *ticket price* must be higher than some point so that not many participants in the network have nodes in too many shards. On the other hand, the maximum possible amount of waste resources increases as the *ticket price* increases since the waste resource of each participant is more than zero and less than the *ticket price* if it exists. This is problematic when adversaries collude so that only honest participants have the waste resource (*i.e.*, be quantized) and its sum is huge. At worst, a pool of honest validators has so many waste resources that adversaries can conquer the network with fewer resources than the fault tolerance bound that the network guarantees. This is feasible enough when considering that the mining pools commonly possess more than 15% of the total resource of the network and collaborate themselves [10]. Therefore, the *ticket price* also should not be too high.

However, most state-of-the-art sharding models assume a democratic environment and ignore the above mentioned problem. In the democratic environment, every participant has the same amount of resources and runs a single node. As our common sense indicates, the actual environment where sharding blockchains will be deployed is not democratic. This can also be ascertained from the current resource distributions of a few popular blockchains. Figure 1 shows this, and we revisit how we can calculate the distribution in Sect. 5. Since the demonstrations and experiments in the prior works are conducted with a single node per participant, it would be invalidated if the model is released in a non-democratic environment where participants run multiple nodes most of the time [22].

In this paper, we first provide background for the identity establishment phase of sharding blockchain and present a taxonomy of sharding blockchain models according to their resiliency bound. After explaining several definitions and notations, we suggest formulae to quantify the security threat from resource quantization and damage to scalability. Having the formulae we suggest, empirical results are presented with four real-world resource distributions captured from Bitcoin [24], Ethereum [5], Ethereum 2.0 [1], and Cosmos [19]. Our contributions can be summarized as follows:

- Formulate resource quantization, a new kind of security threat that only exists in sharding blockchain.
- Present formulae to quantify the scalability and security of sharding blockchain according to its *ticket price*.
- For the first time, build a theoretical background on identity establishment protocols for sharding blockchains and examine the balance between security and scalability.

2   Background

2.1   Sybil-Resistant Identity

In the permissionless setting, sharding blockchain requires a sybil-resistant identity. While permissioned blockchains [7] rely on an external selection process to admit a network member [23], there is no such selection process in permissionless blockchains. Instead, self-selected participants become a validator by paying resources. This mechanism is required to deal with the problem of Sybil attack [9] by restricting malicious entities from populating their nodes and taking over the network. For this purpose, Bitcoin [24] and Ethereum [5] designate computing power as the resource to support Proof-of-Work (PoW). On the other hand, other well-known blockchain systems use Proof-of-Stake (PoS) to define the identity, such as Algorand [11] and Cosmos [19]. As far as a resource of each miner can be split into certain unit pieces, other sybil-resistant identities besides PoW and PoS, such as Proof-of-Burn (PoB) [15] and Proof-of-authority (PoA) [8], also work well with the sharding blockchain.

2.2   Identity Establishment in Sharding Blockchain

Most sharding models rely on the identity (key-block) blockchain [17] in their identity establishment protocol and share the same algorithmic structure with

Table 1. Resiliency bounds.

Group	Protocol name	Total resiliency (θ)
A	Elastico [21] OmniLedger [18] Pyramid [13] Zilliqa [28]	$\frac{1}{4}$
B	RapidChain [31] Ethereum 2.0 [1]	$\frac{1}{3}$

a few differences in implementation details. The identity establishment protocol can be divided into three steps. First, at the end of every round, a shard that served as a leader of the consensus in the previous round announces new randomness for the PoW puzzle to assure that the solution is not precomputed. Second, a participant who wishes to join in the next round should establish an identity by solving the fresh PoW puzzle that consists of the participant's public key, IP, and new randomness. Finally, after the previous leader shard receives the predefined number of PoW solutions, it fixes the network membership for the next round and records it in the identity blockchain. As some of them [18,21] have already pointed out, it is worth noting that this identity blockchain is compatible with any sybil-resistant identity mechanisms (*e.g.*, PoS). In the above protocol we describe, the difficulty of the PoW puzzle is the ticket price. Currently, the ticket price is adjusted according to (i) the number of PoW solutions submitted in the previous round or (ii) the time to solve a single PoW puzzle. However, there is no model that considers the scalability and security problems when controlling the ticket price.

2.3 Taxonomy

We classify sharding blockchain models into two groups, *i.e.*, A and B, according to the total resiliency bound. The group A includes Elastico [21], OmniLedger [18], Pyramid [13], and Zilliqa [28] that have $\frac{1}{4}$ total resiliency with $\frac{1}{3}$ shard resiliency since they adopted the traditional PBFT [6] algorithm for intra-shard consensus protocol. On the other hand, the group B includes RapidChain [31] and Ethereum 2.0 [1] that introduce their own version of BFT consensus protocol [11,16] for intra-shard consensus to achieves $\frac{1}{3}$ total resiliency and the $\frac{1}{2}$ shard resiliency. One of the renowned models in the literature, Monoxide [29], is out of our concern since its Chu-ko-nu mining requires most miners to participate in as many shards as possible to guarantee security, which means that theoretically, it does not allow the single-shard takeover attack. However, it still suffers from power centralization [30], a lack of state sharding [12], and issues associated with PoW [27]. We do not consider Chainspace [3] as well because it relies on the assumption that a shard responsible for processing transactions is honest. We only put the models that do not rely on the solid assumption of

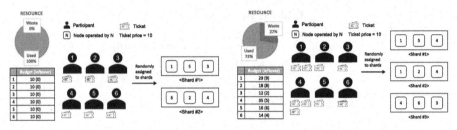

(a) Democratic environment   (b) Non-democratic Environment

Fig. 2. (a) Every participant operates a single node and manages only a part of the whole blockchain. There is no *waste resource* since all participants own the same amount of resource with the ticket price. (b) The bigger budget the participant has, the more nodes it can run. The total amount of *waste resource* is the sum of leftover of all participants.

participants' honesty under our consideration. Table 1 shows the total resiliency bounds of exemplary models from both literature and industry we discuss further.

3   Definitions and Notations

Before we plunge into any details of our formulae, we fix definitions of a few terminologies and introduce some key concepts.

Node vs. Participant. We use the term node distinguished from a participant. A node is a unit of software implementation that can communicate on the P2P overlay network and participate in the consensus. Since most sharding blockchain protocols adopt the PBFT-based [6] algorithm for intra-shard consensus, we generally use the term node to indicate a validator with single voting power. A participant refers to a real-world individual or corporation that owns a resource to invest on a blockchain, such as computing power (PoW) or stake (PoS). This distinction is especially important in the context of sharding blockchain. As discussed earlier, to evenly distribute network members into each shard, mainstream sharding blockchain protocols charge a ticket price to each participant. All participants have to pay a ticket price from their wallets for every node they want to operate. This implies that each participant with more resources than the ticket price might run several nodes. Therefore, unlike other traditional blockchain protocols, participant and node do not mean the same thing in this paper.

Democratic and Non-democratic Environment. The issue of node heterogeneity has been first introduced in RepChain [14] where they pointed out an inefficiency of existing sharding blockchain systems that regard all nodes as the same except for the dissimilarity between honest and malicious ones. Ostraka [22] viewed the heterogeneity in terms of resource possession and first presented a notion of a democratic environment in which every participant has a similar amount of resources. Whereas they focused on dealing with the protection from the shard-targeted Denial-of-Service (DoS) attacks and the problem of limited state sharding, we refer to this term to highlight the trade-off between scalability and security in the sharding blockchain system. Most hybrid blockchain protocols [25], including sharding blockchains, assume a democratic environment where every participant only operates a single node. That is, every participant owns the exact amount of resource by which it can run precisely one node, as shown in Fig. 2a. The size of a shard in this figure is three, and there are six participants in total, each of which is running one node. In contrast, participants in a non-democratic environment operate as many nodes as they can create in proportion to its holding amount of resources, as shown in Fig. 2b.

Table 2. Notations.

Notation	Description
T	Ticket price
N	Total number of nodes
I	Total number of participants
R	Total amount of resources that the participants have
t	Ratio of the ticket price to the total amount of resource (R)
h	Number of adversarial nodes
β	Average amount of waste resources
μ	Average number of nodes per participant
θ	Total resiliency

Other notations for the formulae are shown in Table 2. Note that we use both notations T and t to denote the ticket price. T denotes the quantity of resource for a single ticket. However, due to the diversity of mechanisms to define identities (*e.g.*, hashing power, stake), the choice of unit is somewhat arbitrary, so we favor to use t throughout this paper, which means the ratio of the ticket price to the total amount of resources R.

4 Analysis Models

In this section, we explicate quantitative measurement models to deal with the problem in the identity establishment protocol of sharding in the non-democratic environment from the ticket price perspective. A trade-off between security and scalability arises as the ticket price grows and falls. We discuss both directions one by one.

4.1   Analysing the Effect of Resource Quantization

We present a new security threat, so-called *resource quantization*. The above-mentioned approaches for generating nodes in the sharding blockchain system inevitably accompany resource quantization that does not exist in the traditional blockchain system. As every participant should fully utilize its resource to generate nodes to maximize its incentive, they are likely to pay for multiple tickets as much as possible. However, the ticket price is independently chosen based on a configuration of each blockchain protocol and can vary from time to time under the dynamic environment [32]. Hence, participants who want to take part in the consensus cannot precisely prepare their resource budget as a multiple of the ticket price to avoid wasting resources. For this reason, it is unavoidable to have a surplus resource in every participant's wallet (PoS) or computation cluster (PoW)[1]. This surplus resource is called *waste resource*, and it can be calculated deterministically from all participants' budgets and the ticket price. Nevertheless, this does not mean that we can predict the total amount of the *waste resource* unless every participant reveals their budget ahead of the protocol. Furthermore, it could fluctuate to a great extent even if there is a minute change in the ticket price, and this would be amplified as more participants join the network.

Let us figure out the effect of waste resources on the number of nodes in the sharding blockchain. We denote the expected amount of *waste resource* for each participant as β. Since a *waste resource* can not exceed the ticket price T, β has a value between 0 and T. β is 0 when every participant owns resources precisely a multiple of the ticket price and increases as participants add more resources to their budget but less than the ticket price (T). When a certain non-zero β exists, the sum of I participants' waste resources is $\beta \times I$, and the number of nodes that could have been generated with waste resources is $\lfloor \frac{I\beta}{T} \rfloor$, called *waste nodes*. The total number of nodes running in the network, thus, can be described with Eq. (1) when there is no *waste nodes* and Eq. (2), otherwise.

$$(Ideal) \quad N = \lfloor \frac{R}{T} \rfloor \tag{1}$$

$$(Quantized) \quad N = \lfloor \frac{R}{T} \rfloor - \lfloor \frac{I\beta}{T} \rfloor \tag{2}$$

Note that we cannot calculate β every moment during the consensus, but it is possibly a high value close to the ticket price. Since the higher β means that there may be more redundant resources that honest participants cannot use to generate nodes, this makes their power weaker in the consensus than the power they would have in an ideal environment. Whereas most of the honest commercial participants compete with each other, adversaries can collude so that they can decrease their β to almost zero. As more resources of honest entities become redundant and lose their power, adversaries would get more chances to threaten the entire system's security.

---

[1] https://github.com/DurianStallSingapore/Zilliqa-Mining-Proxy

Threat Model. To further elaborate on the security threat under resource quantization, we describe the threat model. Our threat model is closely built on the classic adversary introduced in the single-shard takeover attack in previous works [18]. This naive adversary cannot launch an attack as long as the protocol's resiliency bound (*i.e.*, Table 1) is maintained. The adversary does not collaborate with other honest entities and behaves arbitrarily until a specific condition is met, such as owning more nodes above the shard resiliency bound (*i.e.*, single-shard takeover attack). Upon this, we additionally assume that they can collude so that they obtain a single summed resource budget. This means that they would not suffer from the resource quantization as much as honest participants do since they can be viewed as a single participant; that is, their total waste resource is at most the ticket price. Normally, the adversary needs more resource than the total resiliency bound of the protocol to make invalid changes on the global state (safety) or delay the protocol (liveness). Here we further assume *rich adversary* owning almost the same resources with the resiliency bound but still under the bound. Having considered the attribute of the blockchain ecosystem, we consider this assumption quite probable [10,20], especially if we think about the mining pools. We show this *rich adversary* still can subvert the protocol in Sect. 5.

Modeling. Considering that the resource quantization only occurs among the honest entities, the ratio of the maximum number of tolerable adversarial nodes (h) in respect to the quantized total number of nodes should be bounded by the total resiliency (θ) that is $\frac{1}{4}$ for group A and $\frac{1}{3}$ for group B.

$$\frac{h}{\lfloor \frac{R}{T} \rfloor - \lfloor \frac{I\beta}{T} \rfloor} < \theta \tag{3}$$

With this inequation, we can capture the minimum number of adversarial nodes exceeding the total resiliency when given the ticket price at a specific moment during the protocol. Intuitively, since the denominator of the left-hand side term is less than the ideal number of nodes, the number of attacker's nodes can surpass the resiliency bound even withholding less resource than the resiliency bound. In Sect. 5, we confirm this threat with more concrete numbers.

4.2 Analysing the Effect of Increasing Nodes to Each Participant

In previous works on sharding [18,21,31], they assumed a non-democratic environment. Their experiments and performance measurements were based on this premise. However, we can only achieve the *approximated democratic environment* where the sharding effects can be maximized. To have this maximal effect, we have to calibrate the ticket price carefully to minimize the number of participants running more than two nodes. In such an environment, every participant's resource reserve is mainly distributed between T and 2T so that they only have to run a single node. If the ticket price is lower than some threshold, most participants will run multiple nodes. This situation is quite undesirable because increasing the number of nodes means increasing overhead regarding network bandwidth, transaction processing, and storage requirement. The overhead increases linearly regarding the number of nodes, and some of the participants probably might not afford it.

Given that these less-competent participants become a bottleneck and can severely hamper the throughput [14], the performance improvements of prior works are hard to hold in a non-democratic environment. One might claim that the throughput could be guaranteed if all participants were capable enough to participate in multiple shards. However, it can be viewed as running multiple independent blockchains, and it would cause another scalability problem that brings us back to the starting point. In addition, although the throughput, among others, is the main factor of assessing the scalability of blockchain, an overhead of storage and latency is also non-negligible element of scalability by itself [12]. Considering that a significant number of participants would run more than two nodes despite the convoluted ticket price calibration, it can be seen that recent sharding models sacrifice other factors of scalability to improve the throughput. Nevertheless, the appointed throughput improvement cannot even be guaranteed in the non-democratic environment due to the heterogeneity of participants in terms of capacity.

Average Number of Nodes Each Participant Runs. There can be many quantitative methods to measure the degree of damage in scalability caused by participants running multiple nodes. The most naive way is to use the number of nodes run by participants owning the average amount of resources as the sole indicator. In this case, one can simply force the ticket price to be a proper amount so that these average participants only run a single node. Another sophisticated way is to derive the bound by calculating the number of nodes that occupies a certain percentage of shards on average (Appendix A). From this formulation, one can limit the ticket price based on the average number of shards that each participant joins. Since this can be regarded as a design choice for regulating the trade-off between scalability and security, we suggest a simple model, the average number of nodes, as a baseline so that future researchers can develop their own scheme upon this.

Modeling. We can calculate the average number of nodes as follow.

$$\mu = \frac{\lfloor \frac{R}{T} \rfloor - \lfloor \frac{I\beta}{T} \rfloor}{I} \tag{4}$$

As the ticket price is getting small, participants should run more nodes, and the network will have a higher average number of nodes accordingly. Note that μ does not mean most participants are running around μ nodes. It varies according to the shape of resource distribution among participants. This becomes more obvious when Fig. 1 is considered. Therefore, we cannot simply get the ticket price bounded with μ, but still it is good starting point to measure the degree of scalability.

5   Numerical Analysis

We show quantitative measures in four resource distributions of a real-world blockchain network with suggested models. We try to answer the following research questions throughout this numerical analysis.

- RQ1: Under the resource quantization, how much is the total resiliency bound changed as the ticket price increases?
- RQ2: How much is the scalability ruined by decreasing the ticket price?
- RQ3: Is this information practically useful to operate sharding blockchain?

5.1   Datasets

Our datasets consist of four resource distributions captured from representative blockchains for each popular consensus algorithm: PoW, PoS, and sharding. In particular, we select Bitcoin and Ethereum since those two PoW blockchains are the biggest network. We have chosen Ethereum 2.0, which recently has drawn much attention for its sharding, and Cosmos, which uses the famous PoS consensus algorithm Tendermint [4]. Having an assumption that a single participant owns a single account, we take a different approach to approximate the actual resource distribution for each dataset.

Bitcoin & Ethereum. We have counted the number of blocks each public key mines for three months and divided it by the total number of blocks to approximate the resource ratio each public key owns.

Ethereum 2.0. Since participants in Ethereum 2.0 should stake 32 ETH from the original Ethereum 1.0 network, we can distinguish each participant with the public key in Ethereum 1.0 and track the amount of ETH each public key stakes in Ethereum 2.0.

Cosmos. Cosmos is a complete PoS-based blockchain, and we can see the voting power of each validator from their website[2].

5.2   RQ1. Upper Bound of Ticket Price

Figure 3 shows the resiliency bound recalculation results for group A and group B. By equating both sides of Eq. (3), we can derive a new equation regarding h, and then the new resiliency bound can be calculated by multiplying h by $\frac{T}{R}$, i.e., the ratio of the ticket price (Appendix B). We can affirm that the newly derived resiliency bound decreases as the ticket price increases. Therefore, the upper bound can be chosen according to the degree of security the blockchain wants to provide. The upper bound will be tighter if the blockchain operator does not want a further decrease in the resiliency bound.

Since the value of β fluctuates randomly, the graph is noisy, and the noise is amplified when the ticket price is high. This is because of the nature of a

---

[2] https://cosmoscan.net/cosmos/validators-stats.

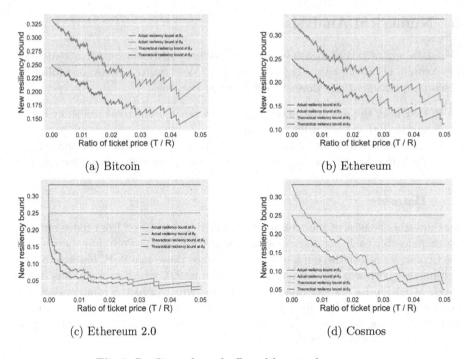

Fig. 3. Resiliency bound affected by non-democracy.

long-tailed resource distribution where the population of rich participants is
sparse. Therefore, the resiliency bound experiences more dramatic change when
the budget of rich participants matches multiples of the ticket price. Unlike
other distributions, in Fig. 3(c), there is a steep drop around 3.6466e−06 which
corresponds to 32 ETH. The reason is that most Ethereum 2.0 participants
buy only one ticket. We admit that the calculation based on the approximated
resource distribution is error-prone, especially in PoS-based blockchain where
participants can adjust their budget more easily than in PoW-based blockchain.
However, we believe that the results are still meaningful in showing that the
influence of non-democracy closely depends on the shape of resource distribution.

The region above 0.01 in Fig. 3, although we have shown up to 0.05, is impractical considering Fig. 1, where participants' budget is mostly distributed between
0 and 0.01. Therefore, we consider a feasible ratio of the ticket price up to 0.01
and find the maximum resiliency drop for each resource distribution. Table 3
shows the affected resiliency bound (θ') under this condition. The results are presented with the percentage drop ($\frac{\theta'-\theta}{\theta} \times 100$) regarding the theoretical resiliency
bound (θ). The results illustrate that sharding models from prior works cannot
keep the ideal fault tolerance bound (θ) under the resource quantization, and it
can be diminished to the extent of −14% to −76% when they are applied in an
environment that has a similar resource distribution with the ones we presented.
Note that in Ethereum 2.0 settings, such a huge resiliency drop is unlikely to

Table 3. Changed resiliency bounds.

Group	Bitcoin	Ethereum	Ethereum 2.0	Cosmos
A	0.215 (−14%)	0.1975 (−21%)	0.06 (−76%)	0.155 (−38%)
B	0.2866 (−15%)	0.2633 (−22%)	0.08 (−76%)	0.2066 (−39%)

happen, as we already pointed out. However, it can still give a meaningful warning to the Ethereum 2.0 community that the ticket price should be changed by having enough time for participants to prepare their budget in accordance with the changed ticket price.

Table 4. Damage to scalability.

Metric	Bitcoin	Ethereum	Cosmos
AN	48.06	16	39.81
MN	397	449	449

5.3 RQ2. Lower Bound of Ticket Price

Figure 4 illustrates the average number of nodes that each participant has to run according to the decrease in the ticket price. The number decreases rapidly from some point of the ticket price where the budgets of the most population are distributed. That explains why Ethereum 2.0 graph (Fig. 4(c)) drops most rapidly. Note that, unlike the resiliency bound graph, the scale of the x-axis here is different for each resource distribution. Since the resource distribution covers a broad range of budgets, it is impossible to make every participant run only a single node. Instead, we can adjust the ticket price to minimize this number. Blockchain operator, therefore, can have their own policy about the scalability regarding the number of nodes running in each participant's server and set the lower bound of the ticket price to prevent the nodes from being too populated.

We suggest using the amount of resources that appeared most frequently in resource distribution (the mode) to select the ticket price. We set the ticket price (t) such that the mode lies between t and $2t$ and show the degree of damage in scalability measured by two metrics for each resource distribution in Table 4. The first metric we use is the **A**verage number of **N**odes (**AN**) that we have introduced above, and the second is the **M**aximum number of **N**odes (**MN**) operated among participants. The metric MN is useful since it indicates the maximum burden that participants are expected to have. We exclude Ethereum 2.0 since we have found that it tells nothing but the lack of middle class partly because of its immature state. The results show that the network members would run more than 15 nodes on average and the richest participant could manage around 400 nodes even when we restricted the ticket price. This reveals that

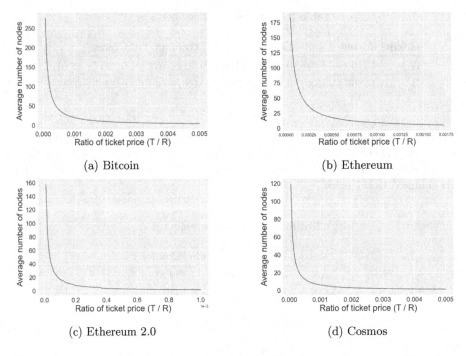

Fig. 4. Average number of nodes per participant. The lines are interpolated based on the diverse ticket prices.

the performance reports assuming homogeneity of participants from the previous sharding research are invalid under the non-democracy. It is impossible to increase the ticket price imprudently to reduce these overheads because of the resource quantization.

5.4   RQ3. The Validity Interval of the Ticket Price

Here, the *validity interval* of the ticket price denotes an interval where the proper level of secure resiliency bound is guaranteed while mitigating the damage to the scalability enough. Specific decisions regarding the trade-off between security and scalability are entirely up to blockchain developers. They only need to adjust the ticket price so as to meet the validity interval. However, we can imagine a more tricky situation where there is no validity interval. Although there seems to be a wide validity interval for each of our four datasets, this does not mean it always exists. According to the design decisions and the shape of resource distribution, there can be no validity interval where the lower bound is larger than the upper bound. In this case, developers should further change their design choices or implement a more complex ticket price adjustment algorithm.

6   Discussion and Future Works

Since, for now, there is no way to measure the total quantity of waste resources (*i.e.,* $\beta \times I$) accurately, we need a way to track the budget of each participant without harming privacy. Also, note that although we insist that inventing a new algorithm for adjusting the ticket price is an indispensable step for sharding blockchain, we see this as an orthogonal work to ours since it should be designed to be able to blend in an overall architecture. Allowing participants to delegate their resources to a small number of trusted participants can potentially resolve the resource quantization issue since the waste resource of honest entities will be summed. Therefore, it can be another possible future work. Also, we only introduced simple models to measure the degree of scalability since a viewpoint on scalability can be diverged in the way one sees the trade-off in there. We believe that more delicate metrics must explain the scalability that is also easily measurable.

7   Conclusion

This paper presented a problem we would encounter when the sharding-based blockchain is deployed in the non-democratic environment, especially in the identity establishment phase. From the ticket price perspective, we introduced mathematical models to quantify the security threat from the resource quantization and the damage to scalability. With the formalized analysis for the trade-off between security and scalability, we confirm that the ticket price takes an important role in calibrating this trade-off. We hope future research on sharding blockchain focuses on the ticket price control problem.

Acknowledgement. This research was supported in part by the MSIT (Ministry of Science and ICT), Korea, under the ITRC (Information Technology Research Center) support program (IITP-2022-2018-0-01441) supervised by the IITP (Institute for Information & Communications Technology Planning & Evaluation), the Office of Naval Research (ONR) under awards N00014-21-1-2409 and N00014-17-1-2232, and the Defense Advanced Research Projects Agency (DARPA) Small Business Technology Transfer (STTR) Program Office under contract W31P4Q-20-C-0052. Any opinions, findings and conclusions or recommendations expressed in this material are those of the author(s) and do not necessarily reflect the views of MSIT, ITRC, IITP, ONR, DARPA, the DARPA STTR Program Office, or any other South Korea and U.S. government agency. We also gratefully acknowledge an "Endeavor" research award from the Donald Bren School of Information and Computer Sciences at UC Irvine.

Table 5. Additional notations.

Notation	Description
S	The number of shards
λ	The target ratio of shards that is occupied on average
α	The amount of resource to achieve the target ratio

A Amount of Resource to Participate in a Certain Number of Shards

To show this, we define additional notations in Table 5. When a participant has α/t nodes, a probability that the participant has at least a node in one of the shards is the complement of the probability that all of the nodes are not in that shard.

$$(1 - (\frac{S-1}{S})^{\lfloor \alpha/t \rfloor})$$ (5)

Now, we can estimate the expected number of shards that a participant with α/t nodes would take part in.

$$S \times (1 - (\frac{S-1}{S})^{\lfloor \alpha/t \rfloor})$$ (6)

Equation (6) should be equal to the target number of shards.

$$\lambda S = S \times (1 - (\frac{S-1}{S})^{\lfloor \alpha/t \rfloor})$$ (7)

Solving for α, we can get the amount of resource with which a participant has nodes in the target number of shards (*i.e.*, λS) on average.

$$\alpha = \frac{t \log(1 - \lambda)}{\log(1 - 1/S)}$$ (8)

B Resiliency Bound Recalculation

What we want to do is to calculate the minimum ratio of resources that is smaller than the total resiliency bound (θ), yet can generate more number of nodes which goes over the bound under the resource quantization. By equating Eq. (3), we can derive the equation for this value and it will be the changed resiliency bounds (θ').

$$\frac{h}{\lfloor \frac{R}{T} \rfloor - \lfloor \frac{I\beta}{T} \rfloor} = \theta$$ (9)

$$\frac{h}{(R - I\beta)/T} = \theta$$ (10)

Solved for h.

$$h = \frac{\theta(R - I\beta)}{T} \tag{11}$$

Multiplied by the ratio of ticket price.

$$\frac{T}{R} \times h = \frac{T}{R} \times \frac{\theta(R - I\beta)}{T} \tag{12}$$

$$t \times h = \frac{\theta(R - I\beta)}{R} \tag{13}$$

$$\theta' = \frac{\theta(R - I\beta)}{R} \tag{14}$$

Thus, the *rich adversary* with the resource more than θ' but less than θ can still subvert the network.

References

1. Ethereum 2.0 ([n d]). https://ethereum.org/en/upgrades/
2. Abdelatif, H., Abdelhakim, S.H., Mustapha, S.: A tractable probabilistic approach to analyze sybil attacks in sharding-based blockchain protocols. arXiv preprint arXiv:2104.07215 (2021)
3. Al-Bassam, M., Sonnino, A., Bano, S., Hrycyszyn, D., Danezis, G.: Chainspace: a sharded smart contracts platform. arXiv preprint arXiv:1708.03778 (2017)
4. Buchman, E.: Tendermint: Byzantine fault tolerance in the age of blockchains. Ph.D. thesis, University of Guelph (2016)
5. Buterin, V., et al.: A next-generation smart contract and decentralized application platform. White Pap. **3**(37) (2014)
6. Castro, M., Liskov, B., et al.: Practical byzantine fault tolerance. In: OSDI 1999, pp. 173–186 (1999)
7. Danezis, G., Meiklejohn, S.: Centrally banked cryptocurrencies. arXiv preprint arXiv:1505.06895 (2015)
8. De Angelis, S., Aniello, L., Baldoni, R., Lombardi, F., Margheri, A., Sassone, V.: PBFT vs proof-of-authority: applying the cap theorem to permissioned blockchain (2018)
9. Douceur, J.R.: The sybil attack. In: Druschel, P., Kaashoek, F., Rowstron, A. (eds.) IPTPS 2002. LNCS, vol. 2429, pp. 251–260. Springer, Heidelberg (2002). https://doi.org/10.1007/3-540-45748-8_24
10. Gencer, A.E., Basu, S., Eyal, I., van Renesse, R., Sirer, E.G.: Decentralization in bitcoin and ethereum networks. In: Meiklejohn, S., Sako, K. (eds.) FC 2018. LNCS, vol. 10957, pp. 439–457. Springer, Heidelberg (2018). https://doi.org/10.1007/978-3-662-58387-6_24
11. Gilad, Y., Hemo, R., Micali, S., Vlachos, G., Zeldovich, N.: Algorand: scaling byzantine agreements for cryptocurrencies. In: Proceedings of the 26th Symposium on Operating Systems Principles, pp. 51–68 (2017)
12. Hafid, A., Hafid, A.S., Samih, M.: Scaling blockchains: a comprehensive survey. IEEE Access **8**, 125244–125262 (2020)
13. Hong, Z., Guo, S., Li, P., Chen, W.: Pyramid: a layered sharding blockchain system. In: IEEE INFOCOM 2021-IEEE Conference on Computer Communications, pp. 1–10. IEEE (2021)

14. Huang, C., et al.: Repchain: a reputation based secure, fast and high incentive blockchain system via sharding. IEEE Internet Things J. **8**, 4291–4304 (2020)
15. Karantias, K., Kiayias, A., Zindros, D.: Proof-of-burn. In: Bonneau, J., Heninger, N. (eds.) FC 2020. LNCS, vol. 12059, pp. 523–540. Springer, Cham (2020). https://doi.org/10.1007/978-3-030-51280-4_28
16. Kiayias, A., Russell, A., David, B., Oliynykov, R.: Ouroboros: a provably secure proof-of-stake blockchain protocol. In: Katz, J., Shacham, H. (eds.) CRYPTO 2017. LNCS, vol. 10401, pp. 357–388. Springer, Cham (2017). https://doi.org/10.1007/978-3-319-63688-7_12
17. Kogias, E.K., Jovanovic, P., Gailly, N., Khoffi, I., Gasser, L., Ford, B.: Enhancing bitcoin security and performance with strong consistency via collective signing. In: 25th USENIX Security Symposium (USENIX Security 2016), pp. 279–296 (2016)
18. Kokoris-Kogias, E., Jovanovic, P., Gasser, L., Gailly, N., Syta, E., Ford, B.: OmniLedger: a secure, scale-out, decentralized ledger via sharding. In: 2018 IEEE Symposium on Security and Privacy (SP), pp. 583–598. IEEE (2018)
19. Kwon, J., Buchman, E.: Cosmos whitepaper (2019)
20. Kwon, Y., Liu, J., Kim, M., Song, D., Kim, Y.: Impossibility of full decentralization in permissionless blockchains. In: Proceedings of the 1st ACM Conference on Advances in Financial Technologies, pp. 110–123 (2019)
21. Luu, L., Narayanan, V., Zheng, C., Baweja, K., Gilbert, S., Saxena, P.: A secure sharding protocol for open blockchains. In: Proceedings of the 2016 ACM SIGSAC Conference on Computer and Communications Security, pp. 17–30 (2016)
22. Manuskin, A., Mirkin, M., Eyal, I.: Ostraka: secure blockchain scaling by node sharding. In: 2020 IEEE European Symposium on Security and Privacy Workshops (EuroS&PW), pp. 397–406. IEEE (2020)
23. Miller, A.: Permissioned and permissionless blockchains. In: Blockchain for Distributed Systems Security, pp. 193–204. Wiley, Hoboken (2019)
24. Nakamoto, S.: Bitcoin: a peer-to-peer electronic cash system. Decentralized Bus. Rev. 21260 (2008)
25. Pass, R., Shi, E.: Hybrid consensus: efficient consensus in the permissionless model. In: 31st International Symposium on Distributed Computing (DISC 2017). Schloss Dagstuhl-Leibniz-Zentrum fuer Informatik (2017)
26. Ratta, P., Kaur, A., Sharma, S., Shabaz, M., Dhiman, G.: Application of blockchain and internet of things in healthcare and medical sector: applications, challenges, and future perspectives. J. Food Qual. **2021** (2021)
27. Stoll, C., Klaaßen, L., Gallersdörfer, U.: The carbon footprint of bitcoin. Joule **3**(7), 1647–1661 (2019)
28. Team, Z., et al.: The ZILLIQA technical whitepaper. Retrieved September 16, 2019 (2017)
29. Wang, J., Wang, H.: Monoxide: scale out blockchains with asynchronous consensus zones. In: 16th USENIX Symposium on Networked Systems Design and Implementation (NSDI 2019), pp. 95–112 (2019)
30. Yu, G., Wang, X., Yu, K., Ni, W., Zhang, J.A., Liu, R.P.: Survey: sharding in blockchains. IEEE Access **8**, 14155–14181 (2020)
31. Zamani, M., Movahedi, M., Raykova, M.: RapidChain: scaling blockchain via full sharding. In: Proceedings of the 2018 ACM SIGSAC Conference on Computer and Communications Security, pp. 931–948 (2018)
32. Zhang, J., Hong, Z., Qiu, X., Zhan, Y., Guo, S., Chen, W.: SkyChain: a deep reinforcement learning-empowered dynamic blockchain sharding system. In: 49th International Conference on Parallel Processing-ICPP, pp. 1–11 (2020)

On the Routing Convergence Delay in the Lightning Network

Niklas Gögge[(✉)], Elias Rohrer, and Florian Tschorsch

Distributed Security Infrastructures, Technical University of Berlin, Berlin, Germany
n.goegge@campus.tu-berlin.de,
{elias.rohrer,florian.tschorsch}@tu-berlin.de

Abstract. Nodes in the Lightning Network synchronise routing information through a gossip protocol that makes use of a staggered broadcast mechanism. In this work, we show that the convergence delay in the network is larger than what would be expected from the protocol's specification and that payment attempt failures caused by the delay are more frequent, the larger the delay is. To this end, we measure the convergence delay incurred in the network and analyse what its primary causes are. Moreover, we further investigate and confirm our findings through a time-discrete simulation of the Lightning Network gossip protocol. We explore the use of alternative gossip protocols as well as parameter variations of the current protocol and evaluate them by the resulting bandwidth usage and convergence delay. Our research shows that there are multiple ways of lowering the convergence delay, ranging from simple parameter changes to overhauling the entire protocol.

Keywords: Bitcoin · Lightning network · Gossip · Convergence delay

1 Introduction

Since its inception in 2008, the Bitcoin [8] network showed an inability to scale to a high volume of transactions [13]. The Bitcoin Lightning Network [11] is a second-layer payment channel network (PCN) that enables a high volume of low-cost off-chain Bitcoin transactions.

In the Lightning Network, nodes route payments by finding a path to the destination based on a local copy of the public channel graph that each node maintains. In order to keep their channel graph views in sync, nodes propagate update messages via a peer-to-peer gossip protocol that utilizes a so-called *staggered broadcast*. As a result of the gossip protocol, it can—in the worst case—take more than 10 min for a message to reach all nodes in the network.

To avoid issues caused by stale routing information, a convergence delay of this magnitude goes against the common goal of routing protocols to reach convergence quickly and reliably. The larger the convergence delay is, the more likely it is for payment attempts to fail since a source node might be computing a route based on stale information. Payment attempt failures stemming from the

© The Author(s), under exclusive license to Springer Nature Switzerland AG 2023
J. Garcia-Alfaro et al. (Eds.): DPM 2022/CBT 2022, LNCS 13619, pp. 203–218, 2023.
https://doi.org/10.1007/978-3-031-25734-6_13

convergence delay currently account for roughly 1.24% of all failures according to [14]. These failures can not be eliminated completely given that message propagation cannot be instant. Moreover, improved routing algorithms such as multi-part payments (MPPs) do not improve the rate at which these failures occur. In fact, they may even increase their occurrences as the probability of such failures only increases with the number of channels involved in a payment.

In this work, we investigate the convergence delay of routing information and its effects on payments in the Lightning Network. Our main goal is to present the current state of the convergence delay in the Lightning Network, the issues it causes, and to layout potential improvement ideas. Our contributions can be summarized as follows:

- We analyze the Lightning Network's gossip protocol in its current state by looking at and comparing CLN and LND, the two most popular node implementations. We measure the delay seen in the real network through a passive experiment and catalog the seen gossip messages (specifically all channel updates) to understand why and when gossip messages are broadcast by nodes. The catalog is also useful to understand which types of channel updates are potentially disruptive to payment routing (Sect. 3).
- We implemented a simulator capable of simulating the Lightning Network's gossip protocol as well as payments in the Lightning Network. We can bootstrap our simulation from historical topology data and replay recorded gossip messages. We use the simulation to gain further inside into how the gossip protocol operates and where its inefficiencies lie (Sect. 4).
- We evaluate the use of alternative message propagation mechanisms in the Lightning Network. Through simulation, we compare flooding, a structured broadcast utilizing the channel graph topology, inventory based gossip, as well as efficient set reconciliation using Minisketch [4] (Sect. 4).

To our knowledge, there exists no prior related work on the convergence delay in the Lightning Network. However, there is a long history of convergence delay research in internet routing through the Border Gateway Protocol (BGP), which we use to draw inspiration for potential improvement ideas [1,2,7]. We discuss these and other related works in Sect. 6. In the following, we give a primer on information propagation and the convergence delay in the Lightning Network.

2   Information Propagation in the Lightning Network

The Lightning Network [11] is a second-layer payment channel network (PCN) that enables a high volume of low-cost off-chain Bitcoin transactions. A payment channel describes a type of smart contract that enables two parties to transact off-chain, with the only bottleneck being the network latency between the two parties. A PCN enables payments between nodes that do not have direct channels with each other by routing payments over intermediary nodes. In order to ensure that payment forwarding requires no trust towards these intermediaries, such multi-hop payments are secured through so-called *Hash Time Locked Contracts*

(HTLCs). Candidate routes are discovered by the originators through a source-routing algorithm operating on a local copy of the network graph, i.e., the routing information base (RIB). These local information are regularly kept in sync by gossiping update messages in the network.

The `channel_announcement`, `node_announcement` and `channel_update` messages are the three main messages of the Lightning Network's gossip protocol. Channel announcements are used by two nodes to prove that there is a channel between them. The proof comes in the form of four signatures tying the nodes to the keys used in the funding transaction. Node announcements are used to provide additional information about a node such as reachable network addresses. Channel updates provide routing information for a channel edge, such as routing fees and lock times. Each channel counterparty is able to broadcast a channel update for its outgoing channel edge. In order for a channel to be operational the network has to see three messages, one channel announcement and two channel updates (one for each edge of the channel).

2.1 Influences on the Convergence Delay

While the details of the information dissemination protocols are left to the implementations, the most common implementations, such as CLN[1] and LND[2], generally follow the same concepts. As we show later, the concepts presented in the following and their concrete parameterizations can have a significant impact on the convergence delay.

Staggered Broadcast. The gossip protocol of the Lightning Network uses a staggered broadcast that acts as a natural rate limiting mechanism to ensure that the network is resistant to certain types of denial-of-service (DoS) attacks. In a staggered broadcast, each node listens for gossip messages for a specified interval (stagger interval) before broadcasting all messages to a subset of peers. While listening, messages concerning the same channels are deduplicated by the timestamp field provided in the messages. If two channel updates for the same channel edge are seen, only the most recent update is kept in the broadcast queue. The value chosen for the stagger interval has a big impact on the convergence delay, since the higher it is the longer messages take to reach a majority of nodes. The specification[3] recommends a 60 s stagger interval.

Gossip Syncers. The `gossip_timestamp_filter` message allows nodes to manage from which peers they want to receive new gossip. Not sending the filter message is equivalent to not requesting any gossip. By default, nodes only send filters to a subset of their peers, which are called *active gossip syncers*, while all other peers are *passive gossip syncers*. The number of active syncer connections each node maintains has an impact on the convergence delay since it determines

---

[1] https://github.com/ElementsProject/lightning.

[2] https://github.com/lightningnetwork/lnd.

[3] https://github.com/lightning/bolts.

Table 1. Comparison of CLN and LND implementation details most influential on the convergence delay.

	CLN	LND
Staggered broadcast	60 s interval	90 s interval, batches are broadcast in 5 s intervals
Gossip syncers	Five syncers, individual rotations every hour	Three syncers, one being rotated every 20 min
Rate limiting	One channel update per day, burst up to 4	One channel update per minute, burst of up to 10

how well nodes are connected. The more active syncer nodes choose the faster messages will propagate.

Rate Limiting. While the staggered broadcast already offers a form of rate limiting, nodes in addition apply a second rate limit on a per-edge basis. Only a certain number of updates from the same edge are allowed for each rate limiting interval. Such policies exist to prevent nodes from spamming the network with channel updates, but also to prevent I/O DoS attacks, since nodes write new channel updates to disk. A third rate limiting applies to redundant channel updates (only differing in the timestamp of the message), which are also considered as *keep alive updates.* A node will broadcast keep alive updates to indicate that its channels are still active and should not be pruned from other nodes' views of the network. To rate limit keep alive updates, nodes usually only allow them in a defined frequency, but the details differ from implementation to implementation.

Comparing Node Implementations. While the Lightning implementations generally follow the concepts just discussed, the specific parameters used by these implementations can differ quite a bit. In the following, we therefore discuss the relevant details of the two most popular implementations of the Lightning Network protocol, CLN and LND.[4]

As shown in Table 1, the behavior of CLN generally sticks to the specification's guidance, while LND differs from it significantly with a stagger interval of 90 s. When the timer expires, all seen messages are split up into batches and broadcast to all relevant peers in 5 s intervals. The function for calculating the batch size from the total number of messages n to broadcast is the following:

$$sb(n) = min\left(10, \frac{n \cdot 5s + 90s - 1}{90s}\right)$$

The number of broadcast batches increases with the number of messages, but is capped at 18 in order to prevent the overlapping of stagger intervals. With 5 s between batches and a maximum of 18 batches, the last message may potentially

---

[4] Note that LND allows configuration of gossip parameters, CLN does not.

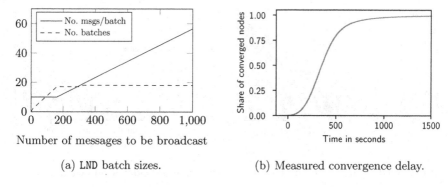

(a) LND batch sizes.   (b) Measured convergence delay.

Fig. 1. LND's broadcast batching and measured convergence delay.

be broadcast $17 \cdot 5 = 85$ s after the stagger timer expires. A plot of $sb(n)$ can be seen in Fig. 1a. Only if there are more than 162 messages seen per 90-s stagger interval, all 18 batches will be filled. If the general rate of messages in the network is lower than that, less batches will be used lowering the convergence delay.[5]

The rate limiting policies of these two node implementations do not play together without friction. If a channel is updated once per minute, a CLN node would disregard all updates after the fourth for up to one hour, while an LND node would accept all updates. The CLN node will not relay disregarded updates, which can cause the convergence delay for these updates to increase. However, this is not an observable issue, since the majority of nodes are running LND.

3   Gossip Traffic Analysis

In the following, we describe our methodology for measuring and analysing gossip traffic in the Lightning Network.

3.1   Measuring the Convergence Delay

In order to measure the convergence delay in the Lightning Network, we used the python pyln-proto[6] package to connect to and communicate with nodes on the network. The node addresses were extracted from a topology snapshot collected from an LND node right before the start of the experiment (Oct. 30, 2021). We connected to as many nodes as possible and chose all of them as our active gossip syncers. We recorded all received messages including at which times $\{t_1, \ldots, t_n\}$ and from which node we got the message. The recorded timestamps can then be

---

[5] The stagger interval was increased in January 2019 from 30 to 90 s with the reasoning to lower bandwidth usage by slowing the propagation of messages [10]. In April 2019, the sub-batch broadcast was introduced with the reasoning to eliminate bursty resource usage after the stagger timer expires [6]. We could not find records of detailed discussion on how the exact parameter values for these changes were chosen.

[6] https://github.com/ElementsProject/lightning/tree/master/contrib/pyln-proto.

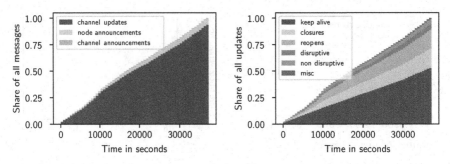

(a) Observed shares of update messages.   (b) Channel updates cataloged by type.

Fig. 2. Categorization of observed gossip messages.

used to estimate the convergence delay in the network by looking at the difference between the first and last timestamp. This estimation method assumes that the first timestamps in these lists correspond to the time of initial broadcast and that all nodes have seen the message after the last timestamp.

In total, we received 69, 942 unique gossip messages from 1, 046 nodes over a time span of close to 10 h. To estimate the convergence delay, we used all messages that were received at least from 500 different nodes. Figure 1b shows the share of nodes that have seen a message in relation to the time since initial broadcast: the average time it takes for a node to see a message is 359.9 s, with 95% of nodes seeing messages after 753 s and 100% of nodes seeing messages after 2, 500 s.

3.2 Dissecting Recorded Gossip

We then categorized the collected data and examined which share of gossip messages are node announcements, channel announcements or channel updates. We also analyzed the contents of all channel updates to understand when nodes send updates and how they typically update channel policies.

As seen in Fig. 2a, the arrival rate of new messages is more or less constant. Of all messages we recorded, 5.13% were node announcements, 0.34% were channel announcements and 94.53% were channel updates. This distribution matches our expectations, as channel announcements are directly rate limited by the blockchain, node announcements only need to be broadcast infrequently to modify network addresses or add new feature announcements, and channel updates change channel policies, which happens regularly over the course of a channel's lifespan. We categorized channel updates into six different categories:

- *Keep-alive* updates only differ in the timestamp field. These updates are meant to tell the network that a channel is still active. They made up 45.32% of all recorded messages.

- *Channel closure* updates close a channel temporarily or permanently. Temporary channel closures can happen if a peer goes offline due to network issues, in which case the other peer will broadcast such an update to inform the network not to route over the offline peer. These updates made up 19.29% of all recorded messages.
- *Channel re-open* updates open a channel that was previously closed. These updates made up 18.66% of all recorded messages.
- *Disruptive* updates change the channel policy in a way that could cause payment failures, if the payment source does not know of the update. Channel closures are excluded because we categorize them separately. Disruptive updates made up 8.57% of all recorded messages.
- *Non-disruptive* updates change the channel policy in a way that could cause a payment source to over-pay on fees or use a higher lock time than needed. These updates made up 7.22% of all recorded messages.
- *Misc.* updates are all other updates that we saw. For example, updates that change the `htlc_minimum_msat` field fall into this category. These updates made up 0.99% of all recorded messages.

The observed amount of keep-alive updates is slightly concerning, as they make up roughly 50% of all seen updates. This amount of keep-alive updates cannot be explained by nodes broadcasting them at a reasonable rate. In theory, a keep-alive only has to be sent for channels that did not have an update within 14 days. Therefore, transmitting a keep-alive update every 13 days should be sufficient to prevent other nodes from pruning the channel. Figure 3a shows the difference in the timestamp field between the keep-alive and the previous update: we observe that for almost all of the keep-alive updates the differences lie between $86,400$ and $88,200$ s, which corresponds to exactly 1 day and 1 day plus 30 min. We found that LND nodes are responsible for these updates, because they check every 30 min if any of their channels had an update within the last day, and will broadcast a keep-alive update otherwise. However, we were not able to explain the large peaks seen in Fig. 3a at the interval boundaries. Moreover, we did not observe any keep-alive updates with a smaller difference, because LND nodes do not relay such updates and therefore they do not propagate through the network.

Looking at the timestamp differences for all updates in our channel re-open category (cf. Fig. 3b), we see that most channels edges that get re-opened were disabled for short periods of time. For example, 60% of edges were closed for less than 22 min. This is likely caused by network issues that lead nodes to temporarily disable edges.

4   Simulation Study

In the following, we discuss the conducted model-based simulation study on the routing convergence delay in the Lightning Network.

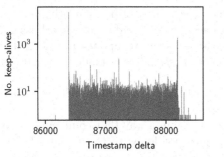 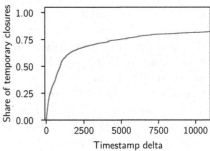

(a) Time since last keep-alive.   (b) Cumulative channel closure durations.

Fig. 3. Timestamp differences of keep-alive and channel closure updates.

4.1 Simulation Model

The behavior of real-world peer-to-peer networks is influenced by many different variables. Nodes participating in such networks can be diverse in geographical location, bandwidth restrictions, software implementation, software version or configuration, and simulating all different permutations is simply not feasible. In the context of investigating the gossip protocol of the Lightning Network, we restrict the scope of our simulation by making the following assumptions: if two nodes are connected through a channel, they have a constant TCP connection. The snapshot we use to bootstrap our simulation contains all nodes and all channels that exist in the network. We ignore any non-listening nodes that were not announced to the network, as well as private channels. Our simulation propagates node and channel announcements, but does not actually add them to the simulated topology. Only channel updates are applied to the simulated topology. The gossip algorithm is the main influence on the convergence delay, and we do not simulate other potential influences such as an overhead caused by cryptographic functions. Payments are atomic and instant. All nodes in each simulation follow the same gossip protocol. All nodes have the same bandwidth of 1 MB/s in up- and download.

We chose to implement our discrete-event simulator[7] in the Go programming language and bootstrap the simulation from historical topology snapshots that were extracted from an LND node with a fully synced network graph. These snapshots contain a list of nodes and channels which we use to build our simulation network. The snapshot we use for all simulations contains 17,332 nodes, 77,921 channels and was taken on Oct. 30, 2021. In order to simulate a realistic amount of traffic, we replay gossip messages that we recorded in the real network. This works well as most gossip messages can be traced back to an origin node in the network as long the snapshot we use to bootstrap the simulation is not much older than the start of the recorded period. For messages for which we could not

---

[7] https://github.com/dergoegge/lnconv-paper-sim.

find an origin in our snapshot we choose a random origin. Bandwidth is modeled by each node having an incoming byte counter that gets incremented with every message that is being downloaded and decremented with every message that is fully received. The arrival time of a new message is calculated based on a fixed bandwidth, the number of incoming bytes and a fixed latency overhead of 100 ms.

4.2   Simulation Results

In this section, we present the data collected on an LND simulation scenario in which we replayed the first hour of the gossip we recorded in Sect. 3, consisting of 7, 217 network messages. We simulate 100, 000 payment attempts which were uniformly distributed over the hour. Payment sources and destinations are chosen randomly and the payment amount is set to 1 *sat* in order to reduce interference by failures originating from anything else than outdated routing information.

Bandwidth. The simulated network transferred a total of 40.77 GB to deliver the 7, 217 messages to all nodes. The theoretical lower bound for bandwidth usage B_{min} is the product of the number of all nodes, the total number of messages and the average message size, i.e.,

$$B_{min} = num\_nodes \cdot num\_messages \cdot avg\_message\_size$$

Assuming all messages are channel updates with a size of 128 *bytes*, $B_{min} = 16.01$ GB. We therefore found that the network uses 2.55 times the theoretically needed bandwidth B_{min}.

Redundancy. 6.29% of messages will be seen only once, 33.28% will be seen twice, 59.93% will be seen three, and 0.5% will be seen four times. All nodes have 3 active gossip syncers which explains why most messages are seen three times or less. A message is only seen 4 times if it is received as part of the initial broadcast, which goes out to all connected peers. On average each message is seen 2.55 times. Note that this is the same factor as the one from our bandwidth calculations: every message that is received more than once is exactly the overhead to a perfect broadcast in which every message is received only once by each node.

Convergence Delay. We measure the convergence delay by recording how long it takes a message to be seen for the first time by every node. This is very similar to the measurements conducted in Sect. 3, but within a simulation we get much more accurate data since we have an omniscient view. Figure 4a compares the convergence delay we recorded in the real network to the one we observed in the simulation. In our simulation, the average time it took for a node to see a message is 291.21 s, with 95% of nodes seeing messages after 510 s and 100% of nodes seeing messages after 1, 075 s. The convergence delay seen in the simulation slightly differs from the delay measured in the real network with messages in the

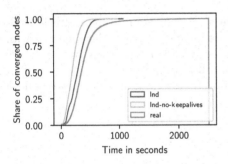
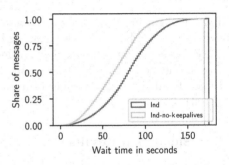

(a) Measured vs. simulated conv. delay.   (b) Queue waiting times.

Fig. 4. Convergence delay and broadcast queue waiting times in a simulated network consisting only of LND nodes.

simulation propagating faster after initially being broadcast and messages taking longer to reach all nodes in the real network. From 20% to 80% of nodes having seen the messages it takes 240 s in the simulation while in took 265 s in the real network.

As mentioned previously, roughly 50% of the messages that we recorded are keep-alive updates. We ran a simulation without the keep-alive updates (lnd-no-keepalives) and found that the convergence delay was significantly reduced, with 95% of nodes converging after 374.19 instead of 510 s.

Waiting Times. Looking at the broadcast queue waiting times of messages we observed that waiting times and hence the convergence delay become larger the more messages are propagating through the network. This is explained by the sub-batch trickling approach that LND has chosen which makes waiting times dynamic to a certain degree. The growth of waiting times is bounded by the maximum number of sub-batches that LND will send. A plot of the waiting times can be seen in Fig. 4b. The minimum waiting time is 0 s and the maximum is 175 s. A message will wait 175 s, if it arrives at the beginning of the 90 s stagger interval and gets broadcast in the last sub-batch, 85 s after the stagger timer ticks.

Failed Payment Attempts. Out of the 100,000 payment attempts, 42% were successful and 58% failed. 0.114% of attempts failed because the payment source did not have a recent update for one of the channel edges in the payment route.

As we have seen, the staggered broadcast is quite inefficient in its bandwidth usage with messages being seen 2.55 times on average by the same node and 95% of nodes converging after 510 s. The share of unconverged payment attempts (0.114%) does not seem that problematic but it could be argued that in absolute numbers the total number of unconverged payment attempts can still be large. The research by Waugh and Holz suggests that this rate is actually higher at around 1.2% [14]. Exploring alternative gossip algorithms seems worthwhile based on these results.

Table 2. Convergence delays (95%), bandwidth usage, and payment attempts.

Algorithm	Conv. delay	Bandwidth usage	Payment attempts
lnd	509.75 s	40.47 GB	602
lnd-t1s	312.65 s	39.36 GB	349
lnd-sb100	266.54 s	38.9 GB	316
lnd-inv	509.46 s	19.26 GB	592
lnd-inv-t1s	313.45 s	19.41 GB	394
lnd-inv-sb100	267.93 s	20.23 GB	274
cln	101.29 s	59.52 GB	171
cln-inv	103.2 s	26.36 GB	161
spanning (BFS)	1.11 s	15.7 GB	5
flooding-4	2.72 s	50.7 GB	3
flooding-8	1.72 s	94.7 GB	1
flooding-16	1.16 s	180.92 GB	2
flooding-32	0.82 s	353.21 GB	4
minisketch-4	19.25 s	19.15 GB	33
minisketch-8	20.24 s	19.84 GB	43
minisketch-16	20.7 s	21.45 GB	43
minisketch-32	20.54 s	21.46 GB	30

4.3 Evaluating Alternative Gossip Strategies

In this section, we layout ideas for potential alternative gossip algorithms that the Lightning Network could employ. We use our simulator to compare the different algorithms and evaluate the feasibility of these alternatives based on bandwidth usage, convergence delays, and their impact on payment attempts. We compare the following alternative strategies: flooding, a structured broadcast using a global spanning tree, inventory based gossip, parameter variations of the current protocol, as well as set reconciliation using Minisketch [4].

We compare all alternative strategies to each other and the simulation data from Sect. 4.2. We specifically compare bandwidth usage, convergence times and the number of unconverged payment attempts and simulate each algorithm using the same snapshot and replaying the same messages as before (17, 332 nodes, 77, 921 channels, 7, 217 messages over 1 h, 100, 000 payment attempts). The convergence delays and bandwidth usage for all the different algorithms are listed in Table 2.

As expected, flooding has the highest bandwidth usage with low convergence delays and the spanning tree algorithm (global tree constructed using breadth-first search) has the lowest bandwidth usage and the lowest convergence delay. With flooding, we see the bandwidth consumption scaling proportionally with

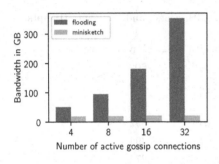

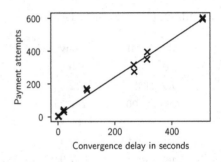

(a) Bandwidth vs. connectivity.

(b) Unconverged payment attempts vs. convergence delay.

Fig. 5. Simulated parameter interdependencies.

increased connectivity (number of active syncer connections). The convergence delay is naturally smaller with increased connectivity.

LND's choice of staggered broadcast parameters results in a roughly five times increase in the convergence delay compared to CLN. While LND's approach leads to a larger convergence delay it also reduces bandwidth usage by about 33%. We simulated two variations of LND's algorithm, one with a minimum sub-batch size of 100 instead of 10 messages (`lnd-sb100`), and one with a sub-batch delay of one instead of five seconds (`lnd-t1s`). Both of these parameter changes lead to faster messages broadcast after the stagger timer expires leading to an decrease in convergence delay of 39% for `lnd-t1s` and 48% for `lnd-sb100`.

Inventory-based protocols announce a shortened version of the full message to give the receiver the chance to only request the full message once. For gossip messages in the lightning network, the size of an inventory message can be 64 bits [12]. We see that inventory based protocols reduce bandwidth usage significantly when compared to their regular variants. With `lnd-inv` requiring 52.4% less bandwidth than `lnd` and `CLN-inv` requiring 55.7% less bandwidth than CLN. The convergence delays however are unaffected by the decrease in bandwidth usage. Usually it would be expected that latency increases with an inventory-based gossip protocol but the extra round trip has no impact here, given that the stagger interval is multiples larger than the round trip time.

In Fig. 5a, we compare the bandwidth usage of flooding and set reconciliation, in relation to the connections made by each node. Our set reconciliation algorithm is based on the Erlay protocol that was proposed for the transaction relay in the Bitcoin network [9]. In our protocol, we implemented no fan-out flooding and hence all messages are exchanged via set reconciliation. We observe that bandwidth usage does not increase proportionally with the number of connections made for the set reconciliation protocol. Instead, the bandwidth usage scales with the rate of messages in the network, just like the Erlay protocol.

We observe that the number of unconverged payment attempts is highly correlated with the convergence delay. We do not distinguish between failed payment attempts and attempts that arise due to opportunity costs, as the combined number of these attempts is sufficient in evaluating different protocols. As seen in Fig. 5b, based on our limited data set of the different algorithms, the relationship between the convergence delay and the number of unconverged payment attempts is linear. The lower the convergence delay, the fewer unconverged payment attempts can be observed.

5 Discussion

The staggered broadcast protocols rate-limit the propagation of channel updates by de-duplicating updates for the same channel with in the stagger interval. This means that a node will only forward one channel update for the same channel edge in every stagger interval. No potentially important updates are discarded, since the newest update that was seen will always be forwarded. This form of rate limiting prevents the network from witnessing rapid changes in channel policies, while still propagating the newest updates. The propagation of the newest updates is significantly delayed as we have shown through the simulations and measured in Sect. 3. We argue that this form of rate limiting implicitly discourages frequent channel updates at the cost of delivering the newest updates with large delays. Explicitly discouraging frequent updates through strict per-channel rate limiting as discussed in Sect. 3 could be well suited for some of our alternative protocols that aim to deliver messages faster. A strict rate limit would discard newer updates that violate the rate limit, so honest nodes should never broadcast messages for the same channel in violation of the limit.

LND's choice of parameters for its staggered broadcast is a bit of a mystery, since there is no public record on how the exact values were chosen. However, broadcasting messages in sub-batches instead of one large batch after the stagger timer expires is a good choice to reduce bursty resource usage. We would however recommend that the LND developers revisit their choice of parameters for the staggered broadcast, because reducing bandwidth usage by 33% while increasing the convergence delay by a factor of five does not seem like a reasonable trade-off (compared to parameters mentioned in the specification). As we have shown through the simulations, adjusting the parameters can have a big impact on the convergence delay. Adjusting these parameters would be the least complex software change to address the large convergence delay, while maintaining the rate limiting properties of the staggered broadcast.

Introducing an inventory-based gossip protocol reduces the bandwidth usage without changing the convergence delay at all. In combination with adjusting the parameters of the staggered broadcast the convergence delay could also be lowered. An inventory-based gossip protocol could remain a staggered broadcast and thereby maintain its rate limiting effect without introducing strict rate limiting. The added software complexity of an inventory-based gossip is fairly low and there already exists a proposal on the specification [5].

Increasing the number of connections that nodes make to gossip (connectivity) can lead to better reliability in adversarial environments. With low connectivity an attacker has to control less connections to be able to censor information from reaching a victim. For some protocols an increase in connectivity can also lead to a reduction in convergence times because the spread factor is higher.

Even though the spanning tree protocol seems great based on the results, it is not a great fit for the real network. As mentioned earlier, the protocol makes the assumption that all nodes agree on the exact same static spanning tree, which would not trivially work in the real network. A single tree is also not going work for security and reliability reasons. If one node in the tree goes offline, none of the nodes in its sub-tree would receive new messages. Introducing multiple trees to gain redundancy would increase the bandwidth usage. A spanning tree protocol with multiple trees would probably turnout to be similar in efficiency to a flooding protocol.

A flooding protocol comes with a small convergence delay of one to two seconds but increases bandwidth usage above that of the current algorithm (lnd). Bandwidth usage increases linearly with increased connectivity. If an increase in connectivity is wanted then flooding would not be suitable. In fact all protocols besides set reconciliation lead to a proportional increase in bandwidth with increased connectivity.

Compared to the other protocols, set reconciliation has a small convergence delay and low bandwidth usage. Increasing connectivity is also possible without increasing bandwidth usage, as the bandwidth usage scales with the rate of messages seen in the network. Introducing set reconciliation comes with much greater software complexity than any of the other protocols. Multiple new message types would need to be introduced and the Minisketch library adds a dependency.

Decreasing the number of unconverged payment attempts can also be done without changing the gossip protocol. Nodes could temporarily allow payments to use old channel policies after broadcasting a new policy. This would work well for fee or lock time adjustments, but would ultimately depend on the channel owners preferences.

6   Related Work

The explosive growth of the internet in its topological complexity as well as user count has led to a lot of research on the convergence delay for routing protocols, such as the Border Gateway Protocol (BGP). Large convergence delays in BGP can cause routing failures similar to how large convergence delays in the Lightning Network can cause payment failures. Labovitz et al. showed through a 2-year study that the convergence delay of BGP was much higher than previously expected. By injecting routing events to simulate failures and collecting data on these events, the authors were able to figure out the convergence delay for different types of events. Convergence delays were primarily caused by different router vendor's implementations of the BGP specification with regard to the choice of timer values [7]. da Silva and Souza Mota suggested ways on how to lower the BGP convergence delay which included adjusting timer values of implementations and centralizing control of networks [2]. Ben Houidi et al. investigated slow BGP table transfers which increase the convergence delay. They found that gaps, in which both sender and receiver are idle, during table transfers are a common occurrence caused by timer driven implementations, with different vendors choosing different timer values [1]. Similar to this BGP research, we found that a big part of the convergence delay in the Lightning Network is driven by the parameter choices for the staggered broadcast of different implementations.

Decker and Wattenhofer measured block propagation times in the Bitcoin network and verified that the propagation time is the primary cause for forks in the blockchain. They measured the propagation times by connecting to a large number of nodes and listening for block announcements. With this setup they recorded when blocks where seen and from which nodes. From this data they are able to estimate how long it takes blocks to traverse the network after the initial broadcast [3]. Our work is methodically similar, since we also measure the convergence delay in the Lightning Network by connecting to many nodes in the network and record arrival times of messages.

Naumenko et al. proposed *Erlay*, a protocol for transaction relay in the Bitcoin network that makes use of efficient set reconciliation in combination with flooding. It aims to lower the bandwidth requirements needed for transaction relay with the trade-off of higher latency. The authors evaluated the bandwidth and latency trade-off of Erlay and compared it to the current flood-only protocol [9]. We used the Erlay protocol as inspiration for simulating a similar protocol in the Lightning Network and specifically used their prior research when choosing the parameters for our protocol.

Waugh and Holz studied availability and reliability properties of the Lightning Network. They tested the network's ability to route payments of different amounts and created a taxonomy of permanent and temporary failures that occurred. They looked at the availability of nodes in the network and measured how much churn (nodes joining and leaving the network) exists [14]. This work listed payment attempt failure types that were caused by outdated routing information, by probing the network with real payments. We only simulated payments to investigate these failure types.

7   Conclusion

In this work, we analyzed the convergence delay in the Lightning Network, described the effect it can have on payments, and evaluated alternative gossip protocols that could reduce the delay. We found the network to have a significant convergence delay, with 95% of nodes only having converged after roughly 10 min. A majority of the gossip traffic consists of redundant channel updates (keepalive messages), which further increase the delay given the parameter choices of the LND implementation. Our simulations show that payment attempt failures due to unconverged routing information are rare (occurring in $\ll 1\%$ of payment attempts). However, the convergence delay may still be lowered while also reducing the bandwidth usage, either by switching to alternative gossip algorithms or adjusting the parameters of the current protocol. By switching to a set reconciliation based protocol, the connectivity of the network could be increased with nodes receiving gossip updates from more peers without suffering from significant increases in bandwidth.

References

1. Ben Houidi, Z., Meulle, M., Teixeira, R.: Understanding slow BGP routing table transfers. In: Proceedings of the 9th ACM SIGCOMM Conference on Internet Measurement, IMC 2009, Chicago, Illinois, USA, pp. 350–355. Association for Computing Machinery (2009)
2. da Silva, R.B., Mota, E.S.: A survey on approaches to reduce BGP interdomain routing convergence delay on the internet. IEEE Commun. Surv. Tutor. **19**(4), 2949–2984 (2017)
3. Decker, C., Wattenhofer, R.: Information propagation in the bitcoin network. In: P2P 2013: Proceedings of the 13th IEEE International Conference on Peer-to-Peer Computing, Trento, Italy, pp. 1–10 (2013)
4. Minisketch Developers: Minisketch: a library for BCH-based set reconciliation. https://github.com/sipa/minisketch/blob/89629eb2c7e262b39ba489b93b111760bade d4b3/README.md. Accessed 5 Dec 2021
5. Drouin, F.: [WIP] BOLT 7: Inventory-based gossip. https://github.com/lightning/bolts/pull/584. Accessed 5 Dec 2021
6. johng: Broadcast gossip announcements in sub batches. https://github.com/lightningnetwork/lnd/pull/2985. Accessed 5 Dec 2021
7. Labovitz, C.: Delayed internet routing convergence. SIGCOMM Comput. Commun. Rev. **30**(4), 175–187 (2000)
8. Nakamoto, S.: Bitcoin: a peer-to-peer electronic cash system (2008)
9. Naumenko, G.: Erlay: efficient transaction relay for bitcoin. In: CCS 2019: Proceedings of the 2019 ACM SIGSAC Conference on Computer and Communications Security, London, UK, pp. 817–831 (2019)
10. Osuntokun, O.: config: increase default trickle delay from 30s to 1m30s. https://github.com/lightningnetwork/lnd/pull/2538. Accessed 5 Dec 2021
11. Poon, J., Dryja, T.: The bitcoin lightning network: scalable off-chain instant payments (2016)
12. Russell, R.: [Lightning-dev] Minisketch and lightning gossip. https://lists.linuxfoundation.org/pipermail/lightningdev/2018-December/001741.html. Accessed 5 Dec 2021
13. Sompolinsky, Y., Zohar, A.: Accelerating bitcoin's transaction processing. Fast money grows on trees, not chains. Cryptology ePrint Archive, Report 2013/881 (2013)
14. Waugh, F., Holz, R.: An empirical study of availability and reliability properties of the bitcoin lightning network. CoRR abs/2006.14358 (2020)

LightSwap: An Atomic Swap Does Not Require Timeouts at both Blockchains

Philipp Hoenisch[1], Subhra Mazumdar[2(✉)], Pedro Moreno-Sanchez[3],
and Sushmita Ruj[4]

[1] CoBloX Pty Ltd., Sydney, Australia
philipp@coblox.tech
[2] Christian Doppler Laboratory Blockchain Technologies for the Internet of Things
Vienna, TU Wien, Vienna, Austria
subhra.mazumdar@tuwien.ac.at
[3] IMDEA Software Institute, Madrid, Spain
pedro.moreno@imdea.org
[4] School of Computer Science and Engineering, University of New South Wales,
Sydney, Australia
sushmita.ruj@unsw.edu.au

Abstract. Security and privacy issues with centralized exchange services have motivated the design of *atomic swap* protocols for decentralized trading across currencies. These protocols follow a standard blueprint similar to the 2-phase commit in databases: (i) both users first lock their coins under a certain (cryptographic) condition and a timeout; (ii-a) the coins are swapped if the condition is fulfilled; or (ii-b) coins are released after the timeout. The quest for these protocols is to minimize the requirements from the scripting language supported by the swapped coins, thereby supporting a larger range of cryptocurrencies. The recently proposed universal atomic swap protocol [IEEE S&P'22] demonstrates how to swap coins whose scripting language only supports the verification of a digital signature on a transaction. However, the timeout functionality is cryptographically simulated with verifiable timelock puzzles, a computationally expensive primitive that hinders its use in battery-constrained devices such as mobile phones. In this state of affairs, we question whether the 2-phase commit paradigm is necessary for atomic swaps in the first place. In other words, is it possible to design a secure atomic swap protocol where the timeout is not used by (at least one of the two) users?

In this work, we present LightSwap, the first secure atomic swap protocol that does not require the timeout functionality (not even in the form of a cryptographic puzzle) by one of the two users. LightSwap is thus better suited for scenarios where a user, running an instance of LightSwap on her mobile phone, wants to exchange coins with an online exchange service running an instance of LightSwap on a computer. We show how LightSwap can be used to swap Bitcoin and Monero, an interesting use case since Monero does not provide any scripting functionality support other than linkable ring signature verification.

A full version of our paper is available in [2].

© The Author(s), under exclusive license to Springer Nature Switzerland AG 2023
J. Garcia-Alfaro et al. (Eds.): DPM 2022/CBT 2022, LNCS 13619, pp. 219–235, 2023.
https://doi.org/10.1007/978-3-031-25734-6_14

Keywords: Blockchain · Atomic swap · Bitcoin · Monero ·
Lightweight applications · Adaptor signatures

1 Introduction

The functionality of atomic swaps [18] was introduced for trading assets between two parties such that each of them holds assets in a different blockchain. The concept of atomicity in such a setting is inspired by database systems where either a multi-step transaction gets committed or it is rolled back in its entirety. In the blockchain setting, it holds similar relevance guaranteeing that the swap either fully occurs or fails entirely [17,44].

As an illustrative example, consider that a user *Alice* has asset α in blockchain $\mathcal{B}_A$ and user *Bob* has asset β in blockchain $\mathcal{B}_B$. An atomic swap is said to be successful when *Bob* transfers asset β to *Alice* on $\mathcal{B}_B$ contingent to the transfer of asset α by *Alice* to *Bob* on $\mathcal{B}_A$. If *Alice* decides to cancel the swap, a refund will be initiated. Upon asset refund, *Alice* will retain α in $\mathcal{B}_A$ and *Bob* will retain β in $\mathcal{B}_B$. A successful swap thereby leads to an exchange of asset's ownership [42]. Hence both the parties need to have accounts in each of the blockchains to enable transfer of ownership [28].

While one can easily envision an atomic swap functionality leveraging a trusted server, the blockchain community has put significant efforts into decentralized protocols for atomic swaps [1,18,26,29,30,35,36,39,44,45]. In a nutshell, these different protocols follow a standard blueprint based on two building blocks: (i) a (cryptographic) locking mechanism that allows one user to locks coins for another user in a given blockchain; and (ii) a timeout mechanism that allows the creator of a lock to release it after a certain time has expired. With these building blocks, current atomic swap protocols are based on the following blueprint: first, *Alice* locks α in $\mathcal{B}_A$ for *Bob* and establishes an expiration time of T_A to such lock. Afterward, *Bob* locks β in $\mathcal{B}_B$ to *Alice* with an expiration time of $T_B : T_A > T_B$. At this point, the atomic swap has been committed and one of the following two outcomes can happen: (i) *Bob* allows *Alice* to unlock β in $\mathcal{B}_B$, which in turn "automatically" allows *Bob* to unlock α in $\mathcal{B}_A$; or (ii) both parties decide to abort the swap by allowing to release the locks at times T_B and T_A respectively.

This blueprint framework used by atomic swaps is based on two crucial properties. First, the (cryptographic) locks should allow to "relate" one to another in the sense that if one party opens one lock in one blockchain, such opening operation automatically reveals enough information to the other party to open her own lock in the other blockchain. Such "correlated locks" have been implemented in practice using different techniques such as leveraging the Turing-complete scripting language of blockchains like Ethereum [40] or more specific scripting functionality like Hash-time lock contract [7,12,18,30], using a third blockchain [21,22,41] as the coordinator or bridge of the two blockchains [3,23,24,34,43] used for the swap , leveraging trusted hardware [6], or designing cryptographic schemes crafted for this purpose such as adaptor signatures [13,39].

The second crucial property is that locked funds must be released to the original owner after a certain time has expired. Surprisingly, all alternative protocols previously mentioned share only two techniques with regard to handling the timelock functionality. They either (i) rely on the scripting language of the underlying blockchain to implement it; or (ii) rely on a cryptographic timelock puzzle [10,33,37] where a secret is saved under a cryptographic puzzle that can be solved after a certain number of serial cryptographic operations are executed. Unfortunately, both of these techniques clearly hinder the adoption of atomic swaps. On the one hand, timelock based on the scripting language restricts its use from those cryptocurrencies that do not have such support, such as Monero [31] or Zcash (shielded addresses) [20]. On the other hand, cryptographic puzzles impose a computation burden on the users that need to compute such a puzzle for each of the atomic swaps that they are involved in. Such a scheme is not suitable for lightweight applications as it would drain the battery of a smartphone or would add a non-trivial cost if outsourced to a third party (e.g., Amazon Web Services [11]).

In this state of affairs, we raise the following question: *Is the timelock functionality a necessary condition to design atomic swap protocols? Or in other words, is it possible to design an atomic swap protocol such that the timelock functionality is not required in (at least one of) the two involved blockchains?*

1.1 Our Contribution

In this work, we present for the first time a secure, decentralized, and trustless atomic swap protocol that does not require any type of timelock in one of the cryptocurrencies. In particular, we present LightSwap, a lightweight atomic swap between Bitcoin and Monero. Similar to previous works, LightSwap leverages adaptor signatures to implement the cryptographic condition that correlates the locks over the committed coins. The crux of the contribution in LightSwap is to depart from the 2-phase paradigm. Instead, we propose a novel paradigm that maintains the security for the users (i.e., an honest user does not lose coins) while removing the need to use timeouts in any form for one of the two cryptocurrencies.

2 Notation and Background

Transactions in UTXO Model. In this work, we focus on the UTXO transaction model, as it is followed by both Bitcoin and Monero.

For readability, transaction charts are used to visualize the transactions, their ordering, and usage in any protocol. We follow the notation in [5]. The charts must be read from left to right as per the direction of the arrows. A transaction is represented as a rectangular box with a rounded corners, input to such transactions is denoted by incoming arrows and output by outgoing arrows. Each rectangular box has square boxes drawn within. These boxes represent the output of the transaction, termed as *output boxes*, and the value within represents

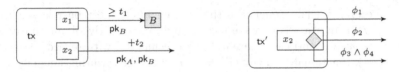

Fig. 1. (Left) Transaction tx has two outputs, one of value x_1 that can be spent by B (indicated by the gray box) with a transaction signed w.r.t. pk_B at (or after) round t_1, and one of value x_2 that can be spent by a transaction signed w.r.t. pk_A and pk_B but only if at least t_2 rounds passed since tx was accepted on the blockchain. (Right) Transaction tx′ has one input, which is the second output of tx containing x_2 coins and has only one output, which is of value x_2 and can be spent by a transaction whose witness satisfies the output condition $\phi_1 \lor \phi_2 \lor (\phi_3 \land \phi_4)$. The input of tx is not shown.

the number of coins. Conditions for spending these coins are written on the output arrows going out of these boxes. The notations and the illustration of the transaction charts are provided in Fig. 1.

The parties that can spend these coins present in the output box are represented below the outgoing arrows in form of a signature. Usually, these are represented as the public keys which can verify this signature. Additional conditions for spending the coins are written above the arrow. Conditions are encoded in a script supported by the underlying cryptocurrency. For our paper, we use the notation "$+t$" or $\texttt{RelTime}(t)$ which denotes the waiting time before a transaction containing an output can be published on-chain. This is termed as the *relative locktime*. If absolute locktime is used, then it is represented as "$\geq t$" or $\texttt{AbsTime}(t)$. It means the condition for spending the output is satisfied if the height of the blockchain is at least t. For representing multiple conditions, if it is a disjunction of several conditions, i.e. $\phi = \phi_1 \lor \phi_2 \lor \ldots \lor \phi_n$, a diamond-shaped box is used in the output box and each sub condition ϕ_i is written above the output arrow. The conjunction of several conditions is represented as $\phi = \phi_1 \land \phi_2 \land \ldots \land \phi_m$.

Adaptor Signatures. We recall the functionality for generation and verification of adaptor signature with respect to a hard relation. This becomes one building block in our approach to substitute the functionality of HTLC. In more detail, given a hard relation $R : (x, X) \in R$, where X is the statement and x is a witness, public key pk having secret key sk, the language L_R and a signature scheme $\Sigma = (\texttt{Gen}, \texttt{Sign}, \texttt{Vrfy})$, an adaptor signature is defined using four algorithms $\Xi_{R,\Sigma} = (\texttt{pSign}, \texttt{pVrfy}, \texttt{Adapt}, \texttt{Ext})$ as follows [4]:

- $\texttt{pSign}(sk, m, X)$: A probabilisitc polynomial time algorithm which on input of secret key sk, message $m \in \{0,1\}^*$ and statement $X \in L_R$, outputs an a pre-signature $\hat{\sigma}$.
- $\texttt{pVrfy}(pk, m, X, \hat{\sigma})$: A deterministic polynomial time algorithm which on input the public key pk, the message $m \in \{0,1\}^*$, the statement $X \in L_R$, and pre-signature $\hat{\sigma}$, outputs a bit b. If $b = 1$, $\hat{\sigma}$ is a valid pre-signature on message m.

- Adapt$(\hat{\sigma}, x)$: A deterministic polynomial time algorithm which on input the witness for the statement X, i.e. x and the pre-signature $\hat{\sigma}$, outputs a signature σ.
- Ext$(\sigma, \hat{\sigma}, X)$: A deterministic polynomial time algorithm which on input signature σ, pre-signature $\hat{\sigma}$ and the statement $X \in L_R$, outputs a witness $x : (x, X) \in R$ or $\perp$.

In this work, we leverage the threshold adaptor signature for ECDSA [27] for the Bitcoin side and the instance defined in [29,38] for Monero. In a 2-of-2 threshold adaptor signature instance, each participant has a share of the secret key sk.

3 Problem Definition

Given a user *Alice* and the service provider *Bob*, the former holds x XMR in Monero blockchain and *Bob* holds y BTC in Bitcoin blockchain. *Alice* wants to exchange x XMR for *Bob*'s y BTC. A generic atomic swap protocol follows a 2-phase commit protocol similar to that used in databases: (i) each user commits their assets and (ii) each user claims the assets of the counterparty. To initiate an atomic swap, both parties need to lock their coins and set a timeperiod within which the swap must be completed. If *Alice* wants to cancel the swap, she will initiate a refund and the locked coins are refunded to the original owner after the designated timeperiod.

Existing Atomic Swap Protocols and Their Drawbacks. We discuss existing approaches as solution for the problem defined above. We denote *Alice* as **A** and *Bob* as **B**.

(i) *Using HTLC based approach.* The simplest trustless exchange protocol widely used across several cryptocurrency exchange is based on *Hash Timelocked Contract or HTLC*. We discuss an HTLC based solution where both **A** and **B** hold their coins at time t_0. The script used in HTLC takes the tuple $(\alpha, h, t, \mathbf{A}, \mathbf{B})$, where α is the asset to be transferred, h is the hash value, and t is the contract's timeout period. The contract states that **A** will transfer α to **B** contingent to the knowledge r where $h = \mathtt{H}(r)$ where $\mathtt{H}$ is a standard cryptographic hash function if the contract is invoked within the timeout period t. If the timeperiod elapses and **B** fails to invoke the contract, the asset α is refunded to user **A**.

A can initiate exchange of x XMR in $\mathcal{B}_A$ for y BTC in $\mathcal{B}_B$ using HTLC. The former chooses a random value r and generates $h = \mathtt{H}(r)$. She next proceeds to lock x XMR in the contract $H_1 = HTLC(x, h, t_5, \mathbf{A}, \mathbf{B})$ at time t_1, where $t_1 > t_0$, and sends h, t_5 to **B**. The timeout period of the contract is t_5. Now **B** will reuse the same terms of the contract but set the timeperiod as $t_4 : t_4 < t_5$. We will explain why the timeout period must be less than the previous contract. **B** locks y BTC in the contract $H_2 = HTLC(y, h, t_4, \mathbf{B}, \mathbf{A})$ at time t_2, where $t_2 > t_1$. **A** knows the preimage of h and claim the coins from **B** by invoking H_2 at time

$t_3 : t_2 < t_3 < t_4$. **B** gets the preimage r which he can use for claiming coins from **A**. If he had used the timeout period t_5 for H_2, then it is quite possible that **A** delays and claims the coins from **B** just at time t_5. This would lead to a race condition and **B** might fail to acquire the coins from **A** if the time at which H_1 is invoked exceeds t_5. Hence he sets the timeout period of the contract H_2 less than the timeout period of contract H_1. **B** claims the coins from **A** by invoking H_1 at time $t_4 : t_3 < t_4 < t_5$. By time t_5, **A** holds y BTC in $\mathcal{B}_B$ and **B** holds x XMR in $\mathcal{B}_A$. This depicts the situation when the swap succeeds and the state transition from time t_0 to t_5 discussed above is termed as *happy path*. If either of the party decides not to co-operate then it will lead to failure of swap.

Incompatibility of HTLC in Scriptless Cryptocurrencies (e.g., Monero). HTLC-based approach requires the use of timelock on both the Monero side as well as the Bitcoin side. The timeout mechanism is essential to allow users to recover their assets in the case the swap does not go through. Thus we require two main building blocks to implement atomic swaps for cryptocurrencies: an atomic locking mechanism and a timeout. However, the main challenge is that Monero does not support hashlock and timelock. Without these two features, it will not be possible for **A** to lock her coins at time t_1. The use of timelock puzzles will make our protocol unsuitable for lightweight applications. Hence none of the paths can be initiated.

(ii) *Without using HTLC for Monero.* A fix for the challenges faced in HTLC based protocol would be to design a protocol without having any hashlock and timelock at Monero side, but **B** uses HTLC for locking y BTC in $\mathcal{B}_B$. In Monero, coins locked in the address can be spend only by the party possessing the private key of that particular address. The modified protocol allows **A** to lock her coins in an address say pk, whose secret key is solely possessed by her. This will allow **A** to initiate a refund at her will. Let the secret key be s. She locks x XMR in address pk at time t_1. Using this secret key, she generates $h_s : h_s = \text{H}(s)$. She shares h_s with **B**. The latter locks y BTC into $HTLC(y, h_s, t_4, \mathbf{B}, \mathbf{A})$ at time t_2. For a successful swap, **A** invokes HTLC using the secret s at time t_3 and claims y BTC. **B** uses the secret key s to spend x XMR locked in address pk at t_4 and transfers it to his address in $\mathcal{B}_A$.

Attack on this Approach. Apparently, it might look like we can accomplish the swap using this approach. However, the problem is now **A** can initiate a refund at any time she wants. Even if she initiates a refund after t_2, she can still invoke the HTLC as $t_2 < t_4$, and claim y BTC from **B**. The service provider **B** will lose his coins. To counter this problem, we can resort to 2-of-2 secret sharing where each half of the secret key s of address pk will be shared with **A** and **B**. This will make **A** dependent on **B** for issuing a refund, violating our objective. If **B** does not lock his coins at t_2, **A**'s coins will remain locked forever.

From the above discussion, it is clear that designing an efficient protocol without any kind of timeout in one of the two chains is a challenging task. We provide a high-level overview of our proposed solution in the next section.

4   Our Approach

4.1   Solution Overview

Our protocol must ensure that the party moving first is allowed to issue a refund without depending on the counterparty. However, it must also be ensured that if the swap is canceled, both parties must get a refund. Since Monero does not support timelocks, we need to design a protocol that leverages the timelock used in the Bitcoin script. We use threshold adaptor signature for seamless redemption and refund of coins without any party suffering a loss in the process.

Signing Refund Transaction in Monero. Consider an atomic swap where *Alice* (or **A**) wants to exchange her monero for *Bob*'s (or **B**) bitcoin. If she locks her coins in an address whose secret key is known to her, she can spend the coins at any time. It is better if the secret key is shared where each half is possessed by **A** and **B**. However, this would mean that **A** has to depend on **B** for initiating a refund. If **B** does not cooperate, then **A**'s coin will remain locked forever. Hence both of them must collaborate and sign the refund transaction even before **A** locks her coins. The signature generated uses *threshold version of adaptor signature*. To generate such a signature, **B** uses his portion of the secret key as well as a cryptographic condition, say R, to generate the incomplete signature. **A** can complete the signature using her share of the secret key and upon fulfilling the hard relation R inserted by **B**. On the Bitcoin side, once **A** invokes the redeem transaction, the coins can be redeemed by her only after a certain timeperiod, say t, elapses. In the meantime, if **B** finds that **A** has refunded her coins but still invoked the redeem transaction at the Bitcoin side, then he can publish his refund transaction within the timeperiod t. A valid signature for a refund transaction can be generated by providing a witness to the relation R. Once **A** has published her refund transaction on $\mathcal{B}_A$, **B** will know the witness and hence, he can claim a refund easily.

We now describe our proposed two-party atomic swap protocol ensuring that none of the parties lose coins in the process.

4.2   Protocol Description

We discuss a lightwieght atomic swap protocol where **A** wants to exchange x_A XMR for y_B BTC of **B**. The protocol consists of six phases: *setup, lock, redeem, cancel, emergency refund* and *punish*. The transaction schema for BTC to XMR atomic swap is shown in Fig. 2. x_A coins are held in blockchain $\mathcal{B}_A$ and y_B coins are held in blokchain $\mathcal{B}_B$.

Setup Phase. In this phase, **A** and **B** jointly create the public key pk in $\mathcal{B}_A$. **A** uses pk to generate an address for locking her coins. Each party will generate one-half of the secret key, i.e., **A** will generate s_A, and **B** will generate s_B. A linear combination of their secret keys will result in s. The latter serves as the private key of the address pk. Additionally, **A** samples an additional secret r_A and generates the statements R_A for $\mathcal{B}_A$ and R_A^* for $\mathcal{B}_B$ (For example,

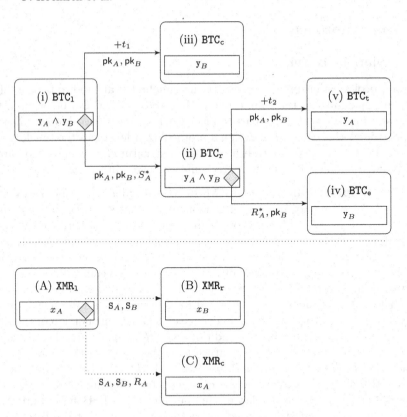

Fig. 2. New transaction schema for BTC to XMR atomic swaps. *Top*: Transaction schema for Bitcoin. *Bottom*: Transaction schema for Monero. Here x_A and x_B denotes the fact that x Monero coins belong to either Alice or Bob correspondingly. Similarly with y_A and y_B in Bitcoin.

$R_A = r_a G$ and $R_A^* = r_a H$ for two different groups having generator G and H respectively). **A** generates a proof π_{r_a} that proves r_A is the witness to both the statements R_A and R_A^*. Similarly, using one half of secret key, s_A, **A** generate the statements S_A and S_A^* for the blockchains $\mathcal{B}_A$ and $\mathcal{B}_B$ respectively. **B** generates a proof π_{s_a} that proves s_a is the witness to S_A and S_A^*. **B** also generates a proof π_{s_b} that proves that s_b is the witness of statement S_B. Both parties share $((\pi_{r_a}, R_A, R_A^*), (\pi_{s_a}, S_A, S_A^*), (\pi_{s_b}, S_B))$. The readers may refer the full version of the paper for details on generation of proof for each statement.

Pre-signing of Monero Refund Transaction: **A** creates a Monero refund transaction $\mathrm{XMR_c}$, box (C) in Fig. 2, where x_A coins locked in address pk is send to another address on $\mathcal{B}_A$ controlled by **A**.

$$\mathrm{XMR_c} : \mathrm{pk} \xrightarrow{x_A} \mathbf{A}$$

Later, **A** and **B** collaborate and pre-sign $\mathrm{XMR_c}$ based on the statement R_A. Both parties provide their share of private spend keys in the process of generating the adaptor signature without revealing it explicitly. This allows $\mathbf{A}$ to opt for a refund anytime she wants.

Exchanging Signatures for the Transactions on Bitcoin Side: $\mathbf{B}$ shares his funding source, tx_{fund}, with $\mathbf{A}$. The source has a balance of at least y_B coins. The transaction BTC_1, box (i) in Fig. 2, is created where $\mathbf{B}$ will lock his coins in a 2-of-2 multisig redeem script, $\mathsf{pk}_{A,B}^{lock}$. The output is denoted as $y_A \wedge y_B$.

$$\text{BTC}_1 : tx_{fund} \xrightarrow{\ y_A \wedge y_B\ } \mathsf{pk}_{A,B}^{lock}$$

The coins can either be redeemed by $\mathbf{A}$ or refunded by $\mathbf{B}$ after a certain timeperiod t_1. $\mathbf{A}$ can publish the transaction BTC_r, box (ii) in Fig. 2, spends the output of BTC_1 and again locks into a 2-of-2 multisig redeem script, $\mathsf{pk}_{A,B}^{redeem}$.

$$\text{BTC}_r : \mathsf{pk}_{A,B}^{lock} \xrightarrow{\ y_A \wedge y_B\ } \mathsf{pk}_{A,B}^{redeem}$$

The output of BTC_r can either be refunded to $\mathbf{B}$, if there is an emergency, or it can be claimed by $\mathbf{A}$ after a certain timeperiod t_2. $\mathbf{A}$ creates the transaction BTC_t, box (v) in Fig. 2, which will allow her to spend the output of BTC_r after timeperiod t_2 and shares it with $\mathbf{B}$.

$$\text{BTC}_t : \mathsf{pk}_{A,B}^{redeem} \xrightarrow{\ y_A\ } \mathbf{A}$$

The latter signs BTC_t and sends it to $\mathbf{A}$. Later $\mathbf{B}$ creates the transaction BTC_c, represented in box (iii) in Fig. 2. It allows him to refund the output $y_A \wedge y_B$ coins of BTC_1.

$$\text{BTC}_c : \mathsf{pk}_{A,B}^{lock} \xrightarrow{\ y_A\ } \mathbf{B}$$

$\mathbf{B}$ sends BTC_c to $\mathbf{A}$ for signature. $\mathbf{A}$ sends BTC_r to $\mathbf{B}$. The latter verifies the transaction, pre-signs the transaction BTC_r based on the statement S_A^* and sends the partially signed transaction to $\mathbf{A}$. Now $\mathbf{A}$ will sign the transaction BTC_1 and send it to $\mathbf{B}$.

Lock Phase. $\mathbf{A}$ creates the transaction XMR_1, box (A) in Fig. 2 where she locks x_A coins into address pk.

$$\text{XMR}_1 : \mathbf{A} \xrightarrow{\ x_A\ } \mathsf{pk}$$

$\mathbf{B}$, upon verification that $\mathbf{A}$ has locked the coins, proceeds with publishing BTC_1 and locks his coins as well.

Redeem Phase. $\mathbf{A}$ knows the witness s_A for the statement S_A^* and thus she generates a valid signature for BTC_r. She publishes the transaction but cannot spend the output before a timperiod of t_2 has elapsed. Meanwhile, $\mathbf{B}$ extracts s_A from the signature on BTC_r. He will create the transaction XMR_r, box (B) in Fig. 2 that will allow him to redeem the coins locked in address pk.

$$\text{XMR}_r : \mathsf{pk} \xrightarrow{\ x_B\ } \mathbf{B}$$

By combining the secret keys s_A and s_B, he will be able to sign $\mathtt{XMR_r}$ and publish it on-chain.

Cancel Swap. If **A** wants to cancel the swap, she will generate a valid signature for $\mathtt{XMR_c}$ using the witness r_A and publish it to claim her coins. Meanwhile, **B** can wait till t_1 has elapsed since $\mathtt{BTC_1}$ was published and **A** has not initiated the swap. He publishes $\mathtt{BTC_c}$ and unlocks his coins.

Emergency Refund. Suppose **A** has initiated the swap by publishing $\mathtt{BTC_r}$ but she has unlocked her coins by publishing $\mathtt{XMR_c}$. Once $\mathtt{XMR_c}$ is published, **B** extracts r_A from the signature on $\mathtt{XMR_c}$. He will create transaction $\mathtt{BTC_e}$, box (iv) in Fig. 2 and spend $y_A \wedge y_B$ coins locked in $\mathsf{pk}_{A,B}^{redeem}$.

$$\mathtt{BTC_e} : \mathsf{pk}_{A,B}^{redeem} \xrightarrow{\;y_B\;} \mathbf{B}$$

Now he will sign the transaction using r_A and publish the transaction on-chain before t_2 elapses.

From the above discussion on *emergency refund*, we emphasize the utility of not allowing **A** to redeem the coins locked by **B**. Instead, a waiting time of t_2 allows **B** to recover his coins, if **A** is malicious. On one hand, **A** can initiate a refund any time she wants but on the other hand, she cannot claim the bitcoins instantly.

Punish. If **B** has published $\mathtt{XMR_r}$ and claimed x_B coins, then **A** waits for t_2 timeperiod to elapse after publishing $\mathtt{BTC_r}$. She will publish $\mathtt{BTC_t}$ and claim y_A coins.

Now, consider that **B** has stopped responding and has neither claimed x_B coins nor initiated a refund. In that case, **A** can *punish* him for remaining inactive by publishing $\mathtt{BTC_t}$. Hence, this phase is called *punish* phase and **B** loses his bitcoins. A detailed description of the protocol can be found in the full version of our paper [2].

4.3   Security and Privacy Goals

- **Correctness**: If both parties are honest, with one party willing to exchange x units of coin for y units of coins of the other party, then the protocol terminates with each party obtaining the desired amount.
- **Soundness**: An honest party must not lose funds while executing the protocol with an adversary.
- **Unlinkability**: Any party not involved with the atomic swap must not be able to link two cross-chain transactions responsible for the atomic swap, except with negligible probability.
- **Fungibility**: An adversary must not be able to distinguish between a normal transaction and a transaction for atomic swap in Monero Blockchain, except with negligible probability.

We discuss how the security properties defined above holds for our proposed protocol:

- **Correctness**: If both parties **A** and **B** are honest, then the atomic swap protocol ensures that if party **A** is able to redeem y_A coins then party B can redeem x_B coins as well within a bounded timeperiod. This is possible since when **A** publishes BTC_r, **B** extracts the secret s_A from signature on BTC_r and uses the same for signing transaction XMR_r.
- **Soundness**: If party **A** initiates the swap but publishes XMR_c before **B** publishes XMR_r, then a relative locktime of t_2 on spending the output of BTC_r allows **B** to opt for an emergency refund by publishing BTC_e and refund his coins.
- **Linkability**: Since Monero transactions are confidential and signatures on transactions are generated from random values, any malicious party observing both the Monero and Bitcoin blockchains will be able to link a pair of Bitcoin and Monero transactions involved in the swap with negligible probability.
- **Fungibility**: There is no structural difference between a normal Monero transaction and a Monero transaction constructed for LightSwap. Any malicious party observing the Monero blockchain can distinguish between such a pair of transactions with negligible probability.

A detailed security analysis of LightSwap in the Global Universal Composability (GUC) [9] framework has been discussed in the full version of our paper [2].

5   Discussion

5.1   Building Monero Transactions

Pre-signing transactions involve signing a transaction where the outputs that need to be spent as input in this transaction have not been added to the blockchain. Since the private spend key and private view key for spending the output of XMR_1 is generated using 2-of-2 secret sharing, it requires both parties to co-operate and generate a valid signature for spending this output. However, if Bob stops responding, Alice will never get back her coins. Pre-signing XMR_c will allow her to go for refund anytime she wants prior to signing of XMR_1 [25]. Unfortunately, it is not possible to implement the pre-signing of Monero transaction in its present form. We specify the key components for building a Monero transaction - (i) a transaction has a ring signature per input to hide exactly which output is being spent, (ii) a unique key image for an input being spent to avoid double-spending, (iii) Pedersen commitments [32] for every input and output, retaining the confidentiality of the transaction, and lastly, (iv) to show that difference in input and output of a transaction is non-negative, bulletproofs [8] are used.

The input of a Monero transaction, denoted as vin, consists of the amount, key offsets, and key image. Since the amount is confidential, it is set to 0. The key offset allows verifiers to find ring member keys and commitments in the blockchain. It consists of the real output public key along with 10 other decoy outputs. The first offset value is the absolute height of the block where the first member is present. Rest are assigned values relative to the absolute value. For example, if the set of 11 public keys forming ring members have real offsets $\{h, h + 4, h + 6, h + 10, h + 20, h + 33, h + 45, h + 50, h + 67, h + 77, h + 98\}$, then it is recorded as $\{h, 4, 2, 4, 10, 13, 12, 5, 17, 10, 21\}$ where h is the height of the block where the first public key can be found and each subsequent offset is relative to the previous. This set is termed as *"ring"* and is stored in the transaction. To ensure that a particular output can only be used once as an input, Monero includes a key image of the output's public key. The key image is constructed using the public key of the output that will be spent. This avoids double-spending attacks in Monero blockchain. Next, we discuss how the input *"ring"* is used for constructing the ring signature CLSAG.

For computing the signature hash $c_{i+1}, \forall i \in \{0, 1, \ldots, 10\}$ where $c_{11} = c_0$, *"ring"* is taken as input along with other parameters and concatenated with L_i and R_i. To generate the signature, the offsets must be known. Offsets are not known until and unless all the outputs in set *ring* have been added to the blockchain. Lack of offsets violates the policy of pre-signing where the transaction must be signed before the output that needs to be spent gets added to the blockchain. To avoid this problem, instead of using the key offsets as input for generating a signature hash, the set of public keys can be used as input. However, this would require changing Monero's codebase but the change is necessary for realizing Layer 2 protocols in Monero blockchain.

5.2 Building Bitcoin Transactions

We created the necessary Bitcoin transactions for LightSwap and deployed these transactions on the Bitcoin testnet. We observed and recorded the size of transactions in bytes, where BTC_1 and BTC_r is 360 B each, BTC_c is 230 B, BTC_e is 231 B, and BTC_t is 229 B. Our result demonstrates the compatibility of the protocol with the current Bitcoin network. The code is available in https://anonymous.4open.science/r/btc_xmr_swap-A7B1, forked from https://github.com/generalized-channels/gc.

6 Related Work

There have been efforts to design time locks on Monero. DLSAG [29] mentions that Monero is locked in a 2-of-2 joint address comprising two different public keys. Any one of the public keys can be used to spend Monero from the address based on certain conditions, for example, pre-defined block height. However, Monero needs to undergo a hard fork to implement DLSAG. Thyagarajan et al. [38] proposed the first payment channel for Monero, PayMo, without requiring any system-wide modifications. Additionally, the authors have also proposed a secure atomic cross-chain swap using PayMo. The payment channel uses a new cryptographic primitive called *Verifiable Timed Linkable Ring Signature (VTLRS)*. The signature scheme uses the timed commitment of a linkable ring signature on a given Monero transaction. However, timed commitment requires a huge computation overhead, making it unsuitable for designing lightweight protocols.

Threshold ring multi-signature proposed by Goodell and Noether [15] was used for spender-ambiguous cross-chain atomic swaps. Their construction doesn't involve any timelock mechanism, it is based on sharing of secret keys - whenever one party goes on-chain for claiming the amount, the other party can reconstruct the secret key completely. However, the paper doesn't formally define the refund method in case one of the parties acts maliciously. Gugger [16] proposed atomic swaps between Monero and Bitcoin. However, as per the concept of the atomic swap, the party which initiates the swap must lock its money first in its native blockchain. However, Gugger's protocol requires the counterparty selling Bitcoin in exchange for Monero to move first. This is not desired as it puts the counterparty at risk. Since there is a timelock involved before which the Bitcoins can be refunded, the buyer of Bitcoin may resort to mounting draining attack [14] by not locking his Monero. We have provided a detailed comparison of Gugger's protocol and LightSwap in Sect. A of Appendix. Hoenisch and Pino [19] provide a high-level sketch of a protocol that mitigates the limitations of Gugger's protocol. However, it avoids any detailed description of the construction of the adaptor ring signature on Monero.

7   Conclusions

We propose LightSwap, a lightweight two-party atomic swap facilitating the exchange of Bitcoin and Monero. LightSwap does not require any type of timeout at one of the two blockchains, without additional trust assumptions. Our protocol is thus efficient, fungible, scalable, and can be used for any cryptocurrency whose script does not support timelock. Either the party can initiate a refund, even if the counterparty does not cooperate. We provide steps for implementing LightSwap that demonstrate the ability to seamlessly deploy the protocol if Monero's codebase is changed to enable Layer 2 protocols. In the future, we are interested to study if a protocol can be designed without using timelock even at the Bitcoin side and what additional trust assumptions would be needed.

Acknowledgments. This work was partially supported by the European Research Council (ERC) under the European Union's Horizon 2020 research (grant agreement 771527-BROWSEC), by the Austrian Science Fund (FWF) through the projects PRO-FET (grant agreement P31621) and the project W1255-N23, by the Austrian Research Promotion Agency (FFG) through COMET K1 SBA and COMET K1 ABC, by the Vienna Business Agency through the project Vienna Cybersecurity and Pri- vacy Research Center (VISP), by the Austrian Federal Ministry for Digital and Economic Affairs, the National Foundation for Research, Technology and Development and the Christian Doppler Research Association through the Christian Doppler Laboratory Blockchain Technologies for the Internet of Things (CDL-BOT). This work has been partially supported by Madrid regional government as part of the program S2018/TCS-4339 (BLOQUES-CM) co-funded by EIE Funds of the European Union, by SCUM Project (RTI2018-102043-B-I00) MCIN/AEI/10.13039/501100011033/ERDF A way of making Europe, by grant IJC2020-043391-I/MCIN/AEI/10.13039/501100011033 and European Union NextGenerationEU/PRTR, and by grant N00014-19-1-2292 from ONR.

A   Detailed Comparison with Gugger Protocol

Gugger proposed a protocol for swapping **B**'s bitcoins for **A**'s monero without using timelocks at the Monero side [16]. **A** locks her monero in an address, whose one half of the private spend key is with **A** and other half with **B**. On the other hand, **B** locks bitcoin in a 2-of-2 multi-sig address having two outputs, one is redeemed and one is for refunding. The redeem script uses a hashlock where the preimage of the hash must be used for claiming Bitcoins. Initially **B** locks bitcoin and upon confirmation, **A** locks her monero. After **A** has verified that **B** has locked bitcoin, she sends the preimage of the hash defined in the redeem script. Using it, **B** publishes the redeem transaction and releases his part of the private spend key to **A**. The latter uses it to construct the private spend key and claim monero. **A** is at risk of losing her deposit forever if **B** refuses to collaborate while refunding. There is no way **A** can refund her coins without **B**'s secret. The schematic diagram of the protocol is shown in Fig. 3.

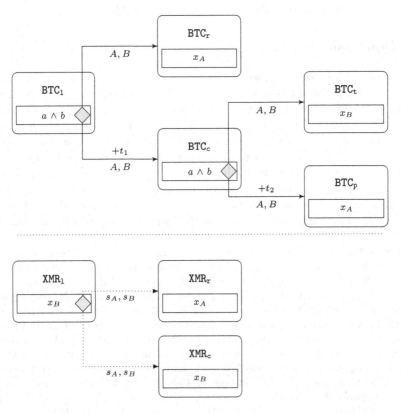

Fig. 3. Transaction schema for BTC to XMR atomic swaps from Gugger et al. [16]. *Top*: Transaction schema for Bitcoin. *Bottom*: Transaction schema for Monero. *Note: Monero view keys are omitted for clarity.*

To address these problems, we propose a protocol that allows **A** to refund instead of depending on **B**. With this guarantee, she can always move first by locking XMR before **B** locks BTC. We use the adaptor ring signature for the refund transaction of Monero. But making this minor change in [16] won't help since providing freedom to **A** puts **B** at risk of losing money. It is quite possible that **A** publishes the refund transaction first and then claims bitcoins. To prevent such a situation, **A** will be allowed to claim bitcoins only after **B** has redeemed monero. Thus once **A** publishes the redeem transaction, the money cannot be spent immediately. A *contest period* is added before she can claim bitcoins.

References

1. Tiernolan. Technical report (2013). https://github.com/TierNolan
2. Anonymous. Lightswap: An atomic swap does not require timeouts at both blockchains (full version) (2022). https://anonymous.4open.science/r/LightSwap-7C07/Final-LongversionXMR_lock_then_BTC.pdf
3. Team Ark. Ark ecosystem whitepaper (2019). https://ark.io/Whitepaper.pdf
4. Aumayr, L., et al.: Generalized bitcoin-compatible channels. IACR Cryptology ePrint Archive 2020:476 (2020)
5. Aumayr, L., Moreno-Sanchez, P., Kate, A., Maffei, M.: Blitz: secure multi-hop payments without two-phase commits. In: USENIX Security 2021 (2021)
6. Bentov, I., Ji, Y., Zhang, F., Breidenbach, L., Daian, P., Juels, A.: Tesseract: real-time cryptocurrency exchange using trusted hardware. In: Cavallaro, L., Kinder, J., Wang, X., Katz, J. (eds.) CCS 2019, London, UK, 11–15 November 2019, pp. 1521–1538. ACM (2019)
7. Borkowski, M., Sigwart, M., Frauenthaler, P., Hukkinen, T., Schulte, S.: DeXTT: deterministic cross-blockchain token transfers. IEEE Access **7**, 111030–111042 (2019)
8. Bünz, B., Bootle, J., Boneh, D., Poelstra, A., Wuille, P., Maxwell, G.: Bulletproofs: short proofs for confidential transactions and more. In: 2018 IEEE Symposium on Security and Privacy (SP), pp. 315–334. IEEE (2018)
9. Canetti, R., Dodis, Y., Pass, R., Walfish, S.: Universally composable security with global setup. In: Vadhan, S.P. (ed.) TCC 2007. LNCS, vol. 4392, pp. 61–85. Springer, Heidelberg (2007). https://doi.org/10.1007/978-3-540-70936-7_4
10. Chvojka, P., Jager, T., Slamanig, D., Striecks, C.: Versatile and sustainable timed-release encryption and sequential time-lock puzzles (extended abstract). In: Bertino, E., Shulman, H., Waidner, M. (eds.) ESORICS 2021. LNCS, vol. 12973, pp. 64–85. Springer, Cham (2021). https://doi.org/10.1007/978-3-030-88428-4_4
11. Amazon Elastic Compute Cloud. Amazon web services. Retrieved November **9**(2011), 2011 (2011)
12. Dai, B., Jiang, S., Zhu, M., Lu, M., Li, D., Li, C.: Research and implementation of cross-chain transaction model based on improved hash-locking. In: Zheng, Z., Dai, H.-N., Fu, X., Chen, B. (eds.) BlockSys 2020. CCIS, vol. 1267, pp. 218–230. Springer, Singapore (2020). https://doi.org/10.1007/978-981-15-9213-3_17
13. Deshpande, A., Herlihy, M.: Privacy-preserving cross-chain atomic swaps. In: Bernhard, M., et al. (eds.) FC 2020. LNCS, vol. 12063, pp. 540–549. Springer, Cham (2020). https://doi.org/10.1007/978-3-030-54455-3_38
14. Eizinger, T., Hoenisch, P., del Pino, L.S.: Open problems in cross-chain protocols. arXiv preprint arXiv:2101.12412 (2021)

15. Goodell, B., Noether, S.: Thring signatures and their applications to spender-ambiguous digital currencies. Cryptology ePrint Archive 2018:774 (2018)
16. Gugger, J.: Bitcoin-Monero cross-chain atomic swap. Cryptology ePrint Archive, Report 2020/1126 (2020). https://eprint.iacr.org/2020/1126
17. Han, R., Lin, H., Yu, J.: On the optionality and fairness of atomic swaps. In: ACM AFT 2019, pp. 62–75 (2019)
18. Herlihy, M.: Atomic cross-chain swaps. In: Newport, C., Keidar, I. (eds.) PODC 2018, Egham, UK, 23–27 July 2018, pp. 245–254. ACM (2018)
19. Hoenisch, P., del Pino, L.S.: Atomic swaps between bitcoin and Monero. CoRR, abs/2101.12332 (2021)
20. Hopwood, D., Bowe, S., Hornby, T., Wilcox, N.: Zcash protocol specification
21. Kiayias, A., Zindros, D.: Proof-of-work sidechains. In: Bracciali, A., Clark, J., Pintore, F., Rønne, P.B., Sala, M. (eds.) FC 2019. LNCS, vol. 11599, pp. 21–34. Springer, Cham (2020). https://doi.org/10.1007/978-3-030-43725-1_3
22. Komodo. Komodo (advanced blockchain technology, focused on freedom) (2018). https://cryptorating.eu/whitepapers/Komodo/2018-02-14-Komodo-White-Paper-Full.pdf
23. Kwon, J., Buchman, E.: Cosmos whitepaper. A Netw. Distrib. Ledgers (2019)
24. Lan, R., Upadhyaya, G., Tse, S., Zamani, M.: Horizon: a gas-efficient, trustless bridge for cross-chain transactions. arXiv preprint arXiv:2101.06000 (2021)
25. Lucas. How to build a Monero transaction (2021). https://comit.network/blog/2021/05/19/monero-transaction/
26. Lys, L., Micoulet, A., Potop-Butucaru, M.: R-SWAP: relay based atomic cross-chain swap protocol. Ph.D. thesis, Sorbonne Université (2021)
27. Malavolta, G., Moreno-Sanchez, P., Schneidewind, C., Kate, A., Maffei, M.: Anonymous multi-hop locks for blockchain scalability and interoperability. In: 26th Annual Network and Distributed System Security Symposium, NDSS 2019, San Diego, California, USA, 24–27 February 2019. The Internet Society (2019)
28. Miraz, M.H., Donald, D.C.: Atomic cross-chain swaps: development, trajectory and potential of non-monetary digital token swap facilities. Ann. Emerg. Technol. Comput. (AETiC) **3** (2019)
29. Moreno-Sanchez, P., Blue, A., Le, D.V., Noether, S., Goodell, B., Kate, A.: DLSAG: non-interactive refund transactions for interoperable payment channels in Monero. In: Bonneau, J., Heninger, N. (eds.) FC 2020. LNCS, vol. 12059, pp. 325–345. Springer, Cham (2020). https://doi.org/10.1007/978-3-030-51280-4_18
30. Narayanam, K., Ramakrishna, V., Vinayagamurthy, D., Nishad, S.: Generalized HTLC for cross-chain swapping of multiple assets with co-ownerships. arXiv preprint arXiv:2202.12855 (2022)
31. Noether, S.: Ring signature confidential transactions for Monero. Cryptology ePrint Archive, Report 2015/1098 (2015). https://eprint.iacr.org/2015/1098
32. Pedersen, T.P.: Non-interactive and information-theoretic secure verifiable secret sharing. In: Feigenbaum, J. (ed.) CRYPTO 1991. LNCS, vol. 576, pp. 129–140. Springer, Heidelberg (1992). https://doi.org/10.1007/3-540-46766-1_9
33. Rivest, R.L., Shamir, A., Wagner, D.A.: Time-lock puzzles and timed-release crypto. Technical report (1996)
34. Stone, D.: Trustless, privacy-preserving blockchain bridges. arXiv preprint arXiv:2102.04660 (2021)
35. Tairi, E., Moreno-Sanchez, P., Maffei, M.: A^2l: anonymous atomic locks for scalability and interoperability in payment channel hubs. IACR Cryptology ePrint Archive 2019:589 (2019)

36. Thomas, S., Schwartz, E.: A protocol for interledger payments (2015). https://interledger.org/interledger.pdf
37. Thyagarajan, S.A.K., Bhat, A., Malavolta, G., Döttling, N., Kate, A., Schröder, D.: Verifiable timed signatures made practical. In: Ligatti, J., Ou, X., Katz, J., Vigna, G. (eds.) CCS 2020, USA, 9–13 November 2020, pp. 1733–1750. ACM (2020)
38. Thyagarajan, S.A.K., Malavolta, G., Schmidt, F., Schröder, D.: PayMo: payment channels for Monero. IACR Cryptology ePrint Archive 2020:1441 (2020)
39. Thyagarajan, S.A.K., Malavolta, G., Moreno-Sánchez, P.: Universal atomic swaps: secure exchange of coins across all blockchains. Cryptology ePrint Archive (2021)
40. Tian, H., et al.: Enabling cross-chain transactions: a decentralized cryptocurrency exchange protocol. IEEE Tran. Inf. Forensics Secur. 16, 3928–3941 (2021)
41. Verdian, G., Tasca, P., Paterson, C., Mondelli, G.: Quant overledger whitepaper (2018). https://uploads-ssl.webflow.com/6006946fee85fda61f666256/60211c93f1cc59419c779c42_Quant_Overledger_Whitepaper_Sep_2019.pdf
42. Wang, G.: SoK: exploring blockchains interoperability
43. Wood, G.: Polkadot: vision for a heterogeneous multi-chain framework. White Pap. 21, 2327–4662 (2016)
44. Zakhary, V., Agrawal, D., El Abbadi, A.: Atomic commitment across blockchains. arXiv preprint arXiv:1905.02847 (2019)
45. Zamyatin, A., Harz, D., Lind, J., Panayiotou, P., Gervais, A., Knottenbelt, W.J.: XCLAIM: trustless, interoperable, cryptocurrency-backed assets. In: IEEE S & P 2019, San Francisco, CA, USA, 19–23 May 2019, pp. 193–210. IEEE (2019)

CBT Workshop: Anonymity, Fault Tolerance and Governance

Preserving Buyer-Privacy in Decentralized Supply Chain Marketplaces

Varun Madathil[(✉)], Alessandra Scafuro, Kemafor Anyanwu, Sen Qiao, Akash Pateria, and Binil Starly

Department of Computer Science, North Carolina State University, Raleigh, USA
{vrmadath,ascafur,kogan,sqiao,apateri,bstarly}@ncsu.edu

Abstract. Technology is being used increasingly for lowering the trust barrier in domains where collaboration and cooperation are necessary, but reliability and efficiency are critical due to high stakes. An example is an industrial marketplace where many suppliers must participate in production while ensuring reliable outcomes; hence, partnerships must be pursued with care. Online marketplaces like Xometry facilitate partnership formation by vetting suppliers and mediating the marketplace. However, such an approach requires that all trust be vested in the middleman. This centralizes control, making the system vulnerable to being biased towards specific providers. The use of blockchains is now being explored to bridge the trust gap needed to support decentralizing marketplaces, allowing suppliers and customers to interact more directly by using the information on the blockchain. A typical scenario is the need to preserve privacy in certain interactions initiated by the buyer (e.g., protecting a buyer's intellectual property during outsourcing negotiations). In this work, we initiate the formal study of matching between suppliers and buyers when buyer-privacy is required for some marketplace interactions and make the following contributions. First, we devise a formal security definition for private interactive matching in the Universally Composable (UC) Model that captures the privacy and correctness properties expected in specific supply chain marketplace interactions. Second, we provide a lean protocol based on any programmable blockchain, anonymous group signatures, and public-key encryption. Finally, we implement the protocol by instantiating some of the blockchain logic by extending the BigChainDB blockchain platform.

1 Introduction

Online marketplaces like Xometry[1] provide a centralized venue for vetted suppliers and customers that significantly facilitate matching customers' needs and

---

[1] Xometry https://www.xometry.com/ is one among many other (e.g., Fictiv, Protolab) online portals for on-demand manufacturing services that match their vetted suppliers with customers interested in 3D printing their unique designs.

Varun Madathil and Alessandra Scafuro are supported by NSF Award #1764025.

© The Author(s), under exclusive license to Springer Nature Switzerland AG 2023
J. Garcia-Alfaro et al. (Eds.): DPM 2022/CBT 2022, LNCS 13619, pp. 239–257, 2023.
https://doi.org/10.1007/978-3-031-25734-6_15

suppliers' offers in the manufacturing domain. On the downside, such an approach requires that all trust be vested in the middleman. This approach centralizes control, making the system vulnerable to bias towards specific providers. Furthermore, both customers and suppliers have no privacy w.r.t. the middleman.

Motivated by these concerns and spurred by the development of blockchain technology, recent work [14,16,28] propose to build *decentralized* online marketplace by replacing the middleman with a smart-contract capable blockchain. A blockchain [25,37] is an immutable ledger that is shared among multiple *peers*. Under the assumption that the majority of the peers follow the protocol, the ledger is guaranteed to be immutable and contain only valid transactions. Validity of a transaction is assessed by the peers by running specific scripts on those transactions. At a high-level, to build a decentralized marketplace, the interaction between customers and suppliers with the middleman could be replaced with smart contracts over blockchain transactions. Correctness would be guaranteed by the transparency and consistency properties of the blockchain, which enforce trust and facilitate dispute resolution.

Existing proposal for decentralized marketplaces [14,16,30,32] mostly target retail marketplaces (e.g., Amazon), where the matching between a customer C and a supplier S can be determined *non-interactively* via a payment transaction from C in favor of S for a certain item. In this work, we are interested in marketplaces where a match between a customer and a supplier is determined after multiple interactions (e.g., request for proposal, bidding, selection, etc.), and some interactions involve *private inputs* from both customers and suppliers. This is typical of outsourcing supply chain marketplaces where some interactions involve customers needing to disclose high-value data e.g. intellectual-property assets like manufacturing designs, software algorithms etc. The process usually involves an initial exploratory phase in which only limited information is shared with a large group of suppliers, followed by a narrowing down of the selection of candidate suppliers with whom subsequent interactions involving additional data that need to be kept private. As a concrete example, a customer might request proposals for the fabrication of a patient-specific craniofacial implant made out of medical-grade titanium alloy, with a 3-week deadline. This initial information may allow suppliers to determine if the request falls within their service capabilities, but yet it does not necessarily divulge high-value information. However, as negotiations proceed and potential suppliers are selected, suppliers will only be able to determine if they can meet the 3-weeks delivery time and what price to charge *after seeing* the complexity of the private implant design. Thus the implant design is shared only with the shortlisted suppliers. In addition, buyers need to keep some of their inputs in interactions private, but they may also want to keep their identities private for some interactions. This is because, in some contexts, the partnerships and collaborations that a company engages in are considered a part of its competitive advantage.

On the other hand, in supply chain marketplaces, suppliers want to share as much information about their capabilities, to be matched as candidates with as many requests as possible. However, they may want to keep their bid values for each request private. Therefore, in the context of blockchains where all transactions and transacting parties are recorded, it is essential to consider how to keep information about buyer identity and some transactional inputs of both buyer and supplier private.

To summarize, in this work, we target interactive marketplaces that present the following privacy properties. 1. *Matching is determined from private inputs.* Private inputs from both the customers (e.g., the private product design) and the suppliers (e.g., the quotes) are required to perform the matching. Hence, the approach of simply publishing requests on a blockchain and having smart contracts matching them is not applicable here. 2. *Customers should be anonymous but accountable.* The matching between the customer and the supplier should remain private. Yet, suppliers need some guarantee that they are interacting with accountable customers, i.e., belonging to a *group of verified customers*. At the same time, suppliers would also want to build a reputation by having a record of successful matches with accountable customers. This is different from the typical marketplace setting where a customer can be completely anonymous, and reputation is built only through reviews. 3. *Matched resources might be exclusive.* A supplier sells the *use* of its resources rather than an item. The marketplace must guarantee that the manufacturer does not overbook its resources.

1.1 Our Contribution

We initiate the study of decentralized interactive marketplaces and we build a proof-of-concept system based on blockchain technology. Specifically, our contributions are:

1. **A Formal Definition of Private Interactive Matching.** We formally capture the correctness and privacy properties of an interactive marketplace, by abstracting it as the problem of private interactive matching in the Universally Composable (UC) framework [7]. Our definitional choices are inspired by the service-oriented marketplaces such as in the manufacturing domain.
2. **A Protocol for Decentralized Private Interactive Matching.** We provide a decentralized protocol based on an ideal ledger capable of a set of validation rules we define, and on anonymous group signatures. We formally prove it is UC-secure.
3. **Implementation and Evaluations.** We provide an implementation strategy for our ledger protocol that involves extending the transaction validation framework of an open-source blockchain database BigChainDB (discussed in Sect. 4). We call the extended platform SmartChainDB.

A Formal Definition of Private Interactive Matching. To formally model the intuitive security guarantees outlined above we use the Universally Composable (UC) framework [7] to define an ideal functionality $\mathcal{F}_{\mathsf{PrivateMatch}}$. The ideal functionality $\mathcal{F}_{\mathsf{PrivateMatch}}$ describes the ideal behavior of a platform that matches customer with the correct suppliers, while guaranteeing anonymity of the customer (within a certain group of well-known customers), correctness of the match, privacy and fairness. We describe the ideal functionality in details in Sect. 2. At high-level the ideal functionality $\mathcal{F}_{\mathsf{PrivateMatch}}$ has the following properties. *Generality:* It captures a variety of settings since there are no fixed roles – a party can sign up as a supplier and customer; and no fixed logic – the ideal functionality is parameterized by external algorithms validResource and canServe that determines validity of the supplier commands. *Customer's (Accountable) Anonymity:* Requests are not associated to a specific customer, but to the group the customer belong to. This means that when a supplier is matched with a customer, the only information leaked to the other parties is that a supplier was matched with a member of a certain group (e.g., the group containing all the implant manufacturing companies). But a misbehaving customer can still be identified within a group and then punished. *Customer's Input Privacy:* Requests contain public values (e.g., the type of resources required, the deadlines, etc), and private values (e.g., the product design). From our example earlier, the suppliers were informed that they were to provide titanium alloy for three weeks. We consider such resources to be public as is the case in the real world. The private values will be revealed only to the suppliers who have *expressed the interest* in fulfilling the request and *possess* the resources to do so. Our ideal functionality allows a supplier to signal interest to all requests just to see the private inputs. Note that this models a behavior that is allowed in real world. However, note that just as in the real world, measures can be added so that if a supplier exhibits this behavior, it can be automatically discarded by the customer. *Supplier's Input Privacy:* The resources offered by a supplier and their interest in serving a request are public. However, details of their quote (e.g., price) are private for everyone, except, of course, for the customer. *Supplier's Transparency:* The resources utilization (e.g., allocation to a certain request) of the suppliers is public. *Correctness and Flexibility of the Match:* Only *capable* suppliers can bid to be matched with the customer. The winner is chosen by the customer according to its own private decision algorithm.

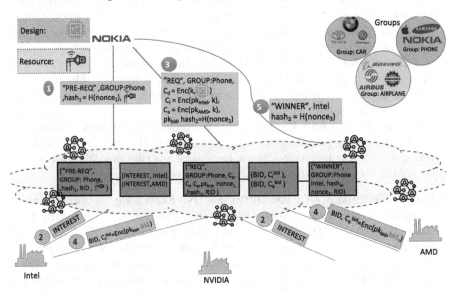

Fig. 1. Example of the protocol overview.

A Protocol for Decentralized Private Interactive Matching. We provide a protocol that securely instantiates the ideal functionality $\mathcal{F}_{\mathsf{PrivateMatch}}$. In the instantiation, we require a blockchain which we abstract as an ideal ledger functionality ($\mathcal{G}_{\mathsf{smartchain}}$). To protect the anonymity of customers while ensuring accountability, we use group signatures [2,5]. These are signatures associated to a group such that a member can generate an anonymous signature on behalf of the entire group. We also assume that there is a registration phase, where the identity of each party and the claimed resources of the suppliers are vetted. This step is application-specific, and we abstract it with an ideal functionality $\mathcal{G}_{\mathsf{reg}}$. After registration, parties can join groups. Group formation is again application-specific; in our protocol we assume groups exist and do not regulate group formation. We describe the stages of the protocol in details in Sect. 3. Below we give an overview of the protocol with a simple example. In Fig. 1 we present an example of the flow of the protocol. We consider three groups of customers as can be seen on the top right. The customers are grouped by their industry - car manufacturers, phone manufacturers and airplane manufacturers. In this example, Nokia (from the PHONE group) wants to build a chip (the design) and needs some chip building equipment (the resource). The suppliers presented below are Intel, Nvidia and AMD. All transactions are sent to a network of validators, that determine if a transaction is valid and then add them to the state of the blockchain. ① Nokia creates a pre-request transaction that details the resources it needs. It only authenticates that it belongs to the group (GROUP:Phone) of phone manufacturers to achieve anonymity within the group. To link next transactions, Nokia they attaches the hash of a random nonce, and reveal the nonce with the next transaction. ② Intel and AMD express interest in serving Nokia by posting an INTEREST transaction. ③ Nokia creates a REQUEST transaction where it encrypts the design with a key k, and encrypts the key k with the public keys of AMD $\mathsf{pk}_{\mathsf{AMD}}$ and Intel $\mathsf{pk}_{\mathsf{Intel}}$. It also attaches a public key $\mathsf{pk}_{\mathsf{bid}}$ for Intel and AMD to encrypt their bids. ④ AMD and Intel retrieve the design and then determine a bid value. They encrypt their respective bids under $\mathsf{pk}_{\mathsf{bid}}$ and post their BID transactions. ⑤ Nokia decrypts to retrieve the bid values and determines a winner - Intel. It posts a WINNER transaction indicating that Intel won. After this step, the interaction between Nokia and Intel will happen off-chain.

For privacy, the sensitive information of the matching is protected as follows. The identity of the customer is protected with the use of group signatures. If the customer misbehaves, they may be de-anonymized by the group manager. This functionality is not easily achieved with other privacy-enhancing techniques such as ring signatures. The private design of the customer is never included directly in a transaction. It is always encrypted. The encryption could even be uploaded to another web location (controlled by the customer) and the transaction only includes the web location. In the transaction, a customer will include encryptions of the key used to encrypt the design, under the public key of the suppliers who have shown interest in doing the job. Finally, the private bids of the suppliers are protected by encrypting them under the customer's ephemeral public key pk_{bid}.

Note that, due to the use of anonymous group signatures, a malicious member of the group can send follow up transactions for the same request. To prevent this, we chain the transactions through puzzles (hash $= H$(nonce)), in such a way that a customer can compute the next transaction in the flow only if it knows the solution (nonce) to the puzzle of previous transactions.

Implementation: SmartChainDB. Our implementation strategy choices were between the use of *smart contracts* on platforms such as Ethereum or the development of native support for these marketplace transactions as first class blockchain transactions. We chose the latter approach which offered several benefits over the use of the smart contracts model. For this reason, we selected to build on a platform BigChainDB [23], which offers an extensible architecture to implement different kinds of blockchain applications. We also implement *group signature* [5] as a possible signature scheme in BigChainDB. We refer to the resulting extended system as SmartChainDB. We undertook a performance evaluation to assess the additional overhead our changes to BigChainDB. We found that latency of our marketplace transaction types took no more than $2.5\times$ (additional 2 s of processing time) that of traditional transactions. The group signature scheme took up to $12\times$ (additional 12 ms) more than the traditional signature scheme.

Some Remark on Our Design Choices. We use a blockchain to allow a seamless interaction between suppliers and customers while maintaining transparency of this interaction. This transparency is critical when disputes occur between entities. In traditional EVM compatible blockchain environments such as Ethereum, Hyperledger Fabric, *"Smart Contracts"* are used to implement general business logic. However, because smart contracts are owned by a single entity, each customer would have to bear the burden of implementing their own contract and face the risks of errors and high economic costs (gas fees) for inefficient implementation. In addition, each supplier would need to discover and study smart contracts as they are made available and make the effort to fully understand their terms since smart contracts are binding and irreversible. We observe that there would be sufficient commonality in behavior in such marketplace smart contracts that they could be generalized and provided as system level operations (i.e. first-class blockchain transactions) which can be reused and parameterized by users as needed. An additional advantage of this approach is that moving functionality away from the smart contract layer into the blockchain transaction layer, avoids the significant additional economic costs of such applications because of the high costs of smart contracts. Given the above mentioned issues, we have pursued a different implementation model that is informed by the factors that led to the success of database systems. More specifically we extend BigChainDB an open-source blockchain database with new transactions that enable matching between suppliers and customers.

Our definition of the ideal matching functionality is inspired by the service-oriented marketplaces (such as Xometry, Fictiv etc). In such domains having the supplier's activities public is considered as a feature for building reputation rather than a drawback. We allow the private input associated to the customer's request to be seen by the suppliers that are interested in bidding, and not only the supplier that is finally matched, since suppliers decide a bid value depending on the complexity of the request. We note that a supplier can try to send an interest transaction to learn the request of the customers. We note that such an interaction is always possible in interactive marketplaces and can occur even today. Furthermore, we note that depending on the application this may not be favorable to the supplier. For example, our system may easily be modified to lock resources of the supplier each time it sends an interest transaction. This will disincentivize suppliers to send interest transactions just to learn the design of customers. To protect the anonymity of the customers we use group signatures. Each group in a group signature scheme is associated with a group manager and this manager can deanonymize users. This is useful in the case of disputes and a customer needs to be de-anonymized. Furthermore, the group manager may be decentralized and we discuss this at the end of Sect. 3.

Related Work. Kosba et al. present Hawk [17], a framework for creating privacy-preserving Ethereum smart contracts. A set of clients describe a functionality that they want to implement, and the framework outputs the code for a smart contract, and programs that is run by a third party who is the facilitator. The data used by the smart contract is encrypted, this ensures on-chain privacy. However, the facilitator must learn the inputs of all clients in order to compute the functionality which is a scenario we avoid.

Benhamouda et al. [3] present a framework on top of the Hyperledger Fabric that allows party to send encrypted inputs to the chain. To compute a function, the parties run an off-chain multiparty computation protocol over the encrypted input. The bidding and match steps in our private match functionality share similarities with sealed-bid auctions. There, bidders simultaneously submit sealed bids to an auctioneer who then announce the winner. A few sealed-bid auctions via smart contracts have been proposed (e.g., Galal et al. [10] on Ethereum and Xiong et al. [38]). However, they cannot be extended to implement the entire flow of private matching. In terms of functionality, the closest work to our is by Thio-ac et al. [33,34]. They integrate a blockchain to an electronic procurement system (a procurement is the process of matching customers with suppliers). However, they do not consider any privacy concern, nor do they present any definitions or proofs. Recent work proposes blockchain-based solutions to decentralize e-commerce retail platforms (e.g., Amazon). In [16,26,28], vendors list their items as input to a smart contract and buyers input their bids. The smart contract computes the output and reveals the winner. None of these schemes consider the anonymity of the buyers. Buyers' anonymity is addressed in Beaver [31] by employing anonymous wallets and the Zcash blockchain [29]. However, this line of work is suitable only for a non-interactive match over public inputs and do not extend to the interactive setting we are interested in this paper.

Finally, a rich body of work has investigated the use of blockchains to increase transparency in the supply-chain management (e.g. [9, 18, 24, 35, 36] just to name a few). However, all such work focusses only on the traceability and provenance of the products.

2   Private Interactive Matching: Formal Definition in the UC-Framework

The ideal functionality $\mathcal{F}_{\text{PrivateMatch}}$ captures a private matching functionality in the UC Framework [7], where *customers* are allowed to request a service *anonymously within a group*, *suppliers* bid to fulfill these services, where the value of the bid is private and eventually a supplier is matched with the customer.

The functionality maintains a global state that will contain all the transactions and can be read by all parties. It also maintains a list (buffer) of transactions that are to be added to state. The functionality keeps of track of the requests in a table $\mathcal{T}$ that is indexed by the request id (denoted RID). To set notation: $\mathcal{P}$ is the set of all parties and the adversary is denoted as $\mathcal{A}$. $\mathcal{G}$ is the list of groups initialized by the environment $\mathcal{Z}$. We denote a set of locked resources as LOCKS and TIMER as the set of times for each request. This set is used to ensure that no time-out (denoted FulfillTime or MatchTime) has occurred. Upon receiving a command from a party, the functionality creates a transaction that corresponds to the command, adds the transaction to buffer and sends the same to the adversary. This reflects the fact that the adversary learns that a command has been invoked.

Overview of the Functionality. Our functionality (Fig. 2) captures the operations that the system should perform, the inputs that the system should protect and the information that the system is allowed to leak to an adversary. We briefly describe the security properties guaranteed by this functionality. Any party that registers with the system as a customer joins a group identified by GID. This party is **anonymous within the group**, since for every command sent by the party (PRE-REQ, REQ, WINNER, RFILL) its identity is not revealed, but only its GID is included. Only the set of suppliers chosen by the customer can see the design as can be observed from the REQ command where the design is sent only to $P_j \in$ bidderSet (a set of suppliers that made bids). This guarantees **service confidentiality**. Similarly, in bid command, the adversary is only notified of the bid and the actual bid value is only revealed to P_i. This guarantees **bid confidentiality** to the bidders. **Request soundness** is the property that a customer participate for a request flow unless it had sent the PRE-REQ command for the request. This is achieved by checking for each command received from a party P_i for request RID, that $P_i \in \mathcal{T}[\text{RID}]$. The canServe predicate checks if a supplier has enough available resources to serve a customer. The functionality accepts bids from bidders only if canServe outputs 1 on their resources. This ensures **supplier completeness**.

$\mathcal{F}_{\text{PrivateMatch}}$

Register : Upon receiving (REG, P_i, [roles]) from P_i, do $\mathcal{P} = \mathcal{P} \cup P_i$. Send (tx = (REG, P_i, [roles])) to $\mathcal{A}$ and do buffer = buffer||tx.

Non-adaptive setup : Receive (CORRUPTED, b) from party P_i

Join Group : Upon receiving (gJOIN, GID) from a party P_i, update $\mathcal{G}[\text{GID}] = \mathcal{G}[\text{GID}] \cup \{P_i\}$. Send (gJOIN, P_i, GID) to $\mathcal{A}$ and (gJOIN, P_i, GID, 1) to P_i.

Update Profile : Upon receiving (UPD, prof, roles) from P_i, verify $P_i \in \mathcal{P}$. If prof = GID, check if $P_i \in \mathcal{G}[\text{GID}]$. If yes, send (tx = UPD, P_i, GID) to $\mathcal{A}$ and do buffer = buffer||tx. Else ignore the message. If prof = res_i, and $(P_i, \cdot) \notin$ LOCKS[RID] for some RID and validResource(res_i, P_i) = 1, update $\mathcal{P}$ as $\mathcal{P} \cup \{(P_i, \text{res}_i)\}$ and remove other instances of $P_i \in \mathcal{P}$. Send (tx = UPD, P_i, res_i) to $\mathcal{A}$ and do buffer = buffer||tx.

PreRequest : Upon receiving (PRE-REQ, GID, res, RID) from P_i
1. Check that $P_i \in \mathcal{G}[\text{GID}]$. If not, ignore.
2. Add $\mathcal{T}[\text{RID}] = (P_i, \text{res}, \emptyset)$.
3. Initialize LOCKS[RID] = $\emptyset$ and TIMER[RID] = 0.
4. Send (tx = PRE-REQ, (RID, res, GID)) to the $\mathcal{A}$ and do buffer = buffer||tx.

Interest : Upon receiving (INTRST, RID) from some supplier P_j:
1. Check if (res $\in \mathcal{T}[\text{RID}]) \subset \text{res}_j$
2. If yes, send (tx = INTRST, RID, P_j) to $\mathcal{A}$ and do buffer = buffer||tx.

Request : Upon receiving (REQ, (RID, [design$_j$]$_{j \in \text{bidders}}$, GID, bidders)) from P_i
1. Check $P_i \in \mathcal{T}[\text{RID}]$ and $P_i \in \mathcal{G}[\text{GID}]$
2. Update $\mathcal{T}[\text{RID}] = (P, \text{res}, \text{bidders})$
3. Send (tx = REQ, RID, GID, bidders) to $\mathcal{A}$ and do buffer = buffer||tx.
4. For each $P_j \in$ bidders, send (REQ, RID, design$_j$).

Bidding : Upon receiving (BID, (RID, bid$_j$)) from P_j
1. Check canServe(RID, P_j, state, LOCKS) = 1 If yes,
2. Send (tx = BID, (RID, P_j)) to $\mathcal{A}$ and (BID, (RID, P_j, bid$_j$)) to P_i. Send TIME to $\mathcal{G}_{\text{refClock}}$ to receive currTime. Set TIMER[RID] = currTime.
3. Add $(P_j, \text{RID}, \text{res})$ to LOCKS

Match : Upon receiving (WINNER, RID, GID, P^*) from P_i
1. Check that $P_i \in \mathcal{T}[\text{RID}]$ and that it belongs to $\mathcal{G}[\text{GID}]$
2. For each $(P_j, \text{RID}, \cdot) \in$ LOCKS[RID], delete $(P_j, \text{RID}, \cdot)$ from LOCKS[RID]. Send TIME to $\mathcal{G}_{\text{refClock}}$ to receive currTime. Set TIMER[RID] = currTime.
3. Send (tx = WINNER, GID, RID, P^*) to $\mathcal{A}$ and do buffer = buffer||tx

Fulfillment from customer: Upon receiving tx = (RFILL, RID, GID) from P_i:
1. Check that $P_i \in \mathcal{T}[\text{RID}]$ and that it belongs to $\mathcal{G}[\text{GID}]$
2. Send tx = (RFILL, RID, GID) to $\mathcal{A}$ and do buffer = buffer||tx

Fulfillment from supplier: Upon receiving tx = (SFILL, RID) from P_i:
1. Send TIME to $\mathcal{G}_{\text{refClock}}$ and receive currTime. Set TIMER[RID] = currTime
2. Delete $(P_i, \text{RID}, \cdot)$ from LOCKS[RID].
3. Send SFILL, RID to $\mathcal{A}$ and do buffer = buffer||tx

Read : Upon receiving (READ) from P_i return state to P_i

Update State : Upon receiving (UPDATE, tx) from $\mathcal{A}$: Delete tx from buffer. Update state = state||tx.

Unlock resources on time-out :
1. If currTime $-$ TIMER[RID] > MatchTime, then delete $(P_i, \text{RID}, \cdot)$ from LOCKS[RID]
2. For RID if there exist WINNER message and no RFILL message and currTime $-$ TIMER[RID] > FulfillTime, then delete all $(P_i, \cdot)$ from LOCKS[RID] and LOCKS[RID]

Fig. 2. An ideal functionality for private matching

Auxiliary functionalities We will use several building blocks such as anonymous signatures, registration authority, ledger, etc. in our protocols. We describe them briefly:

Clock Functionality. $\mathcal{G}_{\text{refClock}}$ (defined in [8]) captures a global reference clock. When queried with (TIME) command it returns currTime to the calling entity. This functionality provides an abstract notion of time and only the environment $\mathcal{Z}$ can update it. Parties do not use this function, only $\mathcal{F}_{\text{PrivateMatch}}$ uses this functionality as a sub-routine. This functionality is a simple counter that is incremented by the environment. For our protocols we only require such an incrementing counter. Alternatively one can also assume that time is realized with respect to block height. For example, a supplier's resources may be locked for k blocks where k is a parameter of the system.

Group Signature Functionality. $\mathcal{G}_{\text{gsign}}$ (defined in [2]) provides an interface of gSETUP, gJOIN, GKGen, gENROLL, gSIGN, gVERIFY, gOPEN, gGET. There are two types of players associated to the functionality. The group manager GM and the set of parties. The functionality allows a party P_j to join the group (using gENROLL) only if the GM gives the approval. After joining P_j can ask the ideal functionality to generate signatures (using gSIGN) on behalf of the group. A party P_l can ask the ideal functionality to de-anonymize ("open" a certain signature (using gOPEN), and the $\mathcal{G}_{\text{gsign}}$ will do so if allowed by GM. An instance of the functionality for group with identifier GID is denoted as $\mathcal{G}_{\text{gsign}}$.

Registration Functionality. $\mathcal{G}_{\text{reg}}$ described in Fig. 3 abstracts the registration process. Command REG allows parties to join the system without any role, that they can later update using the UPD command. $\mathcal{G}_{\text{reg}}$ verifies if the party is eligible for this update by evaluating predicate ValidReg, and if so it returns a certificate cert. Any party verify that a cert is valid by sending a VERIFY command.

$\mathcal{G}_{\text{reg}}$

This functionality is parameterized by a function ValidReg and maintains a list $\mathcal{L}_{\text{REG}}$
- Upon receiving (REG, roles) from a party P_i send (P_i, roles) to $\mathcal{A}$ and get back cert_i. Store $(P_i, \text{roles}, \text{cert}_i)$ in $\mathcal{L}_{\text{REG}}$.
- Upon receiving (UPD, prof, roles) from a party P_i, check if ValidReg$(P_i, \text{prof}, \text{roles}) = 1$. If yes, send $(P_i, \text{prof}, \text{roles})$ to $\mathcal{A}$ and get back cert_i. Update entry $(P_i, \text{roles}, \cdot)$ in $\mathcal{L}_{\text{REG}}$, with $(P_i, \text{roles}, \text{cert}_i)$.
- Upon receiving (VERIFY, cert^*, P^*, roles) from a party P_i or a functionality $\mathcal{F}$, check if $(P^*, \text{roles}, \text{cert}^*)$ exists in $\mathcal{L}_{\text{REG}}$. If yes, return 1 else 0.
ValidReg$(P_i, \text{prof}, \text{roles})$:
- If prof = GID and "customer" $\in$ roles, send gGET to $\mathcal{G}_{\text{gsign}}$[GID] to receive $\mathcal{D}$. If $P_i \in \mathcal{D}$, output 1.
- If prof = res and "supplier" $\in$ roles, check validResource$(P_i, \text{res}) = 1$. If yes, return 1.

Fig. 3. The registration functionality

Smart Ledger Functionality. The smart-ledger functionality $\mathcal{G}_{\text{smartchain}}$ abstract the operations of a shared ledger where transactions are validated and then added to the ledger. The ledger is denoted by the global state state that all parties can read. Upon receiving a transaction from a party, the $\mathcal{G}_{\text{smartchain}}$ functionality first validates (see Fig. 8) the transaction and then adds the transaction to the state.

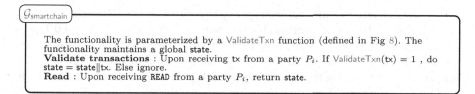

The functionality is parameterized by a ValidateTxn function (defined in Fig 8). The functionality maintains a global state.
Validate transactions : Upon receiving tx from a party P_i. If ValidateTxn(tx) = 1 , do state = state||tx. Else ignore.
Read : Upon receiving READ from a party P_i, return state.

Fig. 4. The $\mathcal{G}_{smartchain}$ functionality

3   The **PrivateMatch** Protocol

In this section we provide a detailed description of our PrivateMatch, and prove that securely realizes the ideal functionality $\mathcal{F}_{PrivateMatch}$. We describe our protocol using the UC formalism below:

Protocol Overview. The protocol PrivateMatch uses the ideal functionalities $\mathcal{G}_{reg}$, $\mathcal{G}_{gsign}$ [2] and $\mathcal{G}_{smartchain}$ described above. Parties create and send transactions to the $\mathcal{G}_{smartchain}$ functionality. If valid, the transaction is added to a global state that can be read by any party.

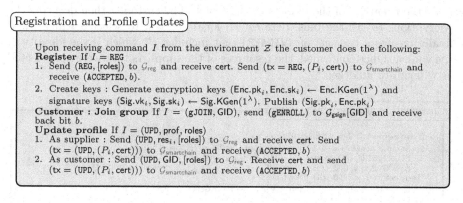

Upon receiving command I from the environment $\mathcal{Z}$ the customer does the following:
Register If $I = $ REG
1. Send (REG, [roles]) to $\mathcal{G}_{reg}$ and receive cert. Send (tx = REG, $(P_i,$ cert)) to $\mathcal{G}_{smartchain}$ and receive (ACCEPTED, b).
2. Create keys : Generate encryption keys (Enc.pk$_i$, Enc.sk$_i$) ← Enc.KGen(1^λ) and signature keys (Sig.vk$_i$, Sig.sk$_i$) ← Sig.KGen(1^λ). Publish (Sig.pk$_i$, Enc.pk$_i$).
Customer : Join group If $I = $ (gJOIN, GID), send (gENROLL) to $\mathcal{G}_{gsign}$[GID] and receive back bit b.
Update profile If $I = $ (UPD, prof, roles)
1. As supplier : Send (UPD, res$_i$, [roles])) to $\mathcal{G}_{reg}$ and receive cert. Send (tx = (UPD, $(P_i,$ cert))) to $\mathcal{G}_{smartchain}$ and receive (ACCEPTED, b).
2. As customer : Send (UPD, GID, [roles]) to $\mathcal{G}_{reg}$. Receive cert and send (tx = (UPD, $(P_i,$ cert))) to $\mathcal{G}_{smartchain}$ and receive (ACCEPTED, b)

Fig. 5. Registration and updates

Registration and Profile Updates. Before participating in the protocol, parties must register with the system by invoking the $\mathcal{G}_{reg}$ functionality and receiving a certificate cert. The party then prepares a transaction with the certificate and its identity tx = (REG, $(P_i,$ cert)) and sends it to the $\mathcal{G}_{smartchain}$ functionality who updates state. Once registered, a party updates its profile as a customer or supplier (or both). To join a group GID, the party sends gENROLL command to $\mathcal{G}_{gsign}$. The party's profile is then updated using the UPD interface of $\mathcal{G}_{reg}$. Similarly the party uses the UPD interface to update its profile as a supplier.

Request for Service. To request resources for an implementation of design the customer first prepares an anonymous PRE-REQ transaction (signed under its group GID) which only includes the resources (denoted res) it would require. Suppliers who are interested in fulfilling this request, send an INTRST transaction, which includes an encryption key pk_j The customer then picks a set of suppliers from the interested set of suppliers and creates the REQ transaction, where the design is encrypted (denoted C_d) with a fresh key k_{RID}. The key k_{RID} is then encrypted (denoted C_{key}^j) under the public keys (pk_j) of the interested suppliers. Lastly, an encryption $\mathsf{pk}_{\mathsf{bid}}$ is also included that will be used by the suppliers to encrypt their bid values. As described earlier, we chain transactions for the same RID using puzzles. Hence, every transaction from the customer for a specific RID contains the output hash of a collision-resistant hash function (CRHF), and any follow up transaction must contain the pre-image of hash. This is done to ensure that the same group member in the group is continuing the protocol. Specifically the transaction is (REQ, (GID, (RID, $\mathsf{pk}_{\mathsf{bid}}$, $\{C_{\mathsf{key}}^j\}_{j \in \mathsf{bidders}}, C_d, \mathsf{hash}_1, \mathsf{nonce}_0), \sigma))$. Note that the design is encrypted and can be decrypted only by the chosen suppliers.

Bidding and Matching. To bid on a request, a supplier first decrypts the encrypted keys to retrieve the symmetric key k_{RID} with which they decrypt the ciphertext and get the design. The supplier then encrypts its bid using the public key pk_{bid}, and send BID transaction containing the encrypted bid, where BID $= \mathsf{Sig}_{\mathsf{sk}_i}((\mathsf{RID}, C_{\mathsf{bid}}))$. Since the bid is encrypted under the pk_{bid}, only the customer can learn the bid value of the supplier. The $\mathcal{G}_{\mathsf{smartchain}}$ functionality *locks* the resources of the bidders at this point. The customer then decrypts the encryptions to get the bids, perform its local decision to select a winner, and finally creates a transaction (WINNER) that includes P^* which is the identity of the winner. Once confirmed, the resources of the suppliers that were not selected as winner are unlocked.

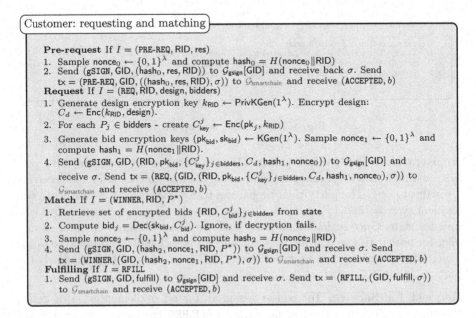

Fig. 6. Customer protocols

Supplier: interest, bid, fulfill and dispute

Interest If $I = (\text{INTRST}, \text{RID})$
1. Read PRE-REQ message from state with RID.
2. Create interest message $(\text{RID}, \text{pk}_i)$ and create a signature $\sigma = \text{Sig}_{\text{sk}_i}(\text{RID}, \text{pk}_i)$.
3. Send $(\text{INTRST}, ((\text{RID}, \text{pk}_i), \sigma))$ to $\mathcal{G}_{\text{smartchain}}$ and receive $(\text{ACCEPTED}, b)$
Bid If $I = (\text{BID}, \text{bid})$
1. From state get $(\text{RID}, \text{pk}_{\text{bid}}, \{C^j_{\text{key}}\}_{j \in \text{bidders}}, C_d, \text{hash}_1, \text{nonce}_0)$
2. Ignore if $i \notin \text{bidders}$. Else compute $k^*_{\text{RID}} = \text{Dec}(\text{sk}_i, C^i_{\text{key}})$ and compute
   design$^* = \text{Dec}(k_{\text{RID}}, C_d)$.
3. Encrypt bid as $C_{\text{bid}} = \text{Enc}(\text{pk}_{\text{bid}}, \text{bid})$. Send $(\text{BID}, \text{Sig}_{\text{sk}_i}((\text{RID}, C_{\text{bid}})))$ to $\mathcal{G}_{\text{smartchain}}$ and
   receive $(\text{ACCEPTED}, b)$
Fulfill If $I = \text{SFILL}$
1. Create $\sigma = \text{Sig}_{\text{sk}_i}(\text{SFILL}, C_{\text{deliveryPrf}}, \text{RID})$.
2. Send $(\text{SFILL}, (\text{RID}, \sigma))$ to $\mathcal{G}_{\text{smartchain}}$ and receive $(\text{ACCEPTED}, b)$

Fig. 7. Supplier protocols

Function ValidateTxn

Unlock Resources As is done in $\mathcal{F}_{\text{PrivateMatch}}$.
Validate registration and updates If tx $= (\text{REG}, v, \text{cert}, \text{roles})$ or $(\text{UPD}, v, \text{cert}, \text{roles})$,
send $(\text{VERIFY}, \text{cert}, P, \text{roles})$ to $\mathcal{G}_{\text{reg}}$. Output the bit returned.
Validate pre-request If tx $= (\text{PRE-REQ}, m, \sigma)$ from a party P_i, send $(\text{gVERIFY}, m, \sigma)$ to
$\mathcal{G}_{\text{gsign}}[\text{GID}]$. Output the bit returned.
Validate interest : Upon receiving $(\text{INTRST}, m, \sigma)$ from a party P_i, check
Sig.Vrf$(\text{vk}_i, m, \sigma) = 1$. If res $\subset$ res$_i$, retrun 1.
Validate request : If tx $= (\text{REQ}, m, \sigma)$ Send $(\text{gVERIFY}, (m, \sigma))$ to $\mathcal{G}_{\text{gsign}}[\text{GID}]$. If 1 re-
turned, check VrfSame$(m, \text{state}) = 1$, if yes, return 1.
Validate bid: If tx $= (\text{BID}, m, \sigma)$ Check Sig.Vrf$(\text{vk}_i, m, \sigma) = 1$. Get RID from m
and check canServe$(P_i, \text{state}, \text{RID}, \text{LOCKS})$, add $(P_i, \text{RID}, \text{res})$ to LOCKS[RID], update
TIMER[RID] $=$ currTime and return 1.
Validate Match: If tx $= (\text{WINNER}, m, \sigma)$ send $(\text{gVERIFY}, m, \sigma)$ to $\mathcal{G}_{\text{gsign}}[\text{GID}]$. If 1 returned,
check VrfSame$(m, \text{state}) = 1$, if yes, return 1. Let P^* be the winner according to m and
res be the resource for RID. For all $P_j \neq P^*$, remove $(P_j, \cdot)$ from the LOCKS[RID] and
update TIMER[RID] $=$ currTime
Validate requester fulfill : If tx $= (\text{RFILL}, m, \sigma)$, check VrfSame$(m, \text{state}) = 1$. If yes ,
send $(\text{gVERIFY}, m)$ to $\mathcal{G}_{\text{gsign}}[\text{GID}]$. If 1 returned, output 1.
Validate supplier fulfill : If tx $= (\text{SFILL}, m, \sigma)$: Get RID from m. Check Sig.Vrf$_{\text{vk}_i}(m)$.
If yes, then return 1, and remove $(P_j, \cdot)$ from LOCKS
Function VrfSame(m, state): Retrieve nonce$_i$ from m. If $\exists \text{hash}_i \in$ state s.t. hash$_i =$
$H(\text{nonce}_i)$, output 1, else output 0.
Function canServe checks if the supplier has sufficient unlocked resources to serve the
customer.

Fig. 8. The validation function

3.1 Security Proof

Theorem 1. (Security in Presence of Malicious Customers) *The protocol*
PrivateMatch *UC realizes the* $\mathcal{F}_{\text{PrivateMatch}}$ *ideal functionality in the* $\mathcal{G}_{\text{gsign}}$, $\mathcal{G}_{\text{reg}}$,
$\mathcal{G}_{\text{smartchain}}$*-hybrid world assuming collision-resistant hash functions [15], secure*
"special" symmetric key encryption [20], EUF-CMA signature [15], secure com-
mitment schemes [15] and CPA-secure encryption [15] in the presence of a PPT
adversary that corrupts a subset of the customers.

Proof. In order to prove UC security we show that there exists a simulator
interacting with $\mathcal{F}_{\text{PrivateMatch}}$ that generates a transcript that is indistinguish-

able from the transcript generated by the real-world adversary running protocol PrivateMatch. We give a high-level description of the simulator $\mathcal{S}_r$ and give an intuition why security is guaranteed. We present detailed proofs in the full version of the paper [21]. For a PRE-REQ command, the simulator only receives the GID and not the identity of the party calling the PRE-REQ command. The simulator simulates the $\mathcal{G}_{gsign}$ functionality and records the message-signature pair without the identity of the party. This guarantees anonymity within the group GID. For the REQ command, the simulator encrypts 0 instead of **design**. By CPA security of the encryption scheme the simulation is indistinguishable from the real-world and thus we achieve **service confidentiality**. The simulator aborts if it is able to create a REQ transaction that corresponds to the RID of an honest user. This occurs with negligible probability since we use CRHF and thus we guarantee **requester soundness**. For the BID command the simulator encrypts 0 instead of the bid value to get **bid confidentiality**. In the case of a malicious customer, the simulator simulates a key-exchange and sends an encryption of 0 to the customer instead of encryption of its secret key.

Theorem 2. *(Security in Presence of Malicious Suppliers) The protocol* PrivateMatch *UC realizes the* $\mathcal{F}_{PrivateMatch}$ *ideal functionality in the* $\mathcal{G}_{gsign}$, $\mathcal{G}_{reg}$, $\mathcal{G}_{smartchain}$*-hybrid world assuming collision-resistant hash functions [15], EUF-CMA signature [15], secure commitment schemes [15] and CPA-secure encryption [15] in the presence of a PPT adversary that corrupts a subset of the suppliers.*

Proof. Like the malicious requesters case we need to show that there exists a simulator $(\mathcal{S}_s)$ interacting with $\mathcal{F}_{PrivateMatch}$ that generates a transcript that is indistinguishable from the transcript generated by the real-world adversary running protocol PrivateMatch. For an INTRST transaction from a corrupt P_i, the simulator aborts with UnforgeabilityError if the signature corresponds to that of an honest party. By the unforgeability property of the signature schemes, this abort occurs with negligible probability. Moreover, when the command is sent to the $\mathcal{F}_{PrivateMatch}$ functionality, it checks the supplier is capable of fulfilling the request. This guarantees the **supplier completeness property**

Remark on Fairness. We do not tackle the problem of fairness or disputes in this work and consider it out of scope. There are numerous dispute resolution solutions in the literature [12,16] and we claim that an appropriate technique could be used in our setting as well.

Implementing Auxiliary Functionalities. We present some intuition on how to realize the auxiliary functionalities - $\mathcal{G}_{reg}$: Verification of identity can be done with systems like CanDID [22] that allows parties to port credentials from legacy systems (e.g. social security numbers) whereas verifying resources of suppliers may be done by some external auditing agencies. $\mathcal{G}_{gsign}$: We use the $\mathcal{G}_{gsign}$ functionality as defined in the work by Ateniese et al. [2] and the protocol realizing this functionality is presented in Sect. 5 of [2]. This protocol has a single group manager(GM) which goes against the spirit of a decentralized setting. One can replace the GM with multiple managers that enable threshold group signatures.[2] [4] present a fair traceable group signature scheme that allow specific fairness authorities to open signatures where the group manager encrypts the identity of the party under the pk of the fairness authorities, and to open, the fairness authorities run a threshold decryption protocol. Similarly [6,11] present protocols for distributed tracing using tag-based encryption to open the signatures of parties.

4 Implementation and Evaluation

Our implementation framework for PrivateMatch focuses on (i.) transactional behavior that captures general marketplace business logic e.g., requesting for quotes, bidding, etc.; (ii.) transaction anonymity using group signatures.

We introduce new blockchain transaction types into an open-source blockchain platform that is amenable to the desired extensions. BigchainDB [23] is a blockchain database that possesses blockchain characteristics. Its architecture involves a fixed set of nodes - *validators*, and is Byzantine Fault Tolerant (BFT) (up to a third nodes may fail). Its key architectural components include Tendermint [19] (for consensus), the BigchainDB Server (for syntactic and semantic validation of transactions), and a local MongoDB [1] database (for blockchain storage) on every validator node.

Extending BigChainDB's Transaction Model. BigChainDB allows transfer of assets, and its transaction model is a "declarative", attribute/key-value model. We refer to our extension of BigChainDB as SmartChainDB. SmartChainDB extends the validator algorithms in BigChainDB according to the ValidateTxn. We implement "locking" of resources as a transfer of resources to an "escrow" account (a designated non-user account used for holding resources). To release the resources, the validators issue a transaction back to the owner. Note that SmartChainDB is deployed as a network of its own with the validators running new validation algorithms. They run the same consensus algorithms (Tendermint) and are incentivized to do as in BigChainDB.

Extending BigChainDB's Privacy Model. We enable parties to use group signatures [5] instead of regular Ed25519 signatures provided by BigChainDB's library. The core building block of this scheme is a re-randomizable signature scheme (Pointcheval-Sanders scheme from [27]) and implemented in [13]. Our implementation is in Rust and uses python-based Cherrypy server as a wrapper to call the Rust cryptographic functions as a service.

The objective of our evaluation of SmartChainDB was twofold: (i.) verify that the newly introduced transaction types can support simulated marketplace workloads under reasonable performance bounds and (ii.) that the overhead of the group signature implementation did not deem the protocol impractical.

---

[2] In threshold group signatures, a signature can be de-anonymized only if a threshold of managers all agree to perform de-anonymization.

Experimental Setup. We set up a private test network on 16 machines with an Intel Westmere E56 Quad-core 3.46 GHz CPU, 8 GB memory, running 64-bit Ubuntu with kernel v4.15.0. We set up 12 validator nodes, with each node running its SmartchainDB server, Tendermint v0.31.5, and MongoDB v3.6 instances. For workload simulations, we set up the driver on 4 VM instances, running the customer and supplier code to trigger different transaction types. The drivers produce 80–100 transactions per second and send them to the validator nodes. The `CREATE` and `TRANSFER` (available in the vanilla BigChainDB implementation) transactions are evaluated under the same workload.

Latency Overhead. We measure the commit latency (time between a validator node receiving a transaction and its commit into the blockchain. We compare the `PRE-REQ` and `REQ` with `CREATE` transactions because those transactions are semantically closest. Similarly, the vanilla `TRANSFER` transaction is similar to `INTRST` and `BID` transaction. Figure 9 shows the average commit latency for every transaction types under the workload discussed above. The blue bars are for the native transactions and the orange ones for the new transactions. Overall, the results show the expected trend with the newer, more complex transactions having higher latency than their traditional "counterparts" due to the required additional validation overhead. In practical terms, these latency differences can be considered as a relatively minor trade-off for supporting more involved market-place events. Note that, these experiments were carried out in the non-private and non-anonymous settings, where we do not consider group signatures, encryptions, etc. Finally for the group signatures, we measure the time taken to sign and verify messages using our implementation of group signatures with the signature scheme used in BigchainDB (eddsa-sha512). We ran 200 sign and verify algorithms and observe that the group signature signing and verification take 10× that of regular signatures.

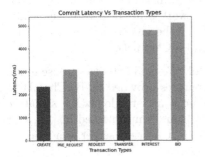

	Mean	Median	Std. Dev
gSIGN ([5] + [28])	9.77	9.65	0.92
BigchainDB Sign	0.75	0.52	0.84
gVERIFY ([5] + [28])	11.13	11.03	0.30
BigchainDB Verify	1.00	0.76	0.64

Fig. 9. Performance comparison of transactions

Fig. 10. Comparing group signatures and BigchainDB signatures (ms)

5 Conclusion and Future Work

In this paper we present a protocol for decentralized private interactive matching and prove that it is UC secure. We also extend an existing blockchain database system (BigChainDB) to implement private matching by introducing new transactions.

An interesting future direction would be to enhance the privacy of the request that is sent by the customer to the suppliers. This may be achieved using techniques such as fully homomorphic encryption or garbled circuits. Another future direction would be to specify protocols and transactions for dispute resolution for the SmartChainDB system.

References

1. MongoDB: the most popular database for modern apps. https://www.mongodb.com/
2. Ateniese, G., Camenisch, J., Hohenberger, S., De Medeiros, B.: Practical group signatures without random oracles (2005)
3. Benhamouda, F., Halevi, S., Halevi, T.: Supporting private data on hyperledger fabric with secure multiparty computation. IBM J. Res. Dev. **63**(2/3), 1–8 (2019)
4. Benjumea, V., Choi, S.G., Lopez, J., Yung, M.: Fair traceable multi-group signatures. In: Tsudik, G. (ed.) FC 2008. LNCS, vol. 5143, pp. 231–246. Springer, Heidelberg (2008). https://doi.org/10.1007/978-3-540-85230-8_21
5. Bichsel, P., Camenisch, J., Neven, G., Smart, N.P., Warinschi, B.: Get shorty via group signatures without encryption. In: Garay, J.A., De Prisco, R. (eds.) SCN 2010. LNCS, vol. 6280, pp. 381–398. Springer, Heidelberg (2010). https://doi.org/10.1007/978-3-642-15317-4_24
6. Blömer, J., Juhnke, J., Löken, N.: Short group signatures with distributed traceability. In: Kotsireas, I.S., Rump, S.M., Yap, C.K. (eds.) MACIS 2015. LNCS, vol. 9582, pp. 166–180. Springer, Cham (2016). https://doi.org/10.1007/978-3-319-32859-1_14
7. Canetti, R.: Universally composable security: a new paradigm for cryptographic protocols. In: Proceedings 42nd IEEE Symposium on Foundations of Computer Science, pp. 136–145. IEEE (2001)
8. Canetti, R., Hogan, K., Malhotra, A., Varia, M.: A universally composable treatment of network time. In: 2017 IEEE 30th Computer Security Foundations Symposium (CSF), pp. 360–375. IEEE (2017)
9. Chang, S.E., Chen, Y.C., Lu, M.F.: Supply chain re-engineering using blockchain technology: a case of smart contract based tracking process. Technol. Forecast. Soc. Change **144**, 1–11 (2019)
10. Galal, H.S., Youssef, A.M.: Verifiable sealed-bid auction on the ethereum blockchain. In: Zohar, A., et al. (eds.) FC 2018. LNCS, vol. 10958, pp. 265–278. Springer, Heidelberg (2019). https://doi.org/10.1007/978-3-662-58820-8_18
11. Ghadafi, E.: Efficient distributed tag-based encryption and its application to group signatures with efficient distributed traceability. In: Aranha, D.F., Menezes, A. (eds.) LATINCRYPT 2014. LNCS, vol. 8895, pp. 327–347. Springer, Cham (2015). https://doi.org/10.1007/978-3-319-16295-9_18

12. Goldfeder, S., Bonneau, J., Gennaro, R., Narayanan, A.: Escrow protocols for cryptocurrencies: how to buy physical goods using bitcoin. In: Kiayias, A. (ed.) FC 2017. LNCS, vol. 10322, pp. 321–339. Springer, Cham (2017). https://doi.org/10.1007/978-3-319-70972-7_18

13. Hyperledger: hyperledger/ursa. https://github.com/hyperledger/ursa/tree/master/libzmix/src/signatures/ps

14. Kabi, O.R., Franqueira, V.N.L.: Blockchain-based distributed marketplace. In: Abramowicz, W., Paschke, A. (eds.) BIS 2018. LNBIP, vol. 339, pp. 197–210. Springer, Cham (2019). https://doi.org/10.1007/978-3-030-04849-5_17

15. Katz, J., Lindell, Y.: Introduction to Modern Cryptography. CRC Press, Boca Raton (2020)

16. Klems, M., Eberhardt, J., Tai, S., Härtlein, S., Buchholz, S., Tidjani, A.: Trustless intermediation in blockchain-based decentralized service marketplaces. In: Maximilien, M., Vallecillo, A., Wang, J., Oriol, M. (eds.) ICSOC 2017. LNCS, vol. 10601, pp. 731–739. Springer, Cham (2017). https://doi.org/10.1007/978-3-319-69035-3_53

17. Kosba, A., Miller, A., Shi, E., Wen, Z., Papamanthou, C.: Hawk: the blockchain model of cryptography and privacy-preserving smart contracts. In: 2016 IEEE Symposium on Security and Privacy (SP), pp. 839–858. IEEE (2016)

18. Kumar, G., et al.: Decentralized accessibility of e-commerce products through blockchain technology. Sustain. Urban Areas **62**, 102361 (2020)

19. Kwon, J.: Tendermint: consensus without mining. Draft v. 0.6, fall 1(11) (2014)

20. Lindell, Y., Pinkas, B.: A proof of security of Yao's protocol for two-party computation (2006)

21. Madathil, V., Scafuro, A., Anyanwu, K., Qiao, S., Pateria, A., Starly, B.: Preserving buyer-privacy in decentralized supply chain marketplaces. Cryptology ePrint Archive, Report 2022/105 (2022). https://ia.cr/2022/105

22. Maram, D., et al.: Candid: can-do decentralized identity with legacy compatibility, sybil-resistance, and accountability. In: 2021 IEEE Symposium on Security and Privacy (SP), pp. 1348–1366. IEEE (2021)

23. McConaghy, T., et al.: BigchainDB: a scalable blockchain database. White paper, BigChainDB (2016)

24. Montecchi, M., Plangger, K., Etter, M.: It's real, trust me! Establishing supply chain provenance using blockchain. Bus. Horiz. **62**(3), 283–293 (2019)

25. Nakamoto, S.: Bitcoin: a peer-to-peer electronic cash system. Decentralized Bus. Rev. 21260 (2008). https://bitcointalk.org/index.php?topic=321228.0

26. Özyilmaz, K.R., Doğan, M., Yurdakul, A.: IDMoB: IoT data marketplace on blockchain. In: 2018 Crypto Valley Conference on Blockchain Technology (CVCBT), pp. 11–19. IEEE (2018)

27. Pointcheval, D., Sanders, O.: Short randomizable signatures. In: Sako, K. (ed.) CT-RSA 2016. LNCS, vol. 9610, pp. 111–126. Springer, Cham (2016). https://doi.org/10.1007/978-3-319-29485-8_7

28. Ranganthan, V.P., Dantu, R., Paul, A., Mears, P., Morozov, K.: A decentralized marketplace application on the ethereum blockchain. In: 2018 IEEE 4th International Conference on Collaboration and Internet Computing (CIC), pp. 90–97. IEEE (2018)

29. Sasson, E.B., et al.: Zerocash: decentralized anonymous payments from bitcoin. In: 2014 IEEE Symposium on Security and Privacy, pp. 459–474. IEEE (2014)

30. Soska, K., Christin, N.: Measuring the longitudinal evolution of the online anonymous marketplace ecosystem. In: 24th {USENIX} Security Symposium ({USENIX} Security 15), pp. 33–48 (2015)

31. Soska, K., Kwon, A., Christin, N., Devadas, S.: Beaver: a decentralized anonymous marketplace with secure reputation. IACR Cryptol. ePrint Arch. **2016**, 464 (2016)
32. Subramanian, H.: Decentralized blockchain-based electronic marketplaces. Commun. ACM **61**(1), 78–84 (2017)
33. Thio-ac, A., Domingo, E.J., Reyes, R.M., Arago, N., Jorda Jr, R., Velasco, J.: Development of a secure and private electronic procurement system based on blockchain implementation. arXiv preprint arXiv:1911.05391 (2019)
34. Thio-ac, A., Serut, A.K., Torrejos, R.L., Rivo, K.D., Velasco, J.: Blockchain-based system evaluation: the effectiveness of blockchain on e-procurements. arXiv preprint arXiv:1911.05399 (2019)
35. Uesugi, T., Shijo, Y., Murata, M.: Short paper: design and evaluation of privacy-preserved supply chain system based on public blockchain. arXiv preprint arXiv:2004.07606 (2020)
36. Westerkamp, M., Victor, F., Küpper, A.: Blockchain-based supply chain traceability: token recipes model manufacturing processes. In: 2018 IEEE International Conference on Internet of Things (iThings) and IEEE Green Computing and Communications (GreenCom) and IEEE Cyber, Physical and Social Computing (CPSCom) and IEEE Smart Data (SmartData), pp. 1595–1602. IEEE (2018)
37. Wood, G.: Ethereum: a secure decentralised generalised transaction ledger. Ethereum Project Yellow Paper **151**(2014), 1–32 (2014)
38. Xiong, J., Wang, Q.: Anonymous auction protocol based on time-released encryption atop consortium blockchain. arXiv preprint arXiv:1903.03285 (2019)

Grape: Efficient Hybrid Consensus Protocol Using DAG

Yu Song[1], Guoshun Fan[1], Yu Long[1(✉)], Zhen Liu[1], Xian Xu[2(✉)], and Dawu Gu[1(✉)]

[1] Shanghai Jiao Tong University, Shanghai, China
{sy_121,fanguoshun,longyu,liuzhen,dwgu}@sjtu.edu.cn
[2] East China University of Science and Technology and Shanghai Key Laboratory of Trustworthy Computing, Shanghai, China
xuxian@ecust.edu.cn

Abstract. One most potential solution to enhancing the performance of the Nakamoto consensus is to utilize the classic Byzantine fault-tolerant protocol running by a rolling committee. However, this hybrid consensus method still faces some challenges. One is that many hybrid consensus schemes use the Nakamoto single-chain, resulting in low throughput and poor scalability. The other is that the committee's internal consensus process has to be interrupted when the committee rotates. To address these challenges, we propose Grape, an efficient hybrid consensus protocol using the Directed Acyclic Graph structure. We prove that Grape is secure when the adversary's ratio of the mining power is less than $1/3$. To demonstrate the feasibility of Grape, we implement a prototype and make the experimental evaluation. The result shows that Grape achieves high transaction throughput with instant confirmation.

1 Introduction

Since Bitcoin [10] was introduced in 2008, the concept of blockchain has become a new and promising tool to build trust in the digital world and has been widely utilized. Bitcoin works in a permissionless setting, and an append-only and hard-to-tamper ledger is publicly maintained by all participants (e.g., miners). The core of Bitcoin is the *Nakamoto consensus*. Despite various kinds of potential applications, one main criticism against Nakamoto consensus comes from its low transaction throughput and high confirmation time. More specifically, to avoid forking attacks, all miners in bitcoin compete to solve a cryptographic puzzle to generate a new block, and the longest-chain rule is applied. As such, the transactions contained in one block will not be confirmed until this block is "buried" deep enough. It is turned out that Bitcoin's throughput is only 7 transactions per second and the transaction confirmation time is as long as 1 h,

This work is supported by the National Natural Science Foundation of China (No. 61872142, 62072305), the Key Research and Development Plan of Shandong Province (No. 2021CXGC010105), and the Open Project of Shanghai Key Laboratory of Trustworthy Computing under grant No. OP202205.

© The Author(s), under exclusive license to Springer Nature Switzerland AG 2023
J. Garcia-Alfaro et al. (Eds.): DPM 2022/CBT 2022, LNCS 13619, pp. 258–274, 2023.
https://doi.org/10.1007/978-3-031-25734-6_16

which is far from being satisfactory compared with VISA. However, due to the security constraint [2,14,20], it is not realistic to simply increase the mining rate and block size to improve its performance.

Many subsequent works have tried to improve Bitcoin's throughput and reduce confirmation time in various ways. A quite promising method is *hybrid consensus*. In a nutshell, hybrid consensus utilizes the fast permissioned consensus, e.g., Byzantine fault-tolerant (BFT) protocol [3,24], to optimize the performance of Nakamoto consensus. In the BFT protocol, once the order of the executions is committed, it will not change. This may endow the hybrid consensus scheme with *instant confirmation* and *responsiveness* [15]. However, the main challenge for the combination of BFT and Nakamoto consensus lies in that the BFT protocol runs in the permissioned setting, where there are strict restrictions on the choice of participants. In the permissionless setting, to defend against Sybil attack and put restrictions on the participation in the committee, the hybrid consensus schemes utilize Proof-of-work (PoW) to select and rotate committee members. In this way, after selecting the current committee from the miners, the committee members run the BFT consensus to confirm transactions.

Despite the fact that the hybrid consensus brings a broader view to the blockchain by greatly reducing the transaction confirmation delay, it still suffers from some bottlenecks. ByzCoin [8] improves the confirmation time of Bitcoin-NG [5]. But it resorts to Nakamoto's single-chain to confirm transactions, which leads to poor scalability. Besides, it was later pointed out by Pass and Shi [14] that it is insecure when the adversary's ratio of mining power exceeds 1/4. HC [14] utilizes a rolling committee to run PBFT [3] in order to confirm transactions responsively. To defend against selfish mining attacks, it proposes to adopt Fruitchains [13] to replace the Nakamoto chain. As a result, when the Nakamoto chain grows to a certain length, the consensus process of the current committee will be interrupted. Solida [1] uses PBFT to confirm transactions and to complete committee reconfiguration. Miners join the committee by solving PoW puzzles and the committee reconfiguration will also interrupt the current consensus process. Thunderella [15] achieves responsiveness and instant confirmation in most cases, but it must resort to Nakamoto consensus to confirm transactions if the "leader" in the current committee misbehaves.

Although the abovementioned hybrid consensus protocols improve on the Nakamoto consensus, the basic blockchain structure is maintained in most of them. That is, a block only refers to a single parent block by a hash pointer, resulting in a *single-chain* eventually. In contrast, in Directed Acyclic Graph-based (*BlockDAG* for short) protocols, one block can refer to all blocks that a miner has received up to certain conditions. Unlike "the longest chain rule" adopted in the Nakamoto consensus, in BlockDAG protocols, blocks outside the main chain can still contribute to the growth of the ledger, which greatly improves transaction throughput. Ghost [20] is the first BlockDAG consensus that adopts the heaviest subtree principle to replace Bitcoin's longest chain to avoid the waste of computing power. But it turns out that Ghost is vulnerable to the balancing attack [2,11]. Conflux [9] proposes a novel sorting algorithm for the DAG structure. However, the global transaction order and transaction validity in Conflux depend on the confirmation of a "pivot chain", which results in a long confirmation delay. Spectre [19] fails to provide a total order over all transactions required by smart contracts. Phantom [21,22] has improved Spectre in this aspect, but it lacks a formal proof of security. Prism [2] has an excessive and complex chain structure which will put a lot of storage pressure on miners. Jointgraph [23] improves consensus efficiency but requires an additional supervisor to monitor member behaviors. Besides, IOTA "Tangle" [16] applies PoW to build the DAG structure, but it has neither instant confirmation nor formal security guarantee. Furthermore, as far as we know, all of the existing BlockDAG protocols lack responsiveness, despite their improvements over the throughput.

In this paper, we explore further the hybrid consensus mechanism with the BlockDAG structure, to achieve responsiveness in the DAG-based permissionless setting. The basic idea is to utilize the rotation committee to construct a single-chain, in which each block will refer to a number of blocks in BlockDAG. This single-chain will serve as a "pivot chain" to sort all transactions in BlockDAG into a total order. Even better, the well-established security definitions of Nakamoto consensus [7] provide it with a rigorous security guarantee. While this high-level idea is straightforward, there are two technical challenges that need to be solved: (1) How to use the "pivot chain" to guarantee the BlockDAG's security? In particular, how to resist selfish mining attacks without sacrificing the optimally resilient property? (2) How to rotate the committee without interrupting the ongoing BFT consensus, namely *smooth rotation*?

Our Contributions. To solve the above challenges, we propose Grape, an efficient hybrid consensus protocol using DAG with formal security proof. To the best of our knowledge, Grape is the first hybrid consensus protocol that achieves all of the following properties:

- **DAG-based.** Grape uses DAG to improve transaction throughput and presents a deterministic transaction-sorting algorithm to help miners get the total order of all transactions.
- **Smooth rotation of the committee.** Grape's committee reconfiguration mechanism can accomplish the committee rotation without interrupting the committee's consensus process.
- **Optimal resilience.** Grape can effectively resist selfish mining attacks and achieve optimal resilience. Through theoretical analysis, we prove that Grape is secure when the adversary's ratio of the mining power is less than $1/3$.

Table 1 compares Grape with other hybrid consensus protocols.

2   Preliminaries

2.1   Permissioned BFT

BFT consensus is a kind of State Machine Replication protocol that can tolerate Byzantine nodes. Specifically, the BFT consensus divides the member nodes into the malicious Byzantine nodes and the honest nodes. Besides the *safety* and the *liveness* as the SMR, some BFT consensus protocols, such as PBFT [3], running in the partially synchronous model, have both instant confirmation and

Table 1. Performance of hybrid consensus protocols

Protocol	Smooth rotation	DAG-based	Responsiveness	% Adv[a]
PeerCensus [4]	✗	✗	✓	1/4
ByzCoin [8]	✗	✗	✓	1/4
Hybrid consensus [14]	✗	✗	✓	1/3
Thunderella [15]	✗	✗	✓	1/4
Solida [1]	✗	✗	✓	1/3
Grape	✓	✓	✓	**1/3**

[a] "% Adv" denotes the adversary's maximum mining power ratio to ensure that the protocol remains responsive and secure against self-mining attacks. A protocol is optimal resilience if the ratio is 1/3 [14].

responsiveness. As discussed in [14,15], a secure and responsive consensus protocol can tolerate at most 1/3 corruption. Thus, in an n-member BFT consensus protocol with *optimal resilience*, the number of the corrupted members f' will not exceed $\frac{n-1}{3}$. In this work, we use the partial-synchronous permissioned BFT protocols satisfying these properties as a building block.

2.2 BlockDAG Consensus and Basic Operations

Instead of the longest-chain rule used in Bitcoin, BlockDAG consensus organizes blockchain into a *Direct Acyclic Graph* (DAG) which can benefit from all blocks mined in parallel by honest miners. Through DAG structure, BlockDAG consensus makes good use of the node's bandwidth and achieves true concurrency. Since there are multiple paths from the genesis block to one block, more operations need to be introduced to define BlockDAG. We use parent(Chain, B) to denote the set of blocks which B references directly, past(Chain,B) to denote the set of all blocks that B references (directly or indirectly), and tips(Chain) to denote the set of blocks with 0 in-degree, i.e., end blocks. Also we call past(Chain,B) the precursor blocks of B, which are blocks traversed on all paths from the genesis block to B. Operation RetrieveEdge(BlockSet) returns the reference relationships between the blocks in BlockSet.

3 Model and Security Definition

3.1 The Security Model

Network Assumption. Grape runs in the *permissionless* setting, which means that participants can join or leave at any time and use their public keys as pseudonyms. To achieve responsiveness, we adopt the *partially synchronous* model defined in [14,15], where a pre-determined upper bound of delay Δ is known to all participants. Meanwhile, any message sent by an honest node is guaranteed to arrive at all honest nodes within the actual network delay δ.

Corruption Model. We assume that there is an environment $\mathcal{Z}(1^\kappa)$ where κ is the security parameter. The role of it is to provide inputs to participants and receive outputs from participants. We use N to denote the set of all participants in our protocol, $S \subset N$ to denote the set of honest participants, and $N \backslash S$ to denote the set of corrupt participants. We use $|N|$ to denote the total number of participants, who do not need to know $|N|$. The ratio of the adversary's mining power is denoted as $\beta = 1 - \frac{|S|}{|N|}$. Honest participants will strictly follow the protocol while corrupt participants can deviate from the protocol arbitrarily. An adversary $\mathcal{A}$ controls all corrupt participants and can see their internal states. The environment $\mathcal{Z}$ cannot see the internal states of honest participants but can see their outputs to the environment. $\mathcal{A}$ is capable of delaying or reordering any messages between participants, but it cannot drop or modify the messages broadcasted by honest participants. We consider the "rushing" adversary $\mathcal{A}$ that can observe other honest participants' actions before taking its actions.

Adversary Model. In the execution of the protocol, the environment $\mathcal{Z}$ initializes all participants, including both the honest and corrupt participants. The adversary $\mathcal{A}$ can adaptively corrupt an honest participant $i \in S$ by sending a corrupt instruction, as long as the ratio of the adversary's mining power does not exceed β. When the honest participants receive a corrupt instruction from the adversary, it takes at least τ time before they are corrupted. The mildly adaptive assumption is necessary in committee-based designs [1,4,8,14,15]. Roughly, this assumption is used to ensure that honest members have left the committee before becoming corrupt participants.

3.2 Definitions of Security and Smooth Rotation

In 2015, Garay *et al.* introduced two security requirements, namely *consistency* and *liveness*, for permissionless consensus. Refer to [7] for formal descriptions.

Definition 1. A permissionless consensus protocol is secure if the *consistency* and *liveness* properties are guaranteed.

Definition 2. A hybrid consensus protocol with a specified committee rotation mechanism is *smooth rotation* if the execution of the consensus among a committee will NOT be interrupted by the rotation of the committee members.

4 Technical Overview

Current hybrid consensus solutions rely on the single-chain in combination with a permissioned consensus protocol to construct fast permissionless consensus. By contrast, Grape uses BlockDAG to organize transactions and a permissioned consensus to agree on a committee that can be *smoothly* rotated constantly. Moreover, we provide an elegant design to prevent Grape from selfish mining attack. All transactions in Grape could be totally ordered.

4.1 Grape Architecture

At the high level, Grape is organized as a double-layer chain, as shown in Fig. 1. Layer 1, TxChain, uses the BlockDAG structure to record transaction blocks.

Layer 2, KeyChain, is a single-chain that provides finality to the whole ledger by referring to blocks in TxChain.

More concretely, miners in Grape use different block structures to package the received transactions and then order them. To fully utilize the throughput of the network, miners use the transaction block to package collected transactions. To achieve instant confirmation and responsiveness, we select miners publicly to form a committee to construct the key blocks for KeyChain.

Since a long-term fixed committee always suffers from bribery attacks, the committee members must be constantly rotated. Thus, key blocks also contain the proofs of the new committee members. In our scheme, the concept identity block stands for the proof. By utilizing the PoW mechanism, miners can construct identity blocks, to avoid selfish mining attacks. In summary, there are three kinds of blocks in Grape as follows.

(1) Transaction block. After the miners receive transactions, they will package them into a transaction block, which contains the hash values of the previous transaction blocks. We use txb to denote transaction block.

(2) Identity block. To join the KeyChain committee, miners must mine identity blocks. To defend against Sybil attacks, the PoW mechanism is utilized to generate a valid identity block. To be more specific, a valid identity block contains the puzzle of the corresponding committee, the miner's public key, and a nonce value as the puzzle solution. In other words, one identity block stands for one member. The identity block is represented as idb.

(3) Key block. The KeyChain is composed of key blocks. Each key block refers some txbs and idbs, and contains the previous key block's hash value. Once the key block is committed via the BFT consensus, all the referenced blocks will be instantly confirmed. key block contains the height of this block in KeyChain and the sequence number of the current committee. We use keyb to denote key block.

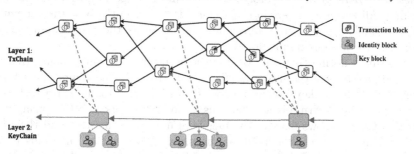

Fig. 1. Grape architecture. 1) Grape contains two layers and three kinds of block structures. 2) The first layer is TxChain, which is the DAG composed of transaction blocks. The second layer is KeyChain, which consists of key blocks committed by each committee. 3) Each key block contains its reference relations to transaction blocks and identity blocks. 4) The black solid arrows denote transaction blocks' reference relationships. The blue solid arrows indicate the reference relationships between key blocks. The blue dashed arrows indicate the references of key block to transaction blocks, and the green dashed arrows to identity blocks. 5) Once a key block is committed, all the referenced blocks get confirmed. (Color figure online)

4.2   Initiation and Reconfiguration of the Key Chain Committee

As described above, in Grape, the KeyChain is maintained by committees who use BFT protocols to construct chained key blocks. However, it is well-known that an immutable committee is not only vulnerable to bribery attacks but also harmful to the decentralized feature of the permissionless blockchain. Our key solution is to utilize a rotating committee publicly maintained by all miners.

Committee Member Participation. Whenever a miner wants to join a committee to construct the KeyChain, a valid solution for a PoW puzzle is needed. The miner packages its identity, the puzzle, and the solution into an identity block and broadcasts it *immediately* to get involved in the next committee. Let n be the committee size (i.e., the number of members in each committee). To bootstrap the entire protocol, the first $n = 3f + 1$ committee members, including no more than f corrupted ones, could be hard-coded in the genesis key block.

In detail, we use $comm_k$ to denote the member set of the k-th committee. When an honest miner mines an identity block successfully, it will immediately broadcast the block to other miners. Thus the current committee $comm_k$ can instantly include all the newly received idbs in a new keyb. Once this key block is committed, all these referenced idbs get committed simultaneously. Members in $comm_k$ use an initially empty set cid_{k+1} to record the (next) committee members. All the creators of these identity blocks, which are referenced by the key blocks generated by $comm_k$, can join the next committee. When the size of cid_{k+1} (i.e., the number of the new confirmed identity blocks) reaches the committee size n, committee rotation is triggered.

Committee Rotation. Assuming the current committee is $comm_k$, the n members of $comm_k$ maintain cid_{k+1} to collect the $(k + 1)$-th committee's members. When the size of cid_{k+1} achieves n when the most recent key block is confirmed, honest members in $comm_k$ broadcast an END message immediately and stop working. All the n members in cid_{k+1} form the $(k + 1)$-th committee $comm_{k+1}$ and run BFT protocol to confirm new keyblocks as the last committee did. Figure 2 provides an example for $n = 7$.

It is worth noting that only when some keyblock is committed such that the collected members of the next committee exceed n, will the committee rotation happen. This is the key point to smooth rotation. Informally, since each committee runs the deterministic consensus to form the fork-free KeyChain, every miner in Grape knows exactly the members in each committee and their first block height. On the other hand, as the previous committee only ends its job after the generation of their last key block, no interruption will happen if only the security guarantee of the BFT consensus could be satisfied. A more detailed analysis could be found in Sect. 6.

Selfish Mining Prevention. Eyal *et al.* [6] has pointed out the existence of selfish mining attacks in Bitcoin. Roughly speaking, attackers may get benefit from mining sequential blocks secretly and broadcasting all of them in the future. In Grape, the attackers may try to launch this attack by mining identity blocks

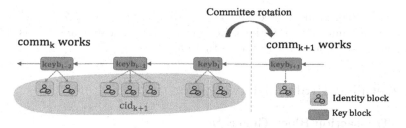

Fig. 2. An example of the committee rotation. Assuming the committee size is $n = 7$, $comm_k$ runs a BFT to commit key blocks, then the referenced identity blocks form the next committee $comm_{k+1}$. For instance, when $keyb_i$ is committed, the size of cid_{k+1} reaches 7, the next committee $comm_{k+1}$ is formed and committee rotation happens. Members in $comm_{k+1}$ take over the work to commit new key blocks.

as much as possible[1], and wish more than $1/3$ new committee members could be selected from them. To prevent this kind of attack, each identity block in Grape is generated in an isolated way. That is, the identity block does not contain a hash pointer to any other blocks. Furthermore, the identity blocks collected in cid_{k+1} contains a puzzle $puzzle(k)$ generated by the $(k-1)$-th committee $comm_{k-1}$. Inspired by Solida [1], we derive $puzzle(k)$ from the set of the $f + 1$ authorized END messages generated by $comm_{k-1}$. In this way, the adversary cannot initiate selfish mining attacks to produce identity blocks contained by cid_{k+1} earlier than other miners, and thus cannot benefit from selfish mining in Grape.

4.3   Transaction Packaging and Sorting

In Grape, we use transaction block txb to package transactions.

Transaction Packaging. Intuitively, we deconstruct the function of the Nakamoto blockchain to enhance the throughput and decrease the confirmation time. All miners in Grape can package transactions to generate transaction blocks. When receiving transactions, the miner firstly puts them into its buffer pool txPool, and then selects transactions from its pool to generate a transaction block txb. Let the block Gen be the first block in TxChain, which will appear in the past set of any valid transaction blocks. If there is only the genesis block Gen in TxChain, miners will only reference Gen. Otherwise, the miners will reference all end blocks in TxChain. It is worth noting that to ensure the responsiveness of the protocol, we do not make any restrictions on the transaction block.

Transaction Sorting. keybs serve as "pivots". When a key block is committed, all the transactions referenced by it, directly or indirectly, get confirmed. Firstly, the transactions blocks referenced by a key block are sorted according to their reference relationship and their hash values. Then transactions contained by

---

[1] Note that based on the security of the underlying BFT consensus, a leader in the committee who tries to stay longer by not including any identity blocks will always be found by other members and be replaced after a view-change phase.

transaction blocks are sorted and appended into the ledger $\mathcal{L}$, which is the set of the committed transactions. Conflicting and replicate transactions will be discarded. See [9] for more of the sorting idea.

5   Detailed Protocol Description

5.1   Transaction Block Generation

Packaging transactions to generate transaction blocks is the main mission for miners. Algorithm 1 provides the pseudocode of the transaction block generation.

In Grape, to generate a transaction block and add new transactions into BlockDAG, miners need to refer to all end transaction blocks in TxChain. Moreover, to reduce the probability of the replicated recording of one transaction, miners randomly select transactions from its local txPool (line 4 in Algorithm 1). The selected transactions constitute the body of a transaction block, and the Merkle-tree root of these transactions is recorded in the head of the transaction block. Then the corresponding miner signs it to creat a new transaction block. The last step is to broadcast it instantly to others.

Algorithm 1: Transaction block Generation

> **Input:** End txbs of the TxChain, miner's public key pk, miner's transaction pool txPool
> **Output:** Transaction block txb
> 1 txb_ref = ∅
> 2 **for** txb ∈ tips(TxChain) **do**
> 3   *add* HashPointer(txb) *to* txb_ref
>
> 4 $T \leftarrow$ SELECTRANDOMLY(txPool)
> 5 txPool $\leftarrow$ txPool\T
> 6 txb_MKroot $\leftarrow$ MerkleRoot(T)
> 7 txb $\leftarrow$< txb_ref, txb_MKroot, pk, T >
> 8 BROADCAST(txb)

5.2   Identity Block Generation

While generating transaction blocks, miners also try to mine valid identity blocks to join the committee. We utilize the PoW mechanism to resist Sybil or selfish mining attacks, and miners need to solve a cryptographic hash puzzle to join a committee. We note that the k-th puzzle puzzle$_k$ is the set of $f + 1$ END messages from the $(k - 1)$-th committee comm$_{k-1}$. For convenience, we assume that each puzzle is collected and provided by environment $\mathcal{Z}$ to miners. Each miner is limited to access the hash oracle $H(\cdot)$ no more than q times. By constantly increasing a local nonce η to compute the hash value, miners compete to mine an identity block. When the hash value h of the identity block is smaller than a given (and globally adjustable) Target and the puzzle is still useful, a valid identity block is mined.

Algorithm 2: Identity block Generation

Input: puzzle formed by the last committee, miner's public key pk
Output: Identity block idb
// The involvement of oracle $H()$ subjects to the q-bound
1 . **while** $\eta \le q$ **do**
2   **if** $H(\text{puzzle}, \text{pk}, \eta) < \text{Target}$ **then**
3        $\lfloor$ idb $\leftarrow\ <$ puzzle, pk, $\eta >$
4   **else**
5        $\lfloor$ $\eta \leftarrow \eta + 1$

6 BROADCAST(idb)

5.3 Key Block Generation and Confirmation

Algorithm 3: Key Block Generation and Confirmation

Input: Current KeyChain height $h - 1$, the number of committee session k,
     unreferenced transaction blocks txbs, newly generated identity blocks
     idbs
Output: Key block keyb, updated KeyChain with keyb in height h
1 keyb_ref $= \emptyset$, RefTo_txb $= \emptyset$, RefTo_idb $= \emptyset$, cid$_{k+1} = \emptyset$
2 keyb_ref $\leftarrow$ HashPointer(KeyChain$[h - 1]$)
3 **for** txb $\in$ tips(TxChain) **do**
4     $\lfloor$ add HashPointer(txb) to RefTo_txb

5 Query environment $\mathcal{Z}$ for Current Puzzle
6 **for** *each unreferenced* idb **do**
7   **if** idb.puzzle $= CurrentPuzzle \wedge H(\text{idb.puzzle}, \text{idb.pk}, \text{idb}.\eta) <$
     Target $\wedge$ idb $\notin$ cid$_{k+1}$ **then**
8   add idb into RefTo_*idb*
9        $\lfloor$ add idb into cid$_{k+1}$
10   **else**
11        $\lfloor$ discard idb

12 keyb $\leftarrow\ <$ keyb_*ref*, RefTo_*txb*, RefTo_*idb*, $h, k >$
13 BROADCAST*(keyb)*
14 BFT*(comm$_k$, keyb)*
15 keyb gets committed by comm$_k$
16 KeyChain$[h] \leftarrow$ keyb
17 SORTTX*(keyb)*
18 **for** idb $\in$ keyb.RefTo_idb **do**
19   **if** $|\text{cid}_{k+1}| < n$ **then**
20        $\lfloor$ add idb to cid$_{k+1}$

21   **else if** $|\text{cid}_{k+1}| = n$ **then**
22   BROADCAST*(END)*
23   Members in comm$_k$ stop working and COMMITTEEROTATION starts

Committee members can generate a key block and run the BFT protocol to commit it. Each new key block will reference all end blocks in TxChain, newly generated valid identity blocks, and the last key block. Besides, the current key chain height h and the committee's session number k are included in each key block.

After the generation of a new key block, a BFT consensus within the ongoing committee will start. If the key block gets votes from more than $2f$ committee members, it is successfully confirmed and will be added to the KeyChain at height h. The safety of BFT consensus ascertain that no more than 1 key block could be confirmed at the same height. Thus, KeyChain is a forking-free single chain.

During the creation of a key block, if n new identity blocks are collected, then all of the next committee's members are publicly known. Thus the ongoing committee stops working only at the end of a BFT consensus, and the committee rotation mechanism will never interrupt any ongoing consensus. Hence the smooth rotation is achieved. Algorithm 3 provides the pseudocode.

5.4 Transaction Sorting

Whenever a committee commits a key block keyb, the transactions within the transaction block referenced by it are sorted and added to the ledger $\mathscr{L}$ in turn. When sorting transaction blocks, we first extract the relevant precursor blocks B_Δ of a given keyb from TxChain, that is the set of transaction blocks "belonging" to keyb (Line 4 in Algorithm 4). By "belonging", we mean that the transaction block is referred to by the key block. Next, the miners will do a topological sorting of the blocks in B_Δ, that is, add blocks with 0 in-degree to BlockSeq according to the reference relationship. So we need to call RetrieveEdge(B_Δ). If there are multiple blocks with 0 in-degree, they are sorted according to their hash values, and then sequentially added to BlockSeq. After that, the miners add the transactions contained in the blocks in BlockSeq to the ledger $\mathscr{L}$.

Algorithm 4: Transaction Sorting

Input: Current committed keyb
Output: The transaction ledger $\mathscr{L}$

1 BlockSeq $\leftarrow \emptyset$
2 $h \leftarrow$ keyb.h
3 $PreviousKeyb \leftarrow$ KeyChain[$h-1$]
4 $B_\Delta \leftarrow$ past(TxChain, keyb) $-$ past(TxChain, PreviousKeyb) $- \{PreviousKeyb\}$;
5 **while** $B_\Delta \neq \emptyset$ **do**
6   TxChain' $\leftarrow (B_\Delta, \text{RETRIEVEEDGE}(B_\Delta))$
7   **if** parent(txChain', txb) $= \bot$ **then**
8   add txb to B'_Δ
9   Sort blocks by their hash values $B'_\Delta \leftarrow \text{SORT}(B'_\Delta)$
10   **for** txb $\in B'_\Delta$ **do**
11   BlockSeq $\leftarrow$ BlockSeq||txb
12     $B_\Delta \leftarrow B_\Delta - B'_\Delta$
13 **for** $B \in$ BlockSeq **do**
14   **for** (tx $\in B$) $\wedge$ (tx $\notin \mathcal{L}$) **do**
15         $\mathcal{L} \leftarrow \mathcal{L}||$tx

6   Security Analysis

In this section, we prove that Grape is both secure and rotation smooth. In the following, we use $n = 3f+1$ to denote the size of each committee and f' to denote the number of the corrupt committee members. Our main idea of the proof is to apply the *Safety* and *Liveness* of the underlying BFT consensus to guarantee the security definitions of the permissionless blockchain. Assuming the first committee comm_1 contains at most $1/3$ corrupted members and the adversary's mining power will never exceed $1/3$ during the execution of Grape, we prove that all the committee meets the $1/3$ byzantine fault tolerance requirements.

Lemma 1. *Assume $f' \le f$. If an honest miner commits a key block* keyb *at height h, then any honest miner will commit* keyb *at height h.*

Proof. Since comm_1 is hard-coded into the protocol, comm_1 is the same for all honest miners. If the BFT protocol we adopt in Grape satisfies *Safety* and *Liveness* and $f' \le f$. It can be proven by contradiction that during the operation of comm_1, all honest miners outside the comm_1 will also commit the same keyb at the same height.

We assume that one honest miner i outside the committee has committed keyb at height h, which means that keyb has received more than $2f + 1$ votes in the BFT consensus process. To find the contradiction, we assume that there is an honest miner j $(j \ne i)$ outside the committee who has committed $\mathsf{keyb}' \ne \mathsf{keyb}$ at height h, which means that miner j has also received more than $2f + 1$ votes on keyb'. Thus there must be an honest member in the committee who votes for both keyb and keyb' during the BFT consensus process, which is impossible.

We conclude that in the working procedure of comm_1, if an honest miner has committed keyb, all honest miners will commit it within Δ time, which means that they will add the same identity blocks to cid_2. So comm_2 is the same for all honest miners. By an inductive argument, comm_k is the same for all honest miners where $k \ge 1$. Therefore, during the working procedure of comm_k, all honest miners will commit the same block at the same height.

Lemma 2. *The adversary can know the* puzzle *of the next committee at most 2Δ time ahead of the honest miners.*

Proof. Recall that the puzzle contains $f + 1$ END messages from the last committee. For the adversary who corrupts at most f nodes in one committee, to learn the puzzle, there must be at least one honest committee member who has broadcasted the END message. Then the adversary can immediately get the puzzle by adding f END messages.

As for the honest miners, once an honest committee member has broadcasted an END message, all other honest members will broadcast the END messages within Δ time. Then after the next Δ time, all honest miners can get these END messages and know the puzzle of the next committee. Therefore, the adversary can know the puzzle of the next committee 2Δ time ahead of the honest miners.

We emphasize that we use Δ to analyze the maximum advantage of the adversary only, our scheme works in a partially synchronous network.

Lemma 3. *Assume $f' \le f$ holds for* comm$_1$. *Then in each subsequent committee, $f' \le f$ holds except for a probability exponentially small in the committee size n, if the adversary's mining power ratio satisfies $\beta < 1/3$.*

Proof. We notice that the probability of the adversary joining the committee is the same as its ratio of mining power, which is β. So the probability of honest miners joining the committee is $1 - \beta$. However, the adversary may try to use its superiority to extend this probability. We will prove that the superiority will not benefit the adversary in practice. More specifically, the adversary's superiority comes from the following two events:

- A: The adversary can know the puzzle of the next committee 2Δ time ahead of the honest miners, as proved by Lemma 2.
- B: The f' corrupted users act as the "leaders" in the underlying BFT consensus consequently, and discard idbs generated by the honest miners.

To benefit the adversary, we assume that the key block proposed by a corrupted leader will not contain any identity blocks proposed by the honest miners. However, it is no use for the adversary if it cannot dominate the committee for a long enough term, because the key blocks proposed by the honest leaders always contain the idb ignored by the corrupt ones. Thus, we only need to consider the case that corrupted members dominate the committee for a long term. In this case, the txb generated by honest miners will be ignored forever and the adversary can get benefits. Although this case happens with low probability, we include it in the following discussion. That is, we are considering the worst case.

The process of mining can be modeled as Poisson distribution since it is a memoryless process [1]. The probability that a miner mines k blocks in a certain period is $p(k, \lambda) = \frac{\lambda^k e^{-\lambda}}{k!}$, where λ is the expected number of blocks mined during this period. In event A, the expected number of blocks mined by the adversary within 2Δ time is $\lambda_A = 2\Delta\beta/D$. Recall that D is the expected time for all miners to find an identity block. Therefore, in event A, the probability that the adversary does not mine a block is $Pr(AdvFindNoBlockInEventA) = p(0, \lambda_A) = e^{-2\Delta\beta/D}$. Similarly, in event B, the probability that the adversary does not mine a block is $Pr(AdvFindNoBlockInEventB) = e^{-f'T(\Delta)\beta/D}$. We use $T(\Delta)$ to denote the longest time that a single corrupted leader can rule the committee for one time. Figure 3 illustrates the adversary's superiority.

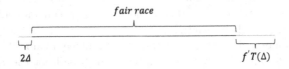

fair race

2Δ $f'T(\Delta)$

Fig. 3. The illustration of the adversary's superiority. The timeline denotes that the adversary gains the superiority during this period. The black timeline denotes the fair race between the adversary and honest miners during this period.

If the adversary did not mine any block in events A and B, then the probability of the corrupt miners joining the next committee is precise β. However, once event A or B happens, the adversary may get more superiority. Precisely, the adversary has the probability of $Pr(adv) = 1 - Pr(AdvFindNoBlockInEventA)$ $\times Pr(AdvFindNoBlockInEventB) = 1 - e^{-(f'T(\Delta)+2\Delta)\beta/D}$ to promote β to β' (β' denotes the adversary's actual mining power). In theory, we can increase D to eliminate the adversary's superiority: as $D \to \infty$, $Pr(adv) \to 0$ and $\beta' \to \beta$. Recall that we assume $\beta < 1/3$, so we can assume $\beta' < 1/3$ in the following.

Now we can prove this lemma by induction. Assume that the number of corrupted miners in a committee comm_k is $f' \leq n/3$. Since whether each miner can join the committee or not is independent of whether other miners can join the committee or not, we can utilize Chernoff inequality to calculatethe probability that f' exceeds f in comm_{k+1}. We have $E(f') = \mu = \beta'n$, where $E(f')$ denotes the expected number of the corrupted members in the committee. Due to the Chernoff bound, we have $Pr(f' \geq (1 + \epsilon)\mu) \leq e^{-\epsilon\mu \log(1+\epsilon)/2}$.

We select $\epsilon = \frac{1}{3\beta'} - 1$, then we have $Pr(f' \geq \frac{1}{3\beta'} \times \beta'n) = Pr(f' \geq \frac{n}{3}) = Pr(f' > f) \leq e^{n(1-3\beta')\log(3\beta')/6}$. Since $(1 - 3\beta')\log(3\beta') < 0$, the above probability is exponentially small in n. Therefore, this lemma has been proved.

Theorem 1. *(**Consistency and Liveness**) Assuming $f' \leq f$ in comm_1, Grape can meet the consistency and liveness in Definition 1 except for a probability exponentially small in n if $\beta' < 1/3$.*

Proof. In Lemma 3, we proved that if $f' \leq f$ holds for comm_1 and $\beta' < 1/3$, then $f' \leq f$ holds for each subsequent committee, where f' denotes the actual number of corrupt members in the committee except for a probability exponentially small in n. In Lemma 1, we proved that any honest miner will commit the same block at the same height if $f' \leq f$. Since the miners use a deterministic sorting algorithm to generate ledger $\mathscr{L}$ according to KeyChain, *consistency* follows in a straightforward manner from Lemma 3 and Lemma 1.

After receiving the transaction tx, the miner will pack it into the transaction block txb and broadcast it. Then txb will soon be referenced by a keyb. When the key block is committed, tx will also appear in the ledger of all honest miners. To prove that the ledger $\mathscr{L}$ meets the *liveness*, we only need that the BFT run by the committee can continuously generate key blocks to include new transaction blocks. Grape's *liveness* follows from Lemma 3 and the BFT protocol's *liveness*.

Theorem 2. *(**Smooth Rotation**) The rotation of the rolling committee never interrupts the underlying BFT consensus.*

Proof. From Theorem 1, the Grape protocol satisfies both consistency and liveness. New valid identity blocks could be contained in blocks in KeyChain, and every user in Grape can agree on the ending of the last commit and the beginning of the next one. In this way, users in Grape agree on the committee rotation. As described in Algorithm 3, the last committee members will quit and the new committee members take over their job immediately. Since the switch of the underlying BFT consensus committee and the generation of the old committee's last block happen simultaneity, there is no interruption of the BFT consensus.

7   Implementation and Simulation

We implement the whole Grape protocol with the Go programming language [17]. Regarding the underlying BFT part, we utilize the same aggregate signature as in Ethereum [18] to reduce the complexity, and the Gnet framework [12] to build the communications among the committee members.

We deploy the Grape protocol on four machines and test its performance. One of the machines has a CPU model of Intel i7-6700 (with 4 cores and 8 threads), and 16 GB of memory. The CPU model of the other three machines is AMD 4800H (with 8 cores and 16 threads), and the memory is 16 GB. The bandwidth employed between these machines is 939 Mbits per second and the bandwidth employed within a single machine is 6.20 Gbits per second. We test the effect of the different committee sizes on the performance of the Grape protocol. It is worth noting that since the Grape protocol confirms transactions by using a fixed-size committee (i.e., value n is constant) to run the underlying BFT, the number of all nodes in Grape has little effect on its performance.

In the experiment, we choose a transaction size of 24B with each transaction block contains 100 transactions, and the size of the transaction block is 2.614 KB. We evaluate the performance of the Grape protocol in terms of transaction latency and transaction throughput.

Table 2. Experimental results of grape

Committee size n	4	7	10	13	16
Transaction throughput ($\times 10^5$ transactions/second)	3.83	3.28	3.02	2.81	2.34
Confirmation latency (seconds)	1.74	3.27	3.38	3.50	4.39

In our simulation, we vary the committee size from 4 to 16. The result shows that the transaction throughput of Grape varies from 3.83×10^5 tps to 2.34×10^5 tps, and the confirmation latency varies from 1.74 seconds to 4.39 seconds correspondingly, as shown in Table 2, which are much better than other approaches [2, 15, 24]. We emphasize that the throughput is the number of blocks multiplyed the containing transactions, where blocks are sent by miners in parallel before selection by committees.

It is worth noting that Grape's performance decreases almost linearly as the committee size grows. In practice, people can determine committee size according to the estimated number of corrupt committee members, and balance between the performance and the security bound.

8   Conclusion

In this paper, we propose Grape, an efficient hybrid consensus protocol using BlockDAG, which gives a new and comprehensive answer to the challenges of promoting the blockchain throughput and reducing the confirmation time. Compared with other hybrid consensus protocols, Grape makes improvements on committee rotation and concurrency. Furthermore, the simulation justifies the availability of Grape.

References

1. Abraham, I., Malkhi, D., Nayak, K., Ren, L., Spiegelman, A.: Solida: a blockchain protocol based on reconfigurable byzantine consensus. arXiv preprint arXiv:1612.02916 (2016)
2. Bagaria, V., Kannan, S., Tse, D., Fanti, G., Viswanath, P.: Prism: deconstructing the blockchain to approach physical limits. In: Proceedings of the 2019 ACM SIGSAC Conference on Computer and Communications Security, pp. 585–602 (2019)
3. Castro, M., Liskov, B., et al.: Practical byzantine fault tolerance. OSDI **99**, 173–186 (1999)
4. Decker, C., Seidel, J., Wattenhofer, R.: Bitcoin meets strong consistency. In: Proceedings of the 17th International Conference on Distributed Computing and Networking, pp. 1–10 (2016)
5. Eyal, I., Gencer, A.E., Sirer, E.G., Van Renesse, R.: Bitcoin-NG: a scalable blockchain protocol. In: 13th USENIX Symposium on Networked Systems Design and Implementation (NSDI 2016), pp. 45–59 (2016)
6. Eyal, I., Sirer, E.G.: Majority is not enough: bitcoin mining is vulnerable. In: International Conference on Financial Cryptography and Data Security, pp. 436–454. Springer (2014)
7. Garay, J., Kiayias, A., Leonardos, N.: The bitcoin backbone protocol: analysis and applications. In: Oswald, E., Fischlin, M. (eds.) EUROCRYPT 2015. LNCS, vol. 9057, pp. 281–310. Springer, Heidelberg (2015). https://doi.org/10.1007/978-3-662-46803-6_10
8. Kokoris-Kogias, E., Jovanovic, P., Gailly, N., Khoffi, I., Gasser, L., Ford, B.: Enhancing bitcoin security and performance with strong consistency via collective signing. In: USENIX, pp. 279–296 (2016)
9. Li, C., et al.: A decentralized blockchain with high throughput and fast confirmation. In: USENIX ATC 2020, pp. 515–528 (2020)
10. Nakamoto, S.: Bitcoin: a peer-to-peer electronic cash system. Technical report, Manubot (2019)
11. Natoli, C., Gramoli, V.: The balance attack against proof-of-work blockchains: the R3 testbed as an example. arXiv preprint arXiv:1612.09426 (2016)
12. Andy, P.: Fast and lightweight networking framework in go (2019)
13. Pass, R., Shi, E.: Fruitchains: a fair blockchain. In: Proceedings of the ACM Symposium on Principles of Distributed Computing, pp. 315–324 (2017)
14. Pass, R., Shi, E.: Hybrid consensus: efficient consensus in the permissionless model. In: DISC (2017)
15. Pass, R., Shi, E.: Thunderella: blockchains with optimistic instant confirmation. In: Nielsen, J.B., Rijmen, V. (eds.) EUROCRYPT 2018. LNCS, vol. 10821, pp. 3–33. Springer, Cham (2018). https://doi.org/10.1007/978-3-319-78375-8_1
16. Popov, S.Y.: The tangle (2015)
17. Pike, R.: The go programming language. Talk given at Google's Tech Talks (2009)
18. Mitsunari, S., Moritz, F.: BLS with compiled static library

19. Sompolinsky, Y., Lewenberg, Y., Zohar, A.: Spectre: a fast and scalable cryptocurrency protocol. IACR Cryptol. ePrint Arch. **2016**, 1159 (2016)
20. Sompolinsky, Y., Zohar, A.: Secure high-rate transaction processing in bitcoin. In: Böhme, R., Okamoto, T. (eds.) FC 2015. LNCS, vol. 8975, pp. 507–527. Springer, Heidelberg (2015). https://doi.org/10.1007/978-3-662-47854-7_32
21. Sompolinsky, Y., Zohar, A.: Phantom: A scalable blockdag protocol. IACR Cryptol. ePrint Arch. **2018**, 104 (2018)
22. Wang, Q., Yu, J., Chen, S., Xiang, Y.: SoK: diving into DAG-based blockchain systems. arXiv preprint arXiv:2012.06128 (2020)
23. Xiang, F., Huaimin, W., Peichang, S., Xue, O., Xunhui, Z.: Jointgraph: a DAG-based efficient consensus algorithm for consortium blockchains. Softw. Pract. Exp. **51**(10), 1987–1999 (2021)
24. Yin, M., Malkhi, D., Reiter, M.K., Gueta, G.G., Abraham, I.: HotStuff: BFT consensus with linearity and responsiveness. In: Proceedings of the 2019 ACM Symposium on Principles of Distributed Computing, pp. 347–356 (2019)

A Game-Theoretic Analysis of Delegation Incentives in Blockchain Governance

Lyudmila Kovalchuk[1,2], Mariia Rodinko[1,3(✉)], and Roman Oliynykov[1,3]

[1] Input Output, Singapore, Singapore
mariia.rodinko@iohk.io
[2] National Technical University of Ukraine,
"Igor Sikorsky Kyiv Polytechnic Institute", Kyiv, Ukraine
[3] V.N. Karazin Kharkiv National University, Kharkiv, Ukraine

Abstract. The paper presents a mathematical description of the vote delegation incentive process for funding proposals in a decentralized governance system using a blockchain-based voting. Two models of bribing a delegate by a proposer submitting proposals for funding are considered: "Rational Delegates" and "Emotional Delegates". In terms of parameters describing the voting process, a sufficient condition for a Nash equilibrium is found to be as follows: if both a proposer and a delegate do not intend to participate in bribery. Moreover, it is shown at what share of the briber's stake this condition is satisfied. The main practical result of the paper is the possibility to define what kind of an attacker (in terms of the bribing capability) we will be able to resist under certain parameters.

Keywords: Blockchain · Blockchain governance · Decentralized voting · Delegation incentives · Vote delegation · Bribery · Nash equilibrium

1 Introduction

Development of an effective on-chain decentralized governance remains one of the most complicated issues in blockchain-based systems design. Some solutions are hybrid off-chain and on-chain systems (e.g., Dash [1]) while others are purely on-chain governance systems (e.g., Tezos [4], Ethereum Classic [12]). More information about blockchain governance can be found in [5,11,13]. The important part of cryptocurrency governance is a self-funding mechanism, often called a treasury system, providing a decentralized funding distribution among projects aimed at cryptocurrency development and growth. One of such funding systems, called Catalyst, is implemented in Cardano [3]. There is a special platform where users can submit their proposals on Cardano improvement [2]. The voting process is carried out on Cardano blockchain using the special voting protocol that provides privacy [17].

As we can see from the past Catalyst Funds (rounds of voting), there are a lot of proposals related to different topics: from development and audit to marketing and global adoption etc. Obviously, stakeholders cannot be experts

© The Author(s), under exclusive license to Springer Nature Switzerland AG 2023
J. Garcia-Alfaro et al. (Eds.): DPM 2022/CBT 2022, LNCS 13619, pp. 275–293, 2023.
https://doi.org/10.1007/978-3-031-25734-6_17

in all proposals' topics of all Catalyst Funds; they do not have enough time and expertise to go through hundreds of proposals and vote for them. In this regard, the problem of constructing an effective delegation incentive scheme arises. Such a scheme should provide:

- high quality decision-making by professional delegates;
- increased stake participation (stakeholders spend less time and may spend less effort in Catalyst);
- higher level of security against treasury attacks (harder attacks to takeover Catalyst control in fully decentralized environment).

So, the proposed delegation incentive scheme aims to satisfy interests of all honest players, minimize risks arising from malicious behavior and provide growth of the overall cryptocurrency value.

Construction, description and security rationale of such a complex process as Catalyst voting [17] requires use of results from various fields of applied mathematics. Most of all it is related to various areas in cryptology, since many symmetric, asymmetric and hybrid cryptosystems, zero-knowledge proofs, secret sharing schemes etc. are used in the voting process.

One of the most important fields of mathematics employed to build the incentive system in Catalyst is game theory. So, the paper [6] describes a probabilistic approach to incentives distribution using a kind of lottery. Existence of a Nash equilibrium for this model is proved, moreover, the proof is constructive, and various properties of this equilibrium are described.

Contributions. The obtained results are also in the field of game theory, but they are related only to analysis of the conditions under which a threat of voter bribery arises.

To analyze the threats related to bribery, we fulfilled the following tasks:

- the mathematical model that fully describes the process of receiving incentives by delegates was built;
- two models of bribing a delegate by a proposer were considered: "Rational Delegates" and "Emotional Delegates";
- all possible conditions of a Nash equilibrium existence for these models were analyzed;
- in terms of parameters describing the voting process, a sufficient condition was formulated and proved that a Nash equilibrium exists only if both a proposer and a delegate do not intend to participate in bribery;
- it was shown at what stake share owned by a briber the above condition is satisfied.

1.1 Related Work

The problem of voting on the blockchain was studied in many papers. One of the most fundamental works in this field is [10]. This paper looks into the blockchain application in electronic voting. It was shown that the blockchain technology can solve some of the issues of electronic election systems, but there are questions regarding privacy protection and scalability. Besides, this paper also contains a large and detailed overview of other papers.

Among other studies dealing with the blockchain-based voting we can list the following ones:

- [16] – on advantages of using blockchain for voting and additional opportunities related to the blockchain application;
- [14] – on principles for building an anonymous decentralized e-voting system using a ring signature mechanism and the blockchain technology to ensure anonymity, integrity and transparency;
- [7] – on distributed protocols that privately compute outcomes of a voting scheme revealing a limited amount of information.

However, it should be noted that the subjects of these papers do not include the issue of bribery.

The book [8] studies many aspects of voting including risks related to bribery using game theory (Chap. 7). Similar issues were discussed in more detail in [9,15], and each of these papers contains its own specific mathematical model corresponding to a certain practical task. However, the results obtained in these papers and recommendations given cannot be used for blockchain-based voting because of the following reasons:

- absence of a "trusted third party";
- identification of a stakeholder offering a bribe is challenging due to blockchain anonymity;
- inability to punish a stakeholder who is bribing because their identity is potentially unknown.

The issues considered in this paper are very different from the above ones as they are related to a completely new model of Catalyst voting developed specially for Cardano. We take into account Catalyst delegate selection scheme, procedure of voting for proposals and stake distribution among voters. So, the results obtained are original and valuable.

2 Preliminaries

There are the following types of participants with specific goals (regarding honest players) in the system:

- *proposers* submit proposals and aim to receive funding for their projects;
- *stakeholders* (aka voters) can either vote for proposals by themselves or delegate this job to delegates (in order for stakeholder to take part in the voting process, their stake must be greater than a given threshold, that is necessary for protection from DoS attacks; the specific value of this threshold is not significant for further analysis); stakeholders are interested in competent decision-making regarding funding (that increases the overall cryptocurrency value and hence the value of their stakes) and rewarding for voting (delegation);
- *delegates* (aka representatives) are authorized to vote on behalf of stakeholders and are interested in competent decision-making regarding funding and rewarding for voting.

- *experts* evaluate proposals and give constructive feedback receiving appropriate rewards for doing this work.

Notations

- $\mathbf{V} = \{V_1, ..., V_m\}$, $m \in \mathbb{N}$ is a set of stakeholders (voters);
- $\mathbf{D} = \{D_1, ..., D_n\}$, $n \in \mathbb{N}$ is a set of delegates;
- $s_1, ..., s_m$, $s_i \in (0, 1)$ are corresponding stake shares of delegates (including a delegated stake);
- $s'_1, ..., s'_n$, $s'_j \in (0, 1)$ are corresponding stake shares of stakeholders;
- $e = const$, $e \in \mathbb{R}_+$ is an escrow that a delegate D_i makes during a registration;
- $\Theta \in \mathbb{R}_+$ is a total treasury fund for one round of voting;
- $\psi \in (0, 1)$ is a share of the treasury fund allocated for delegates' reward (e.g., $\psi = 0.02$);
- $R = \psi\Theta$ is a delegates' total reward;
- $\phi \in [0, 1]$ is a share of the treasury fund allocated for stakeholders' reward (e.g., $\phi = 0.12$);
- $R' = \phi\Theta$ is a stakeholders' total reward;
- $s_{total} \in \mathbb{R}_+$ is a total stake participating in the voting (registered stake);
- $A = \{A_0, A_1, A_2\}$ are shares of the escrow e_i that should be burnt if the delegate D_i has not submitted a ballot, for various delegation levels (e.g. $A = \{0.1, 0.2, 1.0\}$);
- $r_i = Rs_i$ is a total reward of the delegate D_i for honest activity, or if he is bribed but not detected;
- $r^v_j = R's'_j$ is a reward of the stakeholder V_j;
- $\alpha \in [0, 1]$ is a share of a delegates's reward allocated for short-term reward (e.g., $\alpha = 0.7$);
- $r^s_i = \alpha \cdot r_i$ is a short-term reward of the delegate D_i (paid immediately);
- $r^l_i = \begin{cases} r^l_i = (1 - \alpha) \cdot r_i & \text{if Conditions 1 and 2 are satisfied} \\ 0 & \text{otherwise} \end{cases}$,
  is a long-term reward of the delegate D_i (paid at the end of k rounds of voting);

  Condition 1: $s^{av}_i \geq \lambda \cdot s_{total}$, the delegate P_i is delegated with not less than some constant percent of stake on average during k rounds of voting (e.g., $\lambda = 0.02$)
  Condition 2: D_i participated at least in x rounds of voting out of k (e.g., $x = 6$, $k = 8$)
  If a delegate does not participate in any of k rounds of voting, then he will get neither short- nor long-term rewards for this round
- $r_i = r^s_i + r^l_i$;
- $e_i > 0$, efforts paid by D_i for one round of voting;
- p, probability to bribe D_i ($p = Pr(D_i \text{ accepts a bribe})$ for randomly chosen D_i);
- q, probability that bribery of D_i will be detected;
- v, the average funding a proposer gets in k rounds of voting;
- $F \in \mathbb{R}_+$, profit that P gets from bribing;
- $C_i = cs_i$, for some $c > 0$, $C_i \in \mathbb{R}_+$, costs that P proposes to D_i as a bribe;
- $K_i = \kappa s_i$, for some $\kappa \geq 0$, risk cost/moral price if D_i accepts a bribe (with "–"); or interest for refusing (with "+") because D_i is proud of himself (if he is honest).

---

3 Delegation Scheme

A delegation process consists of the following steps.

1. Stakeholders and delegates are registered on a blockchain:
   - each delegate D_i makes an escrow e on registration;
   - decision-making process is supported by experts using their separate platform (currently it is IdeaScale [2]).

2. Stakeholders and delegates vote on proposals:
   - to be rewarded, a delegate D_i must vote (Yes/No) not less than on a fixed number of proposals and write a rationale for each voted proposal on a public resource with its address provided to stakeholders;
   - to be rewarded, a stakeholder V_i must do one of the following:
     - vote (Yes/No) not less than on a fixed number of proposals;
     - delegate their voting power to a delegate who must vote not less than on a fixed number of proposals;
   - the current treasury protocol allows parallel voting providing ballot privacy both for stakeholders and delegates.
3. Rewards are paid to stakeholders (r_j^v) and eligible delegates (r_i):
   - a *short-term* delegate's reward r_i^s is paid immediately after the voting;
   - a *long-term* delegate's reward r_i^l is accumulated and paid at the end of k funds (e.g., 2 years);
   - undistributed delegates' rewards are sent back to further funds.
4. If a delegate sends no ballot (covering necessary amount of proposals) or gets no delegation, he gets no reward and a fine (voting liveness protection):
   - no delegation at all: amount of A_0 of his escrow e is burnt;
   - having delegated less than δ (i.e., 1% of the total stake) tokens and no ballot: amount of A_1 of his escrow e is burnt;
   - having delegated at least δ tokens and no ballot: amount of A_2 delegate's escrow e (100%) is burnt.

3.1 Calculation of a Delegate's Total Reward

To define the value of a bribe that may be interesting for some delegate D_i, we first should define the total reward of D_i that he will lose if the fact of bribery is detected. We assume the following.

- D_i loses at least short-term rewards for the nearest k rounds of voting and one long-term reward, assuming that the long-term reward is paid after every k rounds of voting.
- The value of money that D_i gets now is more valuable than the same value of money that will be received later, with some coefficient $t \in (0, 1)$. More precisely, if D_i gets a short-term reward r_i^s in every voting round, then the value in the nearest voting round is r_i^s, in the next voting round this value is tr_i^s, then $t^2 r_i^s$, $t^3 r_i^s$ etc., respectively.

Then the total reward, R_i, for the i-th delegate (D_i) for the whole "cycle" (k voting rounds or the number of rounds between long-term rewards) is:

$$R_i = r_i^s + tr_i^s + \ldots + t^{k-1}r_i^s + t^{k-1}r_i^l k = r_i^s \frac{1-t^k}{1-t} + t^{k-1}r_i^l k$$
$$= \alpha Rs_i \frac{1-t^k}{1-t} + t^{k-1}(1-\alpha)Rs_i k = Rs_i \left(\alpha \frac{1-t^k}{1-t} + k(1-\alpha)t^{k-1} \right). \qquad (1)$$

The value of t may be taken, in particular, based on deposit interest. For example, if there are 3 months between funds, and the annual interest is 4%, then for every 3rd month the interest is 1%, so $t \approx 0.99$ or so. In this case, and if, for example, $k = 8$, we get the value of the total reward as

$$R_i = Rs_i \left(\alpha \frac{1 - 0.99^8}{0.01} + 8 \cdot (1 - \alpha) \cdot 0.99^7 \right) = Rs_i \left(7.73\alpha + 7.46 \cdot (1 - \alpha) \right) = Rs_i (0.27\alpha + 7.46).$$

4   Bribery Scenario in Pure Strategies

A bribery scenario in pure strategies can be modeled as an asymmetric sequential game among delegates and proposers. Each proposer may play two strategies:

- (B_1) – does not propose a bribe for voting in his interest;
- (B_2) – proposes a bribe for voting.

Each delegate may also play two strategies:

- (S_1) – refuses to take a bribe;
- (S_2) – is waiting for a bribe (after that he votes as a briber wants).

If a proposer plays (B_1), i.e., does not try to bribe a delegate D_i, then D_i gets a payoff R_i – a total reward (1) for participation in k sequential votings, taking into account the fact that different parts of the total reward are paid in different times. But in the case if the delegate was waiting for a bribe, i.e. plays (S_2), he also has some moral suffering κ_i that his expectations were not met. Then the payoff of D_i is:

$$u_i(B_1, S_1) = R_i - ke_i, \tag{2}$$

$$u_i(B_1, S_2) = R_i - ke_i - K_i, \tag{3}$$

where e_i are efforts paid by D_i for one voting.

We also assume that a proposer receives some fixed v that may be considered as the average funding he gets in k funds (we do not care about this value and may assume $v = 0$):

$$u_P(B_1, \cdot) = v. \tag{4}$$

If a proposer plays (B_2), a delegate may play two strategies, and his payoff is:

$$u_i(B_2, S_1) = R_i - ke_i + K_i; \tag{5}$$

$$u_i(B_2, S_2) = C_i + (1 - q)R_i - K_i, \tag{6}$$

where all notations were introduced in *Notations* (Sect. 2).

The payoff of the proposer who plays (B_2) is:

$$u_P(B_2, S_1) = -K_i; \tag{7}$$

$$u_P(B_2, S_2) = F - K_i - C_i, \tag{8}$$

where $F = 0$ iff a stake ratio s_i that briber managed to bribe, is not sufficient to win voting.

The corresponding payoff matrices of the game are:

$$M_i = \begin{array}{c} \\ (S_1) \\ (S_2) \end{array} \begin{pmatrix} \overset{(B_1)}{R_i - ke_i} & \overset{(B_2)}{R_i - ke_i + K_i} \\ R_i - ke_i - K_i & C_i + (1-q)R_i - K_i \end{pmatrix} \qquad (9)$$

payoff for delegate D_i; and

$$M_P = \begin{array}{c} \\ (B_1) \\ (B_2) \end{array} \begin{pmatrix} \overset{(S_1)}{v} & \overset{(S_2)}{v} \\ -K_i & F - K_i - C_i \end{pmatrix} \qquad (10)$$

payoff for proposer.

Note that for case of rational players, we assume $\kappa = 0$, hence $K_i = 0$. From (9) and (10) we get the following trivial Proposition.

Proposition 1 (Nash equilibrium in pure strategies). *The conditions for a Nash equilibrium in pure strategies are the following.*

1. *The point (B_1, S_1) is always a Nash equilibrium.*
2. *The point (B_2, S_2) is a Nash equilibrium iff*
$$\begin{cases} F - K_i - C_i > v; \\ C_i + (1-q)R_i - K_i > R_i - ke_i + K_i. \end{cases}$$
3. *The point (B_1, S_2) is a Nash equilibrium iff* $\begin{cases} K_i = 0; \\ F - C_i < v. \end{cases}$
4. *The point (B_2, S_1) is a Nash equilibrium iff* $\begin{cases} K_i = v = 0; \\ qR_i \geq C_i + ke_i - 2K_i. \end{cases}$

Note that the described voting system is vulnerable to bribery only in the case when (B_2, S_2) is a Nash equilibrium, because in three other points no bribery occurs. Using Proposition 1 and (1), we can formulate the following Corollary.

Corollary 1. *The necessary condition to have a Nash equilibrium (in pure strategies) in the point (B_2, S_2) is:*

$$F > v + K_i + C_i > v + K_i + (R_i - ke_i + K_i - (1-q)R_i + K_i)$$
$$= v + s_i \left(3\kappa + qR \left(\alpha \frac{1-t^k}{1-t} + k(1-\alpha)t^{k-1} \right) - ke_i \right)$$

or

$$s_i < \frac{F + ke_i - v}{3\kappa + qR \left(\alpha \frac{1-t^k}{1-t} + k(1-\alpha)t^{k-1} \right)}.$$

In other words, the necessary condition for a Nash equilibrium in (B_2, S_2) is that the stake that a briber needs to buy to win the voting is not larger than the right part of the equality.

For example, if $F = \$1,000,000$; $k = 8$; $\alpha = 0.15$; $v = \$50,000$; $\kappa = 0$; $e_i = \$2250$; $q = 0.96$; $t = 0.99$; $R = \$360,000$ we get:

$$s_i < \frac{\$1,000,000 + 8 \cdot \$2250 - \$50,000}{0.96 \cdot \$360,000 \cdot \left(0.15 \cdot \frac{1-0.99^8}{0.01} + 8 \cdot 0.85 \cdot 0.99^7\right)} \iff s_i < 0.374.$$

Note 1. According to (7) and (8), to get some profit from bribery, a proposer should bribe some amount of stake, say not less than s, to win voting. As in our model, a bribe is proportional to the amount of stake bribed, the optimal case for him is to bribe delegates $D_{i1}, ..., D_{ik}$ such that:

$$(i_1, ..., i_k) = \arg \min_{j_1,...,j_l} \left\{ \sum_{t=1}^{l} s_{j_t} \geq s \right\}.$$

5   Bribery Scenario in Mixed Strategies

We consider two models for two different types of players behavior: rational players and emotional players. Rational players are interested only in increasing their profit or income and do not pay attention to how moral or how honest their actions are. Emotional players may also try to increase their income in some malicious way, but they feel shame if they do this. And vise versa: they may be proud of themselves if they find strength to resist some profitable proposition that may increase their income. In the model with emotional players, we consider that both sides of the game, the delegate and the proposer, are emotional. And so called "moral price" for them is proportional (with some coefficient κ) to the delegated stake ratio that corresponds to the delegate that briber (proposer) is trying to bribe.

In this chapter we first prove some general statements for two-player game that later we use to obtain results for these two models.

For simplicity, we define elements of the matrices M_i and M_P as:

$$M_i = \begin{pmatrix} d_{11} & d_{12} \\ d_{21} & d_{22} \end{pmatrix}; \quad M_P = \begin{pmatrix} b_{11} & b_{12} \\ b_{21} & b_{22} \end{pmatrix}. \tag{11}$$

For describing a Nash equilibrium in mixed strategies, we need two auxiliary lemmas.

Lemma 1. *Let $a, b \in \mathbb{R}$, $a + b \neq 0$. Define $p = \frac{a}{a+b}$. Then $p \in [0, 1] \iff$*
$$\begin{cases} a + b \neq 0; \\ \left[\begin{array}{l} ab \geq 0; \\ ab \leq 0. \end{array} \right. \end{cases}$$

Proof. Let us consider four cases for a and b.

CASE 1: $a \geq 0$, $b \geq 0$, $a + b \neq 0$.

In this case $0 \leq a \leq a + b$ holds that is equivalent to $0 \leq p \leq 1$.

CASE 2: $a \leq 0$, $b \leq 0$, $a + b \neq 0$.

Define $a = -a_1$, $b = -b_1$. Then $p = \frac{-a_1}{-a_1 - b_1} = \frac{a_1}{a_1 + b_1}$, when $a_1 \geq 0$, $b_1 \geq 0$, $a_1 + b_1 \neq 0$ and, according to Case 1, we get $0 \leq p \leq 1$.

CASE 3: $a > 0$, $b \leq 0$, $a + b \neq 0$.

In this case $a + b < a$ and $p < 0$ (if $a + b < 0$) or $p > 1$ (if $a + b > 0$).

CASE 4: $a < 0$, $b \geq 0$, $a + b \neq 0$.

In this case $p < 0$ if $b + a > 0$ (or $b > -a$), or $p = \frac{-a}{-(b+a)} = \frac{-a}{-a-b} > 1$ if $b < -a$.

In what follows, we will consider mixed strategies $\mu_1 = (p_1, 1 - p_1)$ for the Delegate and $\mu_2 = (p_2, 1 - p_2)$ for the Briber. For simplicity, we say "point (p_1, p_2)" instead of "point (μ_1, μ_2)".

Lemma 2. *Let payoff matrices M_i and M_P be as in* (11). *Then:*

1. *For any p_1, p_2 a point (p_1, p_2) is a Nash equilibrium iff*

$$\begin{cases} d_{21} = d_{11}; \\ d_{12} = d_{22}; \\ b_{21} - b_{22} - b_{11} + b_{12} = 0; \\ b_{12} = b_{22}. \end{cases} \qquad (12)$$

2. *A point $\left(p_1, \frac{d_{12} - d_{22}}{d_{21} - d_{11} - d_{22} + d_{12}}\right)$ is a Nash equilibrium for any $p_1 \in [0, 1]$ iff*

$$\begin{cases} b_{12} = b_{22}; \\ b_{21} = b_{11}; \\ d_{21} - d_{11} - d_{22} + d_{12} \neq 0; \\ \left[\begin{cases} d_{12} - d_{22} \geq 0; \\ d_{21} - d_{11} \geq 0; \end{cases} \\ \left[\begin{cases} d_{12} - d_{22} \leq 0; \\ d_{21} - d_{11} \leq 0. \end{cases} \right. \end{cases} \qquad (13)$$

3. *A point $\left(\frac{b_{12} - b_{22}}{b_{21} - b_{22} - b_{11} + b_{12}}, p_2\right)$ is a Nash equilibrium for any $p_2 \in [0, 1]$ iff*

$$\begin{cases} d_{12} = d_{22}; \\ d_{21} = d_{11}; \\ b_{21} - b_{11} - b_{22} + b_{12} \neq 0; \\ \left[\begin{cases} b_{12} - b_{22} \geq 0; \\ b_{21} - b_{11} \geq 0; \end{cases} \\ \left[\begin{cases} b_{12} - b_{22} \leq 0; \\ b_{21} - b_{11} \leq 0. \end{cases} \right. \end{cases} \qquad (14)$$

4. A point $\left(\frac{b_{12}-b_{22}}{b_{21}-b_{22}-b_{11}+b_{12}}, \frac{d_{12}-d_{22}}{d_{21}-d_{22}-d_{11}+d_{12}} \right)$ is a Nash equilibrium iff

$$\begin{cases} b_{21} - b_{11} - b_{22} + b_{12} \neq 0; \\ \left[\begin{cases} b_{12} - b_{22} \geq 0; \\ b_{21} - b_{11} \geq 0; \end{cases} \right. \\ \left. \begin{cases} b_{12} - b_{22} \leq 0; \\ b_{21} - b_{11} \leq 0. \end{cases} \right. \\ d_{21} = d_{11}; \\ \left[\begin{cases} d_{12} - d_{22} \geq 0; \\ d_{21} - d_{11} \geq 0; \end{cases} \right. \\ \left. \begin{cases} d_{12} - d_{22} \leq 0; \\ d_{21} - d_{11} \leq 0. \end{cases} \right. \end{cases} \tag{15}$$

There are no other Nash equilibria in mixed strategies.

Proof. In our notations,

$$u_i(p_1, p_2) = d_{11}p_1p_2 + d_{12}p_1(1 - p_2) + d_{21}(1 - p_1)p_2 + d_{22}(1 - p_1)(1 - p_2).$$

Then, from equality

$$u_i(0, p_2) = u_i(1, p_2)$$

we get

$$(d_{21} - d_{11} - d_{22} + d_{12})p_2 = d_{12} - d_{22}. \tag{16}$$

CASE 1: $\begin{cases} d_{12} \neq d_{22}; \\ d_{21} - d_{11} - d_{22} + d_{12} = 0. \end{cases}$

In this case (16) has no solutions.

CASE 2: $\begin{cases} d_{12} = d_{22}; \\ d_{21} - d_{11} - d_{22} + d_{12} = 0 \end{cases}$ or $\begin{cases} d_{12} = d_{22}; \\ d_{21} = d_{11}. \end{cases}$

In this case any $p_2 \in [0, 1]$ is a solution of (16).

CASE 3: $d_{21} - d_{11} - d_{22} + d_{12} \neq 0.$

In this case (13) has only one solution

$$p_2 = \frac{d_{12} - d_{22}}{d_{21} - d_{11} - d_{22} + d_{12}}.$$

From condition $p_2 \in [0, 1]$ and using Lemma 1, we get additional restrictions:

$$\begin{cases} \left[\begin{cases} d_{12} - d_{22} \geq 0; \\ d_{21} - d_{11} \geq 0; \end{cases} \right. \\ \left. \begin{cases} d_{12} - d_{22} \leq 0; \\ d_{21} - d_{11} \leq 0. \end{cases} \right. \end{cases}$$

Applying the same considerations to the equality

$$u_B(p_1, 0) = u_B(p_1, 1),$$

we complete the proof.

5.1   Model 1: Rational Players

In this subsection the first model with rational players is considered.

Proposition 2. *For Model 1 (with rational players) the conditions for a Nash equilibrium in mixed strategies are:*

- *a Nash equilibrium in the point* (p_1, p_2) *for arbitrary* $p_1, p_2 \in [0, 1]$ *iff*

$$\begin{cases} qR_i = F - ke_i; \\ F = C_i. \end{cases} \tag{17}$$

- *a Nash equilibrium in the point* $(p_1, 1)$ *for arbitrary* $p_1 \in [0, 1]$ *iff*

$$\begin{cases} qR_i \neq C_i + ke_i; \\ v = 0; \\ F = C_i. \end{cases} \tag{18}$$

- *a Nash equilibrium in the point* $(1, p_2)$ *for arbitrary* $p_1 \in [0, 1]$ *iff*

$$\begin{cases} qR_i = C_i + ke_i; \\ v = 0; \\ F < C_i. \end{cases} \tag{19}$$

- *a Nash equilibrium in the point* $(\frac{F - C_i - v}{F - C_i}, p_2)$ *for arbitrary* $p_2 \in [0, 1]$ *iff*

$$\begin{cases} qR_i = C_i + ke_i; \\ 0 < v \leq F - C_i; \\ F > C_i. \end{cases} \tag{20}$$

- *a Nash equilibrium in the point* $(1, 1)$ *iff*

$$\begin{cases} qR_i \neq C_i + ke_i; \\ v = 0; \\ F < C_i. \end{cases} \tag{21}$$

- *a Nash equilibrium in the point* $(\frac{F - C_i - v}{F - C_i}, 1)$ *iff*

$$\begin{cases} qR_i \neq C_i + ke_i; \\ 0 < v \leq F - C_i. \end{cases} \tag{22}$$

There are no others Nash equilibria in mixed strategies.

Proof. For Model 1 we can rewrite (12) as

$$\begin{cases} R_i - ke_i - (R_i - ke_i) - (C_i + (1-q)R_i + (R_i - ke_i) = 0; \\ R_i - ke_i = C_i + (1-q)R_i; \\ v - (F - C_i) - v + 0 = 0; \\ v = F - C_i \end{cases}$$

that is equivalent to $\begin{cases} R_i - ke_i = C_i + (1-q)R_i; \\ F = C_i \end{cases}$ or $\begin{cases} qR_i = C_i + ke_i; \\ F = C_i. \end{cases}$

Next, (13) can be rewritten as

$$\begin{cases} v = F - C_i; \\ 0 - (F - C_i) - v + v = 0; \\ (R_i - ke_i) - (R_i - ke_i) - (C_i + (1-q)R_i) + (R_i - ke_i) \neq 0; \\ \left[\begin{array}{l} \begin{cases} R_i - ke_i \geq C_i - (1-q)R_i; \\ R_i - ke_i \geq R_i - ke_i; \end{cases} \\ \begin{cases} R_i - ke_i \leq C_i - (1-q)R_i; \\ R_i - ke_i \leq R_i - ke_i \end{cases} \end{array} \right. \end{cases}$$

that is equivalent to $\begin{cases} F = C_i; \\ v = 0; \\ qR_i \neq C_i + ke_i. \end{cases}$

Note that in this case $p_2 = 1$ because of $d_{21} = d_{11}$, so we have a Nash equilibrium as $(p_1, 1)$ for arbitrary $p_1 \in [0,1]$.

Then, the condition (14) can be rewritten as

$$\begin{cases} R_i - ke_i = C_i + (1-q)R_i; \\ R_i - ke_i = R_i - ke_i; \\ 0 - (F - C_i) - v + v = 0; \\ \left[\begin{array}{l} \begin{cases} v - (F - C_i) \geq 0; \\ 0 - v \geq 0; \end{cases} \\ \begin{cases} v - (F - C_i) \leq 0; \\ 0 - v \leq 0 \end{cases} \end{array} \right. \end{cases}$$

or

$$\begin{cases} qR_i = C_i + ke_i; \\ F \neq C_i; \\ \left[\begin{array}{l} \begin{cases} v \geq F - C_i; \\ v \leq 0; \end{cases} \leftrightarrow \begin{cases} v = 0; \\ F - C_i < 0 \end{cases} \quad \Longleftrightarrow \\ \begin{cases} v \leq F - C_i; \\ v \geq 0. \end{cases} \leftrightarrow 0 \leq v \leq F - C_i \end{array} \right. \end{cases}$$

$$\begin{cases} qR_i = C_i + ke_i; \\ \left[\begin{array}{l} \begin{cases} F - C_i > 0; \\ 0 \le v \le F - C_i; \end{cases} \\ \begin{cases} F - C_i < 0; \\ v = 0 \end{cases} \end{array}\right. \end{cases} \iff \begin{cases} qR_i = C_i + ke_i; \\ \left[\begin{array}{l} \begin{cases} F > C_i; \\ 0 \le v \le F - C_i; \end{cases} \\ \begin{cases} F < C_i; \\ v = 0. \end{cases} \end{array}\right. \end{cases}$$

In this case

$$p_1 = \frac{b_{12} - b_{22}}{b_{21} - b_{22} - b_{11} + b_{12}} = \frac{v - (F - C_i)}{v - (F - C_i) + 0 - v} = \frac{F - C_i - v}{F - C_i} = \begin{cases} 1 & \text{if } v = 0; \\ \frac{F - C_i - v}{F - C_i} & \text{if } 0 \le v \le F - C_i \end{cases}$$

and $p_2 \in [0, 1]$.

At last, the condition (15) for Model 1 can be rewritten as

$$\begin{cases} 0 - (F - C_i) - v + v \ne 0; \\ \left[\begin{array}{l} \begin{cases} v - (F - C_i) \ge 0; \\ 0 - v \ge 0; \end{cases} \\ \begin{cases} v - (F - C_i) \le 0; \\ 0 - v \le 0; \end{cases} \end{array}\right. \\ R_i - ke_i - (R_i - ke_i) - (C_i + (1-q)R_i) + R_i - ke_i \ne 0; \\ \left[\begin{array}{l} \begin{cases} R_i - ke_i - (C_i + (1-q)R_i) \ge 0; \\ R_i - ke_i - (R_i - ke_i) \ge 0; \end{cases} \\ \begin{cases} R_i - ke_i - (C_i + (1-q)R_i) \le 0; \\ R_i - ke_i - (R_i - ke_i) \le 0 \end{cases} \end{array}\right. \end{cases} \iff$$

$$\begin{cases} F - C_i \ne 0; \\ \left[\begin{array}{l} \begin{cases} v \ge F - C_i; \\ v \le 0; \end{cases} \\ \begin{cases} v \le F - C_i; \\ v \ge 0; \end{cases} \end{array}\right. \\ qR_i \ne C_i + ke_i; \\ \left[\begin{array}{l} qR_i \ge C_i + ke_i; \\ qR_i \le C_i + ke_i \end{array}\right. \end{cases} \iff \begin{cases} F - C_i \ne 0; \\ qR_i \ne C_i + ke_i; \\ \left[\begin{array}{l} \begin{cases} F - C_i > 0; \\ 0 \le v \le F - C_i; \end{cases} \\ \begin{cases} F - C_i < 0; \\ v = 0 \end{cases} \end{array}\right. \end{cases} \iff \begin{cases} F \ne C_i; \\ qR_i \ne C_i + ke_i; \\ \left[\begin{array}{l} \begin{cases} F > C_i; \\ 0 \le v \le F - C_i; \end{cases} \\ \begin{cases} F < C_i; \\ v = 0. \end{cases} \end{array}\right. \end{cases}$$

In this case

$$p_1 = \begin{cases} 1 & \text{if } v = 0; \\ \frac{F - C_i - v}{F - C_i} & \text{if } 0 \le v \le F - C_i \end{cases}$$

and $p_2 = 1$ as $d_{21} = d_{11}$.

5.2   Model 2: Emotional Players

For Model 2 (with emotional players) we can formulate the following proposition.

Proposition 3. *There exists only one Nash equilibrium in the mixed strategies for Model 2 iff:*

$$\begin{cases} 0 \le v \le F - C_i - K_i; \\ (1-q)R_i \ne K_i - C_i - ke_i; \\ qR_i \le C_i + ke_i - 2K_i. \end{cases} \tag{23}$$

Under the condition (23) the point (p_1, p_2) is a Nash equilibrium, where

$$p_1 = 1 - \frac{K_i + v}{F - C_i}; \quad p_2 = 1 - \frac{K_i}{C_i + ke_i - K_i - qR_i}.$$

Proof. 1. For this Model we can rewrite the first equality in (12) as

$$(R_i - ke_i - K_i) - (R_i - ke_i) = 0,$$

that does not hold because in this Model $K_i \ne 0$.

Then there are no conditions for a Nash equilibrium in (p_1, p_2) for arbitrary $p_1, p_2 \in [0, 1]$.

2. Next, in conditions (13) the second equality can be rewritten as

$$-K_i = v,$$

that does not hold as $v \ge 0$, $K_i > 0$.

3. The second condition in (14) can be rewritten as

$$R_i - ke_i - K_i = R_i - ke_i + K_i,$$

that does not hold as $K_i > 0$.

4. The condition (15) can be rewritten as

$$\begin{cases} -K_i - (F - C_i - K_i) - v + v \ne 0; \\ \begin{bmatrix} \begin{cases} v - (F - C_i - K_i) \ge 0; \\ -K_i - v \ge 0; \end{cases} \\ \begin{cases} v - (F - C_i - K_i) \le 0; \\ -K_i - v \le 0; \end{cases} \end{bmatrix} \\ (R_i - ke_i - K_i) - (R_i - ke_i) - (C_i + (1-q)R_i - K_i) + (R_i - ke_i + K_i) \ne 0; \\ \begin{bmatrix} \begin{cases} (R_i - ke_i + K_i) - (C_i + (1-q)R_i - K_i) \ge 0; \\ (R_i - ke_i - K_i) - (R_i - ke_i) \ge 0; \end{cases} \\ \begin{cases} (R_i - ke_i + K_i) - (C_i + (1-q)R_i - K_i) \le 0; \\ (R_i - ke_i - K_i) - (R_i - ke_i) \le 0 \end{cases} \end{bmatrix} \end{cases}$$

that is equivalent to

$$\begin{cases} F \neq C_i; \\ v \leq F - C_i - K_i; \\ -C_i - (1-q)R_i + K_i - ke_i \neq 0; \\ R_i - ke_i + K_i \leq C_i + (1-q)R_i - K_i \end{cases}$$

or

$$\begin{cases} F \neq C_i; \\ v \leq F - C_i - K_i; \\ (1-q)R_i \neq K_i - C_i - ke_i; \\ qR_i \leq C_i + ke_i - 2K_i = -K_i - (K_i - C_i - ke_i) \end{cases}$$

or

$$\begin{cases} v \leq F - C_i - K_i; \\ (1-q)R_i \neq K_i - C_i - ke_i; \\ qR_i \leq C_i + ke_i - 2K_i. \end{cases}$$

In this case

$$p_1 = \frac{v - (F - C_i - K_i)}{v - (F - C_i - K_i) - K_i - v} = \frac{F - C_i - K_i - v}{F - C_i} = 1 - \frac{K_i + v}{F - C_i};$$

$$p_2 = \frac{(R_i - ke_i + K_i) - C_i - (1-q)R_i + K_i}{(R_i - ke_i + K_i) - (1-q)R_i + K_i + R_i - ke_i - K_i - R_i + ke_i} = \frac{2K_i - C_i - ke_i + qR_i}{K_i - C_i - ke_i + qR_i}$$

$$= 1 - \frac{K_i}{C_i + ke_i - K_i - qR_i}.$$

5.3 Sufficient Conditions for a Nash Equilibrium in Terms of a Delegated Stake Ratio

Here we formulate the condition for a Nash equilibrium in terms of a stake ratio that a proposer needs to buy to be guaranteed to win the voting. First, we formulate some general sufficient conditions based on results from 2.4, 2.5.1 and 2.5.2.

Proposition 4. *Let condition*

$$\begin{cases} qR_i > C_i + ke_i - 2K_i; \\ F < C_i \end{cases} \tag{24}$$

hold. Then:

1. *if $K_i = 0$ then:*
   - *(B_1, S_1) is a Nash equilibrium;*
   - *(B_2, S_2) is not a Nash equilibrium;*
   - *there are no Nash equilibria in mixed strategies;*
2. *if $K_i \neq 0$ then the only Nash equilibrium in both pure and mixed strategies is (B_1, S_1).*

Proof. 1. Let $K_i = 0$. From Proposition 1 it is easy to see that (B_1, S_1) is a Nash equilibrium and (B_2, S_2) is not due to the condition $F < C_i$ from (24) that contradicts the first condition $F - K_i - C_i > v > 0$ from p.2 of Proposition 1. Next, this condition also contradicts (17), (18), (20) and (22) in Proposition 2.

The condition $qR_i > c_i + ke_i - 2K_i$ from (24) contradicts (19) in Proposition 2. And note that the condition (24) entails the fulfillment of the condition (21) in Proposition 2 that means (B_1, S_1) is a Nash equilibrium.

2. Let $K_i \neq 0$. Then from Proposition 1 we again see that (B_1, S_1) is a Nash equilibrium, and there are no other Nash equilibria in pure strategies.

From Proposition 3 we also see that there are no Nash equilibria in mixed strategies, because the first inequality in (24) contradicts the third inequality in (23).

In our notations we may rewrite (24) as

$$\begin{cases} s_i > \dfrac{ke_i}{qR(\alpha \cdot \frac{1-t^k}{1-t} + k(1-\alpha)t^{k-1}) - c + 2\kappa}; \\ s_i > \dfrac{F}{c} \end{cases}$$

or

$$s_i > \max\left\{ \frac{ke_i}{qR(\alpha \cdot \frac{1-t^k}{1-t} + k(1-\alpha)t^{k-1}) - c + 2\kappa}, \frac{F}{c} \right\}. \tag{25}$$

In other words, the condition (25) is sufficient to have a Nash equilibrium only in (B_1, S_1) and not to have it in (B_2, S_2) and in the mixed strategies.

6   Numerical Results

Using the formula from Corollary 1, we calculated the values of the maximum stake share that is necessary for the briber to win voting, under which a bribery is still profitable for them, for the following parameters:

- the total treasury fund for one voting round $\Theta = \$8,000,000$;
- the profit that a proposer gets from bribing $F = \$1,000,000$;
- the number of voting rounds in one cycle: $k = 5, ..., 10$ for Fig. 1 and $k \in [4; 35]$ for Fig. 2;
- the share of short-term reward $\alpha = 0.15$;
- the proposer's average profit in the case of no bribery $v = \$50,000$;
- the moral price $\kappa = 0$;
- the effort spent for voting on all proposals in one voting round, i.e. one Catalyst Fund, $e_i = \$2250$;
- the probability of bribery detection $q = 0.96$;
- the value of a delegate's reward $t = 0.99$;
- the total reward for delegates per one voting round: $R \in [\$136,000; \$1,600,000]$ for Fig. 1 and $R = \$360,000$ for Fig. 2.

The obtained results are summarized in Figs. 1–2.

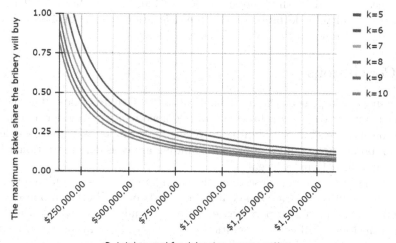

Fig. 1. Dependency of the maximum stake share that is necessary for the briber to win voting, under which a bribery is still profitable for them, on R, the total reward for delegates per voting round (for different k)

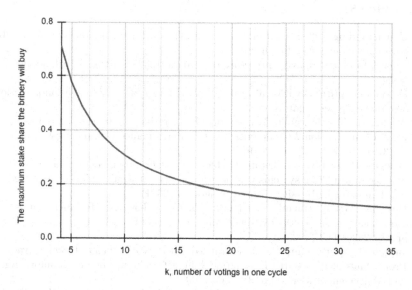

Fig. 2. Dependency of the maximum stake share that is necessary for the briber to win voting, under which a bribery is still profitable for them, on k, the number of voting rounds in one cycle

Let us look at the Fig. 1 and the curve for $k = 8$ (the green one). For $R = \$440,000$, a Nash equilibrium in the point (B_2, S_2) will exist only if the delegates' stake share that a briber needs to buy to win voting is not larger than 0.3057. That means spending the amount of $R = \$440,000$ for the total delegates' reward, we will provide protection of the delegation scheme against a bribery involving buying more than 30% of delegates' stake.

7   Conclusions

In this paper we present the mathematical model that fully describes the vote delegation incentive process for decentralized governance system for funding distribution that uses a blockchain-based voting. Two models of bribing a delegate by a proposer submitting proposals for funding are considered: "Rational Delegates" and "Emotional Delegates".

In terms of parameters describing the voting process, it is stipulated that the sufficient condition that a Nash equilibrium exists only if both a proposer and a delegate do not intend to participate in bribery, and it is shown at what stake share owned by a briber this condition is satisfied. The main practical result of the paper is the possibility to define what kind of an attacker (in terms of the bribing capability) we will be able to resist under certain parameters.

Acknowledgements. We gratefully thank Philip Lazos for fruitful discussions.

References

1. Understanding dash governance (2021). https://docs.dash.org/en/stable/governance/understanding.html
2. Create, fund and deliver the future of cardano (2022). https://cardano.ideascale.com/
3. Fund your project with catalyst (2022). https://developers.cardano.org/docs/governance/project-catalyst
4. Allombert, V., Bourgoin, M., Tesson, J.: Introduction to the tezos blockchain. In: 2019 International Conference on High Performance Computing & Simulation (HPCS), pp. 1–10. IEEE (2019)
5. Balogun, H.O.: Towards sustainable blockchains: cryptocurrency treasury and general decision-making systems with provably secure delegable blockchain-based voting. Lancaster University (United Kingdom) (2021)
6. Birmpas, G., Kovalchuk, L., Lazos, P., Oliynykov, R.: Parallel contests for crowdsourcing reviews: existence and quality of equilibria. arXiv preprint arXiv:2202.04064 (2022)
7. Brandt, F., Sandholm, T.: Decentralized voting with unconditional privacy. In: Proceedings of the Fourth International Joint Conference on Autonomous Agents and Multiagent Systems, pp. 357–364 (2005)
8. Brandt, F., Conitzer, V., Endriss, U., Lang, J., Procaccia, A.D.: Handbook of Computational Social Choice. Cambridge University Press, Cambridge (2016)
9. Dal Bó, E., Dal Bó, P., Di Tella, R.: "plata o plomo?": bribe and punishment in a theory of political influence. Am. Polit. Sci. Rev. **100**(1), 41–53 (2006)
10. Jafar, U., Aziz, M.J.A., Shukur, Z.: Blockchain for electronic voting system - review and open research challenges. Sensors **21**(17) (2021). https://www.mdpi.com/1424-8220/21/17/5874. ISSN 1424–8220

11. Jairam, S., Gordijn, J., da Silva Torres, I., Kaya, F., Makkes, M.: A decentralized fair governance model for permissionless blockchain systems. In: Proceedings of the International Workshop on Value Modelling and Business Ontologies, pp. 4–5 (2021)
12. Kaidalov, D., Kovalchuk, L., Nastenko, A., Rodinko, M., Shevtsov, O., Oliynykov, R.: Ethereum classic treasury system proposal. IOHK RESEARCH REPORT (2017)
13. Kiayias, A., Lazos, P.: SoK: blockchain governance. arXiv preprint arXiv:2201.07188 (2022)
14. Kurbatov, O., et al.: Anonymous decentralized e-voting system. In: CMiGIN, pp. 12–22 (2019)
15. Lianju, S., Luyan, P.: Game theory analysis of the bribery behavior. Int. J. Bus. Soc. Sci. **2**(8) (2011)
16. Liebkind, J.: How blockchain technology can prevent voter fraud, December 2020. https://www.investopedia.com/news/how-blockchain-technology-can-prevent-voter-fraud/
17. Zhang, B., Oliynykov, R., Balogun, R.: A treasury system for cryptocurrencies: enabling better collaborative intelligence. Cryptology ePrint Archive (2018)

CBT Workshop: Short Papers

A Limitlessly Scalable Transaction System

Max Mathys, Roland Schmid, Jakub Sliwinski$^{(\boxtimes)}$, and Roger Wattenhofer

ETH Zürich, Zürich, Switzerland
`jsliwinski@ethz.ch`

Abstract. We present ACCEPT, a simple, asynchronous transaction system that achieves perfect horizontal scaling.

Usual blockchain-based transaction systems come with a fundamental throughput limitation as they require that all (potentially unrelated) transactions must be totally ordered. Such solutions thus require serious compromises or are outright unsuitable for large-scale applications, such as global retail payments.

ACCEPT provides efficient horizontal scaling without any limitation. To that end, ACCEPT satisfies a relaxed form of consensus and does not establish an ordering of unrelated transactions. Furthermore, ACCEPT achieves instant finality and does not depend on a source of randomness.

1 Introduction

The financial world is changing around the globe. With the rise of digital cryptocurrencies like Bitcoin [13] and Ethereum [16], the pressure on the traditional banking system to implement a digital currency on its own is rising. Due to the well-known limitations of permissionless blockchain systems thus far, such a digital currency is mostly envisioned based on permissioned, byzantine fault-tolerant ledger technology. Furthermore, as both central and commercial banks have no interest in a fully distributed solution that can hardly be regulated, the employment of a permissioned system constitutes a good fit to establish such a digital currency.

Previously, revolutionizing the global financial infrastructure was envisioned based on byzantine agreement protocols. Such systems are popular because they provide a reliable and robust way of transferring funds between participants by establishing a total order of all transactions. However, ordering all transactions has proven to be a throughput-limiting factor for these systems, which only achieve throughputs up to tens of thousands of transactions per second even in lab environments [15]. Despite byzantine agreement systems being optimized for high throughput, they only recently matched the demands of leading credit card providers; hence, this technology does not seem future-proof in our increasingly digital world.

Our Contribution: We present a system based on A Cheaper Consensus for Efficient, Parallelizable Transactions (ACCEPT), that features:

© The Author(s), under exclusive license to Springer Nature Switzerland AG 2023
J. Garcia-Alfaro et al. (Eds.): DPM 2022/CBT 2022, LNCS 13619, pp. 297–307, 2023.
https://doi.org/10.1007/978-3-031-25734-6_18

- **Limitless Scalability:** ACCEPT does not order transactions that do not depend on each other. Thus, any number of parallel transactions can be processed given a sufficient amount of hardware.
- **Instant Finality:** ACCEPT confirms transactions in 1 round-trip time to the validator nodes. Confirmed transactions are final and cannot be reversed.
- **Asynchrony:** ACCEPT does not require any network timing assumptions. An adversary having complete control over the network can halt the progress of the system (by simply disabling communication) but otherwise cannot trick the participants in any way, such as reversing a confirmed transaction or pretending that an impermissible transaction is confirmed.
- **Independent Validators:** Validator nodes only need to provide a basic API to accept new transactions, verifying them internally and returning a valid signature in case of success. This makes the nodes' implementations independent, as they only need to interpret other nodes' (and clients') signatures. Validators can parallelize and balance workload as they individually see fit, without changing the way they interact with the system.
- **Simplicity:** ACCEPT does not rely on randomness and is easy to comprehend and implement. Hence, given some deployment scenario, the validators can easily implement the protocol themselves, thus achieving fault tolerance with respect to software bugs in the code. In contrast, existing (complicated) permissioned blockchain systems rely on reference implementations that are used as a black box, where a single bug can compromise the entire system.

We demonstrate ACCEPT's horizontal scaling on common server hardware and showcase its transaction throughput to be orders of magnitudes above byzantine agreement systems.

2   Preliminaries

We assume that conflicting transactions can only be issued by a misbehaving party. Under this crucial assumption, the system can maintain liveness and consistency without solving consensus [8].

In contrast to orthodox blockchain systems, ACCEPT does not support consensus and does not attempt to order conflicting transactions issued simultaneously. If a misbehaving client issues two transactions spending the same funds simultaneously, it is possible that both transactions will be rejected by the system and the misbehaving client will lose the funds.

2.1   Model

ACCEPT is maintained by n different agents called *validators*. Similarly to other byzantine fault tolerant systems, we assume up to $f = \frac{n-1}{3}$ of the validators are adversarial and behave arbitrarily. Any set of $2f + 1$ validators is called a *quorum*. In addition, an arbitrary number of *clients* interact with the system by issuing and receiving transactions.

The network is asynchronous: The adversary controls the network, dictating when messages are delivered and in what order. There is no bound on the time it might take to deliver a message. Under such weak network requirements, an adversary delaying the delivery of messages can delay the progress of the protocol, but otherwise will not be able to interfere.

We assume the functionality of digital signatures where a public key allows the verification of a signature of the associated secret key. We also assume cryptographic hashing, where for every message a succinct, unique hash can be computed. Apart from these primitives, ACCEPT is completely deterministic.

Security and Threat Model. Validators and clients hold public/private key pairs. All participants know the public keys of all validators.

The adversary knows the protocol and controls all adversarial validators and any number of clients. The adversary controls the network and can delay, replay, reorder messages, etc. The adversary does not know the private key of any correct participant.

3   Protocol

The ACCEPT protocol differentiates two main roles:

- **Validators:** Validators are agents that *verify* and *sign* transactions. There is a fixed number of validators. Validators do not have to exchange messages with each other. Validators can be sharded across multiple servers to increase the throughput of the system.
- **Clients:** Clients are end users of the system who *issue/receive* transactions. The system supports an arbitrary number of clients in the system. Clients possess funds that can be sent to other clients via a transaction. Clients may follow the protocol correctly or not; however, it is only guaranteed that they can spend their funds if following the protocol.

Transactions are processed by the system in the UTXO model [7]. The initial state of the system, called *genesis*, consists of (number, public key) pairs, where the number represents the available funds, and the public key identifies the party able to spend them. These pairs are called unspent transaction outputs (UTXO).

If a client (sender) wishes to transfer funds to another client (recipient), the sender issues a transaction. The transaction contains input UTXOs that the sender can spend. The sender specifies output UTXOs, where inputs and outputs sum up to the same amount of funds. For example, a single transaction can specify two outputs, where one output represents the transacted amount and includes the public key of the recipient, and the second output represents the change and includes the public key of the sender. Ultimately, the sender signs the transaction with the private key(s) corresponding to the inputs.

Transaction Pipeline. ACCEPT performs four steps to confirm a transaction from client c_1 to client c_2:

1. **Issuing a Transaction:** The client c_1 composes and signs a transaction. Client c_1 sends the transaction to the validators. If the inputs of the transaction are not part of genesis, the client also sends the confirmations of the inputs to the validators.

2. **Verifying a Transaction:** Each validator v_i verifies the transaction signature and inputs' confirmations (if not part of genesis). Also, v_i checks that it has not validated any transaction spending the same inputs thus far.
3. **Signing a Transaction:** If the transaction is valid, validator v_i signs the transaction and returns the signature to c_1.
4. **Finalizing a Transaction:** A set of $2f+1$ signatures of distinct validators constitutes a *confirmation* of the outputs. The client c_1 can show the corresponding transaction output and the confirmation to c_2 to prove the transfer took place. The client c_2 accepts the transfer after verifying the output and the confirmation.

3.1   Complexity

In Sect. 3.5 we discuss a signature aggregation scheme where a client aggregates all signatures of a given output, such that each validator receives and verifies only one signature for each transaction input. With this improvement, the computational and communication complexity of processing one transaction are both $O(1)$ for each validator.

Without aggregating signatures, each validator receives and verifies $2f+1$ signatures for each input. Thus both the computational and communication complexity of processing one transaction are $O(n)$ for each validator. However, the batch signature scheme we discuss in Sect. 3.4 will be more efficient than aggregating signatures for smaller n, as discussed in more detail in Sect. 4.1.

3.2   Correctness

Double-spending. Suppose some execution of the protocol produced two confirmed transactions t_1 and t_2 that spend the same output. Each confirmed transaction is signed by a validator quorum. Since the adversary controls at most f validators, at least $f+1$ correct validators signed t_1 and t_2. Since there are $2f+1$ correct validators, some correct validator v signed both t_1 and t_2. However, when signing a transaction, correct validators check whether they have not signed any of the inputs previously – a contradiction.

Finality. Given a confirmed UTXO, it can only be invalidated if some validators observe a transaction that spends the UTXO. Only the owner of the UTXO can sign such a transaction.

Liveness. Any $2f+1$ validators can confirm any transaction. Since at least $2f+1$ validators are correct, the correct validators can confirm transactions if the adversary refrains from participating.

3.3   Signature Protocol

Naively, validators can sign each transaction separately and verify separate signatures for each output. In addition to this naive approach, we design two different protocols for batch-processing the transactions, thereby vastly improving the system's performance: the Merkle scheme and the BLS scheme.

3.4 Merkle Scheme

In the Merkle scheme, validators combine many transactions into Merkle trees and only sign the root, effectively signing many transactions at once.

Signing. By *pooling* multiple signing requests, the validator collects a large number p of unsigned outputs. The hashes of the outputs $h_0(i) = h(o_i)$ are hashed in pairs $h_1(i) = h(h_0(i), h_0(i + 1))$, the resulting hashes are hashed in pairs $h_2(i) = h(h_1(i), h_1(i + 2))$ and so on, to create a complete binary tree of hashes, where the leaves are the hashes of the UTXOs to be signed.

The validator signs the root of the tree. For each output o_i, the validator will return to the issuer of o_i the hashes needed to compute the path from $h(o_i)$ to the root: the hash x_1 to compute $h_1(i) = h(h_0(i), x_1)$, the hash x_2 to compute $h_2(i) = h(h_1(i), x_2)$, and so on. These hashes x_j together with the signature of the tree root constitute o_i's signature in the Merkle scheme (see Appendix A.1).

When a validator signs p outputs, only one signing operation is executed (compared to p signing operations with the naive scheme). However, many hash operations must be performed for both signing and verification in this scheme.

Signature verification. As in the naive scheme, for an output to be confirmed, there must be $> \frac{2}{3}n$ signatures from different validators. We verify each Merkle signature $s_i = (\{x_j\}, s_i^{root})$: we reconstruct the hash path to the root using the x_j's and verify the signature of the root. There are p signatures with the same Merkle root; hence, the verification result can be cached in memory by the validator such that the validator only verifies the root signature the first time it is observed. For all $p - 1$ subsequent encounters of the root, it suffices that the validator performs $\log(p)$ hash operations.

Optimal Merkle Tree Size. If the Merkle tree is very large, the hashing time dominates the verification and signing process. However, if the Merkle tree size is small, the cryptographic operations dominate. We omit the work not related to cryptographic operations or hashing and estimate the optimal tree size.

Let q be the quorum size of the system, N the number of leaves in the Merkle tree, c_h, c_s, c_v the costs of hashing, signing, and verification. Let C_{naive} and C_{merkle} denote the average time cost incurred by a validator to process one UTXO under the naive and Merkle signature protocols. Each validator signs a UTXO once and later has to verify the signatures constituting that UTXO's confirmation. Hence, the expected cost for the naive scheme is $C_{naive} = q \cdot c_v + c_s$.

The expected cost of the Merkle scheme is

$$C_{merkle} = \underbrace{q\left(c_h \log N + \frac{c_v}{N}\right)}_{\text{Verification}} + \underbrace{\frac{2Nc_h + c_s}{N}}_{\text{Signing}} = \log N(qc_h) + \frac{1}{N}(qc_v + c_s) + 2c_h.$$

The expression is minimized by $N = \frac{qc_v + c_s}{qc_h} \ln 2$. For example, if the relative operation costs are around $c_h = 1$, $c_s = 63$, $c_v = 107$ and there are 10 validators (quorum size 7), we estimate the optimal number of leaves in the Merkle tree at

$N^{optimal} \approx 80.4$. For binary trees ($\log N$ being an integer), either a Merkle tree with 64 or 128 leaves is optimal.

3.5 BLS Scheme

BLS [6] is a signature scheme where signatures can be aggregated. One verification operation on an aggregated signature can be used to verify all constituent signatures at once. Combining the properties of BLS with Shamir's secret sharing, it is possible to construct a threshold signature scheme. In this scheme, each validator possesses a different private key and signs transactions for clients individually. Once a client obtains at least $2f + 1$ signatures for their transaction, they can use the signatures to compute a unique *master* signature of their transaction. The master signature is unique and the same, irrespective of which $2f + 1$ validators' signatures were used to compute it.

Due to space constraints, we do not describe the working of this threshold scheme in detail (the reader can find an instructive description at [5]).

The BLS signatures are relatively costly to produce and verify. However, the scheme comes with the great advantage that aggregated BLS threshold signatures have a constant verification time, irrespective of the number of validators in the system.

Each validator receives a BLS private key, and the corresponding public keys are publicly known. The master public key is publicly known (or can be computed given the validator public keys). The validators sign the outputs of the clients with their BLS keys, similarly to the naive scheme. The validators' signatures function on their own as usual, so clients can verify that they receive the correct signatures. After receiving $2f + 1$ signatures, a client can compute the unique master signature for their outputs. Most importantly, when validators receive transactions to be signed, they only need to verify one master signature for each input of the transaction.

4 Implementation

The validator node and client are written in Go due to its performance and ease of parallelization. The implementation features the three different signature protocols described in Sects. 3.3–3.5: the naive scheme, the Merkle scheme, and the BLS scheme. For signing and verification, the naive, and Merkle schemes use EdDSA with Curve25519 (Ed25519). A Go library [1] provides bindings to ed25519-donna [4]. Ed25519-donna is written in C++ and provides a fast implementation of the Ed25519 public-key signature system [3]. Batch verification can be used for greater throughput. The BLS scheme is implemented using the `herumi/bls` [11] with Go-bindings [12].

Benchmarking Merkle tree size. The signing and verification times for the Merkle signature scheme have been measured on the AWS reference instance for different Merkle tree sizes and 10 validators. The observed global minimum of around 64–128 leaves matched the conclusion from Sect. 3.4.

4.1 Cryptographic Scheme Comparison

The benchmark of the cryptographic operations executed on a single core on the reference instance is denoted in Table 1.

Table 1. Benchmarks for relevant cryptographic operations for each scheme. Fort the Merkle scheme, the number of leaves is 64.

Scheme	Operation	ns per signature
Naive	Signing	29,967
	Verifying, single	100,663
	Verifying, batch of 64	51,247
Merkle	Signing	2709
	Verifying, no caching	106,771
	Verifying, cached	6473
BLS	Signing	640,205
	Verifying	1,918,578

If multiple signatures are verified in one batch, EdDSA can take advantage of x86 SIMD instructions. This gives verification a speedup of up to ≈ 2. Assuming that the Merkle tree has 64 leaves, the Merkle scheme is about a magnitude faster than the naive scheme. Since verification of threshold BLS signatures is constant for any number of validators, we find BLS to be faster than the naive and Merkle schemes if the number of validators is >37 and >475, respectively. Moreover, for larger quorum sizes, the naive and Merkle schemes yield larger transaction confirmations, whereas BLS confirmations have a constant size.

4.2 Storage

Each validator keeps track of outputs they signed as spent. The spent outputs are stored in a thread-safe and efficient hash map. Golang's built-in thread-safe hash map, sync/map, exhibits excessive lock usage and coroutine blocking; hence, we implemented a purpose-built hash map (see Appendix A.2). Running on the AWS reference instance with one coroutine per processor, Golang's implementation reaches $7.04 \cdot 10^5$ inserts per second, and our implementation about $3.30 \cdot 10^7$ inserts per second.

4.3 Sharding

Crucially, validators can easily shard their workload among multiple machines. Clients are assigned to different shards based on their public keys; in this implementation, inputs corresponding to different public keys cannot be mixed in one transaction. In our implementation, the assignment of clients to shards is publicly known and clients request the machines they are assigned to. Alternatively, validators could use some load balancing approach.

5   Evaluation

We performed end-to-end benchmarks of the system using the Merkle scheme with servers rented at AWS. We tested with 4, 10, and 28 validators. For each number of validators, we experimented with 1, 2, and 4 shards (machines) for each validator. The server instances used in these benchmarks were c3.8xlarge with 32 virtual CPU threads and 60 GiB of RAM. Each test consisted of a preset number of client servers (corresponding to the expected throughput) generating transactions and sending them to appropriate shards of the validators. The duration of each test was ten minutes. The results of the experiment are presented in Table 2. The average CPU utilization observed was 80.9%.

We performed an additional experiment with 4 validators and 37 shards per validator (and otherwise the same setup), yielding a throughput of 1,449,847 transactions per second on average, with an average CPU utilization of 71.9%. The results of this experiment are presented with logarithmic scales in Fig. 1.

Table 2. Average transactions per second in the experiment.

#validators	4	10	28
1 shard	48,667	34,451	22,015
2 shards	92,115	72,079	44,764
4 shards	183,380	141,767	80,917

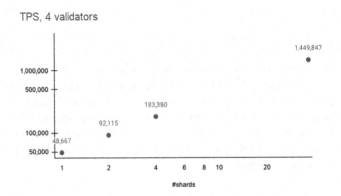

Fig. 1. TPS scalability results for 4 validators, log scales.

6   Related Work

The first work to suggest a simpler, consensus-free approach to processing transactions in a permissioned system was Gupta [9]. Gupta focuses on providing verifiable audit trails. We employ a similar transaction confirmation principle and focus on designing and implementing a system around horizontal scaling without loss of efficiency.

Guerraoui et al. [8] prove that the consensus number of a payment system is indeed 1 in Herlihy's hierarchy [10].

FastPay [2] might be closest related to our work. FastPay provides an implementation of a permissioned settlement system and focuses on interfacing with a preceding, primary system. FastPay is similar in spirit to ACCEPT but more complicated in crucial aspects; for example, FastPay employs a two-phase confirmation protocol that complicates the interaction between the validators. However, FastPay does not implement the efficiency improvements described in Sects. 3.4 and 3.5. Parallel processing in FastPay's implementation is only process-based and hence does not exemplify multi-machine sharding. The performance is also not reported clearly: benchmarks are presented for the two confirmation phases separately, whereas one exhibits a bottleneck in the process-based implementation.

Cascade [14] describes how a consensus-free system can be managed similarly to proof-of-stake blockchains, thus extending the approach to the permissionless setting. Cascade also contributes some features of the protocol, such as pruning redundant contents from the blockchain and discusses some economic aspects of the permissionless setting. However, Cascade does not provide an implementation.

A   Concepts

This section will clarify the concepts of Merkle signatures and hash maps. Merkle signatures are used in Sect. 3.4 to improve the efficiency of validators. A custom hash map is developed to improve the performance of the UTXO store, as described in Sect. 4.2.

A.1   Merkle Signatures

A signature scheme based on Merkle trees is used to optimize the performance of validators when creating and verifying signatures.

Signing. A validator S_i collects n hashes to sign where $n = 2^k, k \in \mathbb{N}$. The hashes are combined into a Merkle tree. The validator S_i signs the Merkle root m using EdDSA, denoted as m_{S_i}. For each hash $h_i, i \in \{1, .., n\}$, the validator calculates the Merkle path and outputs $path_{h_i}$. $path_{h_i}$ consists of the hashes and side (left or right) of the nodes from h_i to the Merkle root (in blue). The resulting signature for h_i by S_i is the tuple $(path_{h_i}, m_{S_i})$. An example can be seen in Fig. 2.

Signing n hashes using Merkle signatures is more efficient than signing n hashes separately: the cost of an EdDSA signing operation c_s is much higher than the cost of a hash operation c_h. The cost of signing n hashes with Merkle signatures is $2n \cdot c_h + c_v$ whereas the cost of signing n hashes separately (without Merkle signatures) is $n \cdot c_v$.

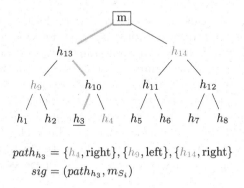

$$path_{h_3} = \{h_4, \text{right}\}, \{h_9, \text{left}\}, \{h_{14}, \text{right}\}$$
$$sig = (path_{h_3}, m_{S_i})$$

Fig. 2. Merkle tree and Merkle signature for hash h_3. (Color figure online)

Verifying. First, the Merkle root m' is reconstructed from the path $path_{h_i}$. If $path_{h_i}$ is a valid path, m' matches m. Finally, m_{S_i} is verified using EdDSA.

Verifying n hashes using Merkle signatures is also more efficient than verifying n hashes separately because the cost of an EdDSA verification operation is high, even higher than an EdDSA signing operation (and thus also higher than the cost of a hashing operation). The Merkle root can be reconstructed with a cost of $\log_2(n) \cdot c_h$ where c_h is the cost of hashing. The Merkle root m only has to be verified for the first encountered Merkle signature, after that, the result of the verification can be cached, making this signature perform very well.

A.2   Hash Maps

Hash maps are used to efficiently calculate set membership in the context of spent UTXO identifiers. Elements $e \in E$ (in our case id_i) are hashed into the hash range $H = \{0, ..., l\}$ and used as an index to an array of linked lists. A linked list at index $i \in \{0, ..., l\}$ contains all items e where hash$(e) = i$. The linked list is then traversed.

Hashing and indexing are implemented as a lock-free operation; traversing and modifying a linked list are protected by a mutex. If l is large enough, the probability of hash collisions is small, minimizing lock contention and the length of the linked list.

References

1. ed25519 - optimized ed25519 for go (2020). https://github.com/oasisprotocol/ed25519
2. Baudet, M., Danezis, G., Sonnino, A.: FastPay: high-performance byzantine fault tolerant settlement. arXiv preprint arXiv:2003.11506 (2020)
3. Bernstein, D., Duif, N., Lange, T., Schwabe, P., Yang, B.Y.: High-speed high-security signatures. J. Cryptographic Eng. **2**, 77–89 (2012). https://doi.org/10.1007/s13389-012-0027-1
4. Bernstein, D., Duif, N., Lange, T., Schwabe, P., Yang, B.Y.: ed25519 donna (2020). https://github.com/floodyberry/ed25519-donna
5. Block, A.: (2018).https://blog.dash.org/secret-sharing-and-threshold-signatures-with-bls-954d1587b5f
6. Boneh, D., Lynn, B., Shacham, H.: Short signatures from the Weil pairing. J. Cryptol. **17**(4), 297–319 (2004). https://doi.org/10.1007/s00145-004-0314-9
7. Delgado-Segura, S., Pérez-Solà, C., Navarro-Arribas, G., Herrera-Joancomartí, J.: Analysis of the bitcoin UTXO set. In: Zohar, A., et al. (eds.) FC 2018. LNCS, vol. 10958, pp. 78–91. Springer, Heidelberg (2019). https://doi.org/10.1007/978-3-662-58820-8_6
8. Guerraoui, R., Kuznetsov, P., Monti, M., Pavlović, M., Seredinschi, D.A.: The consensus number of a cryptocurrency. In: Proceedings of the 2019 ACM Symposium on Principles of Distributed Computing - PODC (2019)
9. Gupta, S.: A Non-Consensus Based Decentralized Financial Transaction Processing Model with Support for Efficient Auditing. Master's thesis, Arizona State University (2016)
10. Herlihy, M.: Wait-free synchronization. ACM Trans. Program. Lang. Syst. (TOPLAS) **13**(1), 124–149 (1991)
11. Mitsunari, S.: BLS threshold signature (2020). https://github.com/herumi/bls
12. Mitsunari, S.: BLS threshold signature for ETH with compiled static library (2020). https://github.com/herumi/bls-eth-go-binary
13. Nakamoto, S.: Bitcoin: a peer-to-peer electronic cash system (2008)
14. Sliwinski, J., Wattenhofer, R.: Asynchronous proof-of-stake. In: Johnen, C., Schiller, E.M., Schmid, S. (eds.) SSS 2021. LNCS, vol. 13046, pp. 194–208. Springer, Cham (2021). https://doi.org/10.1007/978-3-030-91081-5_13
15. Stathakopoulou, C., David, T., Vukolić, M.: Mir-BFT: high-throughput BFT for blockchains. arXiv preprint arXiv:1906.05552 (2019)
16. Wood, G., et al.: Ethereum: a secure decentralised generalised transaction ledger. Ethereum Proj. Yellow Pap. **151**(2014), 1–32 (2014)

Migrating Blockchains Away from ECDSA for Post-quantum Security: A Study of Impact on Users and Applications

Teik Guan Tan[1]([⊠]) and Jianying Zhou[2]

[1] pQCee Pte Ltd., Singapore, Singapore
`tanteikg@gmail.com`
[2] Singapore University of Technology and Design, Singapore, Singapore

Abstract. Blockchains use Elliptic Curve Digital Signature Algorithm (ECDSA) to secure transactions between the wallets and blockchain nodes. Due to the potential threat from quantum computers, these blockchain implementations need to migrate away from ECDSA to a post-quantum algorithm before quantum computers become powerful enough. However, the migration process is long and challenging because replacing the underlying cryptographic implementation will significantly impact several existing use-cases, causing financial losses to users and making applications fail. We study the impact of such use-cases from a user and application perspective. To partly minimize the impact, we observe that use of BIP39 Seed is key to achieving backward compatibility and propose possible strategies in choosing and adapting a BIP39-compatible post-quantum algorithm.

Keywords: Post-quantum cryptography · Bitcoin · Blockchains · Elliptic curve digital signing algorithm

1 Introduction

Elliptic Curve Cryptography (ECC) [10,14] is an asymmetric key cryptosystem that is based on the hard problem of solving a discrete-logarithm problem over an elliptic curve. Using ECC, we construct digital signature schemes such as Elliptic-Curve Digital Signing Algorithm (ECDSA) which can be used to achieve user authentication (where the verifier is able to ascertain the identity of the signer), data integrity (where the verifier is able to know that the message sent by the signer is not modified), and non-repudiation (where the signer cannot deny creating the message).

Classical ECDSA security [2] and vulnerabilities [12] are well studied and the algorithm has been accepted into many standards including American National Standards Institute's (ANSI) X9.63, International Organization for Standards' (ISO) 9796-3 and National Institute of Standards and Technology's (NIST) FIPS 186-4. It is also used widely by many blockchains such as Bitcoin [15] and Ethereum [3] to secure transactions sent from the wallets to the nodes.

© The Author(s), under exclusive license to Springer Nature Switzerland AG 2023
J. Garcia-Alfaro et al. (Eds.): DPM 2022/CBT 2022, LNCS 13619, pp. 308–316, 2023.
https://doi.org/10.1007/978-3-031-25734-6_19

The impending threat to ECDSA comes in the form of quantum computers which can be used to cryptanalyze ECC cryptosystems. An adversary with a powerful-enough quantum computer can use Shor's algorithm [18,23] to compute the ECC secret key K_s when given only the ECC public key K_p. From a blockchain security perspective, this means that this adversary can impersonate any wallet to authenticate successfully against the blockchain and potentially transfer coins and other assets away from the wallet. Clearly, a quantum-secure algorithm is needed to replace ECDSA.

But is taking a technical approach to directly replace ECDSA with a drop-in quantum-secure digital signing algorithm the only challenge we need to take care of? Since the entire migration process will contain many challenging tasks over an extended duration, are there some compatibility or migration issues that we can already take note of? In this paper, we take a deeper look at how ECDSA is used in existing blockchains and examine how applications and users are impacted if such an algorithm change happens. Our contributions are:

- A study on use-cases in blockchains that are impacted by ECDSA migration.
- Identification of strategies to construct a post-quantum digital signing algorithm to partly minimize the impact of migration.

The organization of the paper is as follows. Section 2 covers the background on ECDSA and post-quantum algorithms. Section 3 describes the use-cases where ECDSA is used in blockchains. Section 4 examines the potential issues affecting applications and users if ECDSA is replaced. Section 5 discusses the strategies to construct a suitable algorithm to partly minimize the impact of migration and Sect. 6 concludes the paper.

2   Background

2.1   ECDSA Basics

Definition 1. *We define ECDSA as a digital signature scheme consisting of a collection of polynomial-time functions with the following parameters:*

$ECCKeyGen(1^n) \Rightarrow (K_s, K_p)$ *takes in a security parameter 1^n which typically defines the cryptographic key strength of n, and outputs a secret key K_s and corresponding public key $K_p = ECCPubKey(K_s)$.*

$ECCSign(M, K_s) \Rightarrow (\sigma)$ *takes in a message M and the secret key K_s, and outputs a signature σ.*

$ECCVerify(M, K_p, \sigma) \Rightarrow \{accept, reject\}$ *takes in a message M, the public key K_p and signature σ, and outputs accept if and only if σ is a valid signature generated by $ECCSign(M, K_s)$.*

When used in authentication between a Sender and Receiver,

- The Sender will first call $ECCKeyGen()$ to generate the secret key K_s and provide the Receiver with knowledge of public key K_p.

- To sign a message, the Sender will call $ECCSign()$ to compute a signature σ which is sent with the message M to the Receiver.
- To verify the message from the Sender, the Receiver will call $ECCVerify()$ with the Sender's public key K_p, message M, and signature σ to check that the message is indeed from the Sender.

There are different ECDSA algorithm constructions that vary based of differing curves parameters, use of padding or values. Both Bitcoin and Ethereum run `secp256k1` [19] which make use of elliptic curves belonging to the Koblitz family for digital signing. The blockchain wallet functions as the Sender while the blockchain nodes are the Receiver.

2.2 Post-Quantum Cryptography (PQC)

NIST started a post-quantum standardization exercise back in 2016 where they solicited submissions from both industry and academia for new algorithms that are quantum resistant. With the conclusion of its third round of evaluation [1], a total of one key-exchange and three digital signing (see Table 1) algorithms have been selected for standardization and slated for publication by 2024.

Table 1. NIST PQC digital signing algorithms selected for standardization

Algorithm	Cryptosystem	Remarks
Dilithium	Lattice	www.pq-crystals.org
Falcon	Lattice	www.falcon-sign.info
SPHINCS$^+$	Hash	www.sphincs.org

Work has already been carried out by various researchers to ascertain the suitability of the algorithms to existing real-world applications [25] with Transport Layer Security (TLS) amongst the best studied [17,24]. In the area of post-quantum blockchains, the weakness of ECDSA against quantum computers is well-recognized [5,7] and there are numerous articles [4,6,13,20,21] on how to construct quantum-secure blockchains with additional hashing schemes and new signature algorithms. These articles cover several technical and operational considerations such as additional processing overheads, larger key and signature sizes and potential changes to the consensus algorithm, but lack user and application considerations for existing blockchains which we discuss in Sect. 4.

3 Use of ECDSA in Blockchains

The blockchain is a decentralized computing paradigm made popular by Bitcoin, a cryptocurrency that was introduced by Satoshi Nakamoto [15] in 2008 and has grown over the past 10+ years to one of the most successful distributed systems to date. On a daily basis, the Bitcoin blockchain sees over 400,000 transactions and continues to grow. The overall market valuation of Bitcoin hovers between

$200 Billion to over $1 Trillion, with over 60 million active wallets. The blockchain underwent a major evolution through the introduction of "Smart Contracts" in the Ethereum [3] blockchain. Other notable extensions and improvements include power-optimizing consensus building using Proof-of-Stake [9] and off-chain/side-chain processing for scalability and cost-efficiency.

To use a blockchain natively, a user requires a wallet which essentially contains one or more ECC secret key(s). Using the secret key, the wallet will sign a transaction to spend cryptocurrency tokens associated with the wallet or, in the case of Ethereum-based blockchains, to call a Smart Contract to carry out an operation.

Assumptions. In order for existing blockchains to be quantum-secure, we expect the developers to carry out a series of upgrades on both the wallets and blockchain nodes to make all users migrate to the new platform. New keys may be generated, assets tied to the existing wallets may have to be transferred (if wallet addresses are changed) or bridged to the upgraded blockchain and a hard-fork [11] will have to take place to protect the assets from being compromised by quantum-capable adversaries. As there are large variations of different blockchain implementations, we base our research on Bitcoin (BTC) and Ethereum (ETH), the two largest blockchains by both users and value.

We also assume that readers are aware of cryptographic hash algorithms such as $RIPEMD160()$, $SHA256()$, $KECCAK256()$ and $PBKDF2()$. We will mention the use of formatting algorithms such as $ChecksumEncoding()$ and $Truncate20Bytes()$ for completeness, but they do not materially affect the data content being discussed.

3.1   Key Generation

Most secret keys generated by wallets follow the Bitcoin Improvement Proposal (BIP) 39 [16] process where a sequence of human-readable words are randomly selected from a 2048 wordlist, and used as a deterministic Seed (with an optional user-selected password) to derive the actual ECC secret key (See Eq. (1)). The benefit of using BIP 39 has given rise to the concept of cold wallets or paper wallets which allow blockchain users to store the Seed as a recovery phrase offline, physically secure from the Internet.

$$ECCKeyGen() \Rightarrow \begin{cases} K_s = PBKDF2(Seed + Pwd) \\ K_p = ECCPubKey(K_s) \end{cases}$$

$$Seed = \text{``}s_1\ s_2\ ...\ s_n\text{''}\ :\ s_i \in Wordlist \tag{1}$$

$$Wordlist = \{abandon, ability, ..., zoo\}$$

$$Pwd = \text{Optional user password}$$

3.2   Transaction Signing

While different blockchains use different parameters and formats, the underlying signing operation is a hash-and-sign process as shown in Eq. (2).

$$ECCSign(M, K_s) = secp256k1(Hash(M), K_s)$$
$$M = \text{blockchain transaction}$$
$$Hash() = \begin{cases} RIPEMD160(SHA256()) & \#BTC \\ KECCAK256() & \#ETH \end{cases} \quad (2)$$

Other areas where ECDSA signing is used in the blockchain are:

- *Consensus protocols.* ECDSA is also used in Proof-of-stake and other non Proof-of-work consensus protocol. Blockchain nodes that participate in the consensus protocol are called "validators" and carry out the process of collating the submitted blockchain transactions into a block and signing the block using ECDSA before distributing the signed block to other nodes.
- *Multi-signature schemes.* To support distributed M-of-N control in which more than one secret key is needed to sign a transaction, blockchains support different cryptographic primitives such as Shamir secret-sharing [22] which splits a secret in N shares where M shares can re-constitute the secret key for signing, or a signature quorum natively enforced by the blockchain script where M independent signatures are needed before a transaction is approved. Both these schemes still rely on either one or more ECDSA signatures that will be performed to carry out a transaction.
- *Offchain signing.* A more recent development is the use of side-chains or offchain storage to reduce the processing and/or storage overhead on the actual blockchain. In order for such offchain operations to also claim the same transparency and immutability as onchain transactions, the data results of offchain transactions are typically signed with the same wallet ECC secret key and "rolled-up" into the main blockchain.

3.3 Address Computation

Another area where blockchains are dependent on ECDSA is the computation of wallet addresses. Wallet addresses cannot be arbitrarily chosen by the end-user, but are derived from the ECC public key as shown in Eq. (3).

$$Addr(K_p) = Format(Hash(K_p))$$
$$Hash() = \begin{cases} RIPEMD160(SHA256()) & \#BTC \\ KECCAK256() & \#ETH \end{cases}$$
$$Format() = \begin{cases} ChecksumEncoding() & \#BTC \\ Truncate20Bytes() & \#ETH \end{cases} \quad (3)$$

For programmable scripts and Smartcontract running on the blockchain, their addresses are also not under the control of the user and rely on hash-derivations to be computed. This is shown in Eq. (4).

$$SCAddr(Script) = Format(Hash(Script))$$

$$Script = \begin{cases} Bitcoin\ script & \#BTC \\ K_p + nonce & \#ETH \end{cases}$$

$$Hash() = \begin{cases} RIPEMD160(SHA256()) & \#BTC \\ KECCAK256() & \#ETH \end{cases} \quad (4)$$

$$Format() = \begin{cases} ChecksumEncoding() & \#BTC \\ Truncate20Bytes() & \#ETH \end{cases}$$

4 Migration Issues

We recognize that the entire migration process is huge and highly dependent on several parties working in tandem over an extended duration. In this section, we take an operational approach to identify some possible issues in the post-quantum migration of existing blockchains. We ask the question "what happens when ECDSA is replaced with a different algorithm" and examine its impact to different users and applications based on the use-cases identified in Sect. 3. These are fleshed out in Table 2.

5 Strategies to Minimize Impact

From Sect. 4, we uncovered several areas where the replacement of ECDSA to a post-quantum algorithm will financially impact or disrupt users and applications on the blockchain, thus hindering the success of the migration. Most of these situations are due to inactive or dormant users[1] who are unable to keep up with technological changes needed on the blockchain, or due to the reliance of a static address associated with an identity or smart contract.

An observation is that utilizing BIP39 is key to achieving backward compatibility. Although a quantum-capable adversary can cryptanalyze the ECC public key K_p to obtain the secret key K_s, the BIP39 Seeds or recovery phrases in the hands of existing users are still secure as hashing is resistant to quantum attacks. If we can design the replacement post-quantum algorithm to make use of the Seed to account for inactive users and retain the address mapping, then the impact of migration can be partly minimized assuming users are already using BIP39 for key generation. We propose two possible strategies that can be used:

1. *Adapting from a post-quantum algorithm.* From the algorithms in Table 1, we need to choose an algorithm that can use the Seed to generate a new key. We expect the hash-based post-quantum algorithm, SPHINCS+, to have more flexibility in key generation and can better support BIP39 as compared to

---

[1] A cursory search on Google.com yields estimates where more than 30% Bitcoin wallets are dormant.

Table 2. Impact of replacing ECDSA for different use-cases

Use-case	Affected party	Impact	Remarks
Key Generation	Active user	User will have to upgrade the wallet to generate a new key	Minimal impact
	Inactive cold wallet user	User who does not keep up with technological changes or over-suspiciously mistakes the upgrade for a scam may not generate a new key in time. Then the blockchain nodes have no means to differentiate between such a user's wallet and a quantum-capable adversary trying to impersonate the user	Significant financial losses
Transaction signing	Active user	User will have to participate in the hard-fork process to migrate the assets	Minimal impact
	Dormant user	User may not be aware of the hard-fork and have assets stuck in the old chain which is quantum vulnerable	Significant financial losses
Consensus	Blockchain node	Nodes have to be upgraded with the new algorithm	Minimal Impact
	Previously committed blocks	For non Proof-of-work consensus, some additional blocks may have to be counter-signed with the new algorithm to prevent spoofing	Minimal impact
Multi-Signature	All active users	All users will have to upgrade the wallet to generate a new key	Minimal impact
	Some inactive users	In a M-of-N setting, if the number of inactive users $> N - M$ did not perform the upgrade, then transactions will not be approved	Significant disruptions or financial losses
Off-chain signing	Side-chains	Wallets and nodes in side-chains also have to be upgraded for signature compatibility. Since there are several Ethereum Virtual Machine (EVM) Layer-2 side-chains, not all chains have the community resources to keep up with the upgrade, resulting in some chains being eliminated	Disruptions likely in Layer-2 chains
	Off-chain assets	Assets have to be counter-signed with the new algorithm or risk being compromised. Depending on each implementation, it may not be possible to trace the source of the assets from the blockchain. More analysis to be done on a case-by-case basis	Unable to determine impact holistically
Address Computation	User identity	Some digital identity implementations such as www.proofofhumanity.id tie the identity of users to their wallet addresses. Many users also include their wallet addresses in their social media posts. These will all have to be changed	Some disruption or inconvenience to users
	Smart Contract	Many smart contracts may have hardcoded addresses to reference other smart contracts or payout addresses. These have to be rebuilt (assuming the source codes are available) or risk execution failure or having assets locked up	Significant disruptions or financial losses

the lattice-based algorithms. A needed research direction will be to create a secure two-way mapping function to associate the SPHINCS$^+$ public key to the legacy ECC public key so that the wallet can prove both keys originate from the same BIP39 Seed, and the blockchain nodes can reverse map the legacy ECDSA wallet address to the new SPHINCS$^+$ wallet address.

2. *Zero-knowledge proof-of-key-generation.* When using ECDSA to sign a transaction, if the wallet can securely prove that K_s was generated from a BIP39 Seed, without revealing the Seed, then the blockchain nodes can be certain that the incoming ECDSA signature was not generated a cryptanalyzed K_s. This can be achieved by including a post-quantum zero-knowledge proof of knowledge such as MPC-in-the-head [8] into the signature as demonstrated by Tan and Zhou [26]. Since the legacy ECC key continues to be used, address mapping becomes a non-issue.

6   Conclusion

In this paper, we study possible outcomes when existing blockchains such as Bitcoin and Ethereum migrate away from the use of ECDSA due to security threats caused by quantum computers. While we have only narrowly looked at end-user migration use-cases, we identify additional compatibility issues related to dormant users and the reliance on static wallet addresses that need to be addressed. By relying on BIP39, we have identified two possible strategies to design a suitable post-quantum algorithm to partly minimize the impact of migration.

References

1. Alagic, G., et al.: Status report on the third round of the NIST post-quantum cryptography standardization process. Technical report, National Institute of Standards and Technology Gaithersburg, MD (2022)
2. Brown, D.R.L.: The Exact Security of ECDSA. Technical report, Advances in Elliptic Curve Cryptography (2000)
3. Buterin, V., et al.: Ethereum: a next-generation smart contract and decentralized application platform (2014)
4. Chen, J., Gan, W., Hu, M., Chen, C.M.: On the construction of a post-quantum blockchain. In: 2021 IEEE Conference on Dependable and Secure Computing (DSC), pp. 1–8. IEEE (2021)
5. Fang, W., Chen, W., Zhang, W., Pei, J., Gao, W., Wang, G.: Digital signature scheme for information non-repudiation in blockchain: a state of the art review. EURASIP J. Wirel. Commun. Netw. **2020**(1), 1–15 (2020). https://doi.org/10.1186/s13638-020-01665-w
6. Fernandez-Carames, T.M., Fraga-Lamas, P.: Towards post-quantum blockchain: a review on blockchain cryptography resistant to quantum computing attacks. IEEE Access **8**, 21091–21116 (2020)
7. Giechaskiel, I., Cremers, C., Rasmussen, K.B.: On bitcoin security in the presence of broken cryptographic primitives. In: Askoxylakis, I., Ioannidis, S., Katsikas, S., Meadows, C. (eds.) ESORICS 2016. LNCS, vol. 9879, pp. 201–222. Springer, Cham (2016). https://doi.org/10.1007/978-3-319-45741-3_11

8. Ishai, Y., Kushilevitz, E., Ostrovsky, R., Sahai, A.: Zero-knowledge from secure multiparty computation. In: Proceedings of the 39th Annual ACM Symposium on Theory of Computing, pp. 21–30. ACM (2007)
9. King, S., Nadal, S.: Ppcoin: peer-to-peer crypto-currency with proof-of-stake. Self-Published Paper **19**(1) (2012)
10. Koblitz, N.: Elliptic curve cryptosystems. Math. Comput. **48**(177), 203–209 (1987)
11. Lin, I.C., Liao, T.C.: A survey of blockchain security issues and challenges. Int. J. Netw. Secur. **19**(5), 653–659 (2017)
12. Mayer, H.: ECDSA security in bitcoin and ethereum: a research survey. Coin-Faabrik **28**(126), 50 (2016)
13. Meng, L., Chen, L.: An enhanced long-term blockchain scheme against compromise of cryptography. Cryptology ePrint Archive (2021)
14. Miller, V.S.: Use of elliptic curves in cryptography. In: Williams, H.C. (ed.) CRYPTO 1985. LNCS, vol. 218, pp. 417–426. Springer, Heidelberg (1986). https://doi.org/10.1007/3-540-39799-X_31
15. Nakamoto, S.: Bitcoin: A peer-to-peer electronic cash system (2008). https://bitcoin.org/bitcoin.pdf. Accessed Aug 2022
16. Palatinus, M., Rusnak, P., Voisine, A., Bowe, S.: BIP 0039: mnemonic code for generating deterministic keys (2013). https://en.bitcoin.it/wiki/BIP_0039. Accessed Aug 2022
17. Paquin, C., Stebila, D., Tamvada, G.: Benchmarking post-quantum cryptography in TLS. In: Ding, J., Tillich, J.-P. (eds.) PQCrypto 2020. LNCS, vol. 12100, pp. 72–91. Springer, Cham (2020). https://doi.org/10.1007/978-3-030-44223-1_5
18. Proos, J., Zalka, C.: Shor's discrete logarithm quantum algorithm for elliptic curves. arXiv preprint quant-ph/0301141 (2003)
19. Qu, M.: SEC 2: Recommended elliptic curve domain parameters. Certicom Res., Mississauga, ON, Canada, Technical Report SEC2-Ver-0.6 (1999)
20. Sato, M., Matsuo, S.: Long-term public blockchain: resilience against compromise of underlying cryptography. In: 2017 26th International Conference on Computer Communication and Networks (ICCCN), pp. 1–8. IEEE (2017)
21. Shahid, F., Khan, A.: Smart digital signatures (SDS): a post-quantum digital signature scheme for distributed ledgers. Futur. Gener. Comput. Syst. **111**, 241–253 (2020)
22. Shamir, A.: How to share a secret. Commun. ACM **22**(11), 612–613 (1979)
23. Shor, P.W.: Polynomial-time algorithms for prime factorization and discrete logarithms on a quantum computer. SIAM Rev. **41**(2), 303–332 (1999)
24. Sikeridis, D., Kampanakis, P., Devetsikiotis, M.: Post-quantum authentication in TLS 1.3: a performance study. In: 27th Annual Network and Distributed System Security Symposium, NDSS 2020, San Diego, California, USA, 23–26 February 2020. The Internet Society (2020)
25. Tan, T.G., Szalachowski, P., Zhou, J.: Challenges of post-quantum digital signing in real-world applications: a survey. Int. J. Inf. Security **21**, 1–16 (2022). https://doi.org/10.1007/s10207-022-00587-6
26. Tan, T.G., Zhou, J.: Layering quantum-resistance into classical digital signature algorithms. In: Liu, J.K., Katsikas, S., Meng, W., Susilo, W., Intan, R. (eds.) ISC 2021. LNCS, vol. 13118, pp. 26–41. Springer, Cham (2021). https://doi.org/10.1007/978-3-030-91356-4_2

Verifiable External Blockchain Calls: Towards Removing Oracle Input Intermediaries

Joshua Ellul[1,2]([✉]) [iD] and Gordon J. Pace[1,2] [iD]

[1] Centre for DLT, University of Malta, Msida, Malta
{gordon.pace,joshua.ellul}@um.edu.mt
[2] Department of Computer Science, University of Malta, Msida, Malta

Abstract. It is widely accepted that blockchain and other distributed ledgers cannot initiate requests for input from external systems and are reliant on oracles to provide such inputs. This belief is founded on the fact that each node has to reach a deterministic state. In this paper we show that this belief is a preconceived one by demonstrating a method that supports calls to external systems initiated from the blockchain itself.

Keywords: External calls · Oracle input · Blockchain architecture

1 Introduction

Many have argued that decentralisation is a cure to many woes arising from issues of trust. By removing centralised points-of-trust, one can build solutions which empower participants. Blockchain and other distributed ledger technologies (DLTs) allow for the decentralisation of computational systems and services built on top of them. Whilst there is truth to such statements, the real world lies outside the blockchain, and although data and algorithms residing on the blockchain can be decentralised, any reference to the real world must necessarily break through the event-horizon of the blockchain and interact with the outside world—much of which is centralised out of physical or regulatory necessity. For instance, if one needs to access the temperature at a particular location at a particular time, one must interact with the real world and trust that the correct information has been provided.

Blockchain systems have traditionally addressed these issues through the use of oracles—channels providing information from the outside world into the blockchain. However, the nature of public blockchains allows only for a one way flow of information (from external entities into the blockchain) and any attempt to do this in the opposite direction (i.e. invoke an external entity from within the blockchain) causes problems due to the nature of consensus of such systems. The only alternative solutions available require trusted entities to perform such invocations, which simply delegates the problem one step away.

Blockchain systems require that the decentralised logic encoded within them reaches a deterministic state. It is often said that every node must execute the

© The Author(s), under exclusive license to Springer Nature Switzerland AG 2023
J. Garcia-Alfaro et al. (Eds.): DPM 2022/CBT 2022, LNCS 13619, pp. 317–324, 2023.
https://doi.org/10.1007/978-3-031-25734-6_20

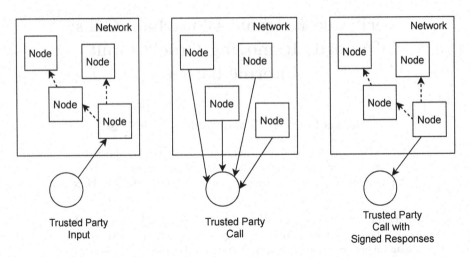

Fig. 1. Left: traditional trusted party input; middle: active calls requiring each node to undertake the external call that must return the same input; right: external calls enabled with verifiable signed responses.

exact same logic in order to achieve consensus—and for this reason, it is the general consensus in the community that Blockchain and DLT systems cannot make calls to external systems/oracles [1–3,5–10,12,14–17]. However, we believe that the general consensus on this matter is not well-founded and is preconceived. Perhaps based upon the often cited statement that deterministic computation is required [13]—yet whilst this statement is true, it is important to highlight that it is the state that computation reaches that must be deterministic, and the computation performed can reach such a deterministic state in different ways.

In this paper, we present initial work on a technique that allows for the interaction with external parties directly in a feasible manner. Figure 1 provides an overview of an oracle input transaction/call flow for: (i) traditional oracle input (on the left); (ii) (inefficient) external calls requiring responses to always be the same—which does not scale up (in the middle); and (iii) the solution proposed herein which makes use of verifiable external calls (on the right).

We have implemented a prototype demonstrating the technique described in Sect. 2 and further present initial gas performance evaluation in Sect. 3. Initial thoughts, motivation and related work have been discussed in [4].

2   Design and Implementation

2.1   Verifiable External Calls

The solution proposed herein is to make use of verifiable external calls—i.e. a request (call) made to an external system that returns back a signed response which: (i) can be verified to truly be a response from the external party in question; (ii) which does not require any further communication (with the external party or other). This can be achieved in the same way how we provide such assurances in traditional applications and how trusted oracle input is verified, by checking whether the response was indeed digitally signed [11] by the external party. Knowledge of the trusted party's public key is required to be known (in the same way that oracle input requires knowledge of the trusted party's address) or can be retrieved from a trusted entity.

To allow for processes to make direct use of external services (in a feasible and efficient manner), which do not require explicit integration from the external parties themselves (with the specific platform), we propose to make use of verifiable external calls which provide a guarantee with respect to the veracity of the origin of the response both at the time of processing as well as for any point in future for which such verification may be required.

A verifiable external call is defined as the following tuple—a request, a public key and a signed response structured as follows:

$$\langle request, \ public\_key, \ signed(response) \rangle$$

The *request* should point to the external system/service endpoint which is to be called (though this is an implementation design decision), and may also comprise of other input data. The *public_key* may be hard-coded into the application logic (e.g. into the smart contract), or it could even be retrieved by a trusted certificate provider. In either case it would need to be recorded by the time when the external call is executed—it will be used to verify the response originated from the respective external party. The *signed(response)* is the response that has been signed using the external party's private key (which is associated with *public_key*.

Indeed, this does require that the trusted data sources provide an end-point that responds back with a signed response which would likely require changes to existing data sources to implement signed responses—however, recent proposals indicate that such a standard may eventually be adopted[1], which if adopted would enable for this approach to integrate with all data sources (that are keeping up with standards).

Furthermore, to avoid old signed responses from being repeated, an incremental number, timestamp, block number or another challenge-response could be made use of which would ensure old responses cannot be repeated—however this is left as an implementation detail. Whilst, the challenge data sent to the external party will be part of the *request*, the verifiable external call's definition may be extended to include the challenge-response. For example, the request can be augmented by a request number to a fresh nonce ν, which is expected to be included unchanged in the response[2]:

$$\langle request \oplus \{nonce \mapsto \nu\}, \ public\_key, \ signed(response \oplus \{nonce \mapsto \nu\}) \rangle$$

---

[1] https://wicg.github.io/webpackage/draft-yasskin-http-origin-signed-responses.html.
[2] We use $\oplus$ to represent function overloading.

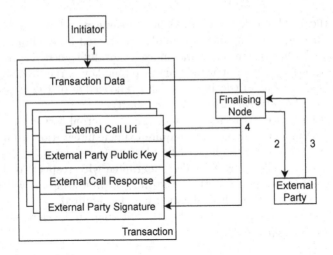

Fig. 2. Transaction finalisation process.

2.2   Transactions

When a transaction is initiated (be it by a user, another system, or the system itself if such a DLT allows this) and accepted for execution, the node which is processing the transaction will establish all external calls which need to be performed, execute them and record the responses received back from the trusted external parties along with associated digital signatures. Indeed, at this point the finalising node must ensure that the response is from the trusted party by verifying the response and signature against the trusted party's public key. Furthermore, if a unique number, date/time, or challenge-response mechanism was used to ensure old data is not repeated, then this would also be validated at this point. A depiction of how a transaction is initiated and attributed with the various data associated with external calls is depicted in Fig. 2.

For responses that are not verified, associated transactions may be deemed to have failed, or depending upon reparation logic, the transaction may still be valid. This is a design decision that each platform would need to consider. The same goes for external calls for which no response is received.

To reiterate, to ensure that a finalising node does not repeat old responses from external parties, the response and signature could be accompanied with the date and time the response was generated and/or a unique response identifier associated with the response (and potentially request as well). One challenge is to ensure that participating nodes indeed execute such external calls rather than simply record failure, which we will delve into in a future paper (since it merits its own paper). However, verifiable external calls could also be undertaken by the transaction initiator (i.e. the party submitting the transaction provides this information as part of the transaction submission process)—however indeed this depends upon the architectural design of the blockchain, smart contract and wallet/dApp software submitting the transaction. By performing the verifiable external call at transaction submission time (on the initiator), the aforementioned problem pertaining to nodes potentially reporting back failed external calls would be eliminated.

2.3   Implementation Details

The Go Ethereum (geth)[3] node implementation (version 1.16.5) was modified to include support for the verifiable external call mechanism described above. The following salient modifications were implemented. A prototype of the approach has been implemented and available from https://github.com/joshuaellul/excalls.

EXCALL Transaction. A new type of transaction, an EXCALL transaction (in `excall_tx.go`), was added (on top of the existing Legacy and Access List transactions) to facilitate storing the additional data associated with external calls (described in Sect. 2.1) in an EXCALL tuple—containing the external call response, signature, and the external party's known public key.

EXCALL Instruction. A new EXCALL virtual machine opcode which instructs the virtual machine to execute the external call was added. Rather than modify the whole programming tool-chain (including the Solidity programming language and Solidity compiler) to support the proposed EXCALL instruction, for the purpose of this prototype it was emulated by replacing PUSH32 instructions (used for string assignments) whose associated data starts with "http" into EXCALL ones.[4]

A miner executes the emulated EXCALL instruction only when finalising a block, and will undertake an external call to the URL specified as a parameter to the instruction (pushed on the stack via the aforementioned PUSH32 instruction). Upon receiving a response and a valid digital signature for the respective public key, the relevant data will be appended to an EXCALL transaction.

Following this, the transaction is stored in the block with the EXCALL transaction data filled in (as depicted in Fig. 2). This then allows for other nodes to verify the external call based upon the stored data (without having to initiate an external call itself).

3   Evaluation

A gambling dApp is used to serve the purpose of a required use-case to evaluate gas performance of the proposed approach against a traditional approach. The evaluation discussed below would also apply to other smart contract use-cases that have similar protocol requirements where a party must first initiate a transaction to a smart contract prior to external oracle data being made available on

---

[3] https://github.com/ethereum/go-ethereum.

[4] Indeed, this means that in the prototype it is not possible to make use of a PUSH32 instruction for data that starts with the string "http", however this does not impact the prototype's purpose to evaluate the proposed technique.

the blockchain (which typically is due to not wanting to reveal that data prior to the initiating transaction).

The use-case requires that these steps are followed to complete a betting transaction: (i) a user initiates interaction with the smart contract by placing a bet; (ii) data from the oracle is retrieved and fed into the smart contract to determine whether the user won. The use-case has been implemented in Solidity and available from https://github.com/joshuaellul/excalls for: (i) a standard Ethereum network that makes use of an external oracle to feed in data; and (ii) a modified Ethereum implementation which supports external calls to directly fetch the oracle input.

Comparing gas costs associated with the two approaches, the standard approach requires 67,599 and 48,222 gas units to execute `beginBetOracle` and `continueBetOracle` respectively. The total gas cost for the standard approach, $standard_{gas}$, amounts to 115,821. Whilst, the total gas computed for the external call approach, $computed\_excall_{gas}$, is 89,071—however, this does not include additional gas associated with actually undertaking the external call.

A gas cost associated with an external call would need to be decided upon for the respective blockchain system. It is not the scope of this work to decide upon an exact value, yet we can make an estimate by breaking down the external call process into: (i) the actual external call undertaken only on the node adding the associated block; and (ii) verifying the external call response which takes place on every node. Based on this the total gas consumption for the approach can be defined as:

$$total\_excall_{gas} = computed\_excall_{gas} + excall_{gas} + verify\_sig_{gas}$$

where $excall_{gas}$ is the gas associated with making an external call; and $verify\_sig_{gas}$ is the gas associated with verifying an external call's response (i.e. verifying an ECDSA signature).

The cost to verify an ECDSA signature ($verify\_sig_{gas}$) was evaluated to be 3,903 gas[5]. Therefore, the total gas required for the external call approach is:

$$total\_excall_{gas} = 89,071 + excall_{gas} + 3,903$$

If the gas costs of an external call approach is equal to or less than a traditional approach, then the external call approach will not be introducing any negative consequences with respect to gas. Therefore, we can identify an upper-bound limit for $excall_{gas}$ to be:

$$standard_{gas} - (computed\_excall_{gas} + verify\_sig_{gas})$$

---

[5] Code from https://solidity-by-example.org/signature/ to verify an ECDSA signature was executed in order to retrieve gas costs. The cost of the verification only was calculated by first executing a function call and then adding in a call to verify a signature, and the difference between the two was used to calculate the signature verification gas cost.

This results in 22,847 gas—which given that the costs of $excall_{gas}$ are only incurred on the node that is adding a block, this amount should be more than justifiable. Based on this, we claim that the external call approach proposed herein should consume equivalent or less gas to that required for the standard approach. However, we leave a full investigation to define appropriate gas costs for such an operation for future work—which may include evaluating differing gas costs according to HTTP Request and Response payload sizes.

4   Conclusions

It is a widely accepted belief that blockchain systems cannot execute calls to external systems due to the requirement for computation to reach a deterministic state. It is often said that blockchain-based computation needs to be deterministic [13], however it is important to highlight that determinism of output can be achieved in different ways. Contrary to the general consensus, in this paper, we have demonstrated a method for Blockchain and DLT systems that allows for direct external calls to be initiated from the Blockchain/DLT itself. We have implemented a prototype and undertaken initial evaluation of gas overheads of a typical dApp requiring external oracle input.

This is only initial work in this direction for which we believe will pave the way for extensive future work in the following directions: (i) investigating novel consensus protocols that better support external calls; (ii) language design for smart contract external calls; (iii) development of novel blockchains that support external calls; (iv) development of novel dApps supported through active external calls; (v) miner/validator incentive mechanisms for external calls; (vi) further performance and evaluation of active external call techniques.

A prototype demonstrating verifiable external calls has been implemented and available from https://github.com/joshuaellul/excalls.

References

1. Adler, J., Berryhill, R., Veneris, A., Poulos, Z., Veira, N., Kastania, A.: Astraea: a decentralized blockchain oracle. In: 2018 IEEE International Conference on Internet of Things (iThings) and IEEE Green Computing and Communications (GreenCom) and IEEE Cyber, Physical and Social Computing (CPSCom) and IEEE Smart Data (SmartData), pp. 1145–1152. IEEE (2018)
2. Caldarelli, G.: Real-world blockchain applications under the lens of the oracle problem. a systematic literature review. In: 2020 IEEE International Conference on Technology Management, Operations and Decisions (ICTMOD), pp. 1–6 (2020). https://doi.org/10.1109/ICTMOD49425.2020.9380598
3. Ellis, S., Juels, A., Nazarov, S.: Chainlink: a decentralized oracle network (2017). White paper (2017)
4. Ellul, J., Pace, G.J.: Towards external calls for blockchain and distributed ledger technology. arXiv preprint arXiv:2105.10399 (2021)
5. Gatteschi, V., Lamberti, F., Demartini, C., Pranteda, C., Santamaría, V.: To blockchain or not to blockchain: that is the question. IT Prof. **20**(2), 62–74 (2018). https://doi.org/10.1109/MITP.2018.021921652

6. Lin, S.Y., Zhang, L., Li, J., Ji, L.l., Sun, Y.: A survey of application research based on blockchain smart contract. Wireless Netw. **28**(2), 635–690 (2022)

7. Liu, X., Muhammad, K., Lloret, J., Chen, Y.W., Yuan, S.M.: Elastic and cost-effective data carrier architecture for smart contract in blockchain. Future Gener. Comput. Syst. **100**, 590–599 (2019). https://doi.org/10.1016/j.future.2019.05.042, https://www.sciencedirect.com/science/article/pii/S0167739X18328334

8. Marchesi, L., Marchesi, M., Tonelli, R.: ABCDE-agile block chain DApp engineering. Blockchain: Res. Appl. **1**(1), 100002 (2020). https://doi.org/10.1016/j.bcra.2020.100002.   https://www.sciencedirect.com/science/article/pii/S2096720920300026

9. Marchesi, M., Marchesi, L., Tonelli, R.: An agile software engineering method to design blockchain applications. In: Proceedings of the 14th Central and Eastern European Software Engineering Conference Russia, pp. 1–8 (2018)

10. Mekouar, L., Iraqi, Y., Damaj, I., Naous, T.: A survey on blockchain-based recommender systems: integration architecture and taxonomy. Comput. Commun. **187**, 1–19 (2022)

11. Merkle, R.C.: A certified digital signature. In: Brassard, G. (ed.) CRYPTO 1989. LNCS, vol. 435, pp. 218–238. Springer, New York (1990). https://doi.org/10.1007/0-387-34805-0_21

12. Rimba, P., Tran, A.B., Weber, I., Staples, M., Ponomarev, A., Xu, X.: Comparing blockchain and cloud services for business process execution. In: 2017 IEEE International Conference on Software Architecture, ICSA 2017, Gothenburg, Sweden, 3–7 April 2017, pp. 257–260. IEEE Computer Society (2017). https://doi.org/10.1109/ICSA.2017.44

13. Sankar, L.S., Sindhu, M., Sethumadhavan, M.: Survey of consensus protocols on blockchain applications. In: 2017 4th International Conference on Advanced Computing and Communication Systems (ICACCS), pp. 1–5. IEEE (2017)

14. Weber, I., Xu, X., Riveret, R., Governatori, G., Ponomarev, A., Mendling, J.: Untrusted business process monitoring and execution using blockchain. In: La Rosa, M., Loos, P., Pastor, O. (eds.) BPM 2016. LNCS, vol. 9850, pp. 329–347. Springer, Cham (2016). https://doi.org/10.1007/978-3-319-45348-4_19

15. Xu, X., Pautasso, C., Zhu, L., Lu, Q., Weber, I.: A pattern collection for blockchain-based applications. In: Proceedings of the 23rd European Conference on Pattern Languages of Programs, EuroPLoP 2018, Irsee, Germany, 04–08 July 2018, pp. 3:1–3:20. ACM (2018). https://doi.org/10.1145/3282308.3282312

16. Xu, X., et al.: A taxonomy of blockchain-based systems for architecture design. In: 2017 IEEE International Conference on Software Architecture, ICSA 2017, Gothenburg, Sweden, 3–7 April 2017, pp. 243–252. IEEE Computer Society (2017). https://doi.org/10.1109/ICSA.2017.33

17. Zhao, Y., Kang, X., Li, T., Chu, C.K., Wang, H.: Towards trustworthy DeFi oracles: Past, present and future. IEEE Access (2022)

Author Index

© The Editor(s) (if applicable) and The Author(s), under exclusive license
to Springer Nature Switzerland AG 2023
J. Garcia-Alfaro et al. (Eds.): DPM 2022/CBT 2022, LNCS 13619, pp. 325–326, 2023.
https://doi.org/10.1007/978-3-031-25734-6

Printed in the United States
by Baker & Taylor Publisher Services

Printed in the United States
by Baker & Taylor Publisher Services